The Language of Constitutional Comparison

ELGAR MONOGRAPHS IN CONSTITUTIONAL AND
ADMINISTRATIVE LAW

Series Editors: Rosalind Dixon, *University of New South Wales, Australia*, Susan Rose-Ackerman, *Yale University* and Mark Tushnet, *Harvard University, USA*

Constitutions are a country's most important legal document, laying the foundation not just for politics, but for all other areas of law. They allocate power among different levels and branches of government, record and promote a society's shared values, and protect the rights of citizens. Countries around the world are adopting written constitutions, though what defines a constitution is evolving to include a variety of sources beyond canonical texts, such as political conventions, statutes, judicial decisions and administrative law norms.

This cosmopolitan monograph series provides a forum for the best and most original scholarship in constitutional and administrative law, with each book offering an international, comparative or multi-jurisdictional approach to this complex and fascinating field of research.

Titles in the series include:

Autonomous Public Bodies and the Law
A European Perspective
Stéphanie De Somer

Constitutional Preambles
A Comparative Analysis
Wim Voermans, Maarten Stremler and Paul Cliteur

Comparative Constitutional Studies
A Comparative Analysis of Regionalist Negotiations
Vito Breda

Judging Regulators
The Political Economy of Anglo-American Administrative Law
Eric C. Ip

Constitutional Crowdsourcing
Democratising Original and Derived Constituent Power in the Network Society
Antoni Abat i Ninet

The Language of Constitutional Comparison
Francois Venter

The Language of Constitutional Comparison

Francois Venter

Extraordinary Professor, Faculty of Law, North-West University, South Africa

ELGAR MONOGRAPHS IN CONSTITUTIONAL AND ADMINISTRATIVE LAW

Cheltenham, UK • Northampton, MA, USA

© Francois Venter 2022

All rights reserved. No part of this publication may be reproduced, stored in a retrieval system or transmitted in any form or by any means, electronic, mechanical or photocopying, recording, or otherwise without the prior permission of the publisher.

Published by
Edward Elgar Publishing Limited
The Lypiatts
15 Lansdown Road
Cheltenham
Glos GL50 2JA
UK

Edward Elgar Publishing, Inc.
William Pratt House
9 Dewey Court
Northampton
Massachusetts 01060
USA

A catalogue record for this book
is available from the British Library

Library of Congress Control Number: 2022931139

This book is available electronically in the Elgaronline
Law subject collection
http://dx.doi.org/10.4337/9781800882584

ISBN 978 1 80088 257 7 (cased)
ISBN 978 1 80088 258 4 (eBook)

Printed and bound by CPI Group (UK) Ltd, Croydon, CR0 4YY

ESTER, who walks every step with me

Contents

Preface		viii
1	Constitutional language spoken here	1
2	The history of contemporary constitutional language	15
3	Nation	55
4	Sovereignty	78
5	The state	101
6	Citizenship and nationality	123
7	Democracy	139
8	Rule of law	170
9	Constitutionalism	185
10	Judicial review	199
11	Constitutional comparison and terminology	221
Epilogue		233
Bibliography		242
Index		261

Preface

As I taught constitutional law to young students over a number of years, I worried about the limited time available in the curriculum to explain what stock words in the standard texts, such as 'legal', 'constitutional', 'national', 'representative', 'jurisdiction', 'rights', and many more actually mean. Eventually I began wondering about it myself, and wrote a bit about it. When I was bitten by the comparative bug, I realized that there are many of these essential constitutional words that peers working in other jurisdictions would understand in different ways.

This caused me to become both intrigued and concerned with the terminological imprecision endemic in public law globally. My concerns were compounded by the reality that lawyers have very little other than language at their disposal to express their views and intentions and, consequently, that it is grossly conceited to assume that those with whom one converses on constitutional matters, especially in a comparative context, should accept one's own, unexplained preferences of meaning of the core concepts.

When the subject matter under discussion is of a theoretical nature, this kind of scholarly arrogance is nevertheless not unusual at all, especially in the social sciences and humanities (as opposed to the empirical natural sciences where precision is usually indispensable). Most obvious in this regard is the notorious phenomenon of philosophers who, as a matter of course, create their own linguistic instrumentation with which to express their profound thoughts. This forces students of their philosophy to first master the philosopher's linguistic creations[1] before proceeding to read practically everything produced by the great mind in order to claim with some confidence an understanding of the implications of the metaphysical cogitations.

Upon the growing little heap of my concerns the realization was added that theorists and philosophers each operated within their own peculiar frame of mind, based on their understanding of the world, which determined the nature and content of their theories and philosophies. This realization gave rise to the apprehension that, in one's own participation in the expanding compara-

---

[1] Witness e.g. the 'categorical imperative' (Kant), 'sphere sovereignty' (Dooyeweerd), the 'veil of ignorance' (Rawls) and 'deconstruction' (Derrida), to name but a few.

tive constitutional discourse, one may be forced to use concepts in a manner unsuited to one's own convictions. This may also sometimes justify the suspicion that what a constitutional lawyer is saying or writing in the standard constitutional vernacular does not necessarily reflect the intended meaning, or that the language is used to accommodate the audience's ignorance of the speaker's constitutional paradigm.

Wondering what is to be done other than frowningly contemplating these worries, the idea came up that it might be fruitful to share a compilation of the most obvious terminological discrepancies, because there must be others who feel the same stirrings of apprehension about constitutional lawyers' means of expressing themselves. In the research reported in the following pages I discovered evidence that the indefiniteness of constitutional language is being noticed.

The issue of terminological instability touches upon a range of intriguing issues regarding fundamental constitutional questions. Among these are what should or must be done to maintain valuable institutions that depend on the notions that are suffering under the vagueness of our language. After all, the benefits of stable statehood, democratic government, sound operation of the law, just adjudication, and so on can hardly be contested. An assumption of this book is that, in order to preserve good constitutional institutions and to improve on them, linguistic ambiguity must be addressed. Accentuating this lack of clarity is therefore deemed to be a worthy cause.

Providing suggestions for the resolution of the many conceptual difficulties caused by the malleability of the arsenal of words in use will require more than such an accentuation, and will require the involvement of a large portion of the community of constitutional scholars.

I am grateful to Edward Elgar Publishing for the professional processing of the manuscript, including its expeditious submission to rigorous prior peer review. The research necessary for the writing of this book was made possible by the financial support generously made available by the Alexander von Humboldt Foundation and the South African National Research Foundation. The initial research necessary for this project could gratefully be undertaken in 2019 during a visit to the Max Planck Institute for Comparative Public Law and International Law in Heidelberg, Germany.

Francois Venter
North-West University
Potchefstroom
July 2021

1. Constitutional language spoken here

1.1 TERMINOLOGICAL DIFFICULTIES

Walking by a restaurant or hotel lobby, one often sees a notice proclaiming ' ... [some foreign language or languages] ... spoken here' for the obvious purpose of inviting in or accommodating tourists from elsewhere. Calls for papers for conferences also sometimes specify the languages in which presentations may be made, or into which papers will be translated or simultaneously interpreted. Most common, however, is an expectation or assumption that participants will be able to function in the universal *lingua franca*, English.

Writing and conversing comparatively about constitutional law would be impossible if a common constitutional vocabulary did not exist. Constitutional law as a topic is however far from isolated linguistically from related fields. Intuitively one links constitutional law to politics. The mention of politics calls forth a range of concepts, from immodest canvassing of support by politicians seeking power and control, to esoteric sociological musings about the condition of human society – en route crossing considerations of economics, psychology, philosophy, demographics and more.

Although the spectrum of possible approaches to constitutional law is potentially as wide as the range of states in existence (currently around 200), one must assume that there is a broad, largely common understanding of what is meant by 'constitutional law', which may, for the purposes of keeping the present discussion and analysis within manageable boundaries, be described as a field of *legal* regulation, practice and scholarship.[1] Within the encyclopaedia of the law, constitutional law is characterized by legal norms primarily concerning the state, simultaneously as its subject and object. In broad terms constitutional law regulates the establishment of the state, its structure, the authorization of persons, offices, bodies and substructures to exercise the powers and functions attributed to the state, the manner in which such authority is obtained, the framework within and limitations under which state

---

[1] Not all notions of 'the state' are legally determined, but constitutional law is inevitably *legal* in its nature, and concerned with the state. From the perspective of other states, considerations of public international law also come into play in the determination of the recognition of an entity as a state (see Chapter 5).

authority may be exercised lawfully, and the legal relationships between the state and its citizens.

From this it is clear that one cannot conceptualize constitutional law without employing a number of concepts essential for communication about the field, such as 'state', 'authority/power', and 'citizenship'. As one delves deeper into the substance of constitutional law, more profound questions regarding variations in attributed meaning to essential constitutional concepts arise, such as diverse understandings of 'law', 'democracy', 'representation', 'rights', and 'justice'. It is this conceptual variation that challenges consistently dependable comparative intercourse on constitutional law.

The terminological difficulties under consideration can best be understood against the background of their history. Although the history of the current constitutional lexis is not limited to the history of what is generally referred to as 'the West', there is no avoiding the reality that the constitutional language currently in global use is deeply rooted in its evolution in the course of Western political and legal history. John Haley holds that virtually all national legal systems share a common heritage, namely Roman law, particularly Roman private law, which has 'determined many of the most basic features of our contemporary public law regimes'. He deems the notion of rights in public law to be based on private law, and therefore that 'Eurocentric conceptions and assumptions generally work reasonably well'.[2]

There is evidence that views such as Haley's do not sit well with some who do not wish to subscribe to 'Western values', and that the possibility of finding sufficient conversational commonality among all participants in a discussion on constitutional law may be endangered thereby. It should also be kept in mind that some (also Western) scholars are critical of what is usually referred to as 'Eurocentrism'.[3] Nevertheless, it is not unrealistic to proclaim that, where constitutional law is under discussion, whether in a municipal or comparative context, a poster stating 'constitutional language spoken here' is appropriate. Such a proclamation would imply that the language will facilitate sound communication, but this cannot be taken at face value, because it conceals significant problems.

---

[2] Haley 'Political Foundations' 3–4.
[3] See e.g. Menski 'Asia and Africa' 32: 'Studying Asian and African legal systems from an internal perspective, attempting to understand "from inside" how they have developed and function today, it becomes impossible to maintain a eurocentric, statist and purportedly universal set of assumptions about "the law".' Also Giri 'Asian Dialogues' 9: 'But much of social theory as it rules in the academic corridors of Europe, Asia and the world is Eurocentric. But now there is an epochal need for realizing social theory as part of a planetary conversation.'

My conclusion at the end of a preliminary study of the challenges inherent in constitutional terminology emphasizes, with some urgency, the need to recognize the shortcomings of the language we use, especially in the context of comparison:

> The identification of some of the terminological difficulties contained in the 'standard' constitutional lexis ... does not as such resolve the inherent difficulties for the practice of constitutional comparison. It does however reveal the need for renewed investigation into a range of fundamental issues, explicitly approached from divergent points of departure. Among these are the assumptions upon which statehood, legal authority, sovereignty, citizenship, judicial authority and constitutionalism are construed.[4]

In an edited volume excellently revealing the problematics under consideration, the editors Michael Dowdle and Mike Wilkinson aptly opened their joint chapter as follows:

> The modern, liberal vision of constitutionalism – what we are calling structural-liberalism – has contributed greatly to the human experience of constitutionalism and has come to dominate the 'comparative' constitutional imagination – that is, 'comparative constitutional law'. But, like all regulatory ideas, it is a product of particular circumstances: Its foci reflect the concerns of time and place. These concerns and prescriptions are important, but at the same time, they inevitably overlook – or conceal – other concerns that can shape constitutionalism in other times and places.[5]

The contention of this book is that the linguistic difficulties under discussion are attributable to the shortcomings of Western constitutional nomenclature. The difficulties are exacerbated by the dominance of what Dowdle and Wilkinson call 'the modern, liberal vision of constitutionalism', which is also what legal scholars such as Günter Frankenberg and Tamas Gyorfi have labelled the 'orthodoxy'.[6] The global dominance of the North Atlantic constitutional lexicon tends to conceal the reality, for better or for worse, that its nomenclature suffers at least partly from ambiguity, irrationality, lack of sufficient explication and some basic historical assumptions rooted in fictional constructs. This book is therefore about the recognition of the difficulties attending the almost universal constitutional vocabulary of the early

---

[4] Venter 'Rethinking' 95.
[5] Dowdle & Wilkinson 'Constitutional Reflexivity' 17.
[6] Frankenberg 'Critique' 13–16 and Gyorfi 'New Constitutionalism' 16–18, identifying the American model at 254 as 'the new constitutionalism' having become 'the almost orthodox intellectual position'.

twenty-first century, as it has been passed down over the previous centuries, with some suggestions for addressing the situation.

1.2 LANGUAGE IS IMPRECISE – SO WHAT?

It is not uncommon in the legal community *not* to be concerned with the vagueness and generalizations characteristic of our constitutional language. Around the globe in national and international fora, courts, conferences, constitutions, international instruments, scholarly debates in print, conferences, colloquia and seminars, in law schools, institutes and faculties, legal terminology is seldom perceived to be a stumbling block hindering the formulation, study or practice of constitutional law: lawyers and academics simply hold forth, argue, state their case, make their points, and generally converse on the apparent assumption that the words they use should be understood by others as they themselves understand them. Many might therefore ask if there really is a problem, and what it actually entails.

Although this book is not primarily concerned with constitutional pedagogics, it is useful for the purposes of contextualization to pose a universally relevant question regarding constitutional law syllabi: what should law students be taught about the essential denotation of the core concepts upon which the constitutional vocabulary is built? It seems to be generally assumed that it would produce confusion in the learning mind to make the point of departure in an introductory course on constitutional law that the meaning of 'the state', 'sovereignty', 'constitution' etc. is uncertain, unclear and unpredictable. Such an assumption seems to underpin a strategy that is widely used in constitutional teaching namely to focus not so much on the niceties of constitutional theory, but to 'teach the constitution', which essentially involves a descriptive, and sometimes analytical discourse based on the text of the national constitution concerned.[7]

On the other hand, one may ask whether it is didactically justifiable for a constitutional law professor to hide the fact from students that the meaning given to the terms used in the prescribed textbook or the lecture is subject to serious theoretical and philosophical contestation, jurisdictional variation and historical contextualization. Wholly irresponsible would be the creation of the impression that one would be able to use the core terms of the field in sensible comparative description, analysis and conceptual utilization without account-

---

[7] There are many examples of this approach. See for example May, Ides & Grossi 'National Power and Federalism' (USA); Pyke 'Constitutional Law' (Australia); Johri 'Lectures' (India); Badura 'Staatsrecht' (Germany); Ryan 'Constitutional Law' (Ireland); and Ferrari 'Italian Public Law'.

ing for the fact that the words are often spelled, translated and pronounced identically, but that the writers, translators and speakers attach significantly diverse meanings to those words.

The claim here is not that it is in any way original to identify the phenomenon of inconsistent constitutional terminology as problematic. There is in fact a rich and growing range of publications by prominent constitutionalists and theoreticians where the matter has received attention. The following examples warrant verbatim consideration.

In 2010 Nicholas Barber (Oxford University) wrote:

> Constitutional theory suffers from an identity crisis. The subject is taught in universities, enjoys the attention of many academics and has a history that can be traced back hundreds, even thousands, of years, and yet its point and method remain obscure. Most disciplines have aims that can be encapsulated in a handful of words ... Constitutional theory is different. There is no consensus about what constitutional theory is for or how it should be done; and, as a consequence of this, no agreement about what a good argument within the discipline would look like. Without some sense of what counts as a successful exercise in constitutional theory, a set of criteria against which accounts can be tested, we cannot judge the merits of any particular piece of work. The problem is exacerbated by the barely concealed belief of some constitutional theorists that they have identified the unique path of constitutional theory and those working outside of their school are fundamentally mistaken. Historically-minded constitutional theorists tend to think that critical constitutional theorists are engaged in political agitation. Critical constitutional theorists tend to think that interpretive constitutional theorists are apologists for the existing order. Interpretive constitutional theorists tend to think that political science-oriented constitutional scholars can do little more than helpfully gather in the facts that are to be the subject matter of their interpretation. And so it goes, with each group doubting the value of the others, and each secretly believing that, really, only they are engaged in constitutional theory.[8]

In 2010 Riccardo Prandini (University of Bologna) made the following statement introducing his chapter in an edited volume on constitutionalism:

> We are living through a new constitutional era, and we are overwhelmed by strange constitutional–constituent experiences. It is not a time of exceptional politics, as exists during the founding episodes of modern constitutions. It does not represent a demise of constitutionalism, since there is no such unique real thing to be demised. And it does not represent a transmutation because nothing is really mutating: there is only an emerging new form. We are facing a living and latent process of morphogenesis which reframes the very idea of constitution in a way which is more adequate to world society. This is a peculiar phase, which is taking place apparently without popular mobilisations and with difficulties in finding either the constituent

---

[8] Barber 'Constitutional State' 1.

powers or the real legal processes of constitutionalisation, and often without clear polities which are to be constituted.[9]

In 2013 the late Patrick Glenn (McGill University) opened his seminal book on cosmopolitan constitutionalism with the following remarks (citing various other authorities):

> How does one think about an institution or concept as large and as widespread as the state? Some would prefer not to. Others have 'succumbed to analysis'. If today the 'question of the state is posed everywhere in the world' it may be difficult not to think about it. Yet, in thinking about it, should one be empirical or normative, theoretical or descriptive? Are we concerned with the essence of the state, or with legitimate or possible functions? There is no agreement on the answers to these questions, yet it has been said that 'it does appear foolish to deny a state tradition'. So the simplest and most basic answer to the question of the state is probably that it exists as a tradition, a body of normative and often inconsistent information that is inevitably instantiated or institutionalized in various and particular forms. This is the case for law in general, and states are legal constructions.[10]

Citing Ran Hirschl, Upendra Baxi and a previous publication of his own, Günter Frankenberg (Goethe-Universität, Frankfurt) in 2018 opened a chapter on the theory of constitutional comparison as follows:

> This chapter 'takes as its premise a simple fact: the unprecedented revival of comparative constitutional studies rides on a fuzzy and rather incoherent epistemological and methodological matrix'. At the heart of this matrix, a widespread naivety – 'the innocence of method' – intersects with unitary constitutional thought that takes its cues 'from the constitutional experience of half a dozen (on a good day) politically stable, economically prosperous, liberal democracies without providing 'equal discursive dignity to non-European-American traditions'.[11]

Despite these authoritative acknowledgments of the imprecision of the current constitutional vernacular, the problem endures, and can even be expected to deepen. It is not a matter that will resolve itself, and therefore permits more blatant exposure, including by means of, but not only through theoretical consideration. Unavoidably this is a minefield of dogmatism, be it orthodox liberalism, militant post-modernism, abstract historicism, convoluted philosophizing or any other unbending approach. Digging epistemological trenches to engage in an intellectual poison gas battle – emulating the tragically tangible World War I skirmishes among the North Atlanteans across sterile marshland

---

[9] Prandini 'Morphogenesis' 309.
[10] Glenn 'Cosmopolitan State' 1.
[11] Frankenberg 'Between Magic and Deceit' 67.

– is likely to again produce more casualties than solutions, more bogging down than advance.

Principled revelation of one's premises is good scholarly form, but to try to use one's ontological beliefs as an absolute for the purposes of denigrating others' will not resolve the challenges presented by our imprecise means of constitutional communication. The strangeness of our language should, it is submitted, be roundly admitted by all, and should, as a universal problem, be positioned at the heart of the global (especially comparative) constitutional endeavour, wherever it may be undertaken.

1.3 WHERE SHOULD WE SEEK SOLUTIONS?

Where should we then look for solutions to the problems inherent in our standard constitutional vocabulary? There is no hope in seeking relief in an attempt to compile a new, revised constitutional dictionary, as it were, because every definition, designation and characterization that anyone may offer, will inevitably call forth contradictions, contestation and theoretical or epistemological qualification or rejection from various directions.

Should one then attempt to compile all meanings and understandings of the relevant concepts and leave it to each user to make their pick, or even add additional or alternative content? This may be an option, but it would not in itself end the constitutional babel, except if all users of the concepts could be persuaded to reveal their choice of meaning whenever they use them. There is a quixotic element in the pursuit of such an ideal – but let it not be discarded out of hand.[12]

Then there is the possibility of surveying the spectrum of meanings attached to constitutional terminology that superficially appears to be monosemic, but which holds concealed levels of polysemic connotations. Such an approach holds some promise, if only for the purposes of creating sensitivity to the problems created by conceptual arrogance, by which is meant a conscious or subconscious attitude that others must simply accept one's subjective or jurisdictional inferences of meaning. Arrogance is however a tenacious opponent sure to be denied, especially by the most arrogant. It will not be defeated, or affected at all, simply by revealing it. More is required if a contribution to the debate is to be made: the weaknesses concealed in assumptive clear language need to be recognized. That is what the discussion in most of the chapters below is aimed at.

---

[12] An argument can actually be made that doing so is advisable: see Venter 'Rethinking' 94.

1.4 ORTHODOXY CHALLENGED

Given the history of contemporary constitutional thought, it should not be surprising that *liberalism* and the *liberal tradition* regularly crop up in discussions of constitutional theory and terminology. No doubt this is due to the reality that the global constitutional language emanated from the age(s) of Liberalism around the North Atlantic. The political, legal and economic dominance of North America and Western Europe for at least the past seven decades undoubtedly caused the constitutional mores of those regions, usually expressed in the blanket term 'liberal democracy', to become a standard for desirable constitutional 'success', emulated around the world by 'new democracies', be they in the 'Third World', Eastern and Central Europe, the 'global South' or in Asia. Contemporary trends may however indicate that the era of 'Western' primacy is slowly coming to a close, or at least that its assumed superiority is increasingly being challenged. Regardless of one's opinions regarding the justification, merits and demerits of liberal democracy, on this overpopulated and polluted planet change in constitutional attitudes is in the air, and this lability opens the way to global instability. Social instability is not our focus here, but the uncertainty of constitutional terminology is symptomatic of the trend and may even contribute to political and economic instability.

Express challenges to the liberal roots of the constitutional vernacular come from different dogmatic perspectives, including (at least) political ideology, epistemological stances and a desire for terminological clarity. The first two of these perspectives may be founded upon animosity towards liberalism, and the last is (usually) either sympathetic or neutral towards the traditions of liberalism, or tolerant towards it.

Ideological challenges to liberalism were for instance expressed directly by Russian President Vladimir Putin in a newspaper interview in June 2019. Putin was quoted as saying[13] that 'the liberal idea' had 'outlived its purpose', and that '[Liberals] cannot simply dictate anything to anyone just like they have been attempting to do over the recent decades,' and that 'The liberal idea has become obsolete. It has come into conflict with the interests of the overwhelming majority of the population.' To this, the (Polish) president of the European Council, Donald Tusk, responded:

> Whoever claims that liberal democracy is obsolete also claims that freedoms are obsolete, that the rule of law is obsolete and that human rights are obsolete. For us in Europe, these are and will remain essential and vibrant values. What I find

---

[13] *Financial Times* 28 June 2019.

really obsolete are authoritarianism, personality cults, the rule of oligarchs. Even if sometimes they may seem effective.[14]

Epistemologically, perhaps the most direct rejection of constitutional liberalism is being expressed by post-modernist critical theorists. Among these, Günter Frankenberg provides the most comprehensible texts,[15] stating for instance[16] that '[c]ritical comparatists don't want to be governed by the dominant discourse'. The post-modernist distaste for liberal language can probably be explained by the fact that the broader postmodern movement (or is it a trend, inclination, attitude?) grew out of influential linguistic and existential ponderings.[17]

One does however not need to be inclined to subscribe to the nebulous argumentation of some strand of deconstructivism or of the associated 'Crits'[18] to see the problem. At the very least, the difficulty presents itself prominently in constitutional comparison,[19] regardless of epistemic preferences. At a deeper level, however, constitutional scholarship must be cognizant of the reality that liberalism is not the only worldview that may found valid legal perspectives on the state and everything it entails. This does not mean that liberalism must be deemed to be the sworn enemy of those who do not unquestioningly subscribe to it. It does however mean that those who prefer to operate only within the liberal paradigm are not justified to assume that (constitutional) thinking that questions the universal validity of liberalism is unsophisticated, retrogressive, fundamentalistic or for some other reason objectionable.

The vulnerability of monolithic liberal constitutionalism is steadily coming to light not only at the hands of the postmodern 'Crits', but more productively from the perspective of a *desire for terminological clarity*, apparent from the

---

[14] *The Guardian* 28 June 2019.
[15] E.g., Frankenberg 'Critique' Chapter 2.
[16] Frankenberg 'Critique' 34. In Frankenberg 'Political Technology' 97–100 he also thoroughly exposed 'the ambivalence of the liberal paradigm' regarding states of exception.
[17] An apt and compact characterization was provided by Petra Gehring 'Mystical Foundation' 151:
> Derrida's deconstructive 'readings' pursue the project of a radical subversion of knowledge; and in this regard they share a certain kinship with the works of authors such as Foucault, Baudrillard, Lyotard, as different as they otherwise are. From a philosophical point of view, the project of deconstruction is directed against 'the' entire tradition of (Western) metaphysics, and from a political point of view against the order of speech, perhaps more precisely against technique, the techniques of speech and of recording (including the techniques of renewal) in science itself.

[18] As Frankenberg 'Critique' at e.g. 26 refers to them.
[19] Venter 'Rethinking' 72–96.

works of the likes of Barber,[20] Prandini,[21] Glenn,[22] Dowdle and Wilkinson,[23] who sometimes state expressly that they are not in the business of denigrating liberalism.[24] Commentators in this category, for example Peter Baofu in his thought-provoking book,[25] (understandably) do tend to indulge in complex cross-disciplinary theorization, often cumbersome and time-consuming to follow and therefore less accessible to many whose focus is primarily on constitutional law or constitutional comparison.

1.5 ADAPT, ... OR CONFORM?

If we then assume that it is no longer tenable to use the common constitutional Esperanto without qualification, the question arises how the expanding constitutional conversation and the growing global comparative constitutional discourse should be adapted in order to maximize cogency and mutual comprehensibility.

It is likely that the strongest instinctive resistance against challenges to the established language of liberal constitutionalism will come from the most influential and fecund scholarly, judicial and political community working in the countries around the North Atlantic (with some cultural colonies elsewhere on the globe), un-geographically referred to as 'the global North', which is, after all, where the dominant constitutional dictionary originated. Interestingly, however, most of the materials that have revealed the problem also emanate from this source, albeit from a broad spectrum of epistemic perspectives. What this means for the present project is that much space will have to be devoted to reviewing as concisely and accurately as possible generally known historical, theoretical and philosophical data required for understanding the origins and attributed meanings of the dominant constitutional vocabulary in order to highlight the attendant problematics.

---

[20] Barber 'Constitutional State'.
[21] Prandini 'Morphogenesis'.
[22] Glenn 'Cosmopolitan State'.
[23] Dowdle & Wilkinson 'Constitutional Reflexivity', not forgetting the works of Martin Loughlin, Neil Walker, Gunther Teubner and their scholarly ilk.
[24] See e.g. Dowdle & Wilkinson 'Constitutional Reflexivity' 1, where they expressly state that their purpose is not 'to dismiss liberal constitutionalism', but 'to explore not just what it does, but also what it doesn't do and what it is unable to account for.'
[25] Baofu 'Authoritarian Liberal Democracy'. The expression 'Autoritärer Liberalismus' was probably coined by Hermann Heller in 1933 in defence of the upcoming Nazi doctrine of 'national socialism' – see Wilkinson 'Reconstitution' 44–5, note 26.

Why go to all the trouble? The motive cannot be, and it is indeed not merely to show up presumed deficiencies in the thinking of liberal democratic theorists. The good ones among them have produced profound insights based on their liberal premises, and the best among them openly confess their foundational belief in 'classical' liberalism. No one can justify condemning another for holding sincere beliefs, whatever they may be, on the grounds of those beliefs being different or oppositional to one's own. Criticism of an attitude that the dominant dogmatic stance is above criticism is however eminently defensible, as is the revelation of inherent inconsistencies in dogmatic terminology of any stripe.

The alternative would be to take the route of least resistance, to conform by assuming that the dominant jargon will endure and continue to prevail – despite the clear signs of a lack of consistent justification and the indications of the ongoing drainage of its persuasiveness. Not conforming in this sense is what this book is about. It is about questioning the wisdom of maintaining the illusion that the only 'proper' language of constitutional law is the kind that conforms to a hegemonic dogma whose foundational premises are demonstrably incongruous.

1.6 THE STRUCTURE OF THE BOOK

1.6.1 Purpose

What is presented in the following chapters is an analysis of the origins and varicoloured dimensions of selected constitutional concepts in an effort to distil their essence. The analyses should reveal some of the difficulties that arise for constitutional comparatists wishing to interact cogently amid the conceptual fluidity of constitutional words while subjectively holding divergent views on the origins and validation of legal authority. In a constitutional conversation involving an idea or notion that has the same name but represents divergent subjective understandings, it would be helpful if the participants felt constrained to reveal their subjective views on the essential meaning of the constitutional notions under discussion.[26] No doubt promoting such openness is an idealistic goal, but although ideals are often not achieved, scholarship tends to proceed from idealism, making it worth the effort.

Although theorization and philosophy cannot be avoided altogether, the objective of the analyses and discussion in the following chapters is reason-

---

[26] Dowdle & Wilkinson 'Constitutional Reflexivity' 33–5 suggest that psychology should come to our aid in crossing the cultural divide in a charitable manner, but that is not the route that will be followed here.

able comprehensibility and accessibility of the complexities of constitutional theory. One should not have any illusions about the fact that almost all of the topics addressed in this book have been traversed innumerable times, both over the centuries and in recent literature. Nevertheless, given the concern that comparative legal language is increasingly becoming confusing, assumptive and fragmented,[27] it is considered worthwhile to assess the conceptual challenges facing constitutional lawyers anew, especially in the interests of those engaged in comparative work.

1.6.2 Chapters

Chapter 2 seeks to sketch, by means of a condensed historical overview, a composite picture of the foundations and gradual diffusion to many parts of the world of key constitutional conceptions conventionally employed in constitutional discourse. Some of the most influential founding doctrines and social changes that inspired the development of the constitutional language currently in vogue, are outlined. The purpose is to provide basic historical background necessary for an assessment of the ability of the vocabulary in vogue to give comparative expression to the current constitutional realities relating to governmental power, the means to limit it, and the emerging social, economic and political trends.

Chapter 3 deals with the role that the idea of 'the nation' has played and continues to crop up in constitutional and international language, despite patently being an anachronism.

'Sovereignty' is a key concept in public law, but it does not adequately explain why states are deemed to have sovereign authority, or in what or whom sovereign power should vest. In Chapter 4 this legal notion and the inconsistent manner in which it is used, despite being an indispensable element in constitutional and public international law, is considered.

Chapter 5 deals with the surprisingly wide range of divergent conceptions of 'the state' and the various flavours of meaning attributed to this quintessential constitutional construct, ubiquitous around the globe.

---

[27] Consider e.g. Olivier Moréteau's remark in Moréteau 'The Words of Comparative Law' 205:
> Legal science does not have a specialty language. Legal terms are given a normative meaning inside each legal order. They are therefore not suitable for comparative work, because there is constant doubt as to whether a term is used in a neutral way or with its normative meaning inside a legal system. Developing a metalanguage requires imagination and may be done at the risk of being rejected by national jurists, who may no longer understand what we are talking about ...

Citizenship and nationality are on the one hand indispensable identifiers of an individual's association with a state, but the perception of the meaning of these related but distinct concepts, their importance in law, their relationship with statehood, and their legal content and configuration are expressed variously in the language of constitutional law, public international law and other legal and extra-legal disciplines. These are the topics of Chapter 6.

Democracy as a term dates back to ancient Greece, but it has since then been reconfigured in many manifestations. Since at least the nineteenth century democracy has been championed as the ideal system of government, but what is the effect of the exponential growth of the size of electorates on the theory that 'the people' are the source and collective repository of legal authority and governmental power in view of the reality that they have a negligible amount of actual control over the constitutional institutions of the state? This question, variation in the manner in which democracy is conceived and the challenges the idea is facing are highlighted in Chapter 7.

The rule of law is a popular sobriquet in the constitutional vernacular of the world, and it (as well as its related notions in other languages –such as *der Rechtsstaat, état de droit, stato di diritto, el estado de derecho, il principio di legalità*) is usually deemed to be characteristic of good governance and constitutionalism. Chapter 8 is concerned with the variation of meanings and the consequences for comparative discourse of the overburdening of the idea.

Chapter 9 addresses the meaning and content attributed to the collective term 'constitutionalism', which is a widely used symbolic expression of a desirable state of affairs in constitutional law, albeit with many adjectives attached to it. The extensive, but undefined use of the term exemplifies the pliability – and concomitant vagueness – of the notions associated with it in the standard constitutional lexicon.

Constitutional adjudication very often involves the resolution of moral issues, political disputes, all based on the prevailing judicial notions of justice. The spectrum of approaches to an ancient phenomenon across cultures, namely closing disputes by means of final and enforceable adjudication and some of the controversies related to the appropriate place of the judiciary in contemporary constitutional structuring of states, form the substance of Chapter 10.

The question confronted in Chapter 11 is what the implications are for comparative constitutional scholarship of the ongoing variance, mutation and diversity of meaning of the words and concepts that our unstable constitutional vocabulary harbours. This involves briefly addressing the nature and methodologies of constitutional comparison, and finally a demonstration of how slippery the foundations of the standard lexicon are, comparatively speaking.

The epilogue is reserved for an indulgence in the declaration of subjective premises and their implications for a personal understanding of constitutional authority. Doing so emphasizes the severe challenges that all constitutional comparatists face, and the need to address them openly.

2. The history of contemporary constitutional language

Writing about legal comparison and its 'neighbouring disciplines' in general, Mathias Reimann's accurate remarks are particularly apt for constitutional comparison:

> It is by now a banality that comparative law and legal history are closely related, in that both look at law beyond the present domestic legal order, the former in space, the latter in time. This kinship has inspired Hein Kötz to call the disciplines 'twin sisters' (leaving it open which 'is the more comely').
> It is also beyond cavil that both disciplines can greatly benefit from each other. Comparative law often needs a historical dimension in order fully to understand the laws, processes, and institutions it considers – modern similarities and differences in judicial decision-making, for example, are fully intelligible only against the background of their historical development.[1]

As recently as 2017 Justin Collings commented on the 'scarcity' and 'slenderness' of comparative constitutional history,[2] and then went on to propose three possible approaches to the field: perspectival (focusing on a single jurisdiction), thematic (with a focus on a single theme across jurisdictions without regard to chronology) and relational (examining multiple jurisdictions within a single chronological frame).[3]

If what follows has to be categorized within Collings' framework, it would probably be similar to the thematic, the theme being the development of constitutional concepts and terminology over the centuries. No more than a cursory overview of the historical background of the constitutional language under consideration is possible here, but the survey should serve the purpose. The focus is on the origins of the relevant terminology, rather than the historiography concerning the unfolding of socio-economic, cultural and political occurrences that propelled the language of the constitutional law of Europe and North America to its enduring position of conceptual hegemony.

---

[1] Reimann 'Neighbouring Disciplines' 22–3.
[2] Collings 'Comparative Constitutional History' 484–5.
[3] Collings 'Comparative Constitutional History' 486–95.

2.1 ANCIENT ROOTS

In and before the heyday of Athenian democracy, generally considered to have been the foundation upon which the current constitutional edifice was erected, there most certainly had been well-established political and social systems in different regions in the world that might, if they had survived and been able to extend their influence, have determined the nature of twenty-first-century statehood. Thus, we have evidence of powerful and sometimes long-lasting ancient empires in regions like Egypt, Mesopotamia, China, South America and parts of Africa.[4]

The constitutional law (or equivalent system of norms) of none of those earlier civilizations survived or has had a significant effect on the way most lawyers think today of law, society, politics or religion. One can speculate whether there might be a decisive element such as the presence or absence of popular participation that distinguishes those past orders from what became Western democracy, but such hypothetical speculation will not be pursued here.

Regarding the conception of constitutional structuring no continuous line can be drawn from pre-history or ancient history to the present. The ancient empires elsewhere in the world and the Hellenic 'city states' were conceived in isolation from each other, and it is also not possible to draw an historical line from the social structures of Sparta or Athens to any later predecessors of modern statehood. In fact, the Aristotelean *polis* was not conceived of as a 'state', but as a collection of lower-order communities.[5] Crucially, however, what did survive over some 25 centuries, was the foundational thinking of some of the ancient Greeks, especially that of Plato and Aristotle. This survival may be attributed to the resurrection of the Greek classics during the Enlightenment by some of the most influential founding thinkers of contemporary constitutional dogma, such as Montesquieu,[6] Machiavelli and Hobbes,[7] (even) Locke[8] and others, who either oriented their own theories and philosophical construction relative to Plato and Aristotle, or were oriented thus by others.[9]

---

[4] See e.g. Aguilera-Barchet 'History' 10–15 on ancient state-like institutions in the Indus Valley, Egypt and China, and even more comprehensively, the four volumes of Glassman 'Origins'.
[5] See e.g. Bates 'Aristotle's Politics' 59–60.
[6] See e.g. Hartmann, Meyer & Oldopp 'Geschichte' 17–32.
[7] See e.g. Finnis 'Natural Law Theory'.
[8] See e.g. Maloy 'Locke's Politics'.
[9] See in general Huppes-Cluysenaer & Coelho.

The first direct and lasting historical impact that Hellenic thinking concerning the *poleis* had, was on ancient Rome. The beginnings of the Roman era (around the sixth and fifth centuries BC) roughly coincided with the emergence of the *poleis* of Athens and Sparta, although there was no connection between them, until the Romans invaded the Greek peninsula and finally subjected the region in the Battle of Corinth in 146 BC. Personalities who were influential in Roman politics and law such as Cicero (106–43 BC) were educated in and diligently studied ancient Greek philosophy, poetry and history. Nevertheless, the idealistic Hellenistic notions of direct democracy could not find practical purchase in any of the periods of Roman hegemony, nor during the Kingdom (753–509 BC), the Republic (509–27 BC), the (Western) Empire (27 BC–476 AD) or Byzantium (395–1453 AD). This may be ascribed to the large extent of the expansion of Roman influence over vast geographical areas and during various historical eras stretching over more than 20 centuries.

The legacies of the Roman Empire and its law had a much more direct impact on later legal and, less directly constitutional, developments that underpin contemporary constitutional concepts. According to Aguilera-Barchet –

> Rome is the model and the political and legal touchstone for most Western countries. If this is patent in the sphere of private law, it is no less evident in the area of public law. Rome is, in short, the first great state in Western history, a manifest source of inspiration for many great intellectuals, including the likes of Montesquieu, Gibbon and Ferrero in their reflections on political society, the leaders of the American Revolution and even for Napoleon, one of the architects of the contemporary Western state.[10]

2.2 THE MIDDLE AGES AND THE INCEPTION OF THE RENAISSANCE

A few ubiquitous characteristics of the legal (especially constitutional) and political structure of any society present themselves even in an epigrammatic consideration of the ebb and flow of the history of humanity. Among these are:

- the existence of *authority* (in its less gracious form, *power*) present in from the smallest social unit (the family) to the most expansive empire;
- the constant presence of *hierarchy*: there are always those (usually a few) in control, and those (the many) being managed or governed;
- various levels of *relative influence* attributed to groups and individuals within the society concerned;
- *relative autonomy* from surrounding or remote social structures.

---

[10] Aguilera-Barchet 'History' 38.

These typical features of human society manifest themselves in a spectrum ranging from the beneficial to the malevolent: from kind and responsible leadership and comity, to subjugation and arbitrary dictatorial abuse of might. The scale of authority (be it geographical, cultural or commercial) is dynamic and never ceases to vary over time and geographical area.

Seen thus, the demise of the Roman Empire left its area of influence politically, economically and socially fractured[11] for more than ten centuries – sometimes referred to as the 'dark' Middle Ages in Europe. The eventual emergence from this 'darkness' during the Renaissance, the age of Enlightenment, can best be understood against the background of the general nature and development of mediaeval governance.

The vacuum that was left in the political and legal order that was maintained by the Roman Empire could not be filled in any consistent form. Localized authority depended on the abilities of a multitude of regional chieftains and feudal lords to impose their (usually tyrannical) authority over the communities in their scattered territories. Between the fourth and sixth centuries multiple wars, epidemics and famines brought about serious demographic and agricultural crises. The optimistic anthropocentric attitude of classical times was replaced by a pessimistic view of the subordination of man to nature, against which the individual needed communal protection. This emphasis on community can be seen as the seed of the later development and emphasis on nationality. In this period migrating groups (Goths, Lombards, Huns, Vandals, Anglo-Saxons, Franks, etc.) moved southward and settled in Western Europe and Britain. The Roman Church expanded its presence across Europe, stepping into the space left by the essentially powerless public authorities, and providing a conceptual vehicle for individual redemption only through the community of the Church (*extra Ecclesiam nulla salus*). Since the feudal lords were not engaged in much more than maintaining their own power, regular social order depended more on the values that the communities adhered to than on intervention by the authorities, such as they were. The notion of a 'state' as a source of legal authority did not exist in this era, but in due course territorially determined, unwritten sets of mores (*consuetudines*) began emerging as the primary source of a legal order.[12]

During the Middle Ages the Roman Church consciously developed its own canonical legal order. Out of a confused conglomeration of ecclesiastical rules, scholars such as Ivo of Chartres consolidated canon law in the eleventh

---

[11] This pattern, fragmentation following the fall of empires, would appear across all history to have been the inevitable sequel to the collapse of consolidated imperial power.

[12] Grossi 'Geschichte' 21–36.

century, elastically taking into account the localized circumstances of the populace. By then social circumstances were changing, brought about by a significant increase of the population, growing urbanization and mobility of people and goods. An important new class, merchants, was established and education and scholarship became more readily available. By the twelfth century universities were founded, leading to more universal – as opposed to inward-looking naturalistic – perspectives and ventures. Legal scholarship emerged, building upon philosophy and theology. Whereas the cultural vacuum now began to be filled, the political vacuum persisted. The role of feudal lords was not understood to be that of arbitrary lawgivers, but ideally as adjudicators entrusted with the responsibility to apply the laws of the community wisely on the basis of *aequitas* (justice).[13]

The first foundations for the forming of states in Europe were laid by the thirteenth-century monarchs in France, Spain and Portugal, where they were able to extend their territorial authority over a growing number of feudal lords. Philippe Auguste was the first to bear the title 'King of France' from 1180 to 1223, gradually beginning to exert legislative authority. Against the background of the persistent fragmentation of customary law Louis IX initiated more decisive legal reform in France by 1254. In Portugal Alfons III (1248–79) and in Spain Alfons X (1265–84) followed suit. Eclectic monarchical edicts were however not suited to deal with the mounting need for economic and legal ordering of the European society, which was steadily becoming more complex.[14]

Enter learning and legal scholarship, which expanded throughout the region, inspiring the formation of a community of scientists and teachers. The advantage that legal scholars had over royal lawgivers was that they could concentrate on the collection of fragmented materials and their consolidation, and then writing commentaries and extract or develop foundational and guiding legal principles. In short, the legal scholars went about establishing law as a respected scientific discipline. In the absence of an overarching contemporary model for legal ordering, the Roman law recommended itself. After lying fallow for five centuries, the Justinian *Corpus Iuris Civilis* was rediscovered to be explored thoroughly by the scholars, who ventured into adaptive interpretation of the texts to render them applicable to the conditions of late mediaeval society. Due to the mobility and intellectual influence of legal scholarship, the development of a (notionally global) common law, the *ius commune*, validated by the example of the Roman (civil) law and simultaneously by canon law, served as a powerful mechanism for legal unification across Europe, based on

---

[13] Grossi 'Geschichte' 42–49.
[14] Grossi 'Geschichte' 49–52.

rationality. Relating territorial ownership and personal association to land in order to exercise authority, *feudal* law was consolidated. By the middle of the twelfth century feudal notions were combined with those found in civil and canon law to form a common European legal order.[15]

The fourteenth century brought both the high and the turning points of the Middle Ages. Amidst devastating wars, epidemics, economic and agricultural crises emerged a shift of focus to the intelligent individual in search of subjective freedom, thereby laying the foundations of modernity. In law the notion of property, not only in physical things (*dominium rerum*), but also in one's person and abilities (*dominium sui*) developed. This trend was driven by voluntaristic theology and philosophy (emphasizing non-coercion) and the object/thing-centred attitude of the previous centuries began evolving into an anthropocentric orientation. Nothing like a state existed yet. Public life still took place amidst a tug of war between the two 'holy' centres of power, the Roman Church and the disjointed *Sacrum Imperium Romanum* since the ninth century comprising much of Western Europe. The struggle for power between pope and emperor became more pronounced, especially in France where the kings expressly claimed primary authority in all worldly affairs, thereby introducing the notion of *sovereignty* and legislative power, albeit initially still understood as the confirmation of customary law based on *aequitas*.[16]

The humanism that originated in fourteenth-century Europe and flowered in the following centuries provides a key to the understanding of our contemporary constitutional language. Against the background of the mediaeval subjection of the person to ignorance of and fear for nature and the supernatural, to the all-encompassing exclusive mediation by the Roman Catholic Church between the divine and the secular, and the unchecked powers of the feudal lords, there developed *humanism*, entailing full trust in the individual as the 'sovereign' over nature and society, owner of goods and body, capable of gaining insight in the workings of creation. No doubt this emphasis on intellectual freedom rendered society receptive to fundamental religious change. Although the Reformation of the early sixteenth century was not primarily driven by notions of humanism (rather the contrary), the idea that not the Church, but the individual conscience and direct personal access to Scripture should replace corrupt ecclesiastical mediation could easily take root in the general atmosphere of humanism.[17] Individual wealth, colonialism and com-

---

[15] Grossi 'Geschichte' 52–68. The mediaeval lawyer was required to interpret both civil law and canon law in order to access the *ius commune*, which incidentally explains the plural (*legum*) in the history of the legal qualification, *baccalaureus legum* (LLB).

[16] Grossi 'Geschichte' 71–81.

[17] See e.g. Van Gelder 'Two Reformations', especially Chapter VI, stating concisely at 227: 'In the religious evolution with the Humanists (and under their leader-

mercial capitalism also originated in this period of 'rebirth' – the *Renaissance*. The explosive expansion of free and innovative scholarship and science and the development by the 'natural philosophers' of 'the scientific method' did not leave legal scholarship untouched: legal learning was thought of by many as a science.[18]

The renaissance lawyers denounced the formalistic methods of the glossators and commentators, who, according to the new notion of juristic humanism, accepted the *Corpus Iuris Civilis* at face value without contextualizing it in its pre-history of ten centuries of the Roman civilization. Following the other sciences, law had to be a *pansophistic* discipline, taking into account the full extent of scientific knowledge. By a renewed analysis of classical Roman law against the background of Greek and Roman logic, legal scholarship developed the law into a systematic and objective structuring mechanism useful for revealing even the mathematical and geometrical architecture of the cosmos. This approach was the precursor of the development of the idea of natural law. Another significant consequence of the new approach to Roman law as belonging in its own historical context was that the importance of contemporary law came to be emphasized (by for instance the sixteenth-century French Protestant lawyer François Hotmann). This facilitated the strengthening of the belief that (among others) the French king should exercise legislative authority, thereby introducing the concept of the national state.[19]

2.3 NATURAL LAW, THE ENLIGHTENMENT AND ABSOLUTISM

The Enlightenment legal scholarship of the sixteenth and seventeenth centuries in Europe perceived itself, like mathematics and the natural sciences, to be in the business of discovering the universal laws governing nature as it is. Thus, lawyers strove to reveal the universal rules regulating the conduct of humanity as inscribed in the nature of man, discoverable by means of objective observation.[20] To achieve this, it was considered necessary to avoid the contamination

---

ship) I called attention to two tendencies: the transition from a doctrine of salvation to a doctrine of living and a dislike or devaluation of sacramentalism.'

[18] Grossi 'Geschichte' 86–90.
[19] Grossi 'Geschichte' 92–7.
[20] Strauss 'Natural Right' 92 captured the essence of this approach, which still endures:
> ... [B]y uprooting authority, philosophy recognizes nature as *the* standard. For the human faculty that, with the help of sense-perception, discovers nature is reason or understanding, and the relation of reason or understanding to its objects is fundamentally different from that obedience without reasoning why that corresponds to authority proper. By calling nature the highest authority, one would

of history, and to investigate humanity in its natural, i.e. original, condition where individuals were assumed to have conducted themselves freely and autonomously, without social structure or limitation. Natural law therefore operated as an abstract model against which the realities of arbitrary limitation of individual freedom were to be measured. This explains the emphasis (by among others Grotius and Locke) on personal freedom and property.[21]

Thus, natural law theories emerged on the one hand as a scientific search for objective truth,[22] but on the other hand as a strategy to satisfy individual demands against those in authority based largely on the sanctity of property. Consequently, the abstraction of the 'state of nature' did not benefit all equally: the wealthy could profit from the protection of their freedom and equality, but equality and freedom did not (and could never) guarantee wealth. Furthermore, the abstract model of the state of nature is incapable of being realized, and therefore reality required free individuals to come to an agreement on how they were to be governed and their rights protected. These were the seeds for the myth of the social contract.

In the Enlightenment of the seventeenth and eighteenth centuries, an intellectual aversion developed against the cluttered and complicated system of customary laws. This attitude appealed to lawyers who did not consider themselves to be philosophers but mere practical experts, and to the lower classes living by custom. Thus, a new legal vacuum occurred, allowing for instance the Prussian, Austrian and Portuguese monarchs to utilize natural law thinking for the justification of their authority to lay the foundations for national legal systems by means of legislation. The monarch assumed the position of a superior person who was capable of objectively perceiving the natural state of the world better than most, including the Church, and to transform those insights into binding norms.[23]

---

blur the distinction by which philosophy stands or falls, the distinction between reason and authority. By submitting to authority, philosophy, in particular political philosophy, would lose its character; it would degenerate into ideology ...

[21] Grossi 'Geschichte' 98–105. Hochstrasser 'Natural Law Theories' 5 also points out that '[i]t has ... often been shown that ["modern" natural law theories] tended to endorse an absolutist view of property rights (of which Rousseau's critique in the *Contrat Social* is only the best-known example)' and that 'these difficulties were inherent in their basic contention that men held subjective rights by *dominium* which could hardly be regulated by any identifiable objective moral standard of justice.'

[22] Chernilo 'Natural Law Foundations' 73–88 demonstrates the significant variance in conceptions of natural law, but holds that the intellectual core of the natural law tradition is to be found in the idea of universalism.

[23] See e.g. Dauchy 'Western Legal Culture' Chapter 3, where the work of more than 80 authors of legal books of the period are introduced in which the ideas related to natural law and especially the process of codification were clearly reflected.

Therefore, the intellectuals attributed to the monarchs sovereign legislative powers as absolute custodians of the common will of all. Ironically, however, every monarch's jurisdiction was limited territorially, inevitably producing diverse 'concretizations' of natural law, contradicting natural universalism by means of territorial particularism. This introduced an era of legalism as a state of mind according to which the law, as an expression of sound human reason posited exclusively by the state and to be enforced and adhered to without question, was deemed to be the unquestionable foundation of the social order. Key philosophers of the Enlightenment such as Montesquieu, Rousseau and Immanuel Kant promoted this approach which still endures to a large extent.[24]

Inevitably, in time, absolutism bred popular resistance.

2.4 FOUNDATIONAL POLITICAL PHILOSOPHY

The list of philosophers that laid the foundations for the development of the prevailing culture of the West is long and their philosophies have been studied, dissected, dismantled and reconstructed, critiqued, and used innumerable times as building blocks to promote more theorization and philosophizing by later scholars. To narrow down the philosophical theories to those that have exerted most influence on (Western) constitutional thinking when it was conceived between the sixteenth and eighteenth centuries, is however not difficult, and the list has in effect become more or less standardized. On such a list of names and works one will typically find Niccolò Machiavelli (Italy, *Il Principe* 1532), Jean Bodin (France, *Les Six livres de la République*, 1576/1583), Thomas Hobbes (England, *Leviathan* 1688), John Locke (England, *Two Treatises of Government* 1689), Baron de Montesquieu (France, *De l'esprit des lois* 1748), Jean-Jacques Rousseau (France, *Du Contrat Social ou Principes du Droit Politique* 1762), and Immanuel Kant (Germany, *Kritik der reinen Vernunft* 1781).

Machiavelli introduced the notion of the modern state, thereby preparing the ground for the emergence of the European nation states. He is credited for linking politics logically to the state and to capitalistic economics.[25]

Bodin construed unquestionable sovereign authority to legislate, vested in the ruler as earthly representative of God, subject only to divine and natural law. Although the exercise of such sovereignty was not to be disobeyed by the people (its purpose being to protect the people and their peaceful co-existence,

---

[24] Grossi 'Geschichte' 105–12.
[25] Voigt 'Der moderne Staat' 5–6.

their lives, property and freedom),[26] Bodin allowed for dethronement of a tyrant in the event of abuse of power, but only by another sovereign.[27]

According to *Hobbes'* fictional construction based on an assumption of human egotism combined with rationality, man without the state, living in a self-destructive state of nature, is like a wolf against others (*homo homini lupus*). Social order is only possible if absolute sovereign power is placed in the hands of a state. This was achieved by a founding agreement (a social contract) expressing the united will of the people to entrust absolute sovereign power in the hands of the monarch.[28] Hobbes depicted the state as a human creation of political wisdom in the form of a 'Leviathan', which is a mortal god, an artificial animal, a machine whose purpose is to ensure the people's peaceful existence and freedom.[29] Hobbes' ruler, as representative (actually replacement) of God in secular matters, was entrusted with absolute power, not bound by the limitations of divine or natural law.[30]

Locke –

> is often regarded as perhaps the preeminent founder of liberalism for to many it is in the account of the state of nature in Locke's *Second Treatise* that modernity was first introduced to the natural rights-bearing, pre-civil individual who made possible the liberal civic person 'constituted by moral sovereignty over one's core beliefs and practices'.[31]

Locke's imagined state of nature was an altogether more peaceful condition where everyone was free, equal and independent, although all had reason to fear interference by others. To ensure a good life and the preservation of freedom and property, humankind came to a voluntary agreement to subject themselves to the exercise of authority over them by entrusting the responsibility to govern according to the will of the majority, to which the minority must, rather than fall back to the state of nature, yield. Locke recognized the tendency in human nature to abuse power, which he suggested should be checked by a separation of powers.[32]

---

[26] Mäder 'Souveränität' 54.
[27] Balke 'Figuren' 33–42.
[28] Weber-Fas 'Staatsdenker' 51.
[29] Balke 'Figuren' 60.
[30] Weber-Fas 'Staatsdenker' 51.
[31] Ward 'John Locke' 65.
[32] Weber-Fas 'Staatsdenker' 87–8.

Montesquieu read Locke's work, and took the notion of the separation of powers to a new level:

> In every government there are three sorts of power: the legislative; the executive in respect to things dependent on the law of nations; and the executive, in regard to things that depend on the civil law.
> By virtue of the first, the prince or magistrate enacts temporary or perpetual laws, and amends or abrogates those that have been already enacted. By the second, he makes peace or war, sends or receives embassies, establishes the public security, and provides against invasions. By the third, he punishes criminals, or determines the disputes that arise between individuals. The latter we shall call the judiciary power, and the other simply the executive power of the state.
> When the legislature and executive powers are united in the same person, or in the same body of magistrates, there can be no liberty; because apprehensions may arise, lest the same monarch or senate should enact tyrannical laws, to execute them in a tyrannical manner.
> Again, there is no liberty, if the power of judging be not separated from the legislative and executive powers. Were it joined with the legislative, the life and liberty of the subject would be exposed to arbitrary control; for the judge would be then the legislator. Were it joined to the executive power, the judge might behave with all the violence of an oppressor.[33]

Montesquieu's thinking influenced the authors of the Constitution of the United States of America, where the separation of powers was canonized, more or less as it is generally understood today. An interesting question to consider, is how 'liberal' (in the meaning attributed later to the word) Montesquieu's thinking actually was. This was a question raised by Céline Spector, who analyzed the 'Spirit of the Laws' with reference to what she indicated to be the classical definition of liberalism as 'a belief in limited government, the protection of individual rights and the positive effects of interest in the absence of virtue'.[34] According to Spector recognition of Montesquieu's careful, courteous style and his admiration of the English constitutional situation reveals that he 'neither defends the individual conceived as a rights-holder, nor advocates the minimal state', but that he advocated moderation as a requirement for the practical reconciliation of state power and individual liberty.[35]

Rousseau observed the unequal distribution of wealth in eighteenth-century France among the social classes and responded by seeking to promote universal equality and everyone's right to directly participate in democratic decision making. In its progression from the ideal natural state (*état naturel*) to the civilized state (*état civil*), his ideas of popular sovereignty were based on the

---

[33] Montesquieu 'Spirit of Laws' Book XI, Chapter VI.
[34] Spector 'Was Montesquieu liberal?' 59.
[35] Spector 'Was Montesquieu liberal?' 72.

idea that a person's humanity is based on liberty. He wrote: 'To renounce your liberty is to renounce your status as a man, your rights as a human being, and even your duties as a human being.'[36] The purpose of the original social contract founding the state was not only to ensure peace and security, but more specifically to protect the weak. Citing three different works of Rousseau, Judith Shklar described Rousseau's rather ironical views as follows:

> Not only are most individuals too weak to protect themselves against the strong among them. They are not even able to see and pursue their own best interest. The general will, the public will of the people does tend to equality, but alas, 'the force of things is always against it.' That is so because 'the people are stupid.' The people are simply a collection of potential victims. They are nevertheless better, healthier, and more decent than the rich and powerful. They are also all that matters. Let all the kings and philosophers disappear and everything would go on much as usual. These are indeed the perennial attitudes of 'populism,' and Rousseau was surely its original voice.[37]

Individuals must be free to do as they wish, while also subjecting themselves to the common will (*volonté générale*). Thereby the sovereignty of the state becomes absolute, since the individual will is unconditionally subject to the common will. Again ironically, the contractual obligations of the individual enforce 'freedom' in the form of being subject to the (absolute) general will: 'Each of us puts his person and all his power in common under the supreme direction of the general will, and, in our corporate capacity, we receive each member as an indivisible part of the whole.'[38]

Defending Rousseau against those who criticize him as illiberal, totalitarian and contradictory, Marco Goldoni argues that his purpose was to transcend and 'utterly dismiss' the social contract of liberalism: 'The only way to overcome the corruptive and dysfunctional logic of liberal (economic) autonomy is to build a different social being upon the bases of the primacy of the public interest and a strong and substantial conception of equality.'[39] Goldoni then goes on to show (convincingly) how the thinking of Karl Marx, and even more so his followers, was supported by Rousseau's work.[40]

---

[36] Rousseau (Bennett's translation at 4) 'Social Contract' Book 1, 4.
[37] Shklar 'Rousseau and Equality' 21–2.
[38] Rousseau (Bennett's translation at 7) 'Social Contract' Book 1, 6. It remains a curiosity of philosophy how apparently indefensible and contradictory notions such as these, produced by an unstable personality (Rousseau), could profoundly influence other great thinkers such as Kant, Goethe, Nietzsche and Marx: see e.g. Weber-Fas (note 28 above) 155–8.
[39] Goldini 'Radical Constitutionalism' 239.
[40] Goldini 'Radical Constitutionalism' 248–50.

Despite the complexity of his work, *Kant*'s influence strongly reverberates in Western thought to this day. Wilson helpfully summarizes Kant's central ambition to be –

> ... to draw a protective ring around the 'unforsakable' core of common, everyday morality. In his view, we are all committed to a belief in human freedom and a belief in the unconditional nature of moral obligation. These beliefs are embedded in the way we act and the way we understand ourselves, even if we routinely betray them both. Neither belief can be theoretically justified, but philosophy must show that we are entitled to them anyway. Morality depends upon it. If these beliefs are groundless, then there is no reason to think we have an inner worth that distinguishes us from the rest of nature – and so no reason to think we truly *owe* anything to ourselves or to each other.[41]

Ascribing everyone an autonomous will as the source of morality, Kant, the supreme rationalist, declared that such will distinguishes humans from the rest of nature, and that the dignity of human nature is founded upon its autonomy.[42] Kant positioned the rational person, the individual entitled to dignity, at the centre of everything. This attitude continues to be perhaps the most essential element of Western thinking, including constitutional theory. Various elements of the current Western mindset, including individual entitlement to act with self-interest, and voluntary submission to legal authority for purposes of personal protection, can be recognized from the following passage, written more than 220 years ago:

> It is not empirical experience from which we learn of human beings' maxim of violence and of their malevolent tendency to attack one another before external legislation endowed with power appears. It is not some empirical fact that makes coercion through public law necessary. On the contrary, however well disposed and law abiding men might be, it still lies *a priori*, in the rational idea of such a condition, that before a public lawful condition is established individual human beings, peoples, and states, can never be secure against violence from one another, since each has its own right to do what seems right and good to it and not to be dependent upon another's opinion about this. So, unless they wish to abolish all civil rights, they must leave the state of nature, in which each follows its own judgment, and unite themselves, subjecting themselves to public lawful external coercion and entering into a civil condition.[43]

Despite his rationalism, Kant therefore fully bought into the notion of an original state of nature and the illusional social contract.

---

[41] Wilson 'Kant' 442.
[42] Wilson 'Kant' 449.
[43] Kant 'Metaphysics of Morals' §44 at 30–1.

The concepts and constructions developed by the above-mentioned philosophers over approximately 250 years continue to form the basis, approximately another 200 years later, of our global constitutional vocabulary. Among these are 'state', 'sovereignty', the 'social contract', the 'separation of powers', 'liberty' and 'dignity'. Directly emanating from these notions are further concepts foundational to the language of constitutional law, including 'citizenship', 'democracy', 'nation', 'constitutionalism', 'rule of law' and 'judicial authority'.

Although it may be a generalization, it is safe to say that the commonly accepted characterization of the dominant constitutional theory of the West based on the key philosophical works of the sixteenth to the eighteenth centuries, is 'liberal democracy'. Boring down to the very essence of this notion, one finds the Kantian proclamation of the autonomy of the individual, the rational person caught between the demand to be free to act in self-interest, and the inescapable reality that everyone forms part of a society which is an encumbrance (necessary evil?) on one's natural autonomy. Jeremy Waldron succinctly explained it thus:

> Although enlightenment for Kant means thinking for oneself, one is only thinking for oneself when one exposes one's views to 'the test of free and open examination.' From this perspective, it is quite likely that individuals, in the state of nature trying to figure out principles of right and justice, will come up with partial or one-sided, and thus, antagonistic, views.[44]

The most curious element of the dominant historically received constitutional thinking is its reliance on the construction of a social contract or compact. Apart from the acknowledged fictional nature of the mass agreement, the indeterminacy of its content has allowed for constant dispute and contestation, essentially because it is construed as the mechanism with which humanity escapes or had escaped 'the state of nature'. *The nature of this fabricated state or condition has proven to be a matter of subjective conjecture and opportunistic construction.* This for instance explains the opposing pessimistic and optimistic views of the human condition offered by Hobbes and Locke, and the ongoing reconstruction of perceptions of pre-contractual circumstances.[45]

---

[44] Waldron, 'Kant's Legal Positivism' 1552 (quoting both Kant and Hannah Arendt).
[45] This is clearly demonstrated in the seminal article by Waldron, 'Kant's Legal Positivism'. See also Ward 'John Locke' 65–100.

2.5 THE REVOLUTIONS THAT BIRTHED CONSTITUTIONALISM

By the late eighteenth century the economic, political and philosophical developments in Europe created ideal conditions for the two iconic revolutions that inspired the solidification of the essentials of modern constitutionalism. Around the globe the French and American revolutions affected the political and constitutional thinking of the nineteenth century, and even today much of our constitutional language can be traced back to those revolutions and their consequences.[46]

The French Revolution of 1789 brought the notions *pouvoir constituant* (the constitution-making authority) and *pouvoir constitué* (the constitutionally instituted authority) into the standard vocabulary. Emmanuel-Joseph Sieyès, who was involved in both the revolution of 1789 and the plot ten years later leading to the elevation of Napoleon Bonaparte to power, claimed (not wholly justified) to have coined these concepts. They give expression to the notion of the sovereignty (and in others' hands, even the dictatorship) of the people.[47] The idea rests on the assumption that the sovereign nation (the 'third estate' in the jargon of the French revolution) is the primary holder of public authority. Where the nation therefore wills a new state, overthrowing the *pouvoir constitué*, it does so unbound by an existing constitution, and as *pouvoir constituant* creates its own, new founding document. In practice it is naturally not possible for the nation as a whole to convene and draft its founding documents, and it must therefore act through a representative body whose work may later be legitimized by popular vote.

In the same period, but on the other side of the Atlantic, and in a colonial context, the same political theories underpinned the American Revolution. Established early in the seventeenth century, the British colonies in North America developed their own style of government over some 170 years. The colonial governors mostly shared their authority with legislative bodies, which, over time, laid claim to representative superiority. Responding to the imposition of limitations by the British authorities around the 1760s, the colonists convened the *Continental Congress* in Philadelphia in 1774, and waged revolutionary war against the British between 1775 and 1783. In 1776 this led to the *Declaration of Independence* by the liberated territories, followed by the resolution to form a confederation. The Congress of the Confederation was however not sufficiently effective, bringing about the impulse to convene the *Constitutional Convention* in 1787. Guided by the thinking of the likes of

---

[46] This section draws on Venter 'Constitutional Comparison' 13–14.
[47] See e.g. Arato 'Adventures' 88–101 and 291–2.

John Locke and Hugo de Groot, this body performed the role of a constitutional assembly which then produced the *Constitution of the United States of America* of 1789.

Having been emulated frequently in many newly established states over the following 230 years, the American Constitution and its added 'Amendments' even today continue to serve as the most prominent standard for liberal constitutionalism. It is not necessarily the wording of the 1789 document as such that serves this purpose, but rather its fundamental characteristics which continue to be followed as leading archetype for modern constitution-making. The most important of these features are –

- a written, consolidated constitutional document serving as the highest law, enforceable by an independent judiciary;
- legal protection of individual rights entrenched in the constitution;
- the separation of the legislative, executive and judicial authority;
- a republican form of state; and
- the vertical distribution of government authority between the national, regional and local authorities (sometimes taking the form of a federation).

2.6 ENGLAND AND THE BRITISH EMPIRE

English constitutional history warrants special historical mention here, even at the cost of an interruption of the chronology. This is so because of the persistence of the effects of key constitutional notions over centuries up to the present that were conceived in London, and which were disseminated widely across the globe, transported along the colonial networks of the British Empire. Among these are the parliamentary and cabinet systems and a separated judiciary.

The fractured and largely chaotic political history of England up to the eleventh century produced no significant elements of constitutional law that survived the Norman Conquest of 1066. The Battle of Hastings left the Norman king William I ('the Conqueror') in a position of centralized power from where the English system could evolve.[48] William introduced feudalism in England. Eventually a contest for power between the Crown on the one hand and the feudal lords on the other, and eventually also the common population, ensued. In 1215 the barons extracted the signature of King John on the *Magna Carta Libertatum* (inter alia to lessen feudal payments to the monarch), which

---

[48] Grossi 'Geschichte' 81–2.

may justifiably be construed as an early manifestation of constitutionalism in the form of written restraints on the power of rulers.[49]

Feudal government was not complicated, since most matters were dealt with locally. The Norman kings brought with them the French concept of an advisory royal council, the *curia regis*, which was concerned with non-local affairs, regardless of whether they were (in the terminology that came in use only later) legislative, judicial, or administrative in nature. A distinction was drawn between the larger *Magnum Concilium*, convened occasionally, and the more influential, more or less permanent but smaller council of close members of the royal court. Over time more specialized institutions dealing with distinct governmental functions such as finance (the 'exchequer') and various adjudicatory functions split off from the smaller *curia*. A cabinet eventually grew out of the smaller council, and with the introduction of representative elements to the larger council, the seeds were sown for the development of a parliament, but it took time for the distinctions to solidify.[50] By the fifteenth century Parliament showed increasing independence from the Crown, and the royal council was being made responsible to Parliament, which was now split into an Upper and a Lower House.[51]

The effects in England of the *Renaissance* and the Reformation were in evidence in the sixteenth-century reign of Henry VIII. The growing influence of the merchant middle class promoted the legislative authority of Parliament[52] to the point of its being described as 'supreme'. Parliament's supremacy did not replace the authority of the monarch because some of the 'high prerogatives' of the Crown were retained. Parliament however became the supreme legislator whose consent came to be considered every Englishman's consent.[53] Seventeenth-century England saw a contest between Calvinist Puritans and Catholic Anglicans, centred around a dispute about the source of government authority: the Anglicans maintained the notion of royal authority being based on divinely ordained *rights*, whereas the Calvinists professed the idea of divine *delegation*.[54] Interestingly, the impact of Calvinistic thought on English constitutional history is controversial, perhaps because of a limited understanding

---

[49] See e.g. Glenn 'Cosmopolitan State' 45–6.
[50] For a concise description of these developments, see e.g. Adams, 'Descendants', and more detailed Lyon 'Medieval England' 329–69.
[51] See Hallam 'Constitutional History' 2 and 18–22; Lyon 'Medieval England' 535–61 and 586–612; Hatschek 'Englische Verfassungsgeschichte' 204 and 215–20; and William Stubbs 'Constitutional History' 375–499.
[52] Cf e.g. Hughes & Fries 'Crown and Parliament' 25–7 and 60–1.
[53] Hughes & Fries 'Crown and Parliament' 99–103 and Hallam 'Constitutional History' 276–84.
[54] Cf e.g. Hughes & Fries 'Crown and Parliament' 143 *et seq*.

of Calvin's teachings. Hughes and Fries for instance refer to different sections of Calvin's *Institutes* that appear to be contradictory, but the authors also show how they may actually be understood to be consistent:

> Very clearly, in the first section Calvin reaffirms the idea of strict obedience to magistrates whose powers are derived from divine commission. But, later, he denies the magistrate's right to require actions of the subject which are not in conformity with divine law ... To him ... political authority was delegated by God to the magistrate, and obedience to legitimate authority was thus the religious duty of every subject.[55]

Following the *interregnum* of Oliver Cromwell, a puritanical protestant, and the restoration of the Crown, the determining constitutional point of balance in favour of Parliament was reached in 1689 with the adoption of the *Bill of Rights*. This document marks not so much the inception of the notion of constitutionally protected individual rights (as the examples of its multiple later and contemporary namesakes suggest), but it recorded, amidst continuing political contestation between Anglicans and Puritans, the achievement of parliamentary precedence over the monarchy and the inception of legally sanctioned religious freedom.[56]

The evolution of the original form of cabinet government (emerging from the advisory councils of mediaeval monarchs) is closely connected to the development of the parliament. In the seventeenth century the word 'cabinet' was associated with a small room where the royal advisors met in confidence with for instance King Charles II. Eventually the cabinet grew in independence from the Crown, and by the early nineteenth century the cabinet was led by a Prime Minister.

Although it is customary to relate the origins of democracy to ancient Hellenic history, its modern form was primarily promoted by the history of the English Parliament, even as far back as 1295, when Edward I summoned the 'Model Parliament' to sanction the raising of general tax. In the subsequent centuries English parliaments were representative in one or another form. Originally local nobles designated county representatives sent to parliamentary meetings, but since the early fifteenth century the right to participate in elections and eligibility for election were regulated by statute, at times open, and in practice typically subject to, corrupt manipulation.[57]

In the seventeenth century the members of the House of Commons became divided into royalists and non-royalists. The *Reform Act* of 1832 stabilized elections, creating a system of single-member constituencies and facilitating

---

[55] Hughes & Fries 'Crown and Parliament' 147.
[56] Hughes & Fries 'Crown and Parliament' 307–15.
[57] Cf e.g. Loup 'Geschiedenis' 44–128 and Lyon 'Medieval England' 408–30.

the establishment of political parties. Now the ministers represented their political support base, and became answerable to Parliament, specifically in the House of Commons.[58]

Although not exclusively, English constitutional history produced 'the emergence of the notions of the popular franchise, a representative legislature, the political party system, [and] an executive government which is responsible to parliament',[59] all characteristics routinely associated with modern constitutionalism.

Although it might be said that British colonialism began in the twelfth century with the Anglo-Norman invasion of Ireland, it was only towards the end of the sixteenth century that, driven by commercial interests, the actual foundations were laid for the establishment of the 'First British Empire', largely represented by pre-independence North America. However, by the time of the American Declaration of Independence in 1776 marking the end of the 'First' Empire, the British flag flew, and English was spoken in many parts of the world, including Canada, the West Indies and India. In England, constitutional thinking was still evolving, but the need for governance in the colonies brought about the imposition of English constitutional ideas and mechanisms, thus founding an empire-wide colonial constitutional law.

Many excellent in-depth renderings of the constitutional history of the British Empire have been published over the centuries.[60] The following resumé provides a compact overview of the development of British colonial constitutional law.[61]

On acquisition, British colonies were usually governed by governors appointed by companies to whom royal charters had been granted. Colonists soon however formed representative assemblies, thereby curbing the autocratic legislative and administrative powers of the governor. Initially the Crown held sole sovereignty over the colonies, but dominance over imperial colonial policy was gradually transferred to the remit of the British Parliament and Cabinet.

Basic legal principles and rules on which the later emancipation of British colonies was based, developed during the First British Empire (lasting from

---

[58] Cf e.g. Setzer 'Wahlsystem'; Mackintosh 'British Cabinet' Chapters 2–6; and Burch 'The United Kingdom' 19–20.
[59] Venter 'Constitutional Comparison' 196.
[60] A recent example is Bowen, Mancke & Reid 'Britain's Oceanic Empire'.
[61] This account draws directly on Venter 'Constitutional Comparison' 66–74.

the late sixteenth century until the loss of the American colonies in 1776). *Calvin's Case* of 1609[62] established the following guidelines:

- The manner in which a colony came under British rule (i.e. by conquest or cession or by settlement) influenced the nature of the constitutional powers vested in the colonial inhabitants and their institutions.
- Where the Crown had granted constitutional powers to the inhabitants of a colony, such powers could not be withdrawn without the approval of Parliament.
- The legal system in existence when a colony was acquired was deemed to remain in force until amended by the Crown.
- If aspects of the local law in a conquered colony were considered to be repugnant to British morals, such rules were not recognized as law.[63]

In time for the next phase, known as the Second British Empire, the following framework for British colonial constitutional law was laid down in *Campbell v Hall* (1774):[64]

- The British Parliament had legislative power over a colony acquired by conquest.
- The 'conquered inhabitants once received under the King's protection, become subjects' of the Crown and therefore ceased to be aliens.
- British subjects were, when in a colony, governed by the same laws as the other inhabitants of such colony.
- 'The laws of a conquered country continue in force, until they are altered by the conqueror.' This was an express confirmation of the rule laid down in *Calvin's Case*.
- '... if the King (... without the concurrence of Parliament) has a power to alter the old and to introduce new laws in a conquered country, this legislation being subordinate ... to his own authority in Parliament, he cannot make any new change contrary to fundamental principles.'

Following the loss of the 13 American colonies, the British Empire extended its grasp on the Canadian territories in competition with France and, by military and bureaucratic means determined by circumstance, be it conquest, cession, purchase, occupation or commerce, gained the Cape of Good Hope (in

---

[62] *Calvin's Case* 7 Co. Rep. 1b (published in Volume 77 of the *English Reports*).

[63] In Part I §144 and §145 of the iconic work of Sir William Blackstone, *Commentaries on the Laws of England* (published shortly before the *American Declaration of Independence*) he provided a contemporary exposition of the colonial constitutional law at the end of the First British Empire.

[64] *Campbell v Hall* 1 Cowp. 205 (published in Volume 98 of the *English Reports*).

1795–1803 and then again in 1806), India (in partnership with the East India Company) and Ceylon (in 1802). In these new acquisitions a range of indigenous and European (Dutch, Spanish and French) legal orders existed. Being administered from London by the Secretary for War, local colonial governance usually started out under the autocratic control of a governor appointed by the Crown.

The emancipation of British colonial constitutional law, often inspired by British immigrants, formed a consistent pattern. A newly acquired territory was usually designated a Crown Colony under the plenipotentiary powers, judicial, legislative and executive, of the governor, ruling in the name of the monarch. Soon officers and officials were drawn in to serve in advisory councils, and eventually also colonists. Governmental power was gradually distributed to other organs such as courts and to a local civil administration and police or militia. As representative legislative councils were established, the example of the Parliament in Westminster was emulated as far as possible. When the local legislative arrangements began taking the form of an elected legislative assembly and an appointed legislative council, it could be said that the crown colony had emancipated to a phase referred to as 'representative government'.

During the reign of Queen Victoria (1837–1901), sometimes referred to as the Third British Empire, the constitutional foundations were laid for many of the currently existing states. Rebellions in Ontario and Quebec in 1837 led to the dispatch of a new governor-general, John Lambton, known as Lord Durham. He was mandated to investigate and resolve the causes of the dissatisfaction of the colonists. In 1839 the Durham Report provided the framework for the next phase in the emancipation of all British colonies. Durham intimated that he based his recommendations on his interpretation of the constitutional arrangements of Britain (which were in themselves still being developed),[65] and therefore introduced an important new principle: the colonial governor should gain the support of the elected majority in the legislative body by entrusting the administration of the colony to people supported by the majority of the inhabitants. This translated mere representative government to responsible self-government, which was gradually extended from Canada to New Zealand and Australia in the 1850s and to the Cape Colony in 1872. The system was solidified in the adoption by the Westminster Parliament of the *Colonial Laws Validity Act* of 1865. Colonial parliaments were now competent to amend the English common law, but not the laws of the British Parliament.

In the subsequent years of the nineteenth century the self-governing colonies achieved increased importance in economic and political terms, and

---

[65] The electoral reforms in England, mentioned above at note 58, had only been introduced in 1832.

geographical consolidation of the colonies in federated proto states became possible in Canada, Australia and Southern Africa. At the colonial conferences held from time to time, the self-governing countries under the British Crown were flexing their muscles, and in 1907 won the elevated status of near-independent 'dominions', constitutionally self-sufficient and recognized as distinct participants in international relations. At the time of the outbreak of World War I in 1914, London in effect dealt with Canada, Australia, South Africa and New Zealand not as imperial possessions, but as allies. After the war, the dominions participated in the Peace of Versailles as independent signatories. At the imperial conference of 1926 the status of the dominions was captured in the following statement:

> They are autonomous communities within the British Empire, equal in status, in no way subordinate one to another in any aspect of their domestic or external affairs, though united by a common allegiance to the Crown, and freely associated as members of the British Commonwealth of Nations.

In the *Statute of Westminster* of 1931 the British Parliament repealed the *Colonial Laws Validity Act* of 1865 thereby empowering dominion parliaments to retain or repeal English parliamentary legislation and to pass their own laws with extra-territorial effect. The dominions had become sovereign states, each mainly symbolically and separately under the British Crown as head of state.

The foundational ideas of the domestic English constitution benefited from the evolution of European theory and philosophy while developing its own unique characteristics. These were influenced by imperial ambitions and limitations placed thereon. These ideas were widely diffused across the world by various means including brute force, economic pressure, negotiated compromises and pragmatism.

The history of British colonial constitutional law as it was steered from London is significant for present purposes because, even in the twenty-first century, the British Commonwealth is still spread over one-fifth of the global land mass, including all continents. Many countries share the colonial constitutional history stretching over five centuries, and various constitutional notions originating in London have been emulated in a large number of jurisdictions not included in the Commonwealth. The impact of English constitutional vocabulary therefore endures in today's world.

2.7 EMERGENCE OF THE NATION-STATE

Returning to Western Europe, the nineteenth century was the age of the emergence of 'nations', although the elements of the notion had by then been developing for some time.

> [I]t is quite clear that after the Peace of Westphalia (1648), the idea of a universal Christian empire was replaced by an international order based on the struggle between different secular 'national monarchies' that would struggle to impose their hegemony through successive wars during the next three centuries.[66]

Sounding a sobering note, Patrick Glenn however unequivocally stated that 'there never has been and, it may safely be added, there never will be, a nation-state'. He argued that all states are 'cosmopolitan', meaning 'having the characteristics which arise from, or are suited to, a range over many different countries'.[67]

In his truly monumental work. Aguilera-Barchet describes the establishment of absolute monarchies in the sixteenth and seventeenth centuries, leading, in concert with the rationalism and empiricism of the scientific revolution of the seventeenth century (Galileo, Newton, Leibnitz, Descartes, Bacon, etc.), to the 'enlightened absolutism' of nations ruled by monarchs.[68]

Under the heading 'The Golden Era of Liberalism and the Apogee of the Nation-State' Chapter 16 tells the story of the emergence of the modern 'nation-state' during the nineteenth century.[69] Following the scheme of that exposition, we can sketch the essentials of the developments of that era that still underpin present-day constitutional notions.

At the dawn of the nineteenth century the United States had been stabilized in the form of a republic, recognized as an independent 'nation' and participant in international affairs. The Westminster constitutional dispensation allowed for a different but distinct notion of a British monarchic 'nation', established as a global colonial power. The French Revolution was soon followed by the Napoleonic regime, which notoriously degenerated into an empire dominating or threatening the neighbouring and some remote national monarchies such as Russia. An initiative by the European monarchies (including Britain, the Tsar of Russia, the King of Prussia and the Emperor of Austria) was taken in 1814–15 to restore absolute monarchism in response to the emerging revolutionary ideas of citizen-nations. When Napoleon was finally defeated by

---

[66] Aguilera-Barchet 'History' 245.
[67] Glenn 'Cosmopolitan State' Preface vii–viii.
[68] Aguilera-Barchet 'History' Chapters 9 and 10.
[69] Aguilera-Barchet 'History' 491 *et seq.*

the end of 1815, the victorious powers formed an alliance for the purpose of preventing the resurgence of a popular revolution in France and the rest of the Continent. These efforts could not be sustained for long.

In France Louis XVIII began following the English example of allowing (albeit not-yet democratic) parliamentary government in 1814, and this inspired similar steps in various German states. These concessions did not prevent popular revolutions occurring across Europe. The major liberal revolutions and rebellions occurred in Spain (which was also troubled at the time by demands for independence in its American territories assisted by the British)[70] and Italy (1820), Greece (1822), Russia (1825) and in 1830 the people of Paris overthrew King Charles X, inspiring similar, but less successful uprisings in Italy, Germany and Poland. The revolutionaries in the Netherlands, Spain, Portugal and Switzerland had better success. Two powerful German territorial regimes, Austria and Prussia, were formed in the first half of the nineteenth century, breeding, especially in the German-speaking states under Prussian control, a growing nationalism. In 1848 'liberal' revolutions broke out in various places in Europe, the most productive occurring in Berlin. The Prussian King Friedrich Wilhelm IV was forced to convene a popularly elected national assembly in Frankfurt to draft a constitution for Prussia. In 1849 a *Verfassung des Deutschen Reiches* (Constitution of the German Empire) was adopted. A key component of the Frankfurt Constitution was its Chapter VI, headed *Grundrechte des deutschen Volkes* (Fundamental Rights of the German nation). The Frankfurt Constitution did not survive long, but especially the catalogue of fundamental rights strongly influenced later liberal German constitutions, notably the Weimar Constitution of 1918 and the current *Grundgesetz* of 1949.[71]

Underpinning the renewed popular revolutionary thought encouraged by the success of the American and French revolutions was the idea based in natural law thinking that the 'nation' was the repository of power which legitimized state power in terms of a social contract. This led to the spread of popular demands for written constitutions and the protection of the rights and *liberties* of all, justifying the label of 'liberal' constitutions. Remarkably these concepts continue to form the basis of constitutional intercourse in the twenty-first century.

---

[70] By 1826, 15 independent republics were established in Spanish America, often attempting to emulate the example of the United States.
[71] See also e.g. Badura 'Staatsrecht' 38 and Hilker 'Frühkonstitutionalismus' 362–3.

The groundswell of nationalism and popular liberty in Europe facilitated the solidification and overlap of the notions of 'nation' and 'state'.[72] The idea of the nation-state was concretized most conspicuously by the success of 'national' unifications in Italy and Germany. By means of meticulous political manoeuvres, patriotic military battles and creative legislative drafting, *Il Risorgimento* (the Resurgence) led to an Italian Parliament being convened in Turin in 1861 to proclaim Victor Immanuel II King of Italy 'by the grace of God and the will of the nation'.

In the 1860s Prussian dominance expanded over first the northern, and later all German states under the shrewd guidance of the Prussian Chancellor (the title of the head of government of the Prussian emperor), Otto von Bismarck. First Prussia defeated Austria in battle in 1866 and then Bismarck instigated a war with France, thereby not only inspiring an upsurge of French nationalism, but also establishing Germany as the dominant power in Europe. After defeating France in 1870, the German Second *Reich* was established in 1871 as a federation under the rule of the Prussian emperor. The limited degree of democracy in Germany was eventually avenged after World War I when the Weimar Republic replaced the Second *Reich* in 1919.

With the various European nation-states instituted in the later decades of the nineteenth century, economic rivalry among and between them became the norm, also inspiring competitive colonial occupation of Africa and large parts of Asia, where the local populace were hardly able to resist European military technology. In effect Europe, fractured into powerful individual nation-states, ruled most of the world, imposing as far as possible, and often with unconscionable brutality and national egoism, their laws and cultures around the globe.

The dissipation of European colonialism within a century left the stamp of Eurocentric (eventually North Atlantic) mentalities, including the notion of nationhood, deeply embedded in the constitutional, political and economic psyche of the world. Nevertheless, the ongoing weakening of Western hegemony and the historical disconnect between twenty-first-century globalization and the ageing precepts of Western constitutionalism do not favour the survival of the idea of the state as the exclusive constitutional seat of a 'nation'.

---

[72] See also Glenn 'Cosmopolitan State' 88–107 for additional background concerning the theoretical and philosophical thinking associated with the upsurge of interest in nationhood.

2.8 THE TWENTIETH CENTURY – FROM DEVASTATION TO LIBERAL DEMOCRACY

With very little coherence and intense rivalry for power and influence in all parts of the globe, the nation-states around the North Atlantic were poised for war among themselves by the end of the nineteenth century. World War I (1914–18) between alliances of Germany, the Austro-Hungarian and Ottoman Empires on the one hand, and Britain, France and the United States on the other ensued, and was fought mostly on European soil. Due to the immense demands on all public and private resources required for this 'total war', on the Continent the progression of nineteenth-century liberal constitutional thinking was checked by the perceived need for the centralization of state power, thereby laying the foundations for later totalitarianism and its branching into socialism and communism.[73]

Following the Peace Conference held in 1919 at Versailles that ended World War I, the League of Nations was established in 1920. Its membership covered many countries, including current and former colonial entities. The purpose of the League was to achieve international peace and security by preventing war. Due to an attitude of isolationism in its Senate the United States did not join, and Germany and Italy withdrew in the 1930s. In terms of Article 10 of the Covenant of the League there was an obligation on all member states to resist external aggression against 'the territorial integrity and existing political independence of all Members' and Article 12 foresaw all disputes arising between members to be resolved by arbitration or judicial settlement. The League failed to achieve these goals, providing the world with some clear lessons: 'The lesson was clear. A purely voluntary commitment to go to the defence of other states if they were attacked was far too feeble to be of any value.'[74]

Despite the involvement of the United States, American liberalism survived the Great War almost untouched, allowing the then most prosperous economy in the world to exert immense influence on the rest of the world, interrupted only in the early 1930s when the world-wide 'Great Depression' occurred.

The rise of German and Italian fascism in the 1930s assisted by the global economic crisis led to the outbreak of World War II, which, despite (or perhaps due to) the global political, economic and social disruption and devastation

---

[73] Wilkinson 'Reconstitution' 40–7 describes how the weaknesses of classical liberalism fed into the democratic decline of the Weimar Republic and the rise of national socialism as a consequence. Since the focus here is on the dominant remains of liberal constitutional language, minimal attention will be given to the precepts and development of socialist thought. Aguilera-Barchet 'History' 536 and 557–99 describes in great detail how the circumstances of World War I led to 'the bolstering of state power'.

[74] Luard 'History of the United Nations' 6.

that followed, opened the way for a post-war revival of liberal constitutionalism led by the United States.

Following this second catastrophic 'total war' in 30 years, it would appear that by the 1940s humankind was ready to establish more comprehensive mechanisms capable of ensuring peace and stability. The conceptual framework within which this noble end could be pursued was at hand: the precepts of liberal constitutionalism entrenched in Western thought, maintained since the eighteenth century by the most powerful and prosperous state among the victors, the United States. Not only was the United States influential in the establishment of the United Nations Organization in 1945,[75] but also in the conceptualization of the post-war constitutions of Japan (1947) and Germany (1949), which soon became major economic powers.[76]

In January 1941 US President Franklin D Rooseveldt famously delivered his 'four freedoms' speech. At the time, the United States had not yet entered the war, as it did after the December 1941 Japanese attack on Pearl Harbor. With this 'state of the Union' speech Rooseveldt prepared the way for the end of American isolationism, while providing a moral justification for first assisting the allies of the United States, and later for direct involvement in most regions of the world.

Already in the preparatory phases of the establishment of the UN (at Dumbarton Oaks in 1944), the United States introduced the idea that the assembly of the new international organization should be empowered to make recommendations for the promotion of the observance of basic human rights.[77] At the time President Rooseveldt's wife Eleanor was a remarkable participant in her own right in internal and international American politics. As the US delegate to the General Assembly of the United Nations from 1945 onward, Eleanor Rooseveldt was the first chairperson of the UN Commission on Human Rights, and a key drafter of the *Universal Declaration of Human Rights* (UDHR), adopted in 1948. Not surprisingly, the second paragraph of

---

[75] Describing the drafting of a document between Britain, Russia and the US beginning in 1944, Luard 'History of the United Nations' 24 states that 'the United States took the initiative, formulating proposals to which the others reacted. And the UN Charter, as it finally emerged, was an only slightly modified form of the original US plan.'

[76] See e.g. Venter 'Constitutional Comparison' 60–6, and Law 'Constitutional Archetypes'.

[77] Luard 'History of the United Nations' 32.

the preamble of this document, colloquially known as the 'International Bill of Human Rights', incorporated the notion of four freedoms:

> Whereas disregard and contempt for human rights have resulted in barbarous acts which have outraged the conscience of mankind, and the advent of a world in which human beings shall enjoy freedom of speech and belief and freedom from fear and want has been proclaimed as the highest aspiration of the common people ...

The UDHR continues to be synonymous with the United Nations:

> The promulgation of the UDHR in 1948 made a difference in how people saw their place in the world and their relations with their state and with each other. This is in itself a valuable contribution, quite apart from the securing of the rights actually listed in the document. Over the decades since 1948, the UDHR has provided the rudiments of a 'common conscience' for humanity. In the words of Immanuel Kant, a violation of rights in any place is now felt all around the world. The international community is continuing to build on this, and the UDHR should be regarded as one of the pillars of an emerging global ethic for our increasingly interdependent world.[78]

The establishment and persistence of the post-war universal human rights regime as a global moral standard may justifiably be recognized as the culmination of the North Atlantic constitutional thinking of the preceding centuries channelled through the twentieth-century dominance of American liberalism. The quotation above from the 2016 Brown Report therefore clearly confirms the reality that the political and constitutional language of the early twenty-first century continues to be the language of Euro-American liberal democracy.

The changes that occurred in the condition of humankind since 1945 have been spectacular. Among these are demographic factors (the world's population tripled in size), massive urbanization (from approximately 65% to 90%), the mopping up of colonialism and its political, moral, economic and constitutional consequences, the third and fourth industrial revolutions, and the rise of Japan, India and China as serious challengers of Western economic, political and epistemic dominance.

In the decades following World War II a great number of former colonies and dependencies of the European powers, Britain and the USSR obtained independence, thereby increasing the number of states qualifying for international recognition[79] and requiring new constitutions.[80] In the flurry of

---

[78] Brown 'Living Document' 23.
[79] The membership of the UN almost quadrupled from the original 51 members to 193 in 2021.
[80] Approximately 90 per cent of the 'national' constitutions in operation in 2019 were adopted after 1945.

constitution-writing since 1945 the sources that were drawn upon as examples for conceptual and terminological inspiration were overwhelmingly the constitutions of the United States, France, Germany and Britain. Although each of these constitutional orders displays unique characteristics distinct from the others, they all emerged from and continue to reflect the ethos of eighteenth- and nineteenth-century liberalism, its banner being borne throughout by the United States, the others more or less following the US lead or having returned to it in the second half of the twentieth century.

Currently the most powerful challenges to Western liberal democracy, and therefore potentially of consistent constitutional language, come from the two leading Communist states, the Russian Federation and the People's Republic of China. It is however remarkable that even these constitutional orders have their roots in North Atlantic constitutional history:

> ... a fundamental difference between China and the West is that for China, modernity is an export rather than something grown from its own tradition. Unlike the West, China was deprived of the chance to walk itself out of its feudalistic tradition and form a modern sovereign state of its own accord. Given such historical context, we would conjecture that China's modernization is a response to external provocation posed by a powerful alien civilization ... To sum up, China, after experiencing Opium War and the First Sino Japanese War, had been jolted onto a course of modernization, a process more a response to external provocation than a spontaneous development.[81]

Through business exposure to the West since the early nineteenth century, political ideas useful in the uprising against the Qing dynasty began taking root, leading to the establishment of the Republic of China in 1912 under a presidency fashioned after the example of the United States. Not only North Atlantic constitutional notions found their way into Chinese constitutional development, but most particularly also that of Soviet Russia. After the communist revolution in Russia in 1917 significant involvement from Moscow occurred in Chinese politics, leading to the establishment of the Chinese Communist Party (CCP) in 1920 and the replacement of the notion of a president with that of General Secretary of the CCP. Under strong Russian guidance (if not instruction), the General Secretary became the Chairman of the Party by 1928.[82] The political history of China since the inception of Communism followed a tortuous route, buffeted between many impulses from abroad. The Stalinist Communism that still prevails in this most populous state is

---

[81] Gao, Zhang & Tian 'Modern China' 1–2.
[82] See e.g. Runhua 'Chinese Presidency' 5–18.

constantly being subjected to the prevailing international, essentially Western conceptual challenges, including the rule of law and human rights.[83]

2.9 THE ROLE OF RELIGION

Theory and philosophy are essential tools for the acquisition of a deeper understanding of the field of constitutional law. The history of constitutional law can best be understood against the background of the unfolding of the philosophies and theories that animated constitutional development. In this context the variously defined term 'religion' constantly crops up. Defining religion conclusively evades all.[84] It is most often associated with concepts such as beliefs, convictions, faith, worship, liturgy, rituals and the like, collectively implying profoundly held ontological views of truth, origins, direction, the human condition and eschatological destination.

For present purposes 'religion' is used in its most comprehensive sense, namely *Weltanschauung*, which includes the express or implied basic premises of those who relegate religion to the level of superstition, irrationality and illusion. Atheists, agnostics, secularists and the like will no doubt take umbrage at the suggestion that their views on constitutional matters are determined by religion, except if they can be persuaded to accept that their anti-religious or religion-sceptical stances actually represent their basic views of the world, their essential worldviews. Fundamentally and inescapably an explanation of the world based on for instance an assumption of a serendipitous big bang, evolutionary chance, coincidental progression of history, mathematical probability or the supremacy of human reason serves the same purpose as any other religion: an attempt to explain the inexplicable. Insofar as any assumption such as these (and there naturally are many more, frequently interlinked ones) constitutes one's actual belief, in other words the basis on which one wishes to explain the world, it can be understood to constitute one's religion. Seen thus, nobody is without religion, because every human needs to deal with the different layers of our surroundings in order to be sentient and sane.

A conspicuous, but often underestimated or ignored element in the evolution of constitutional law over the ages, is the influence of religion – both in the form of personal conviction and institutional dogma. The impact of religion on constitutional thinking was at times – and still is – mostly the product of the influence of religious institutions. Often religion was also, and continues to

---

[83] Runhua 'Chinese Presidency' 204–5.
[84] See e.g. Gunn 'Complexity of Religion'; Witte 'God's Joust'; Tiedemann 'Religionsfreiheit'.

be, utilized as a political tool and it presents courts, governments and all legal orders with many alternative and often inconsistent responses.[85]

Considering that law, and most conspicuously constitutional law, is concerned with the institutional authority to enforce compliance with norms promulgated by the state, it follows that the question of the source or justification of authority lies (or should lie) in the centre of the field. The response to this question is inevitably determined by the responder's religion, be it in its devotional sense or in the comprehensive meaning outlined above.

The decisive role of religion in the history of constitutional theory warrants thorough investigation but here the citation of only a few examples will have to suffice.

2.9.1 Plato

Plato wrote:

> And I was forced to say, when praising true philosophy that it is by this that men are enabled to see what justice in public and private life really is. Therefore, I said, there will be no cessation of evils for the sons of men, till either those who are pursuing a right and true philosophy receive sovereign power in the States, or those in power in the States by some dispensation of providence become true philosophers.[86]

2.9.2 Aristotle

Although Segev's interpretation of Aristotle on this point[87] may be debatable,[88] he convincingly demonstrates the classical philosopher's engagement with religion and the polis:

> Aristotle thinks that religion is required for arriving at the knowledge of first philosophy, which he views as the highest intellectual achievement and the highest human good, and thus its achievement is among the most important purposes for which a polis existing according to human nature itself exists. Aristotle does think that religion is also useful in other ways, e.g., insofar as it encourages the masses to accept and support legitimate social and political authority. But it is its role in enabling individual human beings to come to know and understand the ultimate truths of first philosophy, and thus engage in the highest human good, that he thinks makes religion and its institutions indispensable to any well-ordered polis.

---

[85] Cf Venter 'Constitutionalism and Religion'.
[86] Plato's *Seventh Letter* (written 360 BC).
[87] Segev 'Aristotle on Religion) 86.
[88] See e.g. Lloyd Gerson's review in 2018.

2.9.3 The Roman Empire

Possibly influenced by Aristotelean thought, the Roman emperors employed religion deftly as a means of control over the population. In the first century BC, Julius Caesar for instance assumed the office of *pontifex maximus* and Augustus established an imperial cult, deifying the emperor and imposing this cult on all subjects of the empire. According to Spawforth –

> Flattery of the emperor as such was hardly incompatible with, indeed would surely be eased by, heartfelt sentiments of loyalty and gratitude, sentiments sharing in the widespread ancient perception that the extraordinary power of the Roman emperor was god-like. Emotionally the imperial cult was a particularly compelling vehicle for the expression of loyalty because 'it indicated the exact point at which the subject felt himself to be a subject'.[89]

2.9.4 The Middle Ages

In the unfolding of European constitutional thought Christian religious institutions performed a central role. This is seen in the Roman Catholic Church's political aspirations and its influence over rulers, and in the consequences of the Protestant Reformation beginning in the sixteenth century.

The role of the Roman Catholic Church in society and on the development of modern constitutional law was complex and varied.[90] Broadly speaking, the Church provided a more or less common social and religious framework, centred (most of the time) on Rome. The Eastern Roman emperor Constantine I and the Western Roman emperor Licinius established the *Imperium Christianum* by their agreement to cease the persecution of Christians recorded in the *Edict of Milan* in 313. Later, stepping into the vacuum left by the fall of Rome in the fifth century, the Roman Church, conceiving of itself as universal ('catholic') since the second century, was in many respects the only consistent source of public authority in Europe until the establishment in 800 AD of Charlemagne's 'Holy Roman Empire' – 'holy' because the new emperor was crowned by Pope Leo III.

The question of finding a balance between the authority of the Church and that of 'secular' (non-ecclesiastical) powers exercised the minds of various philosophers whose work later underpinned modern thinking about the state. Building on the teachings of Plato and Cicero, Aurelius Augustinus, the Bishop of Hippo, introduced the mystical notion of 'two cities' in 426 AD, the

---

[89] Spawforth 'Augustan cultural revolution' 49.
[90] Glenn 'Cosmopolitan State' captured this complexity concisely under the heading 'The Church as State' 20–8.

one the city of God where the faithful reside, and the other the city for the rest of sinful humankind.[91] This was followed by the notion of 'two powers', the pope's authority being sacred and that of the emperor (merely) royal. Some seven centuries later it took the form of 'two swords', one in the hands of the spiritual Church, the other in the 'temporal' (non-ecclesiastical) authorities. The Reformers Luther and Calvin built on those foundations to produce the idea that people are involved simultaneously in both of the 'two kingdoms', one secular, the other religious.[92]

2.9.5 Natural Law and the Social Contract

The emergence of natural law thinking marks the birth of the mysticism of liberalism that still underpins our constitutional language. Grossi accurately summarized the original natural law ideas relating to property as follows:[93]

> The new individual on which society founded itself was a direct descendant of the mediaeval subject that had been liberated in accordance with the

---

[91] See e.g. Martin 'Two Cities', who concluded (at 216):
Augustine can be said to have written an anti-politics. His program was to put the things of this world, even the best of states, under the things of the next, to commit oneself wholly only to what is absolute, to idealize nothing. Christian political philosophy, like the Christian himself, is a stranger here below; it can be in the world but not of it. The good state, the 'republic' with meritorious common interests, can be pointed out, but the state is not a church and the church should not become a state. The church must look beyond, to the heavenly republic. This is the basic truth of the Christian religion, as it must be the constant theme of Christian political philosophy. This is, I think, the political theme of the City God. It is the political meaning of the concept of the Two Cities.

[92] Right at the end of his *magnum opus* of 1536, Calvin 'Institutes of the Christian Religion' Book 4, Chapter 20, 1254, Jean Calvin provided the following summary views:
96. The People owe to the Magistrate, 1. Reverence heartily rendered to him as God's ambassador. 2. Obedience, or compliance with edicts, or paying taxes, or undertaking public offices and burdens. 3. That love which will lead us to pray to God for his prosperity.
97. We are enjoined to obey not only good magistrates, but all who possess authority, though they may exercise tyranny; for it was not without the authority of God that they were appointed to be princes.
100. The obedience enjoined on subjects does not prevent the interference of any popular Magistrates whose office it is to restrain tyrants and to protect the liberty of the people. Our obedience to Magistrates ought to be such, that the obedience which we owe to the King of kings shall remain entire and unimpaired.
See also Venter 'Constitutionalism and Religion' 20–1.

[93] Grossi 'Geschichte' 103. The quoted passage is my translation from the German text (which is a translation of the original Italian).

theological-philosophical analyses of the fourteenth century. This subject emerged as free and liberated because he was as *dominus* the owner of material things, especially also of himself. In this distant century a continuous development began which was to find its conclusion in Locke's second treatise and upon which the same fundamental pattern of argument is still founded: possession of goods is undoubtedly *natural* because the emanation of property to myself is the result of the drive for self-preservation and the instrument of self-protection that God had granted me.

The European philosophers who crafted Western constitutionalism over the centuries were all inspired by their religious beliefs, be it Christian or based effectively on the partial or full deification of human reason.[94] Thus, whereas Thomas Aquinas ascribed the nature of the cosmos to the creative power of God, Hugo de Groot considered natural law to be based on rules that are uncontradictably *evident*, objectively observable.[95]

2.9.6 Machiavelli

Machiavelli considered the existence of three characteristics indispensable for stability of the republic, namely *buona religione, buoni leggi, buona milizia*.[96] Enno van Gelder's analysis of Machiavelli's ideas further reveals the role of religion in his work:

> His political ideas are those of the Realpolitiker, who thinks that the moral laws existing in society, governing the behaviour of citizens towards one another, do not need to be observed by the prince, if the interest of the State, that is for him the power of the prince and state, would thereby be endangered ... If he then credits religion with a minor and humiliating function in the community, this can only be explained firstly by the fact that he understands by religion the doctrine believed in by the Church in his day and its application (concerning the latter, he was, with many people at that time, highly indignant); secondly, because Machiavelli no longer believed in everything the Church taught concerning the relationship of man to God: if he really had held that belief, then no political object would have been able to convince him that this religion was no longer necessary for him and society. Even the most immoral person will, as long as he believes in them, fulfil his religious duties. When Machiavelli does not respect the moral laws in the interest of the

---

[94] Crowe & Lee 'Natural Law Theory' 1 aptly capture this divergence in the introduction to their book, most of the chapters of which deal with natural law seen from the perspective of various religious systems: 'The idea that natural law represents a set of rules or commands analogous to positive law, but emanating from God rather than humans, is certainly an influential aspect of the natural law tradition. There is, however, a second and equally important sense of "law" as a teleological notion. Natural law, on this conception, is best analogised, not with positive legal enactments, but with the regularities captured in the "natural laws" of physics or biology.'
[95] Grossi 'Geschichte' 99–101.
[96] Huber 'Guicciardinis Kritik' 50.

state, when he is indifferent with regard to official religion by conviction, this too had its foundation in the new appreciation of life and man ... [97]

2.9.7 Jean Bodin

Van Gelder's analysis of *Jean Bodin*'s work leads him to the conclusion that Bodin sought to distil commonalities from the various monotheistic religions: 'in this deism redemption through the mystery of salvation recedes, the stress is laid on the philosophical and ethical element, dogmas and ritual are reduced to a minimum, the whole is based on rational foundations'.[98]

2.9.8 Thomas Hobbes

Thomas Hobbes was a Protestant and devoted much of his energy, often controversially, to theology. His *Leviathan* was the cause of him narrowly escaping censure and death at the hands of the House of Commons. In 1666 the Commons resolved that –

> ... the Committee to which the Bill against Atheism and Profaness is committed be impowered to receive information touching such books as tend to atheism, blasphemy and profaness, or against the essence and attributes of God, and in particular the book published in the name of one White and the book of Mr. Hobbes called 'The Leviathan,' and to report the matter with their opinion to the House.[99]

Referring to Hobbes' Appendix to *Leviathan*, published in 1668 with the original work in Latin, Wright comments:

> But, while Hobbes, at the age of eighty in 1668, surely did not want to suffer punishment as a heretic, as before, he in no way abandoned positions he had long held in the face of ostracism, intimidation and even possible prosecution. Although, as here, he admits to holding novel views in theology, he defends them as derived from scripture. He evidently never believed he espoused heretical views. He thought he was right.[100]

Ironically, Hobbes resisted the separation of church and state:

> Of course, these ideas – the separation of church and state and limited government more generally – had their detractors. Hobbes, for instance, would have no part of it. Large sections of his Leviathan are devoted to the principle that the sovereign must

---

[97] Van Gelder 'Two Reformations' 58.
[98] Van Gelder 'Two Reformations' 394.
[99] Wright 'Religion, Politics' 10, footnote 30.
[100] Wright 'Religion, Politics' 11.

be 'Supreme Pastor' as well as civil ruler. He must have power to determine the doctrines, sacraments, and personnel of the church. Hobbes recognized that if citizens perceive a contradiction between the commands of God and the commands of the sovereign, they will be inclined to obey the higher authority. This is the main cause of 'Sedition, and Civill Warre' in Christian nations. The solution to this problem, Hobbes argued, is to vest spiritual and temporal authority in the same sovereign. This would not conflict with any rightful claim of conscience, he said, because all that is necessary to salvation is faith in Christ and obedience to the laws.[101]

2.9.9 John Locke

John Locke was also a devout Protestant. According to Young 'The figure of John Locke is central to any investigation into English religious thought during this period, since he dominated, directly and indirectly, much of the discussion about religion in the period from 1690 to circa 1780', and 'Locke was a devout Protestant layman intent on finding "Truth".'[102]

Locke, however, ardently pursued a separation of religion from politics, which explains much of the American 'wall of separation between church and state'.[103] In this, his thinking coincided with that of Rousseau.[104]

2.9.10 Jean Jacques Rousseau

Cladis describes *Jean Jacques Rousseau*'s attitude towards religion as follows:

> Rousseau associated the deepest aspects of the public and private life with religion. Paying attention to Rousseau's religious vocabulary exposes the heart of the middle way. Religion, in Rousseau's view, can enable us to cultivate both a rich public and private life, assisting us to achieve a host of capacities and joys that pertain to various spheres of being – the universal, the civic, the domestic, and the realm of friendship and solitude.[105]

---

[101] McConnell 'First Freedom?' 1248.
[102] Young ' Religion and Enlightenment' 1.
[103] The influence of Locke's work on secular liberalism is unpacked by Quadrio 'Religious Particularism' 34–8. At 36 he states that '... on the basis of a theological anthropology, Locke produces a dualistic moral psychology (a dualistic account of human moral interest) the nodes of which offer us a theocentric and an anthropocentric moment.'
[104] See e.g. Koontz 'Religion and Political Cohesion'.
[105] Cladis 'Public Vision' 187.

In effect, Rousseau devised his own, ideal religion and, in a secularistic manner procured Christian belief for the purpose. Cladis summed it up:

> In [Rousseau's work *Emile*] we are invited to resist all authoritarian voices and to consult the heart, that spiritual center which unites reason, the emotions, and moral wisdom. Jesus embodied the religion of the heart. Rousseau portrayed him as kind, tolerant, honest, sincere, natural, and in the face of death, solitary. This is not the Jesus of traditional Christianity. No miracles, no messianic claims, and no death for the sins of the world. The Jesus of Rousseau is like the Jesus of the deists, only more romantic and less moralistic ... Jesus, then, is the good, sincere individual, uncorrupted by society, who voluntarily dies for it, not for its sin, but for its potential goodness.[106]

In his most influential work, Rousseau engaged directly with the role of religion in matters of state:

> In *The Social Contract*, he wrote that under Christianity 'men have never known whether they ought to obey the civil ruler or the priest.' Christianity gave men 'two legislative orders, two rulers, two homelands,' and it put them under 'two contradictory obligations.' This division, of course, is precisely what commends separation to the liberal. But to Rousseau, '[a]ll that destroys social unity is worthless; all institutions that set man in contradiction to himself are worthless.' He thus would establish a new civil religion, which would 'bind the hearts of the citizens to the State,' and would banish all citizens who refuse to conform. To be sure, Rousseau insisted that citizens 'owe the Sovereign an account of their opinions only to such an extent as they matter to the community,' but that is scant comfort, since he also maintained that 'the Sovereign is sole judge of what is important ... for the community to control.'[107]

2.9.11 Montesquieu

According to Roger Oake, *Montesquieu* deemed it necessary for every society to have a religion: 'he simply cannot conceive of a society without religion, just as he cannot conceive of society's existence if men were not, however imperfectly, just.'[108] In the preface of the iconic *De L'Esprit des loix* Montesquieu wrote:

> For the better understanding of the first four books of this work, it is to be observed that what I distinguish by the name of virtue, in a republic, is the love of one's country, that is, the love of equality. It is not a moral, nor a Christian, but a political virtue; and it is the spring which sets the republican government in motion, as honour

---

[106] Cladis 'Public Vision' 194–5.
[107] McConnell 'First Freedom?' 1249. See also Llanque 'Begriff des Volkes'.
[108] Oake 'Montesquieu's Religious Ideas' 548–9.

is the spring which gives motion to monarchy. Hence it is that I have distinguished the love of one's country, and of equality, by the appellation of political virtue.[109]

Oake describes Montesquieu's view of religion 'as essentially social activity', a 'human ethic' which reinforces the state in the performance of its function to maintain social order.[110]

2.9.12 Immanuel Kant

DiCenso opens his work on *Immanuel Kant*'s views on religion and politics with the following summary statement:

> In Kant's writings, the topic of religion occupies a strategic space at the confluence of epistemology, ethics, and politics. Inquiries into the validity of religious truth claims and the possible meanings of religious writings and images form a vital part of Kant's ethical and political project. This project focuses on advancing human autonomy, both individually and in terms of political concerns with shared worldviews, laws, and rights. In its mature form, this line of inquiry begins with the *Critique of Pure Reason*, is further developed in Kant's ethical writings and the *Critique of the Power of Judgment*, and reaches fruition in *Religion within the Boundaries of Mere Reason*. This body of work constructs an intricate framework for understanding religion not only in relation to epistemological issues, but as relevant to both ethical and political considerations. It shows that religion, as both personal and cultural, is profoundly connected with the ethical and political possibilities of human beings.[111]

Although all the elements of the foundations of the currently dominant constitutional language are not directly dealt with by all the theorists and scholars historically responsible for its development, their engagement especially with religion founded and brought forward the essential tenets of twenty-first-century liberal constitutionalism: *rationalism, liberalism, secularism, popular sovereignty, the nation-state, democracy, rule of law, human rights*. These notions may be deemed to constitute the 'confessional' elements of the religion (in the widest sense of the word) of liberal democracy, simply because their universal validity is assumed to be self-evident. As is typical of religious conviction, liberal democracy is therefore also based on narratives and constructions whose veracity is impossible to prove – they are simply believed to be true.

---

[109] Montesquieu 16.
[110] Oake 'Montesquieu's Religious Ideas' 553.
[111] DiCenso 'Kant' 1.

2.10 CONSTITUTIONAL COMMUNICATION IN THE 2020S

As the twenty-first century dawned, the constitutional landscape of the world was changing and shifts in economic, military and political influence became apparent. Home to more than a third of the world's population, China and India incrementally presented serious challenges to Western economic, political and epistemic hegemony. In addition, the return (after the collapse of the USSR 30 years ago) of the Russian Federation as a major international power contending for international influence, serves to bolster the illiberal thinking of quasi-democracy and 'people's capitalism' that took root especially in China. Lacking consistency, Chinese and Russian epistemology, morality and statecraft cannot (yet?) effectively counter the intellectual hegemony of Western liberalism. Their economic and demographic weight does however present an incremental challenge, despite their inability to present cogent alternative answers regarding the source of governmental power: centralized socialism, large-scale social engineering, an attitude of 'might is right' and securocratic secrecy are age-old markers of autocracy, which has been proven repeatedly not to be sustainable without overbearing might and injustice. What should therefore seriously concern constitutional lawyers who are constrained to continue working with notions that depend on liberal conformism and a disregard for the related inconsistencies and mythology, is that liberal constitutionalism presents an increasingly weakening shield against the onslaught of various forms of extremism.

History does not end in the present. On a planet striding towards the limits of its capacity to sustain all of humanity, constitutional concepts are progressively straining to give coherent expression to the realities of governmental power, the modalities of limiting it, and emerging social, economic and political trends. In public life around the globe, phenomena, not necessarily completely novel, but nevertheless recurring in new forms and intensities, are growing in prominence. These include variable leanings towards populism, quasi-democratic authoritarianism, isolationism, and militarization against the background of globalization, all employing or supported by the phenomenon of a new 'industrial revolution' driven by technology and artificial intelligence.

And then, in 2020, an invisible infectious virus brought about a pandemic which may have instigated the most profound challenges to liberal constitutionalism since World War II. The Covid-19 pandemic necessitated the taking of extreme measures by all governments, with as yet unforeseen, but undoubtedly significant implications for the constitutional life of the world.[112] These measures may be expected to lead to the near-normalization of notions falling in the category of 'state of disaster', 'national emergency' and *Ausnahmezustand*. The extraordinary dystopian experiences of a world in 'lockdown' may realistically be construed as heralds of a future characterized by incremental environmental degradation and the concomitant social challenges involving economics, health, science, education, philosophy and religion. It is to be doubted that the language of liberal constitutionalism generated in a completely different world and society will prove to be capable of meeting the challenges emerging from these unique circumstances.

In the meantime liberal terminological gatekeeping continues unabated among constitutional lawyers,[113] few of whom question the validity of the view that a sovereign state exists in a defined territory where the population lives under a government legitimated democratically by the citizens in accordance with a legal order founded upon a constitution which regulates the extent and limits of executive, legislative and judicial authority.

---

[112] For a contemporary consideration of some of the constitutional implications of the Covid-19 pandemic, see Greene 'Emergency Powers'.

[113] This gatekeeping has recently been exposed and criticized quite effectively by Günter Frankenberg in Frankenberg 'Critique' and Frankenberg 'Between Magic and Deceit'. One does not need to subscribe to Frankenberg's deconstructive leanings to recognize the validity of the various aspects of his analysis of liberal constitutionalism.

3. Nation

Linking 'nation' with 'state', 'the people' and 'constitution' is a common phenomenon.[1] Many constitutions employ the concepts 'the people' and 'the nation' without definition or distinction. A long-standing assumption connects, as a self-evident given, a state to a nation and a people to a constitution. The word 'national' intuitively bears the meaning of domestic as opposed to global, regional or local. 'International' (in for instance 'public/private international law') implies a relationship between or among states (each, according to commonly accepted terminological usage, representing a nation).

Beyond the language of the law, 'nation' is used in various disciplinary and social contexts, including as a cultural, ethnic, historical, sociological or religious concept. In politics 'national' and 'nationalism' can sometimes be used to signify patriotism, inclusivity or exclusivity, and 'nationalistic' usually suggests extremism. Ethnology, a special branch of anthropology, derives its designation from the Greek word 'ethnos' – translated as 'a people' or 'nation'.

While it would be possible to devote much consideration to analyses and representations of learning about the nation, nationhood, nationalism and other related concepts especially from the perspectives of historians,[2] sociologists[3]

---

[1] The American Declaration of Independence of 1776 confirmed the creation of a new nation in its opening paragraph: 'When in the Course of human events, it becomes necessary for one people to dissolve the political bands which have connected them with another, and to assume among the powers of the earth, the separate and equal station to which the Laws of Nature and of Nature's God entitle them, a decent respect to the opinions of mankind requires that they should declare the causes which impel them to the separation.' Since then, the famous opening words of the American Constitution 'We the People ...' have appeared in many constitutions, including those of Ireland (1937), Japan (1946), Nauru (1968), Papua New Guinea (1975), Ghana (1979 and 1992), Liberia (1984/1986), the Russian Federation (1993), Belarus (1994), Eritrea (1997), Afghanistan (2004), Iraq (2005), Swaziland (2005), Kyrgyzstan (2007), Kosovo (2008) and Zimbabwe (2012).

[2] See e.g. Hirschi 'Origins of Nationalism' and Liah Greenfeld, whose main books, commuting between sociology and history, are Greenfeld 'Five Roads to Modernity', Greenfeld 'Spirit of Capitalism' and Greenfeld 'Mind, Modernity, Madness'.

[3] Among the leading publications in this field is Billig 'Banal Nationalism'. See also e.g. the collection of articles by Shlomo Avineri, Montserrat Guibernau, Anton Pelinka, Liah Greenfeld, Aviel Roshwald, Andreas Theophanous, Paschalis M.

and the field of (legal) semiotics,[4] such is not the present intention. While it is indisputable that no field of scholarly endeavour – perhaps least of all legal scholarship – can expect to flourish or produce valid outcomes if it is undertaken with blinkered concentration exclusively on its own sources and literature, it is becoming increasingly difficult to make valid choices about how wide one should venture into other fields. This, naturally, is due to the exponential increase in availability and accessibility of materials from all corners of human science and knowledge. In order to maintain disciplinary integrity the approach followed here is to take the field of constitutional law (as wide as it is in itself!) as the point of departure and eventual destination, venturing only selectively into neighbouring disciplines as may be required to enrich the line of constitutional analysis.

Academic constitutional lawyers have not in recent years performed a leading role in discussions of the nation, nationhood and nationalism. Why this is so, one might hypothesize, is explained by the core problem this book is intended to highlight: our – to my mind unjustified – toleration of the imprecision of the prevailing constitutional vernacular.

In the first section of this chapter the history of the concept 'nation' is traced, followed by a description of the manner in which it is employed in the area of diplomacy and international law. The section is concluded with the finding that, at least in constitutional theory, 'nation' is an anachronism. The second section touches upon the extensive discussion, largely from outside the field of constitutional law, of the notion of 'nationalism' followed by a brief presentation of the appearance of 'nation' as an imprecise concept in constitutions and in constitutional law literature. In the concluding section suggestions are made

---

Kitromilides, Hedva Ben-Israel and Elzbieta Matynia in the special Issue of the 2011 (24, 1–2) *International Journal of Politics, Culture and Society*.

[4] The potential salience of legal semiotics for the current discussion is demonstrated by the statement of Carvalho 'Semiotics of International Law' 197 where he raises the possibility of an investigation '… to examine whether WTO law is a common legal culture that amalgamates all legal inputs coming from its Members, or whether this common legal culture is based on an apparent impartiality that, in fact, masks an actual clash between legal cultures that have been translated into one or another language.' Legal semiotics is however an acquired taste, one important strand of which has its roots in the Critical Legal Studies Movement – see e.g. Balkin 'Promise of Legal Semiotics' 1832–5 and Broekman & Backer 'Lawyers Making Meaning' 122–5. The present discussion is less concerned with the theory of semiotics and the reality that constitutional concepts bear semiotic meaning (which is obvious), than with the fact that the meaning attributed to most of those concepts is fuzzy and variable, and that they therefore hold the potential of confusion, especially in the context of the work of constitutional comparatists. However, some of the contributions found in publications on legal semiotics will no doubt be of assistance. A recent example is Körtvélyesi 'Nation, Nationality, and National Identity'.

regarding the implications for constitutional comparison of the imprecision of the term 'nation'.

3.1 POSTULATION OF THE 'NATION'

3.1.1 Naissance

Peering through the mists of history, it is impossible to establish with certainty where and when the concept of a social unit consisting of a group of people who chose to identify themselves as a coherent entity to be distinguished from other similar units, actually originated. However, it stands to reason to assume that such an idea evolved from the omnipresent natural family as the basic unit of human society. Equally intuitively, it may be assumed to be inevitable that within even the smallest social unit, there is always the need for decision-making authority, however the nature and source of such authority is determined or justified. The family inevitably being a relatively small component of society, the need to provide for and improve the chances for survival, to share resources, divide labour, and eventually to strengthen cultural, religious and economic solidarity, would have led family units and unrelated individuals to unite voluntarily or be incorporated forcefully into larger groups.[5]

Be that as it may, the known ancient history of humankind is peppered with facts and tales about powerful and weak clans, rulers, potentates, dynasties, and the rise and fall of cultures. In his wonderfully wide-ranging work on the Near and Far Eastern history of legal concepts, the Hungarian Scholar Janos Jany traces the emergence of Uruk culture back to the fifth century BC in Mesopotamia, and the city states of Ur, Eridu, Uruk, Sippar, Shuruppak, Girsu, Lagash, and Umma to the third century BC where 'organised labour, established political order and a hierarchic social structure which guaranteed their success' were established, with a social structure in which political rule

---

[5] We will not here venture into the areas of expertise dealing with early social development of humanity such as anthropology, ethnology, archaeology, social psychology, linguistics, economics, education sciences, etc. in order to find justification for these intuitive assumptions, since it will not contribute substantively to the current discussion. However, for a source of constitutional law, see e.g. Fleiner & Basta Fleiner 'Constitutional Democracy' 37 (citing Marsilius of Padua):

> It is only upon the development towards the extended family, the kinship group and the tribe that the need for authoritative and long-lasting leadership becomes apparent. At the former level the problems of living together were primarily resolved within the family, either by the father in a patriarchy or the mother in a matriarchal society (the people of the Tuareg), or sometimes by a council of elders. Supra-familial structures first became necessary when there was greater contact and division of labour between families and tribes.

and religion were inseparably intertwined.⁶ Apparently the ancient Egyptian cultural organization also began taking form around 3500 BC in what is referred to as the 'late predynastic' era.⁷ Jany dates the origins of Chinese law to the thirteenth century BC,⁸ the Persian rule from the ninth century BC,⁹ and the first Japanese proto-constitution of *Shotoku Taishi* to 604 AD.¹⁰

Because the terms 'nation' and 'state' are still quite often used as synonyms, their histories tend to overlap. Closer scrutiny however reveals the confusion – at least when greater linguistic precision (in for instance constitutional as opposed to political conversation) is required – that ensues when these terms are dealt with as interchangeable. Taking into consideration that there was a time when state and nation were deliberately conflated,¹¹ the present focus will be only on the idea and history of nationhood and its forerunners.

Although the ancient history of social structuring into supra-familial entities for economic, cultural and governmental purposes reaches very far back in time and is geographically widely dispersed, the terminology of contemporary constitutional law is rooted in more recent European and North Atlantic history. Relying on among others the seminal work of anthropologist Lewis Morgan,¹² Aguilera-Barchet describes the development of early European social structure as emanating from the manner in which Indo-European societies were organized.¹³ The foundation of society was the *gens* (Latin equivalent of the Greek *genos*), consisting of people who shared a common ancestor. The chances of survival of unaffiliated individuals were enhanced by entering into a sacred pact with a *gens* as 'clients', but servants and slaves were also included. Eventually family groups (*gentes*) could be incorporated in a 'phratry' (*phratria* in Greek, *curia* in Latin), allowing for the appearance of common decision-making assemblies and leadership. In the Greek cities and Rome society was structured into even larger, but distinct, tribes. In

---

⁶ Jany 'Legal Traditions in Asia'. See also Aguilera-Barchet 'History' 10–11 and 13–14.

⁷ See e.g. Brewer 'Ancient Egypt' Chapter 7 and also Aguilera-Barchet 'History' 12–13.

⁸ Jany 'Legal Traditions in Asia' 309. Cf also Aguilera-Barchet 'History' 14.

⁹ Jany 'Legal Traditions in Asia' 83.

¹⁰ Jany 'Legal Traditions in Asia' 376. See also Aguilera-Barchet's 'timeline' stretching from 4.6 billion years ago to the annexation of Greece by Rome in 149–148 BC: Aguilera-Barchet 'History' 29–33.

¹¹ See e.g. Mandelbaum 'Nation/State Fantasy' in general, but specifically 140–57 and Chapter 5 below.

¹² Aguilera-Barchet 'History' footnote 18 on page 18, where he quotes from Morgan, L H *Ancient Society* (The University of Arizona Press, 2003 – photographic reproduction of the 1878 ed) 222.

¹³ Aguilera-Barchet 'History' 17–20 and 41.

Rome a tribal leader was known as *tribuno* and assemblies were called *comita curiata* and *comitia tributa*. In Athens ten tribes were represented in a council of 500 members. As urbanization increased, the *urbs* (where the people lived, assembled and found sanctuary) and *civitas* (which referred to a religious and political association of families and tribes) developed. Further refinement of the social structure gave birth to the Greek *polis*.

However, neither Hellas nor any Hellenic *polis* could be regarded as a 'nation', despite the reality that the cities approached in their nature that of what we may now conceive of as a sovereign state, albeit demographically very small.[14] In 1972 Frank Walbank expertly considered the meaning of the words *gens*, *natio* and *lingua* in his analysis of the works of Cicero and concluded that nationalism did not play much of a role in Roman history. Rome was deemed to be the dominant *civitas*, binding Roman citizens much more closely together than *gens*, *natio* or *lingua*: 'It was the achievement of the Romans to develop and extend the political aspect of that civitas and the binding-forces and emotions inherent in it, until eventually it coincided with the length and breadth of the empire.'[15]

Speaking of *gens* (genitive plural, *gentium*) as a Latin word at a stretch translatable as 'nation', a question arises naturally whether in Roman (legal) literature the notion of *ius gentium* implied the recognition of diverse nations. This question is made particularly relevant if one considers how easily a search for a neutral designation in a universal language for 'international law', 'the law of nations', *Völkerrecht*, *droits des gens*, *diritto internazionale*, *derecho internacional*, and so on, might lead one to *ius gentium*.[16]

The origins of *ius gentium* however do not reflect the notion of a system of public international law. In the final year of World War I, Gordon Sherman understandably considered 'the very existence of international law as a practical element in the conduct of human affairs' to be in danger, and therefore delved into 'the earliest conceptions characterizing international jurisprudence'.[17] Sherman traced the use of the phrase through the works of, among many others, Cicero, Pomponius, and Livy, finding that –

> [w]e are, then, to understand by the term *jus gentium*, in the light of the facts enumerated, a system of law gradually arising through the efforts of the Roman *praetor* to promote a sense of equity and fair dealing by so modifying the *jus civile* as to allow a broader practice in granting forms of action than had been possible under the

---

[14] Walbank 'Nationality as a Factor' 146.
[15] Walbank 'Nationality as a Factor' 168.
[16] This seems to underlie the title of *Jus Gentium: Journal of International Legal History* published since 2016 in New Jersey, USA.
[17] Sherman 'Jus Gentium' 56.

stricter ancient law, for it must not be forgotten that ancient Roman jurisprudence realized itself most strikingly in the theory of formal *actions*.[18]

Writing a century later about the origins and later development of the *ius gentium*, Stanisław Wielgus shows that, originally, *ius gentium* was conceived not as public law, but law regulating mutual relations between individuals. By the second century Gaius 'differentiated *ius civile* (law of a given people [*populus*] made for itself) from *ius gentium* (law established by all peoples on the basis of natural reason and, in this understanding, accepted by all peoples [*gentes*])'. At the hands of mediaeval writers, *ius gentium* obtained the character of universal law.[19] Along the route of, among others, Justinian in the sixth century, followed by the Roman Church's development of legal norms regulating war in terms of canon law, and Thomas Aquinas' *Summa theologiae* in the thirteenth century, *ius gentium* evolved to play a part in the struggle for power between clerical and lay authorities.[20]

Sherman concluded that Grotius, generally understood to be the seventeenth-century founder of public international law, endeavoured in his key work *De Jure Belli Ac Pacis* to develop basic principles for a law applicable to the relations between nations, as opposed to court actions between individuals, simultaneously propounding the principles of equality and fairness in international relations.[21] According to Genc Trnavci, Grotius dealt with *ius gentium* as law regulating the relations between independent states; by 1650 the English law professor Richard Zouche wrote about *ius inter gentes*; and Jeremy Bentham introduced the term 'international law' in 1789.[22]

The apt subtitle of Aguilera-Barchet's comprehensive work on the history of Western public law ('Between Nation and State') provides an accurate framework within which one might develop an understanding of the meaning, also today, of the idea of a 'nation'. Part II of his work, covering more than 700 pages, deals with the origins of the European nations.[23] The headings of Chapters 5, 6, and 7 provide us with the highlights of this history from the fourth to the sixteenth centuries: 'From Germanic Tribes to Kingdoms', 'Popes vs. Emperors: The Rise and Fall of Papal Power', and 'From Public to Private Power: Europe in the Feudal Age'. A consideration of this history makes it clear that neither the Greeks or Romans, nor the Roman Church or the early

---

[18] Sherman 'Jus Gentium' 60.
[19] Wielgus 'Genesis and History' 337. See also Galloro 'Das heutige Völkerrecht' 80, footnote 1.
[20] Described in some detail by Wielgus 'Genesis and History' 339–48.
[21] Sherman 'Jus Gentium' 63.
[22] Trnavci 'Meaning and Scope of the Law of Nations' 206.
[23] Aguilera-Barchet 'History' 93–173.

mediaevalists can be deemed to have used 'nation' as we do today. Although *gens, natio, civitas, lingua* and *populus* were not unknown concepts before 'the nation' became politicized and romanticized, the modern conception of nationhood began taking shape only in the 'golden era of liberalism' when the idea flourished that the power of the state depends for its legitimacy on the approval of 'the people'.[24]

As mentioned before, for the contemporary constitutional lawyer an association between 'nation' and 'state' tends to come to mind almost automatically, probably due to the reality that the concept 'nation-state' has been ingrained in much of our constitutional vocabulary. One might even wonder (perhaps a slightly unproductive idea) about the question which was first: nation or state? In view of the intention to return in Chapter 5 to 'state' as constitutional notion, we will here separate (at least partly) 'nation' from 'state' in order to sharpen the focus. A justification of such an approach is to be found in the relative vagueness of perceptions of nationhood in the early stages of the development of the state.

When the era of feudalism, a time when Europe was governmentally fragmented, began to be phased out around the twelfth century, it became possible for monarchs to consolidate their territorial dominance, and eventually to base their power on compacts with sections of society such as the nobility, the propertied, urbanized and learned classes. During the twelfth to the fifteenth centuries various wars between what might be called proto-states, symbolically represented by monarchs, were waged on the Continent. Those were not primarily inter-*nation* wars but were mostly motivated by monarchical yearnings to expand their territorial rule.[25]

In the first chapter of her seminal work on nationalism, Liah Greenfeld meticulously traced the seeds of English nationhood, especially as an expression since the seventeenth century of a territorial (as distinct from an ethnic) solidarity in opposition to foreign powers and entities. Although still a long road lay ahead before popular sovereignty triumphed in England, terms that were emerging gradually in the English vocabulary, signifying equated meanings, were 'country', 'commonwealth', 'empire', 'nation', and 'people'.

---

[24] See e.g. Aguilera-Barchet 'History' 499–500.
[25] See e.g. Aguilera-Barchet 'History' 177–210. At 183 Aguilera-Barchet describes the imperial drive for expansion with reference to the examples of England's approach to Wales and Scotland, the French kings' gradual assimilation of feudal territories in the twelfth and thirteenth centuries, the Spanish 'Reconquest' towards the end of the Middle Ages of Asturias, León, Castile, the County of Barcelona, the Kingdoms of Aragón, Valencia and Mallorca, the unification of the kingdoms of France and Castile, and the union of realms such as in the cases of the British Crown and the Crown of Aragon.

In official documents of the seventeenth century, for instance, reference was made to 'the two nations' of England and Scotland.[26] Greenfeld describes the English Revolution as 'a confrontation between the Crown and the *nation*' which 'focused on the issue of sovereignty':[27]

> The England that emerged from the civic and religious trials of the mid-seventeenth century was a nation. Its formation in the course of the preceding century and a half represented a tremendous change in the nature and pervasiveness of politics and the first major breakthrough toward democracy. English national consciousness was first and foremost the consciousness of one's dignity as an individual. It implied and pushed toward (though it could not necessitate the immediate realization of) the principles of individual liberty and political equality. These notions were primary in the definition of English nationhood.[28]

Aguilera-Barchet describes the more specific increase of the prominence of the idea of 'nation' in Europe as a process of development from absolutism to liberalism.[29] The emphasis on the nation was facilitated by the rise of powerful monarchies exercising absolute power over the inhabitants of consolidated and demarcated territories.[30] In the meantime, however, the powerful thrust of humanism, natural law thinking, the *Renaissance*, the Enlightenment and the attendant political philosophies discussed in Chapter 2 above[31] occurred, culminating in the American and French revolutions which birthed not only constitutionalism, but also elevated liberalism to the foundational constitutional doctrine, and the nation to the status of the fountain of governmental power.[32] Now, contrary to the teachings of Machiavelli and Bodin, not the monarchs, but the 'nation' claimed sovereignty:

> It was not until the triumph of the Romantic ideal, however, that, as a reaction to the Enlightenment, liberals defended the idea of 'nationality', just as the twentieth century would spawn 'nationalism'. Thus, peoples' right to politically and legally organize themselves in accordance with the precepts of Enlightenment revolutions

---

[26] Greenfeld 'Five Roads to Modernity' 31–44.
[27] Greenfeld 'Five Roads to Modernity' 74.
[28] Greenfeld 'Five Roads to Modernity' 86.
[29] Aguilera-Barchet 'History' 489–554.
[30] Cf e.g. O'Kelly 'Nationalism and the state' 53: 'When absolute monarchs ruled states, states were regarded as legitimate in virtue of the authority of the king, who was thought to receive his authority from God. Solidarity had nothing to do with it. When kings were overthrown across Europe and in America, the question of legitimacy arose.'
[31] Sections 2.2–2.4 of Chapter 2.
[32] See section 2.5 of Chapter 2.

was followed by the flourishing of national sentiments within European groups united by their linguistic, cultural and historic ties.[33]

The appearance of the nation on the constitutional scene may be attributed to the theories of Locke, Voltaire, Rousseau and the like, which inspired the French *Déclaration des droits de l'homme et du citoyen* of 1789. Article 3 provided: 'The principle of any Sovereignty lies primarily in the Nation. No corporate body, no individual may exercise any authority that does not expressly emanate from it.'[34] This wording was, according to O'Kelly, drawn from the constitutions of some American states, and derived specifically from the works of Rousseau.[35] O'Kelly goes on to distinguish the revolutionary conception of the nation in France (civic nationalism) being composed of the people born in France, from the romanticized German notion of the *Volk*, based on ethnic nationalism, which saw the state as subordinate to the nation.[36]

In addition to the conceptual establishment of the French and American nations, the great revolutions of the late eighteenth century inspired the formation of more European nations, in some cases also followed by revolutions during the nineteenth century. Most prominent (and arguably with the most severe long-term implications) was the rise of German nationalism. The progression in German-speaking Europe from multiple territorial monarchies to a unified state was not a smooth process, but at its core was the rise of the demand for the recognition of popular sovereignty. The more than 30 German monarchies were heavily fragmented during the Napoleonic wars, but when Napoleon was dethroned in 1814, a loose German confederation, the *Deutsche Bund*, was established following the negotiations at the Congress of Vienna in 1814 and 1815. The *Bund* consisted of 38 duchies and princedoms (including Denmark, the Netherlands and Luxemburg), but the Austrian *Kaiserreich* and the Prussian Kingdom were the major powers. In all the regions of the *Bund* the authority of the nobility was still dominant.

It is significant that 1814 also saw the publication of Friedrich Carl von Savigny's work *Vom Beruf unserer Zeit für Gesetzgebung und Rechtswissenschaft*. Savigny became hugely influential in the field of legal history and theory and the development of a methodology for legal science,

---

[33] Aguilera-Barchet 'History' 499.
[34] These sentiments are presently still reflected in the first two sentences of Article 3 of the French Constitution of 1958: 'National sovereignty shall vest in the people, who shall exercise it through their representatives and by means of referendum', and 'No section of the people nor any individual may arrogate to itself, or to himself, the exercise thereof.'
[35] O'Kelly 'Nationalism and the state' 54.
[36] O'Kelly 'Nationalism and the state' 54–7.

leading to a unified approach to a common German legal culture.[37] The German Historical School founded by Savigny assumed that the people (nation), and not the political authorities, was the source of the law. Savigny held that the law grew out of the *Volk* and that its actual seat (foundation) was the common consciousness of the *Volk*, the *Volksgeist* or *Zeitgeist*.[38] Although the Historical School was primarily concerned with private law and was preoccupied with resistance to the codification of private law in the French *Code Civil*, the Prussian *Allgemeines Landrecht für die preussischen Staaten* and the Austrian *Allgemeines Bürgerliches Gesetzbuch*, the implications for public law of the professed supremacy of the nation speak for themselves. The idea of *Geschichtliche Rechtswissenschaft* (historical legal science) spread to the rest of Europe and even to the English-speaking world.[39]

Following the example of the second revolution in France in 1848 leading to the downfall of King Louis Philippe, violent uprisings in Berlin and Vienna forced the rulers of the participating members of the *Deutsche Bund* to agree to the assembly of a constitution-making national congregation (*verfassungsgebende Nationalversammlung*) in Frankfurt, composed of elected representatives of the *Volk*. A constitution known as the *Paulskirchenverfassung* was adopted by this constituent assembly claiming to reflect the sovereignty of the nation. The constitutional history of Germany in the century following the Paulskirche assembly is well known to have fluctuated immensely, but 1848 is the date of the universally meaningful formal acknowledgement of German nationhood. That was the year in which the first German equivalent of a Bill of Rights, the *Gesetz betreffend die Grundrechte des deutschen Volkes* (Statute Concerning the Fundamental Rights of the German Nation) was adopted, even before the *Reichsverfassung* which followed in 1849.[40]

The rise of German nationhood was a momentous and influential historical occurrence, but by no means an isolated episode. Many nations were conceived in the atmosphere created in Europe and beyond by the revolutions of the eighteenth and nineteenth centuries.[41] This development inevitably led to

---

[37] Cf Giuliani 'What is comparative legal history?' 33–4.

[38] Rahmatian 'Friedrich Carl von Savigny' 5. The notions of *Volksgeist* and *Zeitgeist* were promoted by various other influential philosophers and literary giants of the German romantic era, such as Hegel, Herder and Goethe. See e.g. Knudson 'Volksgeist and Zeitgeist' 410.

[39] Giuliani 'What is comparative legal history?'47–9 and Rahmatian 'Friedrich Carl von Savigny' 1–4.

[40] For a compact but accurate account of the constitutional history of Germany in the first half of the nineteenth century, see Wilms 'Staatsorganisationsrecht' 1–5.

[41] See e.g. Frankenberg 'Between Magic and Deceit' 163–4, where Günter Frankenberg refers to the spate of national constitutions following the breakthrough of the concept between 1791 and 1815, '[f]rom Norway to Sicily, from the Netherlands to

a convergence of nationhood and statehood, that is to say the solidification of the notion of the nation-state, to which we return in Chapter 5.

3.1.2 The International Perspective

In 1972 Frank Walbank wrote that in the middle of the twentieth century the idea of a nation was 'with its inherent right to political independence, ... among the most potent political forces at work,' despite the difficulty of defining it. He considered Friedrich Meineke's 1929 book *Weltbürgertum und Nationalstaat* to be 'one of the more outstanding contributions' to the identification of the essentials of a nation, arguing that –

> nationhood depends on sharing some – not necessarily all – of the following: a common habitation, a common language, a common spiritual and intellectual life, and a common state or share in a federation of states; and he devised two German terms, *Staatsnation* and *Kulturnation*, to describe the nation existing as it were *in esse* and that existing only *in posse*.[42]

Accepting the validity of Meineke's analysis, Walbank however pointed out that another 'fundamental point' needed to be emphasized, namely 'that ultimately men constitute a nation because and when they believe they constitute one'.[43] Dragoljub Popović distinguishes in summary between the French concept of the nation on the one hand, emphasizing citizenship, i.e. a free association of citizens, and on the other the German accent on the ethnic and cultural characteristics of the people. The Americans and British developed their own views on nationhood closer to that of the French but adapted to their circumstances by for instance considering the will or intention of the people to live together to be the constituent element of a nation.[44]

Very shortly after the declaration of war in 1914, WSM Knight began publishing a remarkable continuous depiction of the ongoing war, the series eventually growing into ten comprehensive volumes. In the preface, Knight described the war as 'an industrial and commercial war of the gravest import imaginable, directly affecting all civilised *nations* and men', and went on to state that '[t]o Britons the fight is one for Right as against Might; for the rights of the lesser independent *nations* as against the aggression of the greater; for *Peoples* as against Dynasties and Absolutism'. He expressed the hope that

---

Greece', and to it spreading to other continents following the examples of France, Spain and Belgium.

[42] Walbank 'Nationality as a Factor' 146.
[43] Ibid.
[44] Popović 'Comparative Government' 19–21.

Britain would rediscover the spirit that 'made this *country* and her Empire of all other *nations* of the world the land of liberty and the advance guard, throughout the earth, of political enlightenment and freedom'[45] (my italics). Throughout Knight refers to the major belligerents as '*Powers*', especially 'the Great Powers of Europe', but also 'even Japan, the Great Power of the Far East'.[46] From this language one can see that the idea of 'nation' had in 1914 already been absorbed in the general vocabulary as something of a synonym for 'people', 'country', 'the land' and 'power'.

After the war the language employed in the establishment of the League of Nations in 1919 shows a similar trend: apart from the name of the League 'nations' appeared only in Article 11 of the *Covenant of the League of Nations* agreed to by 'The High Contracting Parties' where the intention 'to safeguard the peace of nations' was expressed. The exact meaning of 'high contracting parties' is not particularly clear but it stands to reason that the 'High Contracting Parties' that established the League were not actually 'nations', but states as represented by the plenipotentiaries of governments.[47]

The description in section 2.8 of Chapter 2 above of how the *Universal Declaration of Human Rights* came to be adopted suggests that the architects of the United Nations were inspired much less by what may have remained after World War II of the ideas of the 'nation' (despite the appearance of the concept in the name of the Organization), than by liberal individualism. The manner in which the word was used in the founding documents again show that it was no longer done to refer specifically to citizen-nations, nor to ethnic or cultural nations. Consider for instance the language (with my italics) of 'The Atlantic Charter' in which Franklin Rooseveldt and Winston Churchill expressed their joint declaration of principles on which they based their 'hopes for a better future of the world' on 14 August 1941: the second principle was that no *territorial* changes should be effected 'that do not accord with the freely expressed wishes of *the peoples* concerned'; their third principle included respect for 'the right of all *peoples* to choose the form of government under which they will live'; the fourth was an undertaking 'to further the enjoyment by all *states*, great or small' of free trade; the fifth expressed the 'desire to bring about

---

[45] Knight 'History of the Great European War' v–vi.
[46] Knight 'History of the Great European War' 8.
[47] See e.g. the evasive, but frequently cited split judgment of the UK's House of Lords judgment *Phillipson v Imperial Airways* (1939) 63 Ll.L.Rep. 119, where a definition was expressly avoided, but mention is made at 320 of 'the representatives of ... states'. See also the 1939 case note by Beaumont 'Jurisprudence'. In the language of diplomacy and therefore in international instruments 'High Contracting Parties' appears to refer to the signatories to the document concerned, duly authorized thereto by the entities (states, governments) they purport to represent.

the fullest collaboration between all *nations* in the economic field'; the sixth spoke of the 'hope to see established a peace which will afford to all *nations* the means of dwelling in safety within their own boundaries', and in the eighth 'nations' was used three times in relation to the abandonment of the use of force, the employment of armaments and the disarmament of aggressors.[48] From this it appears that no substantive distinctions of meaning were drawn by the drafters of the Charter between 'peoples', 'nations' or 'states' existing within specified territories.

The first phrase of the preamble of the Charter of the United Nations of 1945 (my italics) is 'WE THE *PEOPLES* OF THE UNITED *NATIONS*'. The second paragraph reaffirms 'faith in ... the equal rights of ... *nations* large and small'. Paragraph 2 of Article 1 states as one of the purposes of the UN 'To develop friendly relations among *nations* based on respect for the principle of equal rights and self-determination of *peoples*, and to take other appropriate measures to strengthen universal peace', and paragraph 4 'To be a center for harmonizing the actions of *nations* in the attainment of these common ends'. Article 14 purports to empower the General Assembly to intervene in situations considered 'likely to impair the general welfare or friendly relations among *nations*'. Article 55 (on international economic and social cooperation) promotes 'the creation of conditions of stability and well-being which are necessary for peaceful and friendly relations among *nations* based on respect for the principle of equal rights and self-determination of *peoples*'. Article 76 d states that the basic objective is 'to ensure equal treatment in social, economic, and commercial matters for all *Members* of the United Nations and *their nationals*'. Again, the question arises whether 'nations' and 'peoples' in these provisions of the Charter were intended to refer to anything else than states as members of the Organization.

Still from the perspective of international law, the wording of the *Vienna Convention on the Law of Treaties* of 1986[49] is also revealing. The concept 'nations' is mentioned only once, and in the preamble (italics added):

> *Considering* the importance of treaties between States and international organizations or between international organizations as a useful means of developing international relations and ensuring conditions for *peaceful cooperation among nations, whatever their constitutional and social systems*

---

[48] The full text of the Charter can be found at e.g. www.loc.gov/law/help/us-treaties/bevans/m-ust000003-0686.pdf (accessed 15 June 2021).

[49] *Vienna Convention on the Law of Treaties Between States and International Organizations or between International Organizations* (VCLT II), 21 March 1986 https://legal.un.org/ilc/texts/instruments/english/conventions/1_2_1986.pdf (accessed 15 June 2021).

The qualification 'nations, whatever their constitutional or social systems' makes the intention abundantly clear that reference is not made here to ethnic or any other historic form of 'nations', but to states, as is also apparent from the phrase ' ... treaties between states ...' in the title of the Convention. It would seem that the 1753 definition of 'a treaty' by Emer de Vattel which refers only to the 'state' and its authorities or sovereigns still holds despite the appearance in the following century of the idea of the 'nation':

> A treaty (*traité*), in Latin, *fœdus*, is a compact (*pacte*) entered into by sovereigns for the welfare of the State, either in perpetuity or for a considerable length of time ... Treaties can only be entered into by the highest State authorities, by sovereigns, who contract in the name of the State.[50]

3.1.3 Constitutional Anachronicity

The history of the idea of the nation reveals its close linkage to romantic ideas about the identity of the true seat of legal power: 'the people' composed of a collection of sovereign individuals each lending a portion of their sovereignty to other people of whom they demand to establish and maintain social order within the corpus of the multitude. This congregation of individuals are bound together either by their decision to share citizenship, or by ethnic and cultural commonalities engendering common loyalties. In the process of the crystallization of the state as the entity being both the subject and object of constitutional law, the terminology of nationhood and statehood became intertwined but essentially undefined. Constitutional theory has to date done very little to remove 'nation' as obvious anachronism from its vocabulary. Nevertheless, in the minds of many, especially politicians and diplomats, 'nation' cannot and should not be removed from their vocabulary because of its utility as a sentimental device for mobilizing popular emotions and support. For them the vagueness and terminological pliability is a boon.

3.2 THE CONCEPTUAL DIVERSITY OF 'NATION' AND ITS DERIVATIVES

'Nation' is the obvious root idea from which various more or less related notions are derived, each bearing its own clouds of contextual connotations and associations not always directly linked to the root, but often only vaguely linked to the core concept or to one another. These include 'nationality', a term which should in constitutional law have in its own place and context. Another related concept seldom used in law is 'nationalism'. Care must be taken to

---

[50] As quoted by Dörr & Schmalenbach 'Vienna Convention' 28–9.

consider the conceptual baggage of terms like this in their own milieu, without projecting all of their connotations upon the others. 'Nationality' as a component of a person's legal status is attended to in Chapter 6, but here we will first briefly consider 'nationalism' as an important concept derived from the idea of the 'nation', before considering some examples of how 'nation' is used in constitutional documents and literature.

3.2.1 Nationalism

Typical of '-isms', 'nationalism' is prone to be burdened with connotations (often, but not necessarily linked to extremist abuse) going far beyond the merely legal, although not without legal implications.

There is a comprehensive literature on nationalism, very little of it falling within the ambit of legal scholarship, and much of which does not sufficiently distinguish the development of the idea of the nation as the bearer of constitutional sovereignty from 'nationalism' as such.[51] 'Nationalism' is such a broad concept that it allows for many connotations to be attached to it, both positive and negative. Thus, in 2003 Liah Greenfeld, prominent author on nationalism, summarized the essence of her analysis of the development of nationalism as follows:

> Nationalism is a unique form of social consciousness which emerged in the early sixteenth century in England and subsequently spread, first to the English settlements in America, then, in the course of the eighteenth century, to France and Russia, and in the course of the last two centuries conquered the rest of Europe and the Americas, the antipodes, much of Asia, and some of Africa. At the core of this social consciousness lies a compelling, inclusive image of society, referred to as the 'nation,' an image of a sovereign community of fundamentally equal members. National consciousness is inherently democratic: egalitarianism represents the essential principle of the social organization it implies, and popular sovereignty its essential political principle.[52]

With an emphasis on American nationalism, the central thesis of this book was 'that the factor responsible for the reorientation of economic activity toward growth is nationalism', although she found economic growth not necessarily to be a product of nationalism.[53] Many considerations of a historical, political, sociological and economic nature underpin Greenfeld's findings, including the role of egalitarian liberalism in the unfolding of the idea of the nation.

---

[51] For a selection of important publications on the subject, see Skey & Antonsich 'Everyday Nationhood' 1–13.
[52] Greenfeld 'Spirit of Capitalism' 2.
[53] Greenfeld 'Spirit of Capitalism' 1 and 473.

Greenfeld identified three 'types of nationalisms'. First, the individualistic-civic type, on which national sovereignty is based as a consequence of the freedom and equality of such individuals choosing to share the common nationality, thereby implying liberal democracy. Secondly the collectivistic-civic type which infers the subjugation of the interests of the individuals forming the 'nation as a collective individual', thereby furthering elitist and even dictatorial government. The third, and according to Greenfeld the most common type, is collectivistic-ethnic nationalism, which 'combines the unitary definition of the nation with the ethnic concept of membership' thereby having authoritarian, 'quasi-biological (ultimately racist)' implications leading to the redefinition of the liberty or sovereignty of the nation to mean 'freedom from foreign domination'.[54] A significant conclusion reached in the book was that 'economic globalization is unlikely to undermine the nation either as a polity or as an economy', because 'it could not contribute now to the dismantling of the social system based on nationalism unless a new cultural canon, or paradigm, replaced nationalism', and 'so far there is no such new cultural canon'.[55]

In her introduction to the impressive multi-author, multi-national and multi-disciplinary *Research Handbook on Nationalism* published in 2020,[56] Greenfeld emphasized the diversity of scholarly approaches and perspectives to 'nationalism', which she described as 'a subject of intense interest, transcending academia everywhere around the globe', and about which 'no ... general understanding exists'.[57] Significant for the present discussion, Greenfeld opens her summary of the first part of the Handbook with the remark that it focuses 'on the inconsistencies in the expressions of nationalism today', which are 'concepts and categories that everybody uses but very few, if any, bother to define',[58] concluding, that '[c]learly, no progress has been made in the study of nationalism in the four decades since the subject was brought into fashion again by Gellner (1983) and Anderson (1983)'.[59]

Seen from the perspective of various disciplines, there is no doubt in the world of the twenty-first century that there are clear linkages between nationalism on the one hand and economics, politics, the military and sport on the other. Raving crowds at 'international' sports events probably do in some instances express a form of crude ethnic, even racial nationalistic sentiment under the banners of their states – or is it merely an inherent need to 'belong'

---

[54] Greenfeld 'Spirit of Capitalism' 2–3.
[55] Greenfeld 'Spirit of Capitalism' 482.
[56] Greenfeld & Wu 'Research Handbook on Nationalism' 1–21.
[57] Greenfeld & Wu 'Research Handbook on Nationalism' 1.
[58] Greenfeld & Wu 'Research Handbook on Nationalism' 2.
[59] Greenfeld & Wu 'Research Handbook on Nationalism' 6.

or to live in association with others? Looking at it from the vantage point of constitutional law, however, is a different matter.

Formal economic, international political and military associations have little to do with nationhood, but everything to do with the state as a prime role player in those spheres. Economic, diplomatic or military nationalism thus appears to have some utility in general intercourse, but to associate those forms of nationalism with nationhood can be no more than a symbolic, if not antiquated, usage. Therefore, and due to the entrenched status of the word 'nationalism' in our general language, canvassing for the removal of the word from our vocabulary would be wasted effort.

Using 'nationalism' as a term for sensible communication in constitutional law is however wholly undesirable, because it can mean so many things that it actually has no suitable or stable legal meaning.

3.2.2 'Nation' in Constitutional Literature and Constitutions

In constitutional literature terms such as 'nation', '(nation-)state', 'country', 'territory', 'constitutional order' and the like are often used synonymously, in many cases apparently intended as an enriching stylistic tool and not so much for the inherent significatory content of the various words. Some examples (with my bold italicization, not as criticism, but to demonstrate the issue):

> Each of the world's ***countries*** has a unique history that has impacted its value system. Language, religion, geography, economic and political circumstance influence those principles that are common to the inhabitants of individual ***countries*** and to the members of individual ***nations*** and to the members of individual ***nations***. Nevertheless, as the concept of the ***nation state*** spread and established itself in all parts of the world during the nineteenth and twentieth centuries, a large number of the constitutional texts that were designed to govern those ***territories*** were similar in the wording, concepts and format that they adopted. Many emerging ***constitutional orders*** were merely following the precedents that had been established in the United States, Great Britain and France. In other parts of the world, colonialism, and the fact that many of those texts were either directly written or inspired by European officials and scholars, played their part. The individuality of many post-colonial ***countries*** (although not all, see below) was either ignored or repressed in the process.[60]
> The UK, with its unwritten constitution, historic monarchy and 'untenable' principle of parliamentary sovereignty, is perceived by some as the perfect example of ***a nation*** stuck in the past, unable to transform itself into the contemporary conception of a truly democratic ***nation-state***, complete with the primary symbol (i.e., a written constitution) that virtually all such ***states***, complete with the primary symbol (i.e., a written constitution) that virtually all such ***states*** now possess. Thus,

---

[60] Al-Ali & Thiruvengadam 'The competing effect' 431.

while some ***countries*** have progressed to Constitutionalism 3.0, the UK may not ever have progressed to Constitutionalism 1.0.[61]

The manner in which 'nation' is employed in constitutional texts is edifying. Three examples, Germany, South Africa and Hungary, should provide sufficient illumination for the present discussion.

Germany. The word *Volk* (the people/nation) appears in various provisions of the German *Grundgesetz* of 1949. Article 20(3) proclaims the sovereignty of the *Volk*: '*Alle Staatsgewalt geht vom Volke aus*' (all the authority of the state emanates from the people). In the preamble 'das Deutsche Volk' is mentioned twice, firstly to confirm that the people are the *pouvoir constituant*, and secondly to state that the *Grundgesetz* is the constitution for the whole of the German nation ('*Damit gilt dieses Grundgesetz für das gesamte Deutsche Volk*'). Article 116 provides a constitutional definition for 'a German' ('*Deutscher*') as a person who holds German citizenship (*Staatsangehörigkeit*) or who was admitted to the territory of the German *Reich* as it was in 1937 as a refugee or expellee of German ethnic origin (*Flüchtling oder Vertriebener deutscher Volkszugehörigkeit*).[62]

The German people and the state are not presented by the text as the same entity. Article 1(1) for instance entrusts respect for and protection of human dignity as an obligation of all state authority ('*ist Verpflichtung aller staatlichen Gewalt*'), while Article 1(2) states that *das Deutsche Volk* avows itself ('*bekennt sich*') to inviolable and inalienable human rights, and Article 3(2) instructs the state to ensure equality between women and men. German constitutional doctrine maintains the three-element concept of the state (often ascribed to Georg Jellinek, although he popularized it based on the work of predecessors) consisting of a state-nation (*Staatsvolk*), state power or authority (*Staatsgewalt*) and state territory.[63] This coincides essentially (subject to subtle differences) with the conventional view regarding the requirements for statehood in international law. In international law the human element of the state is referred to as 'a permanent population',[64] and not a *Staatsvolk*, which implies

---

[61] Jones 'Constitutional Idolatry' 12.

[62] These 'status Germans' were acknowledged due to the situation immediately following World War II when many people who considered themselves to be German due to their culture, language and education were driven out of especially East European countries and therefore fled to West Germany in the hope of being reintegrated. See e.g. Wilms 'Staatsorganisationsrecht' 33.

[63] See e.g. Wilms 'Staatsorganisationsrecht' 18–19.

[64] In terms of Article 1 of the *Montevideo Convention* of 1933 'The state as a person of international law should possess the following qualifications: (a) a permanent population; (b) a defined territory; (c) government; and (d) capacity to enter into relations with the other states.'

more than inhabitants, but a nation or people as the sovereign constitutional subject.

German constitutional law is notoriously a highly theorized field which has also drawn the attention of iconic philosophers and theorists such as Immanuel Kant and more recently Jürgen Habermas. Typical of the meticulous analyses of aspects of constitutional law such as popular sovereignty undertaken by among others German political scientists, is the work of Ingeborg Maus. Pertinent to an understanding of the fortunes of the constitutional doctrine of the sovereignty of the *Staatsvolk* she made the following remark in her explanatory analysis of Habermas' celebrated 1992 book *Faktizität und Geltung*:

> Habermas's mediation of rights and popular sovereignty runs counter to a process that is typical of democratic societies as they exist today. These systems isolate basic rights from the context of democratic will-formation and thus transform genuine civil liberties (*Freiheitsrechte*) into legal goods (*Rechtsgüter*) defined by an expertocracy; these are then rationed and allocated to the subjects (*Untertanen*) as the state apparatus sees fit. Habermas, by contrast, reconstructs the 'necessary' connection between liberties and popular sovereignty via a discussion of historically entrenched misinterpretations and deficient realizations.[65]

Given the German choices of constitutional wording and the manner in which the literature tends to focus on the state as bearer of *Staatsgewalt* rather than on the indeterminate idea of the *Deutsches Volk*, it is fair to consider the idea of the *Staatsvolk* to have receded into the historical background in favour of the primacy of the state.

South Africa. The preamble of the South African Constitution of 1996 opens with the frequently used trope 'We, the people' (of South Africa) and states that 'we ... , through our freely elected representatives, adopt this Constitution ...' The preamble also records the intentions to ensure that the 'government is based on the will of the people', to build a South Africa able 'to take its rightful place as a sovereign state in the family of nations', and it closes with the prayer 'May God protect our people'. The word 'nation' appears in section 37(1)(a) which concerns the declaration of a state of emergency when 'the life of the nation is threatened', and in section 83(c) which enjoins the President to promote 'the unity of the nation'. The adjective 'national' appears as a reference to the whole (national flag, national anthem), or as a distinction from the provincial, local and international (national government, national legislation, national taxes).

The manner in which 'nation' and 'people' are used in this constitutional text appears to be expressions of the aspiration to establish national unity

---

[65] Maus 'Liberties and popular sovereignty' 852–3.

amidst the realities of social fragmentation. Various other provisions of the Constitution acknowledge this reality, for instance section 41(1)(a), which obliges all 'spheres of government and all organs of state' to 'preserve the peace, national unity and the indivisibility of the Republic'. Other examples are the declaration of 11 different languages to be the 'official languages of the Republic', the establishment in section 30 of the right of everyone 'to use the language and to participate in the cultural life of their choice' and the right of '[p]ersons belonging to a cultural, religious or linguistic community ... to form, join and maintain cultural, religious and linguistic associations and other organs of civil society' in section 31(1)(b).

These constitutional arrangements clearly indicate acknowledgment of the absence of a South African 'nation' as the concept was understood in nineteenth-century Europe. The Constitution recognizes the reality that the Republic of South Africa did not come into existence as an expression of the desire of a population self-identifying as a coherent nation, but quite the opposite. The notion 'we, the people of South Africa' can therefore at most be understood to refer to those who had the formal legal status of citizens at the time of the adoption of the Constitution. The reality of cultural and social incoherence is also acknowledged in the constitutionally expressed desire of the Republic to *become* a nation 'in the family of nations'. Such a process is usually referred to as 'nation-building', which is a process which cannot be said to have a fixed or stable definition, but Harris Mylonas' description is convincing:

> Nation-building may be defined as the process through which the boundaries of the modern state and those of the national community become congruent. The desired outcome is to achieve national integration. The major divide in the literature centers on the causal path that leads to national integration. Thus, nation-building has been theorized as a structural process intertwined with industrialization, urbanization, social mobilization, etc.; as the result of deliberate state policies that aim at the homogenization of a state along the lines of a specific constitutive story – that can and often does change over time and under certain conditions; as the product of top–bottom processes that could originate from forces outside of the boundaries of the relevant state; and as the product of bottom-up processes that do not require any state intervention to come about.[66]

'Nation-building' against the background of increased migration is an issue also in France, where the granting of permanent residence to migrants is made

---

[66] Mylonas 'Nation-Building' (cross-references omitted).

dependent on signing a 'Reception and Integration Contract'. According to Liav Orgad:

> The *Contrat d'accueil et d'intégration* is an interesting exercise in nation-building. The contract seeks to reflect the core of French identity and its fundamental essentials. It explains that the 'French are attached to a history, a culture, and fundamental values'; that living together means knowing and respecting French values; that the Republic is indivisible, secular, democratic, and social; that sovereignty belongs to the people; and that religion is a private matter. The contract puts an emphasis on gender equality. Migrants must sign that parents are jointly responsible for their children and that women are not subject to the authority of their husbands.[67]

On the next page Orgad points out that '... when nations start to examine what holds a people together, they often conclude that there are more sources of division than unity'.

Hungary. Nationhood is a central theme in the Fundamental Law of Hungary of 2011. The preamble is headed 'National Avowal', and opens with the words 'WE, THE MEMBERS OF THE HUNGARIAN NATION'. The word 'nation' is used multiple times in the rest of the preamble, for instance 'We hold that the family and the nation constitute the principal framework of our coexistence'; 'We honour the achievements of our historic constitution and we honour the Holy Crown, which embodies the constitutional continuity of Hungary's statehood and the unity of the nation', and '[Our Fundamental Law] is a living framework which expresses the nation's will and the form in which we want to live.'

In an introductory part of the constitution following the preamble under the heading 'Foundation', Article D reads 'Bearing in mind that there is one single Hungarian nation that belongs together, Hungary shall bear responsibility for the fate of Hungarians living beyond its borders, ... ' Article XXIX(1) provides that '[n]ational minorities living in Hungary shall be constituent parts of the State. Every Hungarian citizen belonging to a national minority shall have the right to freely express and preserve his or her identity.'

According to Zsolt Körtvélyesi Hungarian discussions on nationality have in recent decades been focused on the Hungarians who are not resident within Hungary, but, due to boundary changes brought about at the end of World War I, live in neighbouring states such as Romania, Slovakia, Serbia and Ukraine.[68] It is said that Hungary is representative of post-Soviet Central European states that had not, despite the tenor of their constitutions, ever been 'real' liberal

---

[67] Orgad 'Cultural Defense of Nations' 120. For perspectives on 'nation-building' in various parts of the world, see also Arjomand 'Constitutionalism and Political Reconstruction' and Grotenhuis 'Nation-Building as Necessary Effort'.

[68] Körtvélyesi 'Nation, Nationality, and National Identity' 772.

democracies, rendering them prone to the current surge of 'old ethnonationalist, populist, right-wing political forces'.[69] The 'Holy Crown' mentioned in the preamble refers to the Hungarian coronation crown dating back to the twelfth century. Following the conclusion of World War I, the Hungarian kingdom was restored (and severed from the pre-war Austro-Hungarian monarchy) in terms of the Treaty of Trianon of 1920, which meant a severe reduction of the territory of Hungary and the size of its citizenry, which now became 'an ethnically close to homogeneous country',[70] with however many Hungarians resident extra-territorially as 'national minorities'.

Hungarian citizenship and the requirements for obtaining the status of non-residential or dual citizenship based on ethnicity has since then been a continuous source of political contention surviving both the Nazi and Communist regimes.[71] What it currently means in detail to be a Hungarian is a point of continued dispute and debate: '[T]he debate on "who counts as a Hungarian" and the relevant policy decisions are not principled discussions about the meaning of the nation, democracy, popular sovereignty, and national identity, but the result of pragmatic considerations on what helps those in power remain in government.'[72] Körtvélyesi argues that 'extraterritorial mass naturalization confuses ethnicity, nationality, and citizenship', and that 'external ethnic citizenship is used to support the illiberal regime internally, by delivering a contingency of votes on national elections. Externally, the new citizenship policy has been used as a transport vehicle for the export of the illiberal regime, creating and maintaining loyalties, domesticating media and cultural institutions through personal and financial influence, often labelled clientelism.'[73] Due to the ambiguities of Hungarian citizenship law, there is a lack of certainty of who qualifies for non-resident naturalization, but also 'who constitutes the nation' under the Fundamental Law.[74]

From this (by no means comprehensive, but frequently occurring)[75] set of examples a diffuse picture emerges of possible and actual applications for the concept 'nation'. Some present it as a synonym or substitute for 'country' and 'state', others link it to citizenship, ethnic or territorial affiliation, or the confirmation of sovereignty. The question that is raised by such polysemiticity, is whether the constitutional comparatist should avoid the word completely,

---

[69] Bugarič 'Central Europe's descent into autocracy' 609.
[70] Körtvélyesi 'Nation, Nationality, and National Identity' 378–83.
[71] Körtvélyesi 'Nation, Nationality, and National Identity' 378–83.
[72] Körtvélyesi 'Nation, Nationality, and National Identity' 786–7.
[73] Körtvélyesi 'Nation, Nationality, and National Identity' 791.
[74] Körtvélyesi 'Nation, Nationality, and National Identity' 793.
[75] See e.g. Joseph Weiler's interesting note 'A nation of nations?' regarding self-determination, nation, nationalities, etc. concerning Catalan secessionism.

and if it proves to be impossible or even undesirable, how to avoid confusion when using it.

3.3 'NATION' IN CONSTITUTIONAL LAW

Historically and in contemporary usage the word 'nation' maintains a close link with and is even quite often deemed to be a synonym for the state. The state is, as the primary subject of constitutional law, however essentially different from, and not even similar to a 'nation', except if an artificial and superannuated meaning is attached to the latter. To assimilate (or confuse) 'nation' with 'state' is at the very least anachronistic and imprecise. It is virtually impossible to defend the view that more than a very few contemporary states are the product of the endeavours of an enduring 'nation' in any of its possible definitions, ranging from nineteenth-century romanticism to twenty-first-century populism. What then, can participants in constitutional conversations, especially the comparative kind, do with the term 'nation'? Three approaches might be suggested.

The first is to remove 'nation' from one's constitutional vocabulary. This should not be difficult at all, since the word cannot be said to bear any useful (or, for that matter, consistent) meaning in law. Such a strategy may however suffer under the pressures of authors of international instruments, constitution-writers and contributors to scholarly works less concerned with terminological precision and with a taste for poignant language.

A second approach would, when finding it unavoidable to use the term, be to make the effort to explicitly provide one's own or another explicitly chosen definition for the purposes of clear communication in the circumstances. Such a strategy may however be quite cumbersome, since the choices of meaning and the concomitant theoretical baggage of each are so wide, that it may require substantial justification for making the preferred choice.

A third approach may be to acknowledge the fact that the word 'nation' often crops up, albeit incongruously, in materials relevant to constitutional intercourse, and then to award a narrowed-down meaning to it, strictly limited to give expression to one component of the phenomenon 'state', for instance its human substance.[76] A pertinent proviso must however be stressed here: the use of 'nation' as a reference to the human element of the state for the purposes of incorporating, even by implication, some sophistic doctrine based on an imagined social compact will defeat the purpose. The likelihood of being (mis-)understood thus, renders the first, or at most the second, approach more attractive.

---

[76] See Chapter 5 below.

4. Sovereignty

Constitutional law (and for that matter the law as such) cannot be developed, practised, theorized or even imagined without giving an account of the reasons for the existence of the authority of the state.[1] This is so, because constitutional law is concerned with power, control, force, structure, agency, compulsion – and the regulation and limitation of all of those. Conventionally these are issues that are addressed under the rubric 'sovereignty'. Because sovereignty is often presented as the ultimate justification for the irrefutable authority of the state to compel compliance with the law, it is a notion which lies at the heart of constitutional law.

The authority to compel appears to be such a ubiquitous element in human society (consider for instance the parent/child relationship as a baseline), that it is accepted instinctively in the normal flow of social life, sometimes with grace, sometimes grudgingly, and at critical times it is challenged, resisted and even destroyed, only to be transferred elsewhere.

The history of the notion of sovereignty in the state tells a general story of the dispersal of coercive power from a centralized, mostly individualized point to a plurality of bearers of governmental and administrative competences, collectively and interdependently exerting authority in the name of the state, notionally the collective depository of the whole.

History has also shown that the justification of these phenomena evokes diverse responses. Justifying power requires a principled posture regarding its source, and the principles underlying the various responses vary greatly. Probably because of the inevitability, ubiquity and indispensability of power relations in human society, responses to the question of the justification of the authority of some over others are intimately bound to basic understandings of human existence – worldviews.

No wonder, then, that great minds that have over the centuries been engaged in constitutional and political theory have developed closely argued analyses

---

[1] Although some (especially those engaged in the field of legal pluralism) prefer to consider 'the law' not to be in the exclusive domain of the state, few will contest the close interdependence of law as a binding set of norms, and the constituted state as the major generator and enforcer of such norms. The various perceptions of the nature of law are rooted in a wide range of ontologies ranging from hard-core positivism to anarchical relativism.

and postulations of the origins, purposes and nature of sovereignty and of notions related to it. The depth and fervour of the cogitations on the subject can be sensed from the titles of some of the salient works on the topic: *Leviathan*,[2] *Qu'est-ce que le tiers-état?*,[3] *Political Theology*,[4] *Human Rights and Popular Sovereignty*,[5] *Sovereign Virtue*.[6]

In the first section of this chapter the foundational theories on sovereignty and its application in the contexts of legislation and international relations are presented. The second section provides descriptions of contextual variation of the phenomenon, using the African and European settings as examples. In the final section brief consideration is given to the implications of the instability of the notion for comparative work in constitutional law.

4.1 THE ROOTS OF SOVEREIGNTY

4.1.1 Foundational Theories

Souverän ist, wer über den Ausnahmezustand entscheidet (sovereign is he who decides on the state of exception). Thus the (in)famous core opening statement by Carl Schmitt in his seminal work first published in pre-World War I Weimar Berlin.[7] Due to Schmitt's association with the Nazi regime during World War II and his subsequent scholarly ostracism after the war, he is considered by some to be '... undoubtedly the most controversial German legal and political thinker of the twentieth century. If his friends and foes agree on nothing else, they both acknowledge his brilliance. Even his detractors concede that he is one of the outstanding intellects of our time.'[8]

Others have little regard for his work,[9] while his influence on current jurisprudential thinking does not seem to abate.[10] Schmitt is known as a fervent critic of liberal constitutionalism,[11] based on his hypothesis that political con-

---

[2] Thomas Hobbes, 1651.
[3] The Abbé Sieyès' revolutionary pamphlet of 1789 'What is the Third Estate?'.
[4] Schmitt 'Political Theology'.
[5] Habermas 'Human Rights and Popular Sovereignty'.
[6] Dworkin 'Sovereign Virtue'.
[7] Schmitt 'Politische Theologie'. An English translation was published in 2005 as Schmitt 'Political Theology'.
[8] Schwab 'Introduction to Schmitt's Political Theology' xxxvii.
[9] See e.g. Frankenberg's review of Mehring.
[10] See e.g. Von Bogdandy 'Carl Schmitt's Homonymous Text'.
[11] Schwab 'Introduction to Schmitt's Political Theology' xxxvii ascribes 'the thesis that democracy negates liberalism and liberalism negates democracy' to Schmitt, and Ackerman 'The emergency constitution' 23 urges us to rescue the concept of emer-

cepts are secularized theological concepts.[12] While rejecting Schmitt's 'existential unity of sovereignty', Johan van der Walt's (post-modernist) analysis finds that the linkage between exception and sovereignty 'cannot be faulted':

> The exceptional case (and a case would not be a case if it were not exceptional) requires and demands a decision and the one who decides may and must for all practical and logical purposes be called 'sovereign.' The extent to which some decisions are and must be accepted as indeed decisive or 'final,' albeit not always for long, renders those decisions sovereign. And the one who is called upon to decide *becomes* the sovereign, the *only* sovereign for the moment.[13]

The equally controversial thinking of Schmitt's contemporary, Hans Kelsen, who coined the concept of the *Grundnorm* (often used to express the notion of a constitution as 'highest' or 'supreme' law) has its followers and detractors.[14] Recently Sandrine Baume described Kelsen's approach as a 'refusal to surrender to any of the mythologies that denature the investigation of legal and political phenomena'.[15] Iain Stewart (whose analysis of the *Grundnorm* reduced it to 'wreckage') however pointed out that Kelsen acknowledged that it was based on a fiction 'presupposed by "the individual" in that the general

---

gency powers from 'fascist thinkers such as Carl Schmitt', 'who used it as a battering ram against liberal democracy'.

[12] In the first paragraph of Chapter 3 of *Politische Theologie*, Schmitt (Schmitt 'Political Theology' 36) stated:
> All significant concepts of the modern theory of the state are secularized theological concepts not only because of their historical development – in which they were transferred from theology to the theory of the state, whereby, for example, the omnipotent God became the omnipotent lawgiver – but also because of their systematic structure, the recognition of which is necessary for a sociological consideration of these concepts. The exception in jurisprudence is analogous to the miracle in theology. Only by being aware of this analogy can we appreciate the manner in which the philosophical ideas of the state developed in the last centuries.

[13] Van der Walt 'Horizontal Effect' 238.

[14] The Canadian Supreme Court, e.g. used 'grundnorm' as a matter of course, linking it to parliamentary sovereignty in *Canada (Auditor General) v Canada (Minister of Energy, Mines and Resources)*, [1989] 2 SCR 49, at 103: 'The *grundnorm* with which the courts must work in this context is that of the sovereignty of Parliament. The ministers of the Crown hold office with the grace of the House of Commons and any position taken by the majority must be taken to reflect the sovereign will of Parliament.'

[15] Baume 'Hans Kelsen'. Kelsen's development of the *Grundnorm* is however interpreted by Aguilera-Barchet 'History' 600 as an historic 'return to the idea of the social pact' because the *Grundnorm* 'is the basis of the legal system's legitimacy because it is the product of said pact, the essential rule by which a social community agrees to abide'.

population presupposes a basic norm and that legal science only brings it "to consciousness"'.[16] The post-modern 'Crits' are also dismissive of liberal thinking, but on completely different grounds.[17] Then there are the exponents of Marxist socialism,[18] Islamic legalism,[19] African communalism,[20] various forms of populism,[21] and more to choose from to motivate arguments in favour of a reconsideration of the liberal democratic notion of state sovereignty.

One's principled position on the nature and source of sovereignty is clearly not merely a matter of analysis of a constitutional text or the consultation of a dictionary, but is determined by one's profound convictions concerning essential ontological questions: how must the existence of the state's authority (power) be understood, and how can its location in the hands of people acting as organs of the state be justified? It is remarkable how many of the theories that have been developed over time rely on unsubstantiatable constructions of the beginnings of power. In the result, acceptance of those theories are fully dependent on the acceptance of their premises.

Despite the wide range of possible responses to the questions concerning the roots of authority, classic liberal language is still often used and presented as axiomatic and self-evident, especially within the globally influential sphere of Euro-American liberalism. Witness for instance the reflection, with perfect Asian simulation, of the constitutional sentiments of Western liberalism in the following *dictum* of the Constitutional Court of (South) Korea in its judgment on the impeachment of President Park Geun-hye in 2017: 'In a representative

---

[16] Stewart 'Critical Legal Science of Hans Kelsen' 295–7.

[17] Frankenberg 'Between Magic and Deceit' 95 e.g. holds that proponents of liberal constitutionalism (one of six forms of constitutionalism he identifies) are fearful or uneasy about public power and self-rule, and therefore tend 'to privilege law-rule over democracy', in critical situations deceitfully dressing the Leviathan in a cashmere overcoat.

[18] Marx and Engels considered democracy as a vehicle for socialism to be used to realize communism. See e.g. Schonfeld 'Classical Marxist Conception'.

[19] Law lies at the core of Islamic teaching, thereby subjecting, in most versions of the Muslim belief, the state and the law to Islamic law. See e.g. Hallaq 'Muslim Rage' 1707–8:

If Islamic civilization, culture, or state ever constituted a regime of any kind, it was one of nomocracy. There has never been a culture in human society so legally oriented as Islam ... we have come to realize – more than ever – that Islamic law was not merely a legal system that resolved conflicts and negotiated social and economic relationships (the role normally assigned to law in the West), but that it was in addition a theological system, an applied religious ritual, an intellectual enterprise of the first order, a cultural pillar of far-reaching dimensions and, in short, a world-view that defined both Muslim identity and even Islam itself.

[20] See e.g. Oduor 'Liberal democracy'.

[21] See e.g. Tushnet 'Varieties of constitutionalism' 385–7.

democracy, a public official is entrusted by the people, the sovereigns, with the power to exercise national authority, and thus must work for the benefit of public interest from a neutral position.'[22]

Popular sovereignty is a kernel, together with individual liberty, in liberal democratic thinking, but 'the people' are also awarded the status of the source of power in various other views and constitutional systems. Who 'the people' actually are, is another matter.[23] Be that as it may, if the people (or anyone or any other institution) is 'sovereign', what must we understand it to mean in constitutional law?

The popes of the Roman Church had by the fifth century established themselves as the highest authorities against whose verdicts no appeal was possible, and that the people had to be led (by the Church), not followed (*ducendus est populus, sed non sequendus*).[24] Some six centuries later, kings in Europe were establishing themselves as independent from emperors and popes, achieving undisputed power within their realms. As an affirmation of such claims, the scholars of Roman law of that era advising the kings cited the maxim *Rex est imperator in regno suo*. Aguilera-Barchet traces the confirmation in France of the monarchs' elevation above all feudal lords to an adviser to Louis VI and Louis VII, Abbot Suger de Saint Denis (1081–1151), and the first appearance of 'sovereignty' as a legal term to the legists of Louis IX (1226–1270).[25]

As the idea of representation began taking root around the twelfth century, assemblies of participating discussants ('parliaments') convened from time to time to provide monarchs with money and to submit requests to the Crown, which could become laws on receiving royal approval. By the fourteenth century the postglossator Bartolus de Saxoferrato –

> ... argued that the state was its own prince (*civitas sibi princeps*) and could legislate 'as it pleases' (*prous sibi placet*) on any matter affecting the public weal, with the crucial consequence that, according to him, legislative sovereignty relied on a 'free people' possessing all law-creating capabilities through its popular assembly.[26]

Around that time Baldus de Ubaldis extended the notion of sovereignty also to Italian city republics, and Niccolò Machiavelli advised rulers in 1513 that they

---

[22] **2016Hun-Na1,** (March 10, 2017), at I.(1)① English translation 15 December 2020 http://search.ccourt.go.kr/xmlFile/0/010400/2017/pdf/e2016n1_1.pdf (accessed 17 June 2021).

[23] This is a question with which Chapters 2 and 3 above and Chapter 7 below are also concerned.

[24] Ullmann 'Short history of the Papacy' 10.

[25] Aguilera-Barchet 'History' 178–9.

[26] Aguilera-Barchet 'History' 194.

could trace their authority to the Roman emperors, leading to Jean Bodin's definition in 1576 of sovereignty in his famous *Six Livres*:

> Sovereignty is that absolute and perpetual power vested in a commonwealth which in Latin is termed *majestas* ... Sovereignty is not limited, in power, responsibility, or in time ... it is necessary for sovereigns not to be subject to anyone else's power so that they may ... impose law upon their subjects and rescind or amend useless laws ...[27]

Bodin's postulation of the sovereign nation was followed by Locke, Voltaire, Rousseau and Von Savigny in the process of the conceptualization of constitutional 'nations' in accordance with the examples of the Americans, French, Germans, Italians and others around the North Atlantic,[28] mechanically following the fictional construct of the 'social contract'.[29] Frankenberg describes this transition from monarchical sovereignty to popular sovereignty appositely: '[P]ower became public, the dynastic principle lost its symbolic frame provided by a holy tradition or sacred right and was secularized. Human rights infiltrated the realm formerly structured by privilege.'[30]

It is at this junction – when sole royal sovereignty was romantically transformed into dispersed popular sovereignty – that logic came to contradict theoretical construction: if sovereignty means the highest, final, indisputable authority, it cannot be derived from elsewhere, it cannot be shared, divided or distributed. How is it then possible for sovereignty to be a shared characteristic of 'the people', composed of an ever-changing multitude of individuals? How can it be that a member of 'the sovereign people' needs protection against the other 'sovereigns', and especially against the institutions supposedly jointly empowered to exercise legal authority and protection over all and on everyone's behalf? Strikingly, the Fleiners posed, and responded as follows, to the question whether history creates legitimacy:

> In some theories on state authority, it can be difficult to separate fiction from historical fact. Some exponents of contract theories such as THOMAS HOBBES and ROUSSEAU do not assert that the people of the original society literally concluded a social contract with each other by which they transferred certain governing powers to the monarch. For these scholars the social contract is rather a theoretical fiction, from which additional rules of state authority can be deduced. This fictitious presupposition of free contractual agreement for the building of a polity and for the transfer

---

[27] Aguilera-Barchet 'History' 217–19.
[28] Summarized in section 3.1.1 of Chapter 3.
[29] See section 2.4 of Chapter 2.
[30] Frankenberg 'Between Magic and Deceit' 158. Presumably the correspondence in this passage with Schmitt's idea that political concepts are secularized theological concepts is coincidental.

of power to rule thus provides the justification or legitimacy for state authority. Other exponents of contract theory on the other hand, such as JOHN LOCKE, are of the opinion that people in primitive times literally concluded a first contract in order to set up a polity, and with a second contract transferred limited authority to the rulers. As one can see, it can be difficult to separate historical facts and fiction. Those who see the state as an essential and immanent institution and corollary of human nature will try to prove that the state has always been a historically significant institution.[31]

On the secularization of sovereignty, they wrote:

> Secularised ethics that were separate from religion developed into a generally applicable, universal ethical code. Rights founded on natural law are inalienable. The original equality before God becomes equality before the law. Out of the natural law that precedes the state, man becomes the creator of the state. In short: from the right to resistance (the capacity to say "no") develops popular sovereignty.[32]

And yet, so much of the world of constitutional law is still operating on the contractarian fiction.[33] Can it then be that the various historical and theoretical attempts to secularize (or de-religionize) authority reflects a universal truth, namely that authority can only be explained in religious terms?[34]

Can one conclude otherwise than that constitutional sovereignty (international legal relations aside for the moment) is a misnomer, a fictional mechanism used to implausibly explain the source of the powers of the institutions of the state over those under its jurisdiction based on untenable logic and agnostic worldviews? And yet – the existence and indisputability of those powers must have a cogent explanation, because they are real.

It is possible to explain, analyze and comment on the many historic and contemporary theories and rationalizations proposed for the explanation of the authority of the state, often labelled 'sovereignty', but when doing so, it would be hardly possible to do so neutrally, disregarding the effects of one's ontological and epistemological precepts. The result will have to be rejection of some

---

[31] Fleiner & Basta Fleiner 'Constitutional Democracy' 34.
[32] Fleiner & Basta Fleiner 'Constitutional Democracy' 133.
[33] See e.g. Rawls 'Justice as Fairness' 192–3: 'Thus however mistaken the notion of the social contract may be as history, and however far it may overreach itself as a general theory of social and political obligation, it does express, suitably interpreted, an essential part of the concept of justice.' See further Lessnoff 'Social Contract'; Beyer 'Making Sieyès Habermas Meet'; Hasebe & Pinelli 'Constitutions, 13; Hidalgo 'Lange Schatten'.
[34] I hold ostensible a-religious secularism, agnosticism and atheism actually to be 'religious' in the sense that, if those attitudes base an authentic worldview, they are no different than any other religion: see Venter 'Constitutionalism and Religion' 47 and 224.

views, selective acceptance of elements of some approaches, or the (unlikely) construction of a fresh approach.

Such being the case, the point to be made here (again) is that a constitutional lawyer's use of the word 'sovereignty' is unavoidably infused with subjective precepts, which, if the account is to be clear and defensible, should be revealed. Assuming that there exists a standard conception of constitutional sovereignty capable of universal subscription would be arrogant and misleading. The ambivalence, pliability and inconclusiveness of the notion was recently captured expertly in an editorial article by Neil Walker while in fact defending its continued utility, writing in his conclusion:

> Whenever and wherever we witness the reshaping or relocation of sovereignty today, whether with a view to the recomposition of the scheme of foundational collective commitment, or to raising new and rival claims from below, or to rationing and redistributing existing claims from above, or to reinforcing the jurisdiction of existing state-based claims, or to reducing these claims to a more primitive form, we are reminded of the strengths and limitations, but also of the self-perpetuating indispensability, of the sovereignty frame to our contemporary political imaginary and practice ... [S]overeignty is by no means the only frame through which we understand and seek to fashion the world of law and politics today. But it remains the most influential one, and generates significant surplus value.[35]

4.1.2 Legislative Sovereignty

It stands to reason that, for an enacted legal norm to be binding, it must be backed by the authority to design, formulate and effectively legislate it. In common law constitutional orders such authority of the primary lawgiver is known as 'parliamentary sovereignty'. The notion originated in the English history of the victory of Parliament over the Crown, rendering, as it were, Parliament's consent to be every Englishman's consent.[36] The doctrine was manifestly expressed by Dicey in the late nineteenth century:

> The sovereignty of Parliament is, from a legal point of view, the dominant characteristic of our political institutions ... The principle ... means neither more nor less than this, namely that 'Parliament' has 'the right to make or unmake any law whatever; and further, that no person or body is recognised by the law of England as having a right to override or set aside the legislation of Parliament'.[37]

---

[35] Walker 'The Sovereignty Surplus' 427.
[36] See section 2.6 in Chapter 2 above.
[37] Dicey 'Introduction' 38.

Parliamentary sovereignty continues to be accepted as a 'fundamental principle of the UK constitution',[38] and has been expressly reconfirmed in the course of the 'Brexit' process. Thus, for instance, a balance between the accountability of the executive to Parliament, the independent jurisdiction of the judiciary (though not to review parliamentary legislation), and parliamentary sovereignty, was well demonstrated in 2019 when the Prime Minister had Parliament prorogued (wielding the royal prerogative) at a critical point of decision making about the United Kingdom leaving the European Union.[39] Since the Brexit process was set in motion by a 'referendum' (technically a plebiscite, because the outcome did not bind Parliament in law), the question of the balance between parliamentary sovereignty and popular sovereignty came into play in academic discourse, albeit inconclusively.[40] The United Kingdom's membership of the EU implied on the one hand the 'expectation of compliance with the European Court of Human Rights rulings', but on the other hand, the adoption by Parliament of the *Human Rights Act* of 1998 (the HRA) was designed to preserve parliamentary sovereignty:

> Commentary on the HRA characterizes its design as the outcome of a prudential attempt to reconcile rights protection with democratic principles. The HRA has been described in dialogic terms, where Parliament is recognized as the hegemonic partner in an inter-institutional project of improving compliance with Convention rights because of the deliberate decision to retain the principle of parliamentary sovereignty.[41]

A 'supreme' constitution containing a charter of fundamental rights is clearly incompatible with parliamentary sovereignty because in its essential nature, sovereignty cannot be shared. Therefore, where constitutions with superior legality were adopted in legal orders based on English constitutional law, the issue of legislative sovereignty was either compromised, or eliminated. In the late colonial era, especially in the early twentieth century, the doctrine of parliamentary sovereignty became embedded in the constitutional arrangements of the British dominions Australia, Canada, South Africa and New Zealand.[42] Before the introduction in South Africa of the constitutional state in 1994, parliamentary sovereignty was an instrument of political abuse, but was fully

---

[38] *R (Miller and Dos Santos) v Secretary of State for Exiting the European Union* [2017] UKSC 5 para 43.

[39] *R (on the application of Miller) v The Prime Minister* [2019] UKSC 41 para 33: 'The fact that the minister is politically accountable to Parliament does not mean that he is therefore immune from legal accountability to the courts.'

[40] See e.g. Douglas-Scott 'Brexit'.

[41] Hiebert 'Human Rights Act' 2266.

[42] See section 2.6 in Chapter 2 above.

removed when the Constitution became the 'supreme law';[43] federalism and the adoption in Canada of the *Constitution Act* of 1982 provided for a compromise,[44] the Canadian courts exercise a measure of deference and allow for a 'margin of appreciation' in adjudicating legislative choices;[45] in New Zealand the legislative sovereignty of Parliament persists, but is sometimes subjected to stringent academic scrutiny;[46] Australian regional and aspirational human rights charters 'present a new compromise between the protection of human rights and the maintenance of parliamentary sovereignty'.[47]

The primacy of the highest legislature is routinely qualified by the role of the executive in the legislative process, which is understandably substantial. In this regard it is instructive to note the distinction that can be made in constitutional law between monism and dualism (to be distinguished from the use of these terms in international law indicating whether a particular legal order incorporates international law automatically in its legal system, or requires specific legislative action for it to be incorporated). A constitutional system characterized by parliamentary sovereignty modelled on the United Kingdom example should be monist in the sense that the executive emanates from and is dependent upon the support of the elected component of parliament, is exposed to rejection and replacement at the next general election, but enjoys for the time being reasonable certainty that its legislative initiatives will receive the approval of the parliamentary majority. On the other hand, typical of a dualist system is that it operates under a supreme constitution, deemed to express 'the will of the people' until 'the sovereign people' decide to amend the constitution, therefore rendering all executive conduct – regardless of its having been elected by the majority vote – reviewable under the constitution.[48]

---

[43] See e.g. Hoexter & Olivier 'The Judiciary' 30–31, section 4 of the 1993 Constitution and section 2 of the current (1996) Constitution.

[44] In 2018 the Supreme Court of Canada stated in *Reference re Pan-Canadian Securities Regulation* [2018] 3 SCR 189, para 56: 'While the principle of parliamentary sovereignty is an equally important feature of Canadian law, various aspects of our written Constitution have qualified the basic Diceyan rule that Parliament has the power "to make or unmake any law whatever". One such qualification lies in the federal structure of the Canadian state, which restricts the subject matters over which each legislature has jurisdiction.' Section 33 of the *Canadian Charter of Rights and Freedoms* (attached to the *Constitution Act, 1982*) allows Parliament and provincial legislatures to exclude the operation of sections of the Charter from operation by expressly declaring such to be the case.

[45] Venter 'Constitutional Comparison' 185–7. See also *Reference re Pan-Canadian Securities Regulation*, 2018 S.C.R. 189 (2018) 193.

[46] See e.g. Geddis 'Parliamentary government in New Zealand'.

[47] Dalla-Pozza & Williams 'Constitutional Validity' 38.

[48] See e.g. Ackerman 'We the People' 6–10 and Gyorfi 'New Constitutionalism' 151.

Be that as it may, the delegation or abdication of legislative power is regulated differently in the dualist United States and the presumably monist Canada functioning in the Westminster style. Article I Section 7 of the US Constitution in effect prohibits, as a function of the separation of powers, Congress to delegate its legislative powers to the executive, whereas in Canada, such delegation occurs frequently and Mark Mancini argues that, due to the principle of parliamentary sovereignty, the exercise of delegated legislative powers must be subject to parliamentary control.[49] In newer constitutions adopted on the monist foundations of British colonial constitutional law while asserting the supremacy of the constitution writ large in the image of the dualist American example, confusion regarding parliamentary legislative primacy, presidential imperialism, and judicial review jurisdiction frequently occurs.[50]

Considering this motley picture of legislative sovereignty, various uncertainties arise regarding the actual significance of the term 'sovereignty' in relation to legislative authority. The answers to for example the following questions depend on assumptions regarding the nature of sovereignty:

> In a monist dispensation, is legislative sovereignty and popular sovereignty to be distinguished or merged somehow using for instance an argument that the elected legislature, legislating by majority vote is rendered 'sovereign' by the (majority of the) actual sovereign, the people, for one electoral period at a time?
>
> Is duly enacted legislation adopted by the legislature in a dualist system binding in the same manner as under parliamentary sovereignty, therefore requiring unqualified obedience on pain of retribution?
>
> Can a legislature empowered to adopt amendments to a superior constitution following due process (currently the vogue in most states) be deemed to have been authorized by the 'sovereign people' in whom the constituent power is vested to do so indefinitely?
>
> Is the argument that legislatures (and executives for that matter) are subject to the sovereignty of the 'people' because they are accountable to regularly subject themselves to blunt democratic instruments such as elections, public comment and criticism, referenda and plebiscites, opinion polls and surveys and eventually to acquiesce in judicial findings against them credible?

Given these and similar considerations, can the constitutional lawyer, especially the comparatist, risk using the expression 'legislative sovereignty' and hope to be understood correctly without introducing the discussion with clear disclaimers or delimitations regarding the intended meaning?

---

[49] Mancini 'Non-Abdication'.
[50] Venter 'Separation of powers in new constitutions' 120–2.

4.1.3 Sovereignty and Self-determination in International Law

Since we are here primarily concerned with constitutional law the matter of sovereignty in the international setting can be dispensed with in a few words, the most important consideration being that the concept is fundamentally different in respectively constitutional and international law.

In international relations sovereignty is a more consistent and therefore a more tenable notion. It simply signifies that an authority legitimately representing a particular state *vis-à-vis* other states and the world community has the (almost)[51] exclusive authority to take decisions about those relations. A frequently quoted definition of sovereignty in international law was coined by Swiss diplomat and lawyer Max Huber, sitting in 1928 as arbitrator on the bench of the Permanent Court of Arbitration:

> Sovereignty in the relations between States signifies independence. Independence in regard to a portion of the globe is the right to exercise therein, to the exclusion of any other State, the functions of a State. The development of the national organisation of States during the last few centuries and, as a corollary, the development of international law, have established this principle of the exclusive competence of the State in regard to its own territory in such a way as to make it the point of departure in settling most questions that concern international relations.[52]

As the colonial empires, economic hegemonies and dictatorships of the major powers were shattered, diffused or challenged following the two global wars and the post-war arousal of collective human rights consciences, the twentieth century saw the emergence of a multitude of newly sovereign states.[53] In this

---

[51] In an encyclopaedic dictionary, translated as a chapter in Kelsen 'Sovereignty', Hans Kelsen addressed the qualification of sovereignty under international law as follows at 525–6:
This sovereignty of the state becomes problematic when international law is brought into the picture as a legal system imposing obligations and conferring rights on the state. That international law imposes obligations and confers rights on the state to behave in a certain way does not mean, as sometimes assumed, that international law imposes obligations and confers rights on a being that is not human but a kind of superman or superhuman organism. ... [O]nly the behaviour of human beings can be the content of legal obligations and rights ... in their capacity as organs of the state ... who are to fulfil the obligations imposed and to exercise the rights conferred by international law.
International protection of the internationally legitimized human rights of individuals and groups in effect challenge notions of exclusive state sovereignty: see e.g. Coomaraswamy 'Contemporary challenges to international human rights' 130.

[52] *Island of Palmas case (Netherlands, USA)* 23 December 2020 https://legal.un.org/riaa/cases/vol_II/829-871.pdf at 838 (accessed 18 June 2021).

[53] To quantify this trend: the League of Nations had 63 members by 1939 and the United Nations' membership grew from 51 in 1945 to 193 by 2021.

process, sovereignty in international law came to be accompanied by the notion of the 'self-determination' of ethnic communities, nations and peoples as a right to be recognized internationally.[54] Interestingly (though without particular significance) self-determination is mentioned in the Charter of the United Nations[55] before sovereignty.[56] Zsolt Körtvélyesi recently provided the following useful precis:

> Nation-states continue to be the central players on the international scene, protecting their role with changing vocabulary. Sovereignty had long been the term around which discussions on state power centered, with the notion of self-determination gaining ground after the world wars and ultimately its inclusion in the United Nations legal regime. The notion of 'peoples' include, prominently, the population of existing states, while, in an international regime defined by nation-states, international law remains hostile to secessionist attempts under the same label. Both notions came to include a strong democratic element: popular sovereignty and the peoples' right to self-determination imply legitimacy based on popular consent. The 'new cloth' of sovereignty-references is cut from the fabric of identity talk and politics of recognition, with notions like national identity, cultural identity and constitutional identity. These expressions, especially the latter, can be applied to different, often conflicting purposes: constitutional identity can serve the goal of constitutional protection against encroachment but can also be put to use to shove off external criticism based on human rights, democracy and the rule of law. The latter case can be exemplified by references of national governments and constitutional courts against European criticism where relying on sovereignty would seem to be insufficient.[57]

Although sovereignty as a legal construct in international law, depending on external determination rather than indisputable reality, is not a static or uncontested concept,[58] its essential meaning (independence and freedom from external domination) appears to be substantial enough to make it useful for the purpose. Sovereignty, seen from the perspective of international law, however, does not cover the range of uses of the term within the ambit of constitutional law. The international definition of 'sovereignty' can therefore not be transferred to the domain of constitutional law. To demonstrate: it is for instance quite possible that a plenipotentiary can be recognized in international law as competent to represent and act on behalf of a sovereign state in international

---

[54] See e.g. Van der Vyver 'Right to Self-determination' and Friedberg 'Brexit'.
[55] Article 1, 2 subscribes to 'the principle of equal rights and self-determination of peoples'.
[56] Article 2, 1 states that the UN 'is based on the principle of the sovereign equality of all its Members'.
[57] Körtvélyesi 'Nation, Nationality, and National Identity' 774–5.
[58] See e.g. Worster 'Territorial status'.

relations without such a person having any status constitutionally as the bearer of any of the forms of constitutional sovereignty.[59]

Ongoing claims of sovereignty and self-determination – and the denial thereof – are not an uncommon feature of the world of international relations in the twenty-first century. Palestine, Taiwan, Western Sahara and Kosovo are examples on a potentially long and dynamic list. From the perspective of international relations (which is not the present focus) compromises are sometimes reached regarding recognition as practical (functional) arrangements for the time being.[60]

Approaching the question of contested sovereignty over territorial entities from the perspective of constitutional law, recognition or quasi-recognition of their status can only be of peripheral importance, because constitutional sovereignty is not conditioned on internationally recognized sovereign statehood, the granting of which under unusual circumstances is routinely controversial. Conversely, international recognition of statehood calls for the ability of the authorities representing the state to do so, which is compromised if those authorities cannot convincingly claim constitutional independence, for instance due to political instability and ongoing military and other forms of conflict. Such is the case with the State of Palestine, which was granted 'non-member observer State status in the United Nations' in 2012 on the basis of the 'reaffirmation' of 'the right of the Palestinian people to self-determination and to independence in their State of Palestine on the Palestinian territory occupied since 1967'.[61]

For present purposes, the matter of contested sovereignty of territorial entities is too vexed and unstable a notion, that, to pursue it further does not promise assistance in our present quest for conceptual and terminological clarity in constitutional law.

---

[59] According to the preamble to the (Maastricht) *Treaty on European Union* (1992), the agreement was entered into by three queens, two kings, one grand duke and six presidents as heads of state, and each 'designated as their plenipotentiaries' two ministers of their governments, who signed the treaty in confirmation of the 'decision' of the heads of state. Consider further the following statement by Bartlomiej Krzan, in Krzan 'Poland and International Courts' 108:
> In all proceedings before the European Court of Human Rights, Poland is represented by a government agent, i.e. a government plenipotentiary situated within the structure of the Ministry of Foreign Affairs and being also responsible for the coordination of the execution of ECtHR judgments. It was decided to vest the power of the representation of Poland before the European Court of Human Rights in the Ministry of Foreign Affairs and not in any of the sectoral ministers.

[60] See e.g. Worster 'Territorial status'.

[61] UN General Assembly Resolution 67/19 on 29 November 2012. Regarding internal stability, see e.g. Arake 'Independent State of Palestine'.

4.2 CONTEXTUAL VARIATIONS

In an article published in 2017 dealing with the legitimacy of the outcome of consultative referenda in the Netherlands, Geerten Boogaard posed (with a play on the arresting banner '*Wir* sind das Volk!' (*we* are the people) used in the protest marches of the East Germans preceding the fall of the Berlin wall) the question 'Wer ist das Volk?' (who is the nation?). He concluded that the referendum can be abused to become a dangerous, absolutistic threat to representative democracy.

Boogaard lamented the fact that the question where the ultimate sovereignty lies in the legal order of the Netherlands has never been clearly answered – not in the constitution, nor in the erection of a monumental building symbolizing popular representation. Choices between the theories on royal sovereignty, divine sovereignty, sovereignty of reason or popular sovereignty had not been made before World War II, and after the war nationalist sovereignty was seen in a bad light, causing the 'positivistic constitutional law' to lose interest in the matter. Those Dutch constitutional lawyers who did show some interest in the question to whom sovereignty belonged preferred to imagine a sovereign transcending the concrete legal order, therefore not being a collection of juridical competences, but just an idea about the foundation of the legal order as a whole and the source of the authority of the state.[62]

Although unique in its own way, it is not only in the Netherlands where uncertainty about the place and nature of sovereignty can be detected. A textual void such as in the Netherlands is however rare, elsewhere being filled richly with idealistic liberal democratic phrases with varying degrees of sincerity and clarity.

4.2.1 Fault Lines in Africa

In various African constitutions, where language pertaining to popular sovereignty, such as 'the people', 'nation' and 'democracy', constitutionalized idealism has become a common feature. These liberal ambitions are however constantly being exposed to contention, among various reasons also due to the artificiality of externally imposed state boundaries in the colonial era. Internal and international state borderlines were, at the time of the transformation from colonies to independent states, an almost unalterable given.

At the time of independent constitutionalization, remaining fragments of pre-colonial political, ethnic and economic social orders that may have survived the ravages of colonialism could hardly be revived in modern con-

---

[62] Boogaard 'Wer ist das Volk?' 146.

stitutional configurations. The drafters of African constitutions were left to determine global best practice, and to follow it. Consequently, federal configurations, partial decentralization or deconcentration, and mostly symbolic acknowledgment of the existence of indigenous mores (largely in tension with liberal constitutionalism) represent attempts to accommodate cultural, racial, religious or geographic diversity in African constitutions. In the end, 'We, the people', purportedly unified as a 'nation', serve in many cases as a more or less vague identification of an often disparate, 'sovereign' constitutional subject.

Some examples of the employment in current African constitutional texts of the received notion of sovereignty reveal the mechanical replication of liberal democratic concepts (italics added): in Namibia and Zambia 'all power' is vested in the people of the state concerned to 'exercise their *sovereignty* through the democratic institutions of the State';[63] the '*sovereignty* of Ghana resides in the people of Ghana in whose name and for whose welfare the powers of government are to be exercised in the manner and within the limits laid down in this Constitution;[64] the People of Uganda are recorded to be the authors of their Constitution by 'exercising our *sovereign* and inalienable right to determine the form of governance for our country';[65] the Federal Republic of Nigeria is 'a State based on the principles of democracy and social justice' in which '*sovereignty* belongs to the people of Nigeria from whom government through this Constitution derives all its powers and authority';[66] Kenyans adopted their Constitution being 'proud of our ethnic, cultural and religious diversity, and determined to live in peace and unity as one indivisible *sovereign* nation'[67] and consistent therewith, 'all *sovereign* power belongs to the people of Kenya and shall be exercised only in accordance with this Constitution'[68] and 'Parliament manifests the diversity of the nation, represents the will of the people, and exercises their *sovereignty*;[69] in South Africa 'We, the people of South Africa ... believe that South Africa belongs to all who live in it, united in our diversity'[70] and the 'Republic of South Africa is one, *sovereign*, democratic state'.[71]

---

[63] Article 1(2) of the *Constitution of the Republic of Namibia*, 1990; Section 1(2) of the *Constitution of the Republic of Zambia*, 1991.
[64] Article 1(2) of the *Constitution of the Republic of Ghana*, 1993.
[65] Preamble to the *Constitution of the Republic of Uganda*, 1995.
[66] Section 14 of the *Constitution of the Federal Republic of Nigeria*, 1999.
[67] Preamble to the *Constitution of Kenya*, 2010.
[68] Article 1(1) of the *Constitution of Kenya*, 2010.
[69] Article 94(2) of the *Constitution of Kenya*, 2010.
[70] Preamble to the *Constitution of the Republic of South Africa*, 1996.
[71] Section 1 of the *Constitution of the Republic of South Africa*, 1996.

Troubling fault lines in African constitutional life superficially cast in the mould of liberal constitutionalism have been revealed in the recent three or four decades. These are due to the social, economic and political circumstances on a continent with no indigenous history of individualistic liberalism. This must not be understood to be a derogatory assessment, but recognition of the cultural devastation of indigenous mores wrought by colonialism. Various examples exist of constitutional mechanisms ostensibly meant to enhance liberal constitutionalism in Africa, but they are proving to have been in the nature of mere tactical concessions made to external role players at the time of the writing of the constitutions, or even elitist presumptuousness on the part of those in power.

Witness for instance Article 1(4) of the Kenyan Constitution of 2010, which provides that the 'sovereign power of the people' is exercised at both the national level and county levels and Chapter Eleven as a whole is devoted to 'devolved government'. The process of devolution has however not received much support from and has apparently even been subjected to intentional fiscal smothering by the central government. In 2019, Samuel Ngigi and Doreen Busolo for instance listed the shortcomings attending the process of devolution demanded by the Constitution: disagreement between the national and county governments over funding, insufficient consultation, little technical support for the county authorities, delayed disbursements of funds to the counties by the fiscus, corruption, and more.[72] This lack of enthusiasm on the part of the ruling majority for the realization of transformational idealism captured in the supreme law reveals, at the least, a deficit of constitutionalist conviction.

Adepoju and Basirue argue that 'multiple identities' undercut citizenship in contemporary Africa, making 'the journey to nationhood tortuous and challenging'.[73] A common identity is subsumed in the idea of the sovereignty of the people. Speaking historically, culturally, ethnically and economically, the fractured nature of the citizenry of most African states therefore suggests that Africa is unlikely to be a fertile environment for the constitutional reception of notions of popular sovereignty as perceived in the West.

It is nevertheless possible to make an argument that constitutional identity in Africa, at least in those countries where constitutions were fashioned in the image of the North Atlantic paragons of liberal democracy, reflects a received constitutionalism comparable to the best in the world. When observers are confronted with the reality of the strains and contradictions in the constitutional lives of the citizens and governments of those countries, it might even be possible to defend the view that much progress has been made towards their

---

[72] Ngigi & Busolo 'Devolution in Kenya'.
[73] Adepoju & Basiru 'Crisis of citizenship' 210.

inclusion in the family of liberal-democratic nations. Local adaptations and innovations might be understood to represent developmental progress towards the confirmation of the merits of Western constitutionalism, including popular sovereignty, albeit in a slightly syncretistic form.

The persuasiveness of such a construction however suffers under the indications that important elements of the constitutional texts of Africa that seem to hold the theoretical standards of liberal democracy high, do not reflect lived experience. Those standards have been proven over recent decades not to be so readily transferrable. Thus for instance, Pius Mosima, a Cameroonian philosopher, holds that African development should be approached from 'an African communitarian perspective', development being 'inclusive when it allows values and incorporates the contributions of all stakeholders', and that development efforts on the continent should be 'grounded in the spirit of African communitarianism'.[74] Contrary to the liberalism which promoted the construction of popular sovereignty on the basis of individual liberty, communitarianism is primarily concerned with society as a collective entity, not a conglomerate of free individuals.

4.2.2 Contested Sovereignty in the European Union

The fortunes of the notion of sovereignty in Europe reveal yet another form and arena of contestation over final decision-making authority. The establishment of the EU introduced the concept 'supra-national' (as opposed to 'national' and 'international'), thereby also creating new angles of analysis of notions central to constitutional law, such as statehood, citizenship and nationality, democracy, judicial review – and sovereignty.

Much has been written on the effects of the arrangements of the European Union on sovereignty – much too much to deal with here in any measure of detail.[75] Suffice it to sketch some of the considerations dealt with in a series of widely discussed judgments of the German Federal Constitutional Court, the *Bundesverfassungsgericht* (hereafter 'BverfG') concerning the precedence or otherwise of Community law over the national law of member states.[76]

Article 24(1) of the German *Grundgesetz* (1949) (hereafter 'GG') empowers the Federal Republic to transfer sovereign powers to international organizations by legislation. In 1963 and 1964 the Court of Justice of the European

---

[74] Mosima 'Inclusive Development' 85.
[75] To mention only one secondary source (with emphasis on materials published in German), see the bibliographies at the end of each of the ten chapters in Abbas, Förster & Richter 'Supranationalität'.
[76] The expertly encapsulated review by Dieter Grimm, former justice of the BverfG in Grimm 'Long Time Coming', provides useful guidelines.

Union with its seat in Luxembourg (CJEU) declared that EEC law takes priority over the national law of member states. In the *Solange I* judgment of 1974, the BVerfG however determined that such would the case only as long as European law did not offend against fundamental rights protected under the GG. By 1986 the BVerfG could be convinced that the European human rights regime had been developed sufficiently to accept that the Court should not intercede in questions of applicability of secondary Community law, as long as the conditions of rights protection by the CJEU continue in a manner compatible with the protection of fundamental rights in terms of the GG (the *Solange II* judgment). In 2009 the BVerfG confirmed (in the *Lisbon Judgment*) that the precedence of Community law in Germany was based on the conferral of authority on the EU by legislation adopted by the German federal legislature in accordance with articles 24(1) and 59(2) of the GG, approving the European Treaties.

Grimm explains that, according to the *Lisbon Judgment*, for the BVerfG 'it is key that the European Union is a union of sovereign states, which make up its foundation, and that it must respect their identities, which are reflected primarily in their national constitutions', because the competences of the EU were not *transferred* by the member states, but *conferred*.[77] The first paragraph of Article 1 of the *Treaty on European Union* establishes the Union 'on which the Member States confer competences to attain objectives they have in common', and Articles 4(1) and 5(2) confirm that 'competences not conferred upon the Union in the Treaties remain with the Member States'.

The CJEU however continued to challenge the sovereignty of member states by applying Community law on the supposition that it precedes the national law of member states: 'the EU's level of legitimation is compromised ... by the influence the CJEU has created for itself by declaring the precedence of EU law'.[78] This has led to a 'democracy problem' in the EU, exacerbated by the jurisprudence of the CJEU.[79] In May 2020, the BVerfG drew a distinct line afresh in what has become known as the 'PSPP judgment'.

The background of the PSPP judgment was the 'Weiss judgment' handed down in 2018 by the CJEU, declaring that the European Central Bank's quantitative easing programme (public sector asset purchase programme) had been conceived lawfully. The BVerfG however found that the CJEU's judgment was *ultra vires* in Germany, re-emphasizing the unresolved (though usually low-intensity) disputes over sovereignty in the EU. According to Kyriazis the judgment 'might bring forth a new era in the relationship between the German

---

[77] Grimm 'Long Time Coming' 945–6.
[78] Grimm 'Long Time Coming' 946. See also Kyriazis 'PSPP judgment'.
[79] Grimm 'Long Time Coming' 947.

FCC and the ECJ, and thus between EU law supremacy and Member State sovereignty'.[80] This is borne out by various dicta in the PSPP judgment, such as:

> Art. 23(1) first and third sentence GG affirms that the right to democratic self-determination enshrined in Art. 38(1) first sentence in conjunction with Art. 20(1) and (2) and Art. 79(3) GG applies, in principle, also with regard to European integration (*Integrationsverantwortung*). The democratic legitimation by the people of public authority exercised in Germany belongs to the essential contents of the principle of the sovereignty of the people and thus forms part of the Basic Law's constitutional identity protected in Art. 79(3) GG; it is therefore beyond the reach of European integration in accordance with Art. 23(1) third sentence in conjunction with Art. 79(3) GG ... It follows that the Basic Law does not authorise German state organs to transfer sovereign powers to the European Union in such a way that the European Union were authorised, in the independent exercise of its powers, to create new competences for itself ... The manner and scope of the transfer of sovereign powers must satisfy democratic principles.[81]

Article 22(2) of the GG cannot be more explicit in its subscription to popular sovereignty: 'All state authority is derived from the people. It shall be exercised by the people through elections and other votes and through specific legislative, executive and judicial bodies.' For as long as this explicit form of popular sovereignty prevails, the legitimacy of norms and the exercise of authority by the supra-national structures of the EU will have to be open to contestation. This is not only a dogmatic issue, but also has structural and procedural characteristics, lucidly captured by Grimm:

> The EU derives its democratic legitimation primarily from the Member States, which are organised according to democratic principles and which, by way of the European Council and the Council of Ministers, play the central role in the system of European institutions. At the same time, the EU's own legitimation, derived from the election of the European Parliament, is relatively weak. On the one hand, this is because the European Parliament's powers lag behind those of the national parliaments; on the other hand, and primarily, it is because the turnout of EU citizens in European elections is low and the participation in such elections barely influences European policy. This is due to the fact that only national parties can be elected in European elections, yet these parties do not play an independent role in the European Parliament. Rather, work in the European Parliament is dominated by the European parliamentary groups, which do not stand for election, do not have roots in any European society and only determine their political platform once the elections have taken place.[82]

---

[80] Kyriazis 'PSPP judgment', 'Conclusion'.
[81] C.I.2. (para 101) of the judgment, English translation available 26 December 2020 at www.bundesverfassungsgericht.de/SharedDocs/Entscheidungen/EN/2020/05/rs20200505_2bvr085915en.html (accessed 19 June 2021).
[82] Grimm 'Long Time Coming' 946.

It therefore emerges that neither the EU, nor any of its organs can claim to be 'sovereign'. Nevertheless, the existence and operation of the EU constitutes a constant conceptual, if not legal, qualification of the sovereignty (both in the constitutional and international legal senses) of the member states.[83] No wonder then that British politicians with a populist turn could convince a majority of voters in 2016 to support Brexit in order to 'regain' UK sovereignty – whatever that might mean.[84]

4.3 SLIPPERY ESSENTIALITY

Constitutional law is inconceivable without some notion of sovereignty, not only because it is so firmly ensconced in our specialist language developed over centuries to explain the foundations of and justification for the ubiquitous presence of state authority, but also because the absence of such authority, essential for the maintenance of social order, is unthinkable. The wide range of explanations and qualifications of the idea furthermore suggests incontrovertibly that one's stance on sovereignty is fully dependent on one's ontological premises: we observe the phenomenon of authority without being able to provide an obvious or consistent explanation for its existence.

When placed on a virtual dissection table, the notion of 'sovereignty' presents itself in constitutional law as yet another relic from the history of the evolution of modern statehood. Remembering that the word as such finds its roots in the Old French *soverain*, derived from Vulgar Latin *superanus*, indicating the chief, lord, superior, master, ruler,[85] suggesting incontestable power, and that it is a remnant of the process of transferral by force or agreement of such power from popes, emperors and kings claiming sovereignty as a divine right, to persons and institutions claiming authority as representatives of the popular multitude, it is to be expected that it has lost at least some of its impact and much of its consistency. On the one hand the discarded concept of divinely mandated royal power asserts its indivisibility, whereas its dispersal to a crowd of faceless individuals on the other hand negates the idea that it is irreducible or indissoluble.

'Popular sovereignty' is therefore another constitutional misnomer, even where it is elevated and entrenched in a constitution which is acknowledged as

---

[83] Interestingly – perhaps more on the level of public perception than in terms of national, supra-national and international law – both the President of the European Union and the President of the European Council were core participants in the 2021 summit of 'G7 countries'.

[84] See e.g. Verovšek 'Brexit and the misunderstanding of sovereignty'.

[85] See e.g. the *Online Etymology Dictionary* www.etymonline.com/search?q=sovereign (accessed 28 December 2020).

incontrovertible supreme law. 'The people' simply cannot be a collective sovereign in the essential sense of the word – the statement that the people are the sovereigns entails a contradiction in terms because the idea that those subject to authority are simultaneously the bearers of the same authority defies reason. Historically and notionally 'sovereignty' does not suggest charitable sharing.

Despite the deft theorizations of great minds over centuries to construct explanations for the 'sovereign people' being subject to their rulers, those explanations inevitably rely on fictional assumptions and constructions.[86] If the social contract were presented as a hypothesis for scientific analysis, it has consistently and irredeemably been found to be false.

The range of possible explanations for the reality of state authority, each depending on its own set of understandings of truth and existence, is wide – and the accounts are often mutually exclusive. There can be no single, universally accepted notion of constitutional sovereignty – and it is misleading to the level of intellectual condescension to assume or pretend that the most canvassed version (popular sovereignty) represents universal truth or reality.

Further taking into consideration that the constancy and reliability of mechanisms (such as elections) devised for notional popular legitimation of authority placed in the hands of a select few to be dispersed among them are open to doubt,[87] one might despair over the further utility of the notion of sovereignty in constitutional comparison.

However, regardless of the inconstant, qualified and elastic meanings attached to sovereignty, it is so thoroughly entrenched in the constitutional vocabulary that a quest to rid ourselves of it would be futile. An argument can be made for avoidance, as far as possible, of the word in especially comparative constitutional work, to be replaced by concepts that do not presume to convey the notion of quasi-absolute authority. Choices for such a vocabulary that come to mind are for instance 'competencies', 'authority', 'jurisdiction',

---

[86] Hegel 'Philosophy of Right' 315–16 endeavoured in 1820 to explain sovereignty as an 'ideality' whereby social conflict is resolved lawfully.

[87] One of Heinz Kleger's conclusions at the end of an insightful book captures this concern well: Kleger 'Demokratisches Regieren' 453:
Je größer die politische Gemeinschaft und je komplexer der politische Handlungskontext – von der Mikroebene der Familien und Kommunen über die Mesoebene der Gesellschaft und des Staates vermittelt durch organisierte Interessen, Parteien und Massenmedien bis hin zur Metaebene der Globalisierung und einer nach wie vor weitgehend anarchischen Staatenordnung – desto schwieriger ist es für die Bürger, selbstbestimmt ihre Souveränität einzufordern und auszuüben.
[The larger the political community and the more complex the context of political conduct . . . . the more difficult it is for the citizens to claim and exercise their sovereignty in a self-determined manner.]

'remit' and 'discretion', where appropriate enhanced with adjectives such as 'circumscribed', 'accountable', 'defined', 'limited', etc. One might also plead for the qualification or explanation of the envisioned meaning when sovereignty is mentioned, especially in constitutional comparison. Failing such contextualization the comparatist's audience is constrained to take their refuge in conjecture regarding the intended connotations.

5. The state

The state has become a defining and omnipresent construct of human society. Not many social activities can escape the presence, influence, and often the indispensable involvement of the state (and the law). Closely associated with statehood are sovereignty as the validation of its authority and citizenship (or nationality) as the human basis (by many signified by the notions of 'the nation' or 'the people') of its substance and its *raison d'être*. Nevertheless, the manner in which the notion 'state' and associated conceptions are employed in constitutional (and political) discourse, is volatile.

The state is a structure by which the 'success' of its component society may be measured according to a variety of considerations, but the character and qualities of states around the world are diverse and changeable. Some of the evident standards that come to mind for the measurement of the quality of statehood are the degree of successful maintenance of social peace and civil satisfaction, the preservation of law and justice, protection of individual freedom and welfare, and the protection of the state's physical assets, both geographically and economically.[1]

No doubt any cogent measurement of the comparative quality of statehood would reveal great variance. A comparative constitutional study seeking either similarity or difference can therefore not be simple and, if approached as though it were simple, it can hardly be expected to produce objectively persuasive results.

The difficulties attending variations in the nature of statehood have caused loose classifications to be made, such as democratic/undemocratic, developed/developing/underdeveloped, free market/managed economy, etc. A different approach is to distinguish between states in pre-modern areas where 'statehood never had or has lost meaning', the modern world 'where states, acting in competition with each other, continue to operate in a familiar manner' and a post-modern component where statehood is in a process of dissolution due to supra-national integration, although not leading to some form of superstate.[2] Such distinctions are but blunt instruments whose wielding cannot on their

---

[1] Venter 'Rethinking' 80–1.
[2] Himsworth 'In a State No Longer' 646, summarizing Cooper 'The post-modern state and the world order' 15–23.

own be expected to produce refined results in comparative constitutional studies.

Without case-specific explication, wholesale references to 'states' (and associated concepts) in constitutional comparison (and in related fields) are bound to generate not only misunderstanding, but it may also reduce the comparative effort to neutral superficiality. Some pertinent questions are being raised about statehood.

> Prominent scholars have in recent times begun to raise the question whether the state can survive these times of globalization. Has the state indeed become 'too small for the big problems and too big for the small problems of life?' Is it justifiable to declare, as Michiel Scheltema did that constitutional law must be reinvented, that the state for which constitutional law was conceived, does not exist anymore and that each state is practically delegated by the international community to realize the values of the democratic constitutional state?[3]

In section 2.7 of Chapter 2 a fleeting account was given of the emergence of the modern 'nation-state'. The fragility of the link between 'nation' and 'state' beyond at least nineteenth-century Europe is beyond doubt. Patrick Glenn for instance remarked:

> Th[e] picture of the emergence of the European state is complicated in a major way ... by the realities of colonialism, empire, and the development of contemporary state structures beyond Europe. It is striking, moreover, that what is usually described as the period of emergence of the contemporary state in Europe from, say, the sixteenth century, coincides exactly with the expansion of European authority across the seas. This may not have been accidental. It has clear consequences, however, for our understanding of the cosmopolitan state, since the state beyond Europe was and remains a very different institution from the state within Europe. They are all, however, states, with their peculiarities.[4]

And yet in general, close 'congruities between nation and state, cultural and political boundaries, territory and citizens' are constantly construed. This is ascribed to the need of political communities to draw boundaries between them and others based on real, perceived or idealized homogeneity.[5]

Enquiring into the nature of the phenomenon 'state' justifies deep investigation, as is attested to by the extent of the published literature on the matter.[6] It

---

[3] Venter 'Global Features' 12.
[4] Glenn 'Cosmopolitan State' 64.
[5] Körtvélyesi 'Nation, Nationality, and National Identity' 775.
[6] See e.g. among many more Dunleavy & O'Leary 'Theories of the State'; Wimmer 'Modernisierung'; Hameiri 'Regulating Statehood'; Haldén 'Stability without Statehood'; the range of contributions in Cornelissen, Cheru & Shaw 'Africa

is a complex enquiry involving stances taken on profound philosophical questions concerning the justification of coercive authority,[7] explanations of the basis of sovereignty,[8] the nature of the constitutive 'material' or 'substance' (human and corporeal) of the state,[9] and more.

The diversity of attributed meanings of 'the state' motivated Dragoljub Popović to employ the term 'government' as a connecting conception, a 'lever' to study the nature and elements of the state:

> The scholars researching the characteristic features of a modern state differ in their approaches and consider various concepts to be essential for their respective analyses, definitions and classifications ... An effort to achieve a synthesis in the presence of such a variety of opinions leads us to conclude that there are at least three main characteristic features of a modern state, all of which concern the government as the essential constitutive element of the notion of 'state' in general.[10]

While acknowledging the logic of this approach in the particular context, it is for present purposes proposed to maintain a clear distinction between 'state' and 'government', the latter being an organ of the former.

The concept 'state', as it is currently employed in constitutional and political discourse, is essentially European in nature and origin, although historically associated with various terms: examples are the *poleis* of Greek 'city-states' of the fifth century BC, the *civitas* (body of citizens) and *res publica* (things and matters of a public nature) during the six centuries BC of the Roman Republic, the *imperium* (empire) and *regnum* (kingdom) of the Middle Ages, the German notions of *Reich* (a legal order under a sovereign) and *Land* (the territory where a legal order obtains). Etymologically the term 'state' is rooted in the ancient Roman *status rei publicae*, a designation that was revived in central and northern Italy during the time of the Renaissance to identify a commune (city-state).[11]

Elsewhere in the world historical entities reflecting characteristics associated with the general notion of a state abound. These include the Indian state-like entities apparently stretching back to the fourth millennium BC (to

---

and International Relations'; Voigt 'Der moderne Staat'; and Chinkin & Baetens 'Sovereignty, Statehood and State Responsibility'.

[7] See e.g. Reidy & Riker 'Coercion'.

[8] See Chapter 4 above and publications such as Beckenbach & Klotter 'Gleichheit und Souveränität'; Lombardo 'Critique of Sovereignty'; and Sevastik 'Aspects of Sovereignty'.

[9] See e.g. Moltchanova 'National Self-Determination'; Gible 'Territorial Peace Borders', especially Chapter 3 *Individual, state, and territorial issues* at 25–46.

[10] Popović 'Comparative Government' 7–8.

[11] See e.g. Ferrari 'Italian Public Law' 7.

which the classical Greeks had possibly been exposed), the 'divine kingdoms' of Egypt over 3,000 years since approximately 3500 BC, the consecutive Mesopotamian empires, including the era of the Sumerians (3500–2400 BC), the Accadian empire of Sargon I (2568–2513 BC), the Babylonian empire (1850–1600 BC), the Assyrians (1300–612 BC), the Chaldeans (until 539 BC) succeeded by the Persians, the long Chinese history of various empires and dynasties contesting and expanding their rule since at least 2000 BC, and many more.[12] No, or very few lines of historical development from these examples can be drawn to the global, Europe-based conception of the contemporary state.

Despite its diverse historical sources and range of possible theoretical justifications, the word 'state' is used universally, mostly without question or comment concerning the exact meaning intended to be attached to it. It would normally be assumed that the context will determine the meaning. Thus, for instance, the statement 'the state is responsible to ...' may refer, inter alia, to a subject of international law, the authority-bearing legal subject established and regulated by a constitution, a governmental entity, an administrative authority or a regional component of a federation.

Given the amount of published scholarly work on this topic, it is not the intention here to develop an additional or new definition of the state, but to touch upon the difficulties brought about by its multi-faceted manifestations, especially for constitutional comparison. In the first section we are primarily concerned with the articulation, insofar as it may be possible, of the meaning that has been given in constitutional discourse to the notion 'state' before proceeding in the second section to a consideration of the diversity of understanding of the concept in different contexts. This leads to a brief presentation of an essential, inevitably reduced, conceptualization that might satisfy constitutional comparatists wishing for a more solid terminological foundation.

5.1 THE STATE IN CONVENTIONAL CONSTITUTIONAL THEORY

Admittedly, reference to 'conventional' constitutional theory is not a very precise indication of what is being referred to. The point here is that the word 'state' and its equivalents in other languages must be one of the most frequently occurring terms in contemporary constitutional texts. In fact, in the Germanic languages, '*Staat*' serves as a prefix to the designation of the field

---

[12] See e.g. Aguilera-Barchet 'History' 10–15.

of constitutional law itself to distinguish it from other disciplines of law.[13] 'State' also occurs as an adjective, for instance in 'state religion',[14] 'state institutions', and 'state policy'. But what exactly is meant by the term in every case is usually left open, suggesting that the meaning should be self-evident, or perhaps considered to be clear enough in the context of the particular script to make the intended meaning clear.

The use of the concept 'state' is central not only in constitutional law, but also in the vocabularies of political scientists, international lawyers, and practitioners of various other fields such as economics and sociology. To separate the development of its meanings according to scholarly disciplines is impractical, difficult if not impossible to disentangle, because inter-disciplinary pollination has been extensive.

Moran Mandelbaum's critique (following the post-modernist thinking of philosopher Michel Foucault and the psychoanalyst Jacques Lacan) of the 'nation/state fantasy' provides us with an interesting contemporary perspective on the state. He holds that the nation-state concept is 'so endemic to modern thought, that modern history seems to be the history of the rise of "nation-states" and indeed the homogenisation of states/nations'.[15] But, says he, the congruency of nation and state is a fantasy.[16] He concludes that 'as all fantasies, [the state] must maintain the national subjectivity in a form of anxiety, suspended between the promised utopia of congruity and security, and the Other, the obstacle hindering "our" project of becoming whole'.[17] Mandelbaum's work may require the acquisition of a taste for critical thinking and extraordinary interdisciplinarity, but he succeeded well in fleshing out the many inconsistencies attached to the employment of state-related language.

More conventional thinking about the state is to be found in the complex and ground-breaking work of Georg Jellinek. Jellinek expressed his views on the state in detail in a monumental book *Allgemeine Staatslehre* first published in 1900, but, even after more than a century, his work is said, among others by Oliver Lepsius, to have 'retained its scientific attraction to the present day'.[18]

---

[13] *Staatsrecht* in German and Dutch, *staatsreg* in Afrikaans (directly translatable to 'state law'). Interestingly also, the Indonesian Constitutional Law Journal has 'STAATSRECHT' as its main title, reminiscent of Indonesia's Dutch colonial history.

[14] E.g. article 2 of the Constitution of Pakistan, 1973: 'Islam shall be the State religion of Pakistan'.

[15] Mandelbaum 'Nation/State Fantasy' 9.

[16] The 'congruency' having been captured by Ernest Gellner in the phrase 'one nation, one state': Mandelbaum 'Nation/State Fantasy' 48–51.

[17] Mandelbaum 'Nation/State Fantasy' 228.

[18] See e.g. Lepsius 'Georg Jellinek'; Spadafora 'George Jellinek'; Von Bernstorff 'Georg Jellinek'; and Kelly 'Georg Jellinek'.

Udo di Fabio also finds more analytical clarity in Jellinek's work than in many contemporary constitutional law dissertations.[19]

Jellinek distinguished in the first place between phenomena in society that depend on a coherent expression of the human will, and those that exist without human intervention. The state, he said, is the most important social manifestation of the expression of the human will.[20] Being only feasible as a product of organized human association, the law (legal science, *Rechtswissenschaft*) is a discipline of the science of the state (*Staatswissenschaft*). He pointed out that a range of disciplines in the social sciences were engaged in the study of the state, and that they all interacted. In his scheme *Allgemeine Staatslehre* (translatable only in awkward terms as 'the general doctrine of the state') covers both the state as social construct (*soziale Staatslehre*) and the state approached from the perspective of the law, *Staatsrechtslehre* translatable as the doctrine of state law.[21] In the English legal vernacular, 'constitutional law' is the closest equivalent to *Staatsrecht*. A further refinement is however made in German scholarship and practice, namely *Verfassungsrecht*, which essentially amounts to the study of the constitutional text, including its effects in the many non-statal areas of its operation such as property, education, artistic freedom, etc.[22]

Jellinek famously propounded a theory of the state as having two sides. He formulated (in my free translation) its core meaning as follows:

> *Staatslehre* must investigate all sides of the essence of the state. It has two main areas according to which the state can be viewed. On the one hand the state is a social structure, and on the other a legal institution. Consequently, *Staatslehre* is split between social *Staatslehre* and constitutional doctrine. The general *Staatslehre* as such thus has two branches: social doctrine regarding the state in general and general constitutional law.[23]

---

[19] Di Fabio 'Staatsrechtslehre' 29: 'Wer heute beispielsweise Georg Jellineks Lehre von den Staatenverbindungen oder seine Staatslehre liest, findet mitunter mehr analytische Klarheit als in manchen staatsrechtlichen Abhandlungen der Gegenwart'.

[20] References here are to the third revised edition published by his son, Walter Jellinek: Jellinek 'Allgemeine Staatslehre' 1–4.

[21] Jellinek 'Allgemeine Staatslehre' 9–12.

[22] See e.g. Hesse 'Grundzüge des Verfassungsrechts' 10–11.

[23] Jellinek 'Allgemeine Staatslehre' 10:
Die Staatslehre hat den Staat nach allen Seiten seines Wesens zu erforschen. Sie hat zwei Hauptgebiete, entsprechend den zwei Gesichtspunkten, unter denen der Staat betrachtet werden kann. Der Staat ist einmal gesellschaftliches Gebilde, sodann rechtliche Institution. Dementsprechend zerfällt die Staatslehre in die soziale Staatslehre und in die Staatsrechtslehre. Die allgemeine Staatslehre insbesondere hat demnach zwei Abteilungen: die allgemeine Soziallehre des Staates und die allgemeine Staatsrechtslehre.

Jellinek's minute interdisciplinary analysis of the state as object of scholarly investigation revealed and emphasized a perennial truth about the multi-faceted nature of the core conceptions of constitutional law. While the vital concepts of constitutional law as field of theoretical and practical endeavour – be it municipal, trans-jurisdictional or comparative – can be greatly enriched by the perspectives of other disciplines, the plethora of possible extra-legal significances of terms indispensable to constitutional law can, and do, detract from their accuracy and undermine constancy in the constitutional conversation. The difficulty is enhanced by the impracticability of withdrawing into a constitutional law bastion from which non-legal language is banished. Ignoring this difficulty by not providing your constitutional law interlocutors with some guidance regarding your chosen meaning of a word such as 'the (or a) state' is bound to undermine the value of one's comparative work.

Oliver Lepsius' profound rendering of Jellinek's two-sides theory and of its critics presents us with some valuable foundation blocks upon which the constitutional visage of the state might be construed. He shows that Jellinek wrote in the new-Kantian idiom by presenting the state simultaneously as an abstract idea (an 'ought'), and as a factual phenomenon (an 'is'):

> The State is an epistemological object that is typically associated with the 'Is' as well as to the 'Ought'. Not uncommonly, the attractiveness of the State as an epistemological object is due to the fact that one can amalgamate statements on the status quo and the desired status.[24]

Jellinek's perception of the state as a real legal entity is a particularly useful route to follow in conceiving its nature in constitutional law. The only way for the state to be understood as legal concept, he wrote, is as a legal subject in the form of a corporate body (*Körperschaft*) consisting of people forming a unified association whose guiding will is expressed by its members. The concept of a corporate body is purely juristic in nature, which as all legal concepts does not conform to anything objectively observable in the world of facts. It is a form of juristic synthesis giving expression to the corporate entity's legal relations within the legal order. Ascribing legal personality to the state, he said, is no fiction, because personality is the same as legal subjectivity, meaning a relative position in the legal order.[25]

---

[24] Lepsius 'Georg Jellinek' 24.
[25] Jellinek 'Allgemeine Staatslehre' 183:
Seiner juristischen Seite nach kann der Staat nach den vorausgegangenen kritischen Erörterungen nur als Rechtssubjekt gefaßt werden, und zwar ist es näher der Begriff der Körperschaft, unter den er zu subsumieren ist. Das Substrat der Körperschaft sind stets Menschen, die eine Verbandseinheit bilden, deren leitender Wille durch Mitglieder des Verbandes selbst versorgt

Considering the criticism (often with reluctant admiration) of Jellinek's work,[26] his views cannot be presented as the current standard theory of the state in constitutional law. At the same time, it is not possible at all to identify any theory of the state being representative of the current universal thinking on the subject – constitutionally or otherwise.

This leaves us with a concept which is in constant, universal use, indispensable especially in constitutional law, while a consistent definition persistently evades us. Patrick Glenn provides us with a cogent response to this dilemma, warranting a closer look. His central contention is that all states fit into a 'cosmopolitan' mould consisting of characteristics suited, but adaptable, to all countries,[27] although states exist 'in a remarkable variety of forms, and ... in some instances it has even become evanescent'.[28]

In 2004 Glenn compactly argued for legal *tradition* instead of what some constitutional comparatists refer to as 'system', 'culture', 'family' etc. as an epistemological notion. Tradition, he wrote, is 'non-genetic information which influences but does not control legal practice', it is 'tolerant of argument', 'a useful antidote to reification and homogenisation', and allows for peaceful dispute resolution.[29] The 'state tradition' he finds in the common elements of states, showing how the cosmopolitanism of the state emerged amidst the uniqueness of every state.[30]

The contemporary cosmopolitan state evolved on the basis of European history: 'The Greeks were cosmopolitan, moreover, not only in the universalistic dimensions of their thought, but in their legal practice, and the law of other city-states was simply used, wherever it seemed appropriate, and without much concern for its source.'[31] Antecedents of a state tradition ('irresistibly cosmopolitan in character') were the Catholic Church (an 'early European state'), the rise of eventually failing empires, cities as states, and 'affirmative

---

wird. Der Begriff der Körperschaft aber ist ein rein juristischer Begriff, dem, wie allen Rechtsbegriffen, in der Welt der Tatsachen nichts objektiv Wahrnehmbares entspricht; er ist eine Form der juristischen Synthese, um die rechtlichen Beziehungen der Verbandseinheit, ihr Verhältnis zur Rechtsordnung auszudrücken. Schreibt man daher dem Staate wie der Körperschaft überhaupt juristische Persönlichkeit zu, so hat man nach keiner Richtung hin eine Hypostasierung oder Fiktion vorgenommen, denn Persönlichkeit ist nichts anderes als Rechtssubjekt und bedeutet daher, wie oben ausgeführt, eine Relation einer Einzel- oder Kollektivindividualität zur Rechtsordnung.

[26] See e.g. Paulson 'The Very Idea of Legal Positivism'.
[27] Glenn 'Cosmopolitan State' Preface vii–viii.
[28] Glenn 'Cosmopolitan State' 185.
[29] Glenn 'Legal Cultures' 20.
[30] Glenn 'Cosmopolitan State' 12–13 and 115–16.
[31] Glenn 'Cosmopolitan State' 19.

crowns'.³² These antecedents underlie the contemporary state, not by means of establishing unity, but as a demonstration of cosmopolitanism as reaction to the idea of unity.³³ The development of the law in the Middle Ages led to the crystallization of the 'mutually supporting concepts of constitutionalism and common law'.³⁴ The sources of constitutionalism discernible in this era included the Greek and Roman idea of the need for the consent of the ruled, the notion of divine or natural law and the inalienability of the royal domain. The combination of common and particular laws inspired the emergence of specific states.

Using 'closure' as a metaphor for finding consistent elements of the cosmopolitan state, Glenn identifies the reduction of norms to consolidated and written languages (creating national laws and constitutions as 'markers for successful revolution'), confirmation that hierarchical state structures underpin the continuity of the state (despite changing authorities), and the drawing of maps to establish stable territories, to be 'elements of closure'.³⁵ In due course constitutionalism emerged to justify the existence of the state and to provide limits to the exercise of authority.³⁶ Constitutionalism has proved to be 'the most visible of the cosmopolitan methods' facilitated by written constitutions, constitutional drafting that 'invite resort to sources beyond themselves and cosmopolitan methods of interpretation', structural accommodation of population differences such as federalism, and judicial review.³⁷ In the end, Glenn found that the contemporary state is cosmopolitan in nature, allowing for a wide range of diversity: 'Originality is found in detail and combination, but no state has been free from the influence of diverse strands of state tradition.'³⁸

Writing about 'the state of statehood' some 20 years ago after considering the rising challenges to which the notion of the state was being subjected by the end of the twentieth century, I concluded that '[n]evertheless, the essentialia of the constitutional regulation of the distribution of authority, the protection of rights and the legally controlled processes of legislation, management, administration and adjudication associated with the constitutional state continue to be irreplaceable'.³⁹

---

³² Glenn 'Cosmopolitan State' 27–36.
³³ Glenn 'Cosmopolitan State' 38.
³⁴ Glenn 'Cosmopolitan State' 43.
³⁵ Glenn 'Cosmopolitan State' 43–85. At 291 he finds in conclusion that '[c]losure is inherently problematic, and remains constantly vulnerable to surrounding texture and the challenge of new and different forms of closure'.
³⁶ Glenn 'Cosmopolitan State' Chapter 7.
³⁷ Glenn 'Cosmopolitan State' 204–7.
³⁸ Glenn 'Cosmopolitan State' 291.
³⁹ Venter 'Constitutional Comparison' 261–2.

5.2 CONTEXTUAL VARIATIONS

The state (and its predecessors) has been a key institution of human society for centuries. Over more recent times it morphed from the peace-keeping (night-watchman) state to what should be a serving and protective state in this era, having gone through various phases, including the establishment of the state through and for law (the *Rechtsstaat*), the constitutional state (*Verfassungsstaat*) and the social state (*Sozialstaat*).[40] Not all existing states have however gone through these (native European) phases and the manner in which statehood manifests itself *in loco* depends on the historical and prevailing social conditions, autochthonous constitutional arrangements and the vagaries of the political incumbents. We are here concerned with the *constitutional* denotation of the state, but the extra-constitutional, international and sub-national contexts, being the general conceptual backdrop inevitably present when dealing with constitutional statehood, first need to be considered very briefly.

5.2.1 The State Beyond the Law

This category is not our primary concern, but perhaps useful for the purposes of narrowing down law-related meanings of the state. In the hands of journalists, novelists and politicians there are of course very few limits to the range of meanings that can be attached to the state, usually, but not consistently, associated with some entity empowered to exercise public authority such as a government, administrative office or taxation service.

The notion of 'state aid' was an important consideration in the Brexit process.[41] For this, the European Union has a specific definition (italics added):

> State aid is defined as an *advantage* in any form whatsoever conferred on *a selective basis to undertakings* by national public authorities. Therefore, subsidies granted to individuals or general measures open to all enterprises are not covered by this prohibition and do not constitute State aid (examples include general taxation measures or employment legislation).[42]

---

[40] Voigt 'Der moderne Staat' 44:
Vom Friedensstaat über den Rechtsstaat, den Verfassungsstaat und den Sozialstaat ist der moderne Staat zum Leistungs- und Gewährleistungsstaat geworden. Damit ist ein hohes Leistungsniveau verbunden, das nicht jeder Staat der Erde erreichen bzw. aufrechterhalten kann.

[41] See e.g. Parker, Brundsen & Fleming 'Brexit trade talks'.

[42] European Commission, STATE AID CONTROL https://ec.europa.eu/competition/state_aid/overview/index_en.html (accessed 20 January 2021).

In the interests of fair competition, therefore, in 2020 (unspecified) 'national public authorities' capable of providing some advantage constituted 'the state' for the EU.

Adjectival descriptions to specify the nature and purposes of state-related conduct or policies abound. Examples are the 'social welfare state',[43] and the 'developmental state'.[44] These do not contribute much to a legal perspective on the state as constitutional construct.

5.2.2 States in International Law

In section 4.1.3 of Chapter 4, sovereignty as an essential requirement for the recognition of statehood in international law was mentioned. Although states continue to be the basic building blocks of international legal regulation as the primary subjects of international law, they are no longer the only, or necessarily the most important entities performing international legal acts.[45]

The first ten articles of the *Montevideo Convention*,[46] concluded in 1933 among American states, both North and South, are still recognized globally as a lasting codification of customary international law regarding the nature of states. Article 1 characterizes the state as 'a person of international law' with four characteristics: (a) a permanent population; (b) a defined territory; (c) government; and (d) capacity to enter into relations with the other states. Article 3 explicitly asserts a state's 'right to defend its integrity and independence, to provide for its conservation and prosperity, and consequently to organize itself as it sees fit, to legislate upon its interests, administer its services, and to define the jurisdiction and competence of its courts'. The 'simple fact of its existence as a person under international law' is all Article 4 requires for a state to be 'juridically equal' to all other states, and Article 8 disallows any state 'to intervene in the internal or external affairs of another'. Article 10 declares the 'primary interest of states' (in international relations) to be 'the conservation of peace'.

---

[43] The expression indicates the phenomenon of the state taking on responsibility for the care and welfare of its citizens: see e.g. Förster 'Philanthropic Foundations' 1. Chapter 17 of Aguilera-Barchet 'History', under the heading 'The Triumph of the State Over the Nation: From Totalitarianism to Interventionism', provides valuable insights into the reasons for the emergence of the idea of the social welfare state.

[44] Apparently implying close involvement of the state in economic development: see e.g. Kim, Kyung Mi 'The Korean Developmental State' 6, note 1.

[45] See e.g. Von Bogdandy, Wolfrum, Von Bernstorff, Dann & Goldmann 'The Exercise of Public Authority'.

[46] League of Nations – Treaty Series https://treaties.un.org/doc/Publication/UNTS/LON/Volume%20165/v165.pdf (accessed 20 January 2021).

Of particular interest for present purposes is that legal subjectivity, meaning the competence or capacity to perform legal acts, is an indispensable element of statehood in international law.

5.2.3 Federal States

Article 2 of the *Montevideo Convention* of 1933 provides that the 'Federal State shall constitute a sole person in the eyes of international law'. From a constitutional law point of view federalism however brings another perspective and poses another terminological challenge. The most recognizable instance is the use of the word 'state' to indicate the 50 federated components of the federal republic known as the 'United States of America'.

Since the inception of modern constitutionalism there have been, and still are many federations each designating their federal components in their own way. Thus we find ten *provinces* in Canada, 16 *Länder* in the Federal Republic of Germany, five *states* in the Federal Commonwealth of Australia, 36 *states* in the Federal Republic of Nigeria, the Swiss Confederation is formed by 26 *cantons*, and interestingly, Article 5(1) of the Constitution of the Russian Federation of 1993 provides that (italics added) 'The Russian Federation shall consist of *republics, krays, oblasts, cities of federal significance*, an *autonomous oblast* and *autonomous okrugs*, which shall have equal rights as *constituent entities* of the Russian Federation'.

Federalism as such is a huge topic in its own right.[47] Although the constitutional position of the constituent entities of federations is no doubt a significant subject in a segment of constitutional law (especially in federal states), further pursuit of the theme of federalism will not produce much further insight here into the constitutional meaning of 'state' as primary subject of constitutional law. Suffice it to conclude that, where 'state' is used to indicate a constituent component of a federation, it bears a different and case-specific meaning that is best distinguished from the meaning of the word when used to signify the primary bearer of sovereign constitutional authority.

5.2.4 Constitutional Variants

Unsurprisingly, the word 'state' often appears in constitutional texts, adorned with many-faceted connotations, determined by the context. The malleability of the concept in constitutions can best be demonstrated with reference to a

---

[47] See e.g. Gagnon & Tremblay 'Federalism and National Diversity' and Heidemann & Stoppenbrink 'Join, or Die'.

(nonexhaustive) list of categories with examples from a few current constitutions, each speaking for itself.

5.2.4.1 Explicit definition of the state

'State' is seldom explicitly defined in constitutions, leaving interpreters to derive the meaning by other hermeneutical means. A rare exception is Article 7 of the Constitution of Pakistan, where the definition is not intended to be comprehensive, but specific for the purposes of Part II dealing with fundamental rights and principles of policy:[48]

> In this Part, unless the context otherwise requires, 'the State' means the Federal Government, [Majlis-e-Shoora (Parliament)], a Provincial Government, a Provincial Assembly, and such local or other authorities in Pakistan as are by law empowered to impose any tax or cess.

5.2.4.2 Characterization of the constitutional order

In the foundational description of the kind of constitutional order being established or regulated by a constitution, 'state' often appears as the described subject. The following are typical examples, often reflecting the unique circumstances and motivations prevailing at the time of the design of the constitution concerned:

> The name of the state is Éire, or, in the English language, Ireland. Ireland is a sovereign, independent, democratic state.[49]

> The Federal Republic of Germany shall be a democratic and social federal state.[50] The constitutional order in the Länder shall conform to the principles of the republican, democratic and social state governed by the rule of law within the meaning of this Basic Law.[51]

> ... that Pakistan would be a democratic State based on Islamic principles of social justice[52]

> Russia is a democratic federative law-governed state with a republican form of government. The federal structure of the Russian Federation shall be based on its State integrity, the unity of the system of State power, the division of matters of authority and powers between State government bodies of the Russian Federation and State government bodies of constituent entities of the Russian Federation, the equality and self-determination of peoples in the Russian Federation. The Russian Federation

---

[48] *The Constitution of the Islamic Republic of Pakistan*, 1973.
[49] Articles 4 and 5 of the *Bunreacht na hÉireann* (Constitution of Ireland), 1937.
[50] Article 20(1) of the *Grundgesetz für die Bundesrepublik Deutschland*, 1949.
[51] Article 28(1) of the German *Grundgesetz*.
[52] Preamble to the Constitution of Pakistan.

shall be a social state whose policy is aimed at creating conditions ensuring a worthy life and a free development of Man.[53]

The Republic of South Africa is one, sovereign, democratic state.[54]

5.2.4.3 Constitutional obligations

Where constitutions impose obligations on 'the state' (usually as a whole as distinct from specific components, entities, offices or structures), it requires some contextual interpretation to determine who or what is actually burdened with the obligations. Thus for instance the German *Grundgesetz* states it as a commitment of the German state to ensure equal treatment of men and women and to remove existing disadvantages.[55] Other state obligations include the 'special protection' of marriage and the family by the state,[56] and the protection of natural resources in accordance with its responsibility for present and future generations.[57] These provisions appear to bind every component and element of the state, whatever 'state' may signify. In German constitutional dogma this does not really present a problem, since an elegant, and mostly supported understanding of 'state' is that it is a juristic person, an accountable legal subject endowed legally with specific competencies and acting through its organs.[58]

Article 2 of the Russian Constitution of 1993 provides that the recognition, observance and protection of human and civil rights and freedoms is an obligation of the state, and Article 41.1 grants 'everyone' the right to health protection and medical care, requiring medical care in state and municipal health institutions to be rendered free of charge to citizens.

Section 6(2) of the South African Constitution of 1996 imposes the obligation on the state to take practical and positive measures to elevate the status and advance the use of indigenous languages, and various provisions of the Bill of Rights require the state to take reasonable legislative and other measures, within its available resources, to realize the advantages of fundamental rights.

Article 3 of the Constitution of Pakistan of 1973 demands of the state to ensure the elimination of all forms of exploitation and the gradual fulfilment of

---

[53] Articles 1.1, 5.3, and 7.1 of the *Constitution of the Russian Federation*, 1993.
[54] Section 1 of the *Constitution of the Republic of South Africa*, 1996.
[55] Article 3(2) second sentence, which gives expression to what is known in German constitutional law as a *Staatszielbestimmung*. The doctrine of *Staatszielbestimmungen* deals with the responsibilities and purposes of the state: see e.g. Starck 'v.Mangoldt/ Klein/Starck' 18–20 and 442–4.
[56] Article 6(1) of the *Grundgesetz*.
[57] Article 20a of the *Grundgesetz*.
[58] See e.g. Ipsen 'Staatsorganisationsrecht' 3–5.

the fundamental principle 'from each according to his ability to each according to his work'.

Article 40.3.2 of the Constitution of Ireland of 1937 imposes the task on the state to, 'by its laws, protect as best it may from unjust attack and, in the case of injustice done, vindicate the life, person, good name, and property rights of every citizen'.

Clearly constitutional obligations tend to be aspirational and often couched in general terms. Whether, in any particular constitutional order, it is possible to enforce obligations of the state or to prevent them from being ignored or poorly pursued, depends on the effectiveness of the legal mechanisms available to individuals and non-state entities to do so.

5.2.4.4 Loyalty to the state

Citizenship normally implies loyalty to the state concerned. Some constitutions contain explicit provisions to this effect.[59]

5.2.4.5 The state bound by law

As a principle of constitutionalism, constitutional provisions and other laws should be binding on all to whom they apply, including the state and its organs. Perhaps as a clear rejection of the famous adage *princeps legibus solutus est* (the prince is not bound by the laws) ascribed to Ulpianus in the Justinian Digesta (1.3.31), some constitutions make the principle explicit.

Article 15.2 of the Russian Constitution of 1993 simply states: 'State government bodies, local self-government bodies, officials, citizens and their associations shall be obliged to observe the Constitution of the Russian Federation and laws.'

Section 8(1) of the South African Constitution of 1996 provides that 'The Bill of Rights applies to all law, and binds the legislature, the executive, the judiciary and all organs of state', and, with regard to everyone's right to just administrative action, section 33(3)(b) instructs that 'National legislation must be enacted to give effect to these rights, and must – (b) impose a duty on the state to give effect to the rights.'

The binding of the state to the constitution sometimes takes the form of a proscription, such as Article 28.3.1 of the Irish Constitution: 'War shall not be declared and the State shall not participate in any war save with the assent of Dáil Éireann', and section 9(3) of the South African Constitution: 'The state may not unfairly discriminate directly or indirectly against anyone.'

The German *Grundgesetz* of 1949 incorporates a range of provisions of the Weimar Constitution of 1919 relating to matters of religion, Article 138 of

---

[59] See some examples in section 6.2 in Chapter 6.

which places the responsibility on the *Länder* to legislate for the satisfaction of the claims of religious communities based on statute, contract or special legal titles against the state.

5.2.4.6 State control over resources

The protection of material and incorporeal interests of the state (however construed) is attended to in some constitutions. Thus, Article 10.1 of the Irish *Bunreacht na hÉireann* provides:

> All natural resources, including the air and all forms of potential energy, within the jurisdiction of the Parliament and Government established by this Constitution and all royalties and franchises within that jurisdiction belong to the State subject to all estates and interests therein for the time being lawfully vested in any person or body.

Article 24(3) of the Constitution of Pakistan provides that 'Nothing in this Article shall affect the validity of – (d) any law providing for the taking over of the management of any property by the State for a limited period, either in the public interest or in order to secure the proper management of the property, or for the benefit of its owner.'

Article 29.4 of the Russian Constitution provides for the right to information but qualifies it in the next sentence: 'The list of types of information, which constitute State secrets, shall be determined by federal law.'

Access to 'any information held by the state' is a fundamental right in terms of Article 32(1)(a) of the South African Constitution, which may (as all other rights in the Bill of Rights) however be limited (in terms of section 36) 'only in terms of law of general application to the extent that the limitation is reasonable and justifiable in an open and democratic society based on human dignity, equality and freedom'.

5.2.4.7 State control over non-state entities

Governmental responsibility for, and therefore control over, public education is a characteristic of the contemporary state. This responsibility is cast in the form of an international human right to free and compulsory primary education in for instance Article 13 of the *International Covenant on Economic, Social and Cultural Rights* of 1966. However, not all education is public, bringing about constitutional regulation in some instances of governmental control over private education.

Examples include Article 7(1) of the German *Grundgesetz*, which places education as a whole under the oversight of the state. Article 7(4) then goes on to guarantee a right to establish private schools on the one hand, followed on the other hand with the requirement that the establishment of 'private schools replacing state schools' requires state approval.

Similarly, in South Africa section 29 of the Constitution affords everyone a right to education, and 'to establish and maintain, at their own expense, independent educational institutions' that do not discriminate on the basis of race, are registered with the state and maintain standards that are not inferior to standards at comparable public educational institutions.

Arrangements such as these do allow for a degree of autonomy of privately managed educational institutions as non-state entities, but at the same time they authorize close control over them in the name of 'the state'.

5.2.4.8 International relations in constitutions

Given the distinction between states as subjects of international law with its own norms for state conduct on the one hand, and the state as constitutional entity on the other, it is interesting that constitutions often contain provisions dealing with state conduct in international relations. It seems unlikely that provisions such as the examples mentioned below can be construed as norms of international law, but their municipal application is beyond doubt.

Section 37 of the South African Constitution deals with the declaration of a state of emergency, allowing for the limited 'derogation' of certain fundamental rights during a state of emergency, including limitations on detention without trial. Section 37(8) excludes non-citizens 'who are detained in consequence of an international armed conflict' from the protective provisions of the limitations, but 'the state must comply with the standards binding on the Republic under international humanitarian law in respect of the detention of such persons'.

Article 32(1) of the German *Grundgesetz* explicitly reserves the authority to conduct relations with other states for the federal authorities, but sub-article (3) allows the *Länder* to enter into treaties with foreign states with the permission of the federal government which, interestingly, do not result in such *Land*-foreign state instruments to be deemed federal agreements.

In Ireland, Article 29.3 of the *Bunreacht na hÉireann* provides that 'Ireland accepts the generally recognised principles of international law as its rule of conduct in its relations with other States'.

Article 40 of the Constitution of Pakistan provides some insight in the international priorities of the drafters:

> The State shall endeavour to preserve and strengthen fraternal relations among Muslim countries based on Islamic unity, support the common interests of the peoples of Asia, Africa and Latin America, promote international peace and security, foster goodwill and friendly relations among all nations and encourage the settlement of international disputes by peaceful means.

5.2.4.9 Organs and sub-structures of the state

Where constitutions deal with components, entities, offices or structures of the state (usually distinct from the whole), a range of concepts offer themselves to describe them. The federal, composite or unitary structure of the state naturally has a bearing on the choice and relevance of such concepts, as does the distribution of authority among the branches of government, but other more or less unique structural arrangements also come into play. Some of these may have specific designations, and others are sometimes referred to in generic terms, such as 'organs of state'. The following examples (italics added) speak for themselves:

The *Bunreacht na hÉireann*:

> Article 6: '1. All powers of government, legislative, executive and judicial, derive, under God, from the people, whose right it is to designate the *rulers of the state*. ... 2. These powers of government are exercisable only by or on the authority of the *organs of state* established by this constitution.'; Article 15.2.1: 'The sole and exclusive power of *making laws for the State* is hereby vested in the Oireachtas: no other legislative authority has power to make laws for the State.'; Article 28.4.2: 'The Government ... shall be collectively responsible for the *Departments of State* administered by the members of the Government'; and Article 31.1: 'There shall be a *Council of State* to aid and counsel the President ... '

The *Grundgesetz*:

> Article 24(1a): 'Where the *Länder* have the right to exercise *state powers* and discharge *state functions* they may with the consent of the Federal Government transfer sovereign powers to transfrontier institutions in neighbouring regions'; and Article 34: 'Should anybody, in exercising a public office, neglect their duty towards a third party liability shall rest in principle with *the state* or the public body employing them.'

The Constitution of Pakistan:

> Article 29(1): 'The Principles set out in this Chapter shall be known as the Principles of Policy, and it is the responsibility of each *organ and authority of the State*, and of each person performing functions on behalf of an organ or authority of the State, to act in accordance with those Principles in so far as they relate to the functions of the organ or authority.'

Constitution of the Russian Federation:

> Article 11.1: '*State power* in the Russian Federation shall be exercised by the *President* of the Russian Federation, the *Federal Assembly* (the Council of Federation and the State Duma), the *Government* of the Russian Federation, and *the courts* of the Russian Federation.'

The South African Constitution:

> Section 41(1): 'All *spheres of government* and all *organs of state* within *each sphere* must ... '; section 47(1)(a): ' ... anyone who is *appointed* by, or is *in the service* of, *the state* ... '; section 55(2): 'The National Assembly must provide for mechanisms – (a) to ensure that all *executive organs of state* in the national sphere of government are accountable to it'; section 83: 'The President – (a) is the *Head of State* and head of the national executive'; and Chapter 9 is headed '*State Institutions* Supporting Constitutional Democracy'.

5.2.4.10 The state as geographical entity

Apart from some constitutions that describe or define the extent of their territorial jurisdiction,[60] references to geographical boundaries of a state also occur for other purposes. Article 12.9 of the *Bunreacht na hÉireann* for instance provides: 'The President shall not leave the State during his term of office save with the consent of the Government.'

A different purpose is served by Article 67.2 of the Russian Constitution:

> The Russian Federation ensures protection of its sovereignty and territorial integrity. Any actions (except delimitation, demarcation, re-demarcation of the state border of the Russian Federation with bordering states) aimed at alienation of the part of the territory of the Russian Federation, as well as calls upon such actions are precluded.

5.2.4.11 Religious confession and the state

It is not unusual to find religious confessions in constitutions, some quite specific, others in vague, ecumenical terms sometimes irreverently relegated to the status of 'ceremonial deism', for instance the preamble to the Canadian Charter of Rights and Freedoms of 1982 ('Whereas Canada is founded upon principles that recognize the supremacy of God and the rule of law').

The role of religion in the history of the emergence of the modern state, the oppositioning of 'church and state' or the fragile relationship of many states with religion need not be addressed here.[61] For present purposes the following examples of specific constitutional confessions to specific religions or a-religious attitudes should suffice:

---

[60] It was for instance necessary for South Africa, having undergone a consolidation and reconfiguration of its national and provincial boundaries, to meticulously define the provinces jointly forming the national territory (section 1(2)) in Schedule 1 of the (transitional) *Constitution of the Republic of South Africa*, 200 of 1993.

[61] See e.g. Carey & Gascoigne 'Church and State'.

The preamble to the *Bunreacht na hÉireann*:

> In the Name of the Most Holy Trinity, from Whom is all authority and to Whom, as our final end, all actions both of men and States must be referred, ...

Article 31(2) of the Constitution of Pakistan:

> The State shall endeavour, as respects the Muslims of Pakistan, –
> (a) to make the teaching of the Holy Quran and Islamiat compulsory, to encourage and facilitate the learning of Arabic language and to secure correct and exact printing and publishing of the Holy Quran;
> (b) to promote unity and the observance of the Islamic moral standards; and
> (c) to secure the proper organisation of *zakat [ushr,] auqaf* and mosques.

Article 14.1 of the Russian Constitution:

> The Russian Federation shall be a secular state. No religion may be established as the State religion or as obligatory.

And (apparently incongruously) Article 67.2:

> The Russian Federation, united by the millennium history, preserving the memory of the ancestors who conveyed to us ideals and belief in God, as well as continuity of development of the Russian state, recognises the unanimity of the State that was established historically.

The staggering range of possible meanings attributed to 'state' in constitutional texts provides no relief if one strives to distil a single, manageable definition from those texts. To achieve such a goal, one will have to attempt to gain perspective by standing as far back as possible when assessing the significance of this concept which lies at the heart of constitutional law.

The veritable sponginess of the word 'state' and the range of possible meanings it is made to convey in constitutional texts seem to be without bounds. But again, the constitutional lawyer cannot do without it, because constitutional law is the *law relating to the state*. Fortunately, it is not all that difficult to demarcate the boundaries of constitutional law as a discrete field of study. It is a field not within the categories of private or international law, nor of criminal or commercial law; it is undoubtedly concerned with written documents known as 'constitutions', but is not limited to those texts, since its norms, principles, rules, values, theories and dogma are not confined to the content of constitutions; constitutional law moves closer to extra-legal disciplines, especially those focused on politics, than most other disciplines in the legal encyclopaedia, but still remains primarily concerned with the *law relating to the state*.

Being unconcerned and indifferent about the lack of consistency of meaning of 'state' can therefore not be defended legitimately, not only as a matter of tidiness, but specifically because constitutional law has become a comparative discipline in the practice of which the cavalier use of a core concept such as 'the state' will inevitably devalue the outcome of a comparative project.

Recognizing the problem of the uncertainties connected to the meaning of 'state' and what he calls 'the identity crisis of constitutional theory', Nic Barber presented an optimistic perspective, namely that 'constitutional theory requires an interpretative account of constitutional institutions', and that 'there is no single way of undertaking constitutional theory, but a variety of complementary methods which can help to enhance our understanding of constitutional institutions'.[62] Both of these statements are of course correct, but it should not go unnoticed that they imply that they impose an obligation on constitutional theorists to reveal their interpretative approaches with honesty, and to openly acknowledge that the nature of their theoretical methods diverges from others, complementary or otherwise. Obtaining an understanding of others' understanding of constitutional institutions depends on the identification of their interpretative methodology. Assuming that a core concept of constitutional law such as 'the state' bears a self-evident meaning is entirely inappropriate.

5.3   ESSENTIAL MEANING

Given that constitutional law without the state is inconceivable despite the lack of consistent signification, it may for the purposes of comparative communication be useful to outline the baseline requirements for the existence of a state, constitutionally speaking. A flippant response to the question what that would entail, might be that it depends on the constitutional law of the constitutional order from whose perspective the question is being posed. A better reply is essential if constitutional law as a discipline, also in its comparative manifestation, is to make sense.

Granted, the constitutional law of every state is unique, because it is not 'made', interpreted and applied from outside, but exists for and within the specific state. The remarkable if counter-intuitive fact that constitutional law is created by the state, and the state is created by constitutional law must be accounted for. The law constitutes the state, and the state is the lawgiver. This appears to be an inescapable reality, seemingly based on circular logic – a dilemma of causality. However, it is possible to trace the origins, development, configuration and reconfiguration of every state through its history to its source. No state miraculously flashed into existence, emanating from a mys-

---

[62]   Barber 'Constitutional State' 15 and 16.

terious singularity. Having been developed, refined, reconceived, revised and confirmed since its inception, constitutional law in its current manifestation indeed determines the existence, structure, character and legal minutiae defining a particular state.

Were the constitutional law of a state such a loose concept that it might not be recognizable from the vantage point of another constitutional order, the flippant response suggested above would have been correct. Such is however not the case. Constitutional law can be recognized as such from within the most dissimilar of legal orders, exactly because no legal order is possible without the state. This is not a construction of legal positivism, but one based on a condensation of the essence of statehood and the law. It is not a view which carelessly discards theories of legal pluralism and the realities of extra-legal normativity, but these theories are not considered to be helpful for present purposes, being an attempt to grasp the crux of statehood.

So, again, what is required in constitutional law for the existence of a state? This question is, as the discussion in this and other chapters intimate, the stuff of profound and interminable theorization. Reducing it all to a few elements that one cannot imagine to be absent from any legal conception of the state, we find the following attributes:

- establishment of a particular state as an incorporeal creature of legal (constitutional) regulation, mostly but not necessarily recorded in a recognizable foundational document or set of documents; and
- essential components, namely a corpus of humans (by law identified as citizens), a clear geographical space or spaces within which the particular state exists, and identified persons or bodies of persons endowed by law with governmental authority.

Where these elements are present, it is submitted, constitutional comparison with reference to other states becomes possible. Examining them as they are manifested in two or more states can reveal elemental differences, similarities, dogmatic and doctrinal contradictions and historical explanations for the uniqueness of the constitutional law of each. Discovering those characteristics of unique constitutional statehood is the ultimate goal of the craft of constitutional comparison: knowledge of the possibilities of variance and resemblance of constitutional norms regulating states as key constructs within which human societies function as both the subjects and the objects of legal regulation.

6. Citizenship and nationality

How does one determine, in public law, who or what constitutes the state, or for those who prefer, the nation or the people? In addition to, but apart from considerations of the nature and composition of the state and a nation, the status of individual natural persons (and increasingly also of corporate (juristic) persons)[1] is determined by their citizenship and nationality.[2] In the circumstances of the mounting pressures generated by accelerated migration, especially from the 'global south' to the 'global north', the significance of the 'national' status or non-status of a migrant can have immense implications, politically, economically, legally and personally, even determining life or death.[3]

Is citizenship 'constitutional' and nationality 'international', or do both serve the same purpose?[4] Be that as it may, the granting or withholding of the status both of citizenship and nationality depends on internal legal regulation by the state concerned. It is not clear whether a consistent terminological distinction between citizenship and nationality can be pursued without contributing to the pervasive confusion. On the one hand, the legal traditions of different legal orders vary,[5] and on the other, statutory distinctions between citizenship and nationality are hard to find, and often referred to interchangeably.

Confusing the issue from the perspective of the law even more, the merits of these concepts also attract extra-legal application and ruminations, especially where globalization is taken into consideration.[6] Mention is for instance made

---

[1] See e.g. Butler 'Diversity Jurisdiction and Juridical Persons'.
[2] See e.g. Di Lizia 'More than Just a Humble Abode'.
[3] See e.g. Koulish 'Sovereign Bias, Crimmigration, and Risk' 1–12.
[4] See e.g. the distinction made by John Dugard in Dugard 'International Law' 282–3.
[5] In English legal history the allegiance of the subjects of the Crown more or less performed the function of citizenship and nationality until 1914 when Parliament adopted the *British Nationality and Status of Aliens Act*. Currently the *British Nationality Act* of 1981 regulates the acquisition of British *citizenship*.
[6] Mitra 'Citizenship as Cultural Flow' 2 suggests –
> that the variation in levels of citizenship in time and space is the result of the entanglement of two different forces. Firstly, the primary influence on the state of citizenship is the result of the evolution of the concept of citizenship germane to local culture, tradition, and religion of a specific country, refracted by social evolution and political power, articulated and written onto the statute book by the

of de-territorialized, bi-national, transnational and global citizenship brought about by 'a dispersal of sovereignty' due to what is perceived as the demise of the nation-state, leading to 'postnational citizenship'.[7] Linda Bosniak (a self-confessed exponent of 'critical', deconstructive theory)[8] stated on the first page of her widely renowned book published in 2006:

> Political and legal thought today are suffused with talk of citizenship. Whether the focus is equal citizenship or democratic citizenship or social citizenship or multicultural citizenship, whether the preoccupation is with civil society citizenship or workplace citizenship or corporate citizenship or postnational citizenship, some version of *citizenship* is now vital to the intellectual projects of scholars across the disciplines.[9]

Approaching the matter from the perspective of political science and international relations, the Centre for Citizenship, Globalization and Governance of the University of Southampton explains their approach as follows:

> The field of citizenship is changing in response to global forces and this brings new governance demands. Migration, human rights, issues of global warming, pandemics of ill health and a looming crisis in energy provision are challenges that cannot be contained or addressed within national boundaries ... The Centre focuses on the central political questions of today's world about power, cooperation, security, inequality and democracy.[10]

In economics it is not uncommon to find citizenship (not legally regulated) being attributed aspirationally to commercial enterprises, particularly for the purposes of national and international trade and business. Ingo Pies for instance holds that –

> ... companies who act as corporate citizens (can) take on 'ordo-responsibility' in that they participate in processes of political rule-setting and public rule-finding, thus not abandoning the win-win logic of value creation but, instead, strengthening this role by contributing to improving the (deficient) political rules of the game of the economy.[11]

---

state. The second major influence on citizenship are the forces of globalization, for no nation of the world today is an island, and national citizenship is quickened by the global flow of the concepts of freedom, equity and empowerment.

[7] See e.g. Benhabib 'Transformations of citizenship' 33, 63 and 69.
[8] See e.g. Bosniak 'Making Sense of Citizenship' 3–7.
[9] Bosniak 'The Citizen and the Alien' 1.
[10] C2G2 'About Us' https://web.archive.org/web/20170827033857/http://blog.soton.ac.uk/c2g2/about-us/ (accessed 17 February 2021).
[11] Pies 'Introduction: Corporate Citizenship and New Governance' 2.

Despite the terminological confusion (or heedlessness) found in many juridical and other academic texts using 'nationality' and 'citizenship' interchangeably, as synonyms or as quasi-legal concepts, let us for the present begin by examining them separately and as distinct legal notions. What needs to be determined is whether the use of the terms 'citizenship' and 'nationality' has deteriorated to such a level of vagueness that they have become unusable for the purposes of constitutional comparison. Or have the attributes of both been merged technically to the degree that maintaining a distinction between them is no longer viable? More constructively, can an approach be construed to assist in the redemption of relevant constitutional meaning to support coherent comparative work in law?

Seeking answers to these questions, in what follows 'nationality' is considered in its international and supra-national applications before the historical roots and current constitutional manifestations of 'citizenship' are discussed. Then a common attribute of both, the perception of 'belonging', is considered, followed by concluding remarks on the distinction between nationality and citizenship, and a possible definition of citizenship in terms of its essential elements as a basis for constitutional comparison.

6.1 NATIONALITY

The nature and legal effects of nationality have engaged the international community on various occasions, most concretely and precedent-setting in 1955 in the *Nottebohm Case*:

> The character thus recognized on the international level as pertaining to nationality is in no way inconsistent with the fact that international law leaves it to each State to lay down the rules governing the grant of its own nationality. The reason for this is that the diversity of demographic conditions has thus far made it impossible for any general agreement to be reached on the rules relating to nationality, although the latter by its very nature affects international relations. It has been considered that the best way of making such rules accord with the varying demographic conditions in different countries is to leave the fixing of such rules to the competence of each State. On the other hand, a State cannot claim that the rules it has thus laid down are entitled to recognition by another State unless it has acted in conformity with this general aim of making the legal bond of nationality accord with the individual's genuine connection with the State which assumes the defence of its citizens by means of protection as against other States.[12]

Of particular interest in this dictum is the analysis of the interplay between national and international law. A person's nationality is not established by the

---

[12] *Liechtenstein v Guatemala* [1955] ICJ Rep 4 (6 April 1955) 23.

norms of international law because, historically, the granting of nationality lies within the exclusive purview of the sovereign state. In order to merit international recognition the state is nevertheless not completely free to structure its nationality laws as it pleases, because international law requires proof of a 'genuine connection' between the state and its nationals to qualify as their protector against other states. Disconcertingly, however, the quoted paragraph sets out to characterize *nationality*, but refers in the end to the international defence of states' *citizens*!

A positive interpretation of this last apparent equation of citizenship with nationality might be that it links nationality to citizenship without necessarily rendering the one identical to the other. Put differently, it is an indication that citizenship might be construed as including nationality, without the two having the same legal consequences.

Article I 1 of the 1954 *Convention relating to the Status of Stateless Persons* suggests the most coherent indication of what a person with nationality is deemed to 'belong to' by defining a 'stateless person' as 'a person who is not considered as a national by any State under the operation of its law': nationality as a legal status is established by legal regulation – regulation by a state.

If that were a full reflection of the use of the term, it would have resolved the matter neatly. However, 'nation' is the root concept of 'nationality' and, as has been argued in Chapter 3, the notion of the nation hardly contributes to clarity in constitutional discourse. At best, a precarious conceptual link between 'nation' and 'state' can be construed to acknowledge the observation that the state is composed of (among other elements) a corpus of identifiable humans (as is proposed in Chapter 5). The definition of 'statelessness' suggests that, for the purposes of international law, nationality is the identifying factor linking people to the state.

Although such a construction provides some clarity, the matter can unfortunately not be dispensed with so easily. The 'nation' in '*nation*ality' may also in some cases bear an ethnic, racial and cultural connotation. Such is for instance the case in Myanmar as Su Yin Htun recently described it.[13] In the *Constitution of the Republic of the Union of Myanmar* (2008) one finds a number of references to 'National races'. Reflecting the multi-ethnic composition of the population of Myanmar, section 3 of the Constitution reads: 'The State is where multi-National races collectively reside.' The applicable citizenship legislation (the *Burma Citizenship Law* of 1982) awards citizenship in section 3 to 'nationals' belonging to ethnic groups that settled before 1823 in the territories composing the state, and their descendants acquire citizenship based on the principle of *ius sanguinis* in terms of section 5: 'Every national

---

[13] Htun 'Legal Aspects of the Right to Nationality'.

and every person born of parents, both of whom are nationals are citizens by birth.' People inhabiting the country who do not belong to any one of the identified ethnic groups (such as the Rohingya) are stateless, and therefore do not 'belong' to Myanmar – or for that matter to any other state.

These arrangements demonstrate the definitional difficulties clearly. The 'nationality' in the law of Myanmar explicitly signifies ethnicity and it serves as a foundational qualification for the acquisition of citizenship. This does not resonate with Article 15 of the Universal Declaration of Human Rights (UDHR), which purports to guarantee 'the right to a nationality' and the right to change one's nationality, of which one may not be arbitrarily deprived. Changing one's ethnic origins is not possible, which leads to the conclusion that the notion of nationality with which the UDHR operates is not intended to be related to ethnic association, but to legal regulation by states. In many constitutional orders the acquisition and loss of citizenship is a prerequisite for the acquisition and loss of nationality, or vice versa. This linkage of the acquisition and loss of nationality in conjunction with citizenship however does not necessarily mean that the two concepts or their implications for the holder of citizenship or nationality are the same.

The extraordinary arrangements in the European Union significantly contribute to the definitional confusion. Sara Iglesias Sánchez summarized the European situation concisely:

> Nationality has traditionally been claimed to be one of the spheres in which Member States retain full sovereignty. The incipient conception of citizenship of the Union has found itself anchored to the sole will of States, since its acquisition and loss is determined solely by reference to the nationality of the Member States. It is thus ensured that States remain not only the gatekeepers of membership with regard to their own political communities, but are also the ultimate architects of the composition of EU citizenry. The mainstream approach to which the perception of Union citizenship is still anchored rests upon two basic premises: (1) citizenship of the Union derives from Member State nationality; (2) Member State nationality is the exclusive competence of Member States. *Ergo*, citizenship of the Union is in the exclusive hands of the Member States.[14]

Following this résumé, Sánchez points out that, due to the wording of the Lisbon Treaty and its judicial interpretation, EU citizenship has achieved a growing 'autonomy' as 'the vertical relationship between the Union and its citizens' and even rendering 'EU law as the legal parameter for national decisions regarding nationality'.[15]

---

[14] Sánchez 'Nationality' 65.
[15] Sánchez 'Nationality' 66–7. More or less ignoring the textual distinction between EU citizenship and member state nationality, Pfetsch 'European Citizenship'

In a comprehensive comparative work on the acquisition and loss of nationality in 15 European states, the editors appended a glossary in an attempt to provide 'a standardised terminology that allows comparing modes of acquisition and loss of nationality across countries', hoping to help 'to overcome some of the terminological confusions that are widespread in the comparative study of nationality law'. Where they define citizenship as the 'legal rights and duties of individuals attached to nationality under domestic law', they add that they 'distinguish citizenship from nationality, which signifies a legal status recognised under international law'. Nationality or the status as a national they define as follows: 'Legal relationship between a person and a state (country) as recognised in international law', followed by the remark that '[i]n some countries, the status may be called citizenship rather than nationality and the persons holding the status are referred to as citizens rather than nationals'.[16]

The European conception of member state nationality bears quasi-cultural connotations vaguely reminiscent of the Myanmar-style ethnic nationalism. This may appear to be a gratuitous conceptual leap, and to equate the nationality of member states of the EU with ethnic affiliation would no doubt offend many a European. However, elements of the rise of nationhood and nationalism in nineteenth-century Europe survive in the legal nomenclature relating to nationality, for instance *Nederlanderschap* in the nationality legislation of the Netherlands, *das Deutsche Volk* and *die deutsche Staatsangehörigkeit* in the German *Grundgesetz*. In multi-lingual Belgium, the difference in the French, German and Flemish concepts used for Belgian nationality (citizenship?) in Article 8 of the Consolidated Belgian Constitution of 1994 is interesting: *la qualité de Belge, die belgischen Staatsangehörigkeit, de staat van Belg*. This kind of terminology suggests that, when the concept 'nationality' crops up in the European discourse, belonging to the *nation* associated with a member state is instinctively implied despite the ostensible dogmatic distaste for cultural exclusivity – except that it constitutes the extra-legal stuff of rising populism and isolationism among sections of the citizenry of Europe and the United States.

---

99 ventured to explain the situation as follows:
> European citizenship is dual: it is in addition to the national citizenship of member states and does not replace national citizenship. There is no exclusive European citizenship, only a citizen of a European member state can become a European citizen and not vice versa. The borderline between in and out is clear: only citizens of a member state acquire European citizenship. The question of identity is left to individual legal arrangements.

[16] Bauböck, Ersbøll, Groenendijk & Waldrauch 'Acquisition and Loss of Nationality' Volume 1, 485.

The national and supra-national legal constructions of EU citizenship and member state nationality respectively do not contribute to the clarification of the meaning of and distinction between citizenship and nationality in the language of constitutional law. In fact, the European arrangements are unique and insular, not replicable elsewhere, and it seems that EU citizenship is steadily growing in legal effect at the expense of member state nationalities. Within Europe it has become the subject of a significant volume of scholarly literature, litigation and political contestation, especially due to the patterns of growing global migration.[17]

Beyond Europe, nationality is also hardly amenable to a solid definition, and it would appear that international law is understood to ever more intrude on the sovereign or autonomous sphere of states to regulate the acquisition and loss of nationality, especially in the context of international human rights law.[18]

6.2 CITIZENSHIP

In his portrayal of the Roman political model, Bruno Aguilera-Barchet points out that *res publica* did not indicate the (republican) form of the Roman state, but it 'designated the affairs (also the patrimony) of the *Populus*, conceived as a group of citizens'. He goes on to describe the legal effects of the conquering of other peoples by the Romans, leading to them being 'Romanized' by means of their subjection to Roman law, and the opportunity to obtain the benefits of becoming a Roman *civis*[19] as opposed to a *hostis* (stranger or enemy) or a *peregrinus* (foreigner):

> First one became a Roman citizen for having served as a magistrate, later it sufficed to form part of the corresponding urban assembly and, finally, in 212 AD, Emperor

---

[17] See e.g. Wesemann 'Citizenship in the European Union'; Neuvonen 'Democratic Critique of EU (Citizenship) Law'; De Groot & Luk 'CJEU Jurisprudence on Citizenship'; Gerhard & Lengfeld 'Wir, ein europäisches Volk?'; Strumia 'Supranational Citizenship and the Challenge of Diversity'; Bauböck 'Migration; and Citizenship' and Klingemann & Fuchs 'Citizens and the State'.

[18] See e.g. Human Rights Committee, *Views adopted by the Committee under article 5 (4) of the Optional Protocol, concerning communication No. 2918/2016* https://tbinternet.ohchr.org/_layouts/15/treatybodyexternal/Download.aspx?symbolno=CCPR%2fC%2f130%2fD%2f2918%2f2016&Lang=en (accessed 15 February 2021).

[19] See also Walbank's remark (also cited in section 3.1.1 Chapter 3 above relating to the idea of the nation) that *civitas* was a much stronger bond among Romans than *gens, natio* or *lingua*: Walbank 'Nationality as a Factor' 168.

Antoninus Caracalla granted Roman citizenship to all inhabitants of the Empire, who thereby became *cives romani*.[20]

Although the origins of the notion of citizenship may therefore be associated with Rome and the Roman Empire, the etymology of the modern use of the word 'citizen' and its linguistic predecessors appears not to go back much further than the thirteenth century:

citizen (n.)
c. 1300, *citisein* (fem. *citeseine*) 'inhabitant of a city or town,' from Anglo-French *citesein, citezein* 'city-dweller, town-dweller, citizen' (Old French *citeien*, 12c., Modern French *citoyen*), from *cite* (see city) + *-ain* (see -ian). According to Middle English Compendium, the *-s-/-z-* in Anglo-French presumably replaced an earlier *-th-*. Old English words were *burhsittend* and *ceasterware*.
Sense of 'freeman or inhabitant of a country, member of the state or nation, not an alien' is late 14c. Meaning 'private person' (as opposed to a civil officer or soldier) is from c. 1600. As a title, 1795, from French: During the French Revolution, *citoyen* was used as a republican alternative to *Monsieur*.[21]

The first four letters in the term 'citizenship' clearly imply a link to a 'city', which should be understood against the background of the centrality of the city

---

[20] Aguilera-Barchet 'History' 56–7. In note 56 at 57 he provides further interesting details, which indicates the importance of *civitas* as the condition of having the rights of a Roman (references omitted):

As Treggiari ... indicates, citizens had the right to marry other citizens (*conubium*), the right to enter into contracts according to Roman law (*commercium*), the right to appeal against actions by elected officials (*provocation*), and, if male and adult, the vote, the right (in theory) to stand for public office and follow a *cursus honorum*. All the citizens constituted the Roman People (Populus Romanus) which, through their different assemblies, were sovereign to pass laws, decide on war or peace, and elect magistrates to annual office. To be recognized as a Roman citizen, it was necessary to be registered in the official census. Dupont ... mentions how every 5 years each male Roman citizen had to register for the census, declaring his family, wife, children, slaves and riches. If he failed to do so, his possessions would be confiscated and he himself would be sold into slavery. Throughout the entire Republican era, census registration was the only way that a Roman could ensure that his identity and status as a citizen were recognized. Fathers registered their sons, employers their freedmen. An employer wishing to free one of his slaves needed only to enter him in the census register.

See further the Latin meaning of the related words *civicus, civilis, civis, civitas, hostis* and *peregrinus* in e.g. Simpson 'Cassell's Latin Dictionary'.

[21] *Online Etymology Dictionary* www.etymonline.com/search?q=citizen (accessed 19 February 2021).

of Rome in the Roman era. However, since the Latin for city is *urbs*, the link emerged only later in Europe:

> Between Latin and English the sense was transferred from the inhabitants to the place. The Latin word for 'city' was *urbs*, but a resident was *civis*. *Civitas* seems to have replaced *urbs* as Rome (the ultimate *urbs*) lost its prestige ... A different sound evolution from the Latin word yielded Italian *citta*, Catalan *ciutat*, Spanish *ciudad*, Portuguese *cidade*.[22]

In Chapters 2 and 3 above various instances of the use of the notion of citizenship when dealing with the history of constitutional law language and interrelated constitutional concepts were mentioned. To recapitulate: Machiavelli considered moral laws to govern the behaviour of *citizens* among themselves, but elevated the interests of the prince above those laws;[23] Rousseau's idea of a 'civil religion' was that it should 'bind the hearts of the *citizens* to the State', and insisted that *citizens* 'owe the Sovereign an account of their opinions only to such an extent as they matter to the community';[24] the American and French revolutions provided the foundations for the idea of '*citizen*-nations';[25] during the nineteenth-century development of the idea of the nation-state, the French placed the emphasis on the free association of *citizens* while the Germans were primarily focused on ethnic and cultural attributes.[26]

In a chapter headed 'The Dialectics of Citizenship' Maria Tzanakopoulou remarked:

> The modern concept of the citizen relies on the idea of the free individual who enjoys civil and political rights. Seen from this angle, constitutionalism and citizenship are hardly distinguishable from one another, as the free and equal individual becomes the foundation upon which both institutions emerge in the eighteenth century.[27]

'Citizen' and 'citizenship' are also terms that frequently appear in contemporary constitutional texts, often in connection with fundamental rights. Probably the oldest example is that of the United States. The American Revolution caused the populations of the 13 revolting territories to be deemed to have

---

[22] *Online Etymology Dictionary* www.etymonline.com/search?q=city (accessed 19 February 2021).
[23] Van Gelder 'Two Reformations' 58 (relevant passage quoted in section 2.9 of Chapter 2 above).
[24] McConnell 'First Freedom?' 1249 (relevant passage quoted in section 2.9 of Chapter 2 above).
[25] Cf section 2.7 in Chapter 2 above.
[26] Popović 'Comparative Government' 19–21.
[27] Tzanakopoulou 'Reclaiming Constitutionalism' 64.

withdrawn their allegiance from the British Crown, confirming their choice by continuing their residence in the newly independent colonies.[28]

Article IV of the Articles of Confederation (1778–81) provided: 'The better to secure and perpetuate mutual friendship and intercourse among the people of the different States in this union, the free inhabitants of each of these States, paupers, vagabonds, and fugitives from justice excepted, shall be entitled to all privileges and immunities of *free citizens in the several States*' (italics added).

This provision was (and still is) reflected in Article 4, Section 2 1 of the US Constitution (1789). However, as interpreted by the Supreme Court in the (in)famous *Dred Scott* case (1856), slaves and black people were excluded from obtaining US citizenship. This changed after the American Civil War when the 'reconstruction amendments' were adopted, including the Fourteenth (1866–68), which provides in the first section: 'All persons born or naturalized in the United States, and subject to the jurisdiction thereof, are *citizens of the United States and of the State* wherein they reside. No State shall make or enforce any law which shall abridge the privileges or immunities of *citizens of the United States*' (italics added).

To this many examples from other constitutions adopted over a century and a half and currently in operation can be added to demonstrate the common constitutional use of the concepts 'citizen' and 'citizenship', for instance:

Argentina:

> The citizens of each Province shall be entitled to all rights, privileges, and immunities inherent in the condition of citizen in the other Provinces.[29]

Luxembourg:

> Luxembourgers are equal before the law.[30] The law guarantees the right to work and the State sees to [the] assurance to each citizen [of] the exercise of this right.[31]

Iceland:

> No one may be deprived of Icelandic citizenship. Loss of citizenship may, however, be provided for by law, in the event a person accepts citizenship in another State. An alien can only be granted Icelandic citizenship according to law.[32]

---

[28] Bierbach 'Frontiers of Equality' 81–2.
[29] Section 8 of the *Constitution of the Argentine Nation*, 1853.
[30] Article 10bis of the *Constitution of the Grand Duchy of Luxembourg*, 1868.
[31] Article 11(4) of the *Constitution of the Grand Duchy of Luxembourg*, 1868.
[32] Article 66 of the *Constitution of the Republic of Iceland*, 1944.

Namibia:

Chapter 2 of the Constitution is headed 'Citizenship' and provides in Article 4(1) to 4(5) for the acquisition of citizenship by birth, descent, marriage, registration and naturalisation, and Article 17 provides that '[a]ll citizens shall have the right to participate in peaceful political activity intended to influence the composition and policies of the Government'.[33]

Czech Republic:

Any citizen of the Czech Republic who has the right to vote and has attained the age of twenty-one is eligible for election to the Assembly of Deputies.[34]

Vietnam:

1. A citizen of the Socialist Republic of Vietnam is a person with Vietnamese nationality. 2. A Vietnamese citizen shall not be expelled or handed over to other nations. 3. A Vietnamese citizen residing abroad shall be protected by the Socialist Republic or Vietnam.[35]

The conventional utilization of the notion of citizenship in constitutional texts confirms that statehood and citizenship are universally closely associated with one another. This unfortunately does not assuage the omnipresent and confusing use of the term as a synonym for 'nationality' – a tendency exacerbated by the phenomenon in the EU of associating citizenship with a non-state (the Union) and nationality with (the member) states. Keeping this practice in mind, the following summary by Harald Waldrauch of the usual routes to the acquisition of nationality is directly (actually more appropriately) applicable to citizenship in its traditional (non-EU) sense:

> There are numerous forms, ways, types and modalities of *acquisition of nationality*: it can be acquired at birth or after birth, acquisition can be automatic (*ex lege*) or non-automatic (requiring an initiative on the part of the target person and/or some public authority), and acquisition may become effective from the time all conditions are met, from the time the responsible authority makes a decision; it may even be acquired retrospectively (mostly from birth). If the acquisition is automatic, the main types are acquisition by descent, by birth (on the territory of the state), by legitimation, by marriage, by adoption, upon reaching majority, or by establishing residence in the relevant country. If acquisition is non-automatic, the granting of nationality can be at the responsible authority's discretion or be dependent upon the target person meeting certain conditions. That means that acquisition can become

---

[33] *Constitution of the Republic of Namibia*, 1990.
[34] Article 19(1) of the *Constitution of the Czech Republic*, 1992.
[35] Article 17 of the *Constitution of the Socialist Republic of Vietnam*, 1992.

effective either as soon as all conditions are met or only after a decision by the responsible authority. The type of procedure may then be called acquisition by naturalisation, grant (conferment) or extension of grant, declaration, notification, registration, option or similar. None of these distinctions actually say anything about the numerous potential conditions themselves that have to be met in order to be eligible for acquisition of nationality. In addition, the actual procedures, responsible authorities, possibilities for appeal, etc., may vary considerably from country to country.[36]

Citizenship as a status affording the bearer specifically protected rights and access to the protection and services of the state also has a complexion of distinct obligations. Citing the work of Alan Forrest, Aguilera-Barchet traces the historical origins of the obligations attached to citizenship to the war on which revolutionary France embarked in 1792. Military service was first –

> regarded as an essential aspect of citizenship, incumbent upon all equally, without distinction based on income or property ownership. For the first time the law recognized only one single form of citizenship. Not only were the young men of military age who had to serve in the armies to do their patriotic duty, but the rest of the population as well, as they were assigned a variety of support roles in the country's war effort.[37]

In some cases blanket loyalty to the state is demanded by constitutions. Thus, for instance, Article 9.3 of the Constitution of Ireland of 1937 provides 'Fidelity to the nation and loyalty to the State are fundamental political duties of all citizens' and Article 5(1) of the Constitution of Pakistan of 1973 states that 'Loyalty to the State is the basic duty of every citizen'. Loyalty being a subjective attitude which can hardly be legislated into existence, disloyal conduct towards the state of one's citizenship can no doubt have concrete consequences, for instance in the form of a criminal charge of treason or sedition.

In considering the features of constitutional law in the context of globalization, I have suggested elsewhere that citizenship might serve as a barometer for the observation of changing tendencies in public law.[38] The generalized concept is indeed constantly suffering a loss of solidity, perhaps due to overuse attributable to its attractiveness as a vessel capable of holding many possible, especially extra-legal, meanings.[39] In 2009 Rogers Smith wrote:

> Scholars and policymakers must recognize the proliferation of differing kinds of citizens or quasi-citizens, such as dual nationals, members of subnational, national

---

[36] Waldrauch 'Methodology for comparing acquisition and loss of nationality' 105.
[37] Aguilera-Barchet 'History' 398, note 54.
[38] Venter 'Global Features' 119–30.
[39] See Linda Bosniak's remark quoted at note 9 above.

and supranational forms of political communities, resident aliens with local voting privileges, multinational corporate citizens, and much more.[40]

Be that as it may, constitutional comparison is in need of more solidity if comparatists are to have a workable mutual understanding of what is under comparative discussion when it involves citizenship.

6.3 'BELONGING'

It is safe to say that *belonging* constitutes a foundational element shared by citizenship and nationality. Consider for instance the following remark by Zsolt Körtvélyesi:

> The fundamental question of who belongs to the political community continues to make waves throughout the world. The recent demonstrations in India and the atrocities that followed show to what extent citizenship laws can become contested fields of the struggle for recognition.[41] Citizenship legislation is also unique in that it makes it unavoidable that otherwise loosely defined notions like the nation or the people get concrete, applicable content, a definition of who is in and who is kept out.[42]

Determining what it is that citizens and nationals *belong to* due to their status as such may be the key to finding the underlying and distinguishable meanings of the concepts. Körtvélyesi's remark implies that there are (at least) three possibilities of 'belonging': to a 'political community', a 'nation' and 'the people'. Because of their indeterminacy, none of these 'loosely defined notions' is however particularly helpful for the purposes of legal communication.

Regarding the question of the *belonging* of a citizen and a national in terms of the law, more specifically constitutional law, a construction that a state is the entity to which citizens and nationals 'belong' is the most reasonable. The condition of 'belonging' has various components, typically involving the attribution in law of a range of identifiable rights, privileges, duties, and claims to the individual citizen or national *of a particular state*. In more concrete terms, citizenship and nationality determine a person's *status* in law.

---

[40] Smith 'Beyond Sovereignty and Uniformity' 912.
[41] This is a reference to an amendment of the Indian citizenship legislation adopted in December 2019 allowing persons belonging to Hindu, Sikh, Buddhist, Jain, Parsi or Christian groups from Afghanistan, Bangladesh and Pakistan – pertinently excluding Muslims – to naturalize as Indian citizens.
[42] Körtvélyesi 'Nation, Nationality, and National Identity' 778.

This is not the place to delve into the origins of the notion of juridical or legal status. Suffice it to cite a standard dictionary entry:

> **status** *n.* A person's legal standing or capacity. The term derives from Roman law, in which it referred to a person's freedom, citizenship, and family rights. Status is an index to legal rights and duties, powers, and disabilities.[43]

The title of Chapter II of the *UN Convention Relating to the Status of Refugees* is 'Juridical Status'. Article 12 of the Convention is headed 'Personal Status', and provides as follows (italics added):

> 1. The *personal status* of a refugee shall be governed by the law of the country of his domicile or, if he has no domicile, by the law of the country of his residence.
> 2. *Rights* previously acquired by a refugee and *dependent on personal status*, more particularly rights attaching to marriage, shall be respected by a Contracting State, subject to compliance, if this be necessary, with the formalities required by the law of that State, provided that the right in question is one which would have been recognized by the law of that State had he not become a refugee.

Juridical status of a natural person is determined by a range of factors, including age, (in)solvency, mental capacity, sex, circumstances of birth, marital condition – and nationality and citizenship. Obviously the status of a juristic person cannot be determined by conditions such as age and marriage, and there may be unique considerations in different jurisdictions, such as manner and form of incorporation.

Nick Barber's approach to an explanation of the nature of citizenship as a determinant of status is helpful:

> Citizenship is an institution of the state. As such, it is defined by a sub-set of the rules of the constitution, those rules that constitute the state. It is an institution which particular individuals can enter into; an office of the state. It therefore endows individuals with a particular status. They are no longer merely group members of the state, they are members of a particular sort: citizens.[44]

Barber accepts that it is possible 'to see citizenship both as a process ... with a social and an active element, but also as an institution and a status, constituted by rules'. He bases this duality on the recognition that some scholars prefer to emphasize the social, rather than the legal character of citizenship because the latter does not account for 'the significance of social rules in the construction of citizenship'. Therefore he considers it necessary to accept the

---

[43] Law 'A Dictionary of Law'.
[44] Barber 'Constitutional State' 49.

proposition that there is an 'interaction within the citizenry ... more commonly constructed through social rules backed by social pressure' than by the law.[45]

It stands to reason that, when one deals with citizenship in constitutional law intercourse, not only this 'social' component, but a range of other possible connotations may have to be accounted for, including historical, cultural, religious, economic and political considerations. However, I would argue that citizenship as a status determining attribute generated by the operation of legal rules must be seen as the essential point of departure, not merely as a desiccated conception created by law, but as one with a plethora of legal and extra-legal connotations.

6.4 NATIONALITY AND CITIZENSHIP AS CONSTITUTIONAL STATUS

If citizenship and nationality indicate belonging, it would on the face of it be only reasonable to ask whether the citizen belongs to the state, or if the state belongs to the citizen. Such a question would imply either that the citizens have ownership of the state to deal with as they wish, or that the state rules over the citizenry as a collective body of people subject to the will of the state as it is expressed by its governmental authorities.

But if 'belonging' is to be understood here in the sense of possession, the answer to the question should be neither, nor. Belonging should rather be used in relation to citizenship in a *constitutive* sense, and in relation to nationality as bearing *associative* meaning. Such a construction requires us to recall the essential attributes of the state and of the nation respectively.

Since it appears to be impossible to erase the words 'nation' and 'nationality' from our legal vocabulary, regardless of the conceptual confusion with notions that they entail, such as 'state' and 'citizenship', it may prove to be useful to link the one with the other. The root of 'nationality' is 'nation', from which it follows that a person who is identified as possessing a specific nationality can best be understood to be a person who has the status of being associated in law with a particular nation, however understood.[46] The status of nationality may entail variable, jurisdictionally determined status-determining rights, obligations and privileges. Although there are frequent overlaps regarding the legal acquisition, loss and substance of nationality and citizenship, the most profitable (in the sense of consistency) employment of 'nationality'

---

[45] Barber 'Constitutional State' 50.
[46] See Chapter 3 above.

in constitutional comparison would be as a reference to a person's status of interest in inter*national* law.⁴⁷

Thus at least partially liberated from the burden of double meaning, 'citizenship' could best be used to indicate the status of the citizen as constituting, with the rest of the citizenry, the human substance of the state. Such a construction is premised on the view (as stated in Chapter 5) that 'a corpus of humans' is an indispensable component of the state. It furthermore suggests that the authority of the state, which is essentially a fictional or imaginary legal construct (albeit associated with – as distinguished from 'composed of' – delimited physical territory), can only be exercised by human hands acting as the organs of the juristic person composed of the totality of citizens.

Against the background of this construction, the following formal definition of citizenship, at least for the purposes of consistent meaning in constitutional comparison, is proposed:

> Citizenship is a status-determining juridical condition which occurs where an individual person satisfies the relevant legal requirements; citizenship generates a legal relationship and specific competencies, rights and obligations for both the citizen and the state, which is a juristic person created through the operation of constitutional law.⁴⁸

---

⁴⁷ Had it not been that EU law is the joker in this conceptually unstable pack of cards, it might here have been apposite to add supra-*national* to 'inter*national*'.

⁴⁸ See also Venter 'Global Features' 119–30.

7. Democracy

For a state, a government, a political party, or a leader being accused of not being 'democratic' is widely recognized as being a serious slur. It implies autocracy, or even dictatorship, corruption, disrespect for the popular will, disregard for fairness and wilful promotion of selfish interests as opposed to the welfare of the people, the masses, the grass-roots, of those subjected to authority.

What, however, does it mean to be democratic? By what means and processes can and should the popular will, governmental fairness to all, public welfare and the transparent exercise of authority be determined? How is it possible that the same word is used in appellations such as the *Democratic* Party (in the United States), the *Democratic* People's Republic of Korea, and 'democracy' in the United Nations' aspirational *2030 Agenda for Sustainable Development*,[1] each doubtlessly conveying a different, albeit undefined meaning? Additionally, the word appears to be amenable to a wide range of adjectival qualifiers, for instance liberal, social, open, consensus, constitutional, deliberative, and many more.

A random perusal of constitutions readily reveals the frequency, and simultaneously the conceptual porousness, of reference to democracy as a cipher. In Canada, we find the phrase 'justified in a free and democratic society'[2] (echoed in various African constitutions, for instance in those of Botswana, South Africa, Kenya and Zimbabwe); the constitution of China proclaims the People's Republic of China to be 'a socialist state under the people's democratic dictatorship';[3] Pakistan's Constitution strives 'to establish an order ... [w]herein the principles of democracy, freedom, equality, tolerance and social

---

[1] UN General Assembly resolution A/RES/70/1 adopted on 25 September 2015. Paragraph 9 of its Declaration envisages a world '... in which democracy, good governance and the rule of law, as well as an enabling environment at the national and international levels, are essential for sustainable development ...'

[2] Section 1 of the *Canadian Charter of Rights and Freedoms* of 1982: 'The Canadian Charter of Rights and Freedoms guarantees the rights and freedoms set out in it subject only to such reasonable limits prescribed by law as can be demonstrably justified in a free and democratic society.'

[3] Article 1 of the *Constitution of the People's Republic of China* 1982: 'The People's Republic of China is a socialist state under the people's democratic dictatorship led by the working class and based on the alliance of workers and peasants.'

justice, as enunciated by Islam, shall be fully observed';[4] the Constitution of Greece[5] allows Parliament to limit the exercise of national sovereignty (for the purposes of being a member state of the EU) insofar as such limitation does not infringe upon 'the foundations of democratic government'; the Moroccan Constitution[6] confirms that 'Morocco is a constitutional, democratic, parliamentary and social Monarchy'.

No doubt democracy is a monumental idea, but it is not monolithic in the sense of uniformity or solidity.[7] Furthermore, various considerations and phenomena are associated with, and influence the nature, quality, and practice of a democratic system. Among these are: different and changing notions of representation by a few of the many;[8] the 'paradox of (democratic) constitutionalism';[9] the escalating challenges brought about by the technological revolution;[10] the plurality of electoral systems and political cultures; variations in the transparency of the exercise of governmental power and access to information; alternative methods for the expression of popular preference, including mass demonstrations, and so on.

---

[4] Preamble of the *Constitution of the Islamic Republic of Pakistan*, 1973.
[5] Article 28 3 of the *Constitution of Greece*, 1975.
[6] Article 1 of the *Constitution of Morocco*, 2011.
[7] Höffe 'Democracy' 69–78 e.g. distinguishes nine 'elements of conceptions of democracy' and mentions 'the now endless debate on the topic of democracy'.
[8] See e.g. Holmberg 'Dynamic Representation' 75:
> The lesson opinion-policy research can draw from our results is that public opinion in many cases may not be as exogenous as it is often assumed in the mainly American research tradition. The public opinion that supposedly influences policy can in turn have been influenced by politicians. What appears to be representation from below, from opinion to policy, might thus instead be representation from above – from elite opinion via mass opinion to policy. Appearances can be deceiving.

In raw numbers the estimated size of the world's population increased by a factor of at least seven since 1800. The numerical size of the electorates has consequently exploded. Taking the United States as an example: the total American population when the first general elections were held in the late 1780s was less than 4 million, and by 2019 it was around 329 million. There may therefore now be around 80 times more American voters than at the time of the adoption of their constitution.

[9] In Loughlin & Walker 'Paradox of Constitutionalism' 1, the editors wrote: 'Modern constitutionalism is underpinned by two fundamental though antagonistic imperatives: that governmental power ultimately is generated from the 'consent of the people' and that, to be sustained and effective, such power must be divided, constrained, and exercised through distinctive institutional forms'.

[10] Allenby 'Information Technology' 412 e.g. suggests that 'the ideas, assumptions, and institutions behind today's democratic structures and practices may already be obsolete, if not simply failing. Indeed, many have already failed. If there is a way forward, it necessarily requires inventing new narratives, norms, and institutions, not hoping for old ones to return or stabilize.'

The topicality for constitutional law of these and other considerations regarding democracy was illuminated with great clarity at a symposium organized by the German Law Journal, Cambridge University Press, and the London School of Economics on 'Populism and Constitutionalism' held in London on 25/26 April 2019. In her introduction to the published papers, Rosalind Dixon wrote:

> We are living in an age of profound democratic anxiety. The last year alone saw the publication of a range of books on the future of democracy by leading political scientists, philosophers, and constitutional lawyers ... And it saw wide-ranging attention to the current crisis in constitutional democracy in many countries worldwide. Constitutional lawyers, however, are still grappling with the relationship between public law and the current actual and perceived threats facing constitutional democracy in countries worldwide. Is constitutional law a bulwark against democratic "backsliding," "retrogression," "rot," or "decay"? Or has it contributed to the current democratic malaise, or the rise of various forms of illiberal and authoritarian populism?[11]

In the first section below the link between democracy and governmental authority is surveyed. In the second section representative manifestations of democracy and associated challenges are discussed for the purposes of revealing the significant malleability of the concept, rendering contextual definition indispensable if it is to have a useful core meaning in constitutional law and constitutional comparison. This is followed by a conclusion regarding the utility of the term 'democracy' in constitutional law and its implications for constitutional comparison.

7.1 DEMOCRACY AND AUTHORITY

In Chapter 2 the assumption was mentioned that Athenian direct democracy was the foundation of modern democracy despite the impracticality of its replication in more advanced societies.[12] Reference was also made to Rousseau's ideal of promoting equality by means of a universal right to participation in democratic decision making,[13] and the reality that the history of the English

---

[11] Dixon 'Public law and populism' 125.
[12] Section 2.1. For an analysis of the merits and shortcomings of Hellenic democracy, see Glover 'Democracy in the Ancient World' Chapter IV, ending (at 96) with the following remark: 'Democracy is the form of government that asks the most of every citizen; the Greeks taught us that lesson in all their triumphs, and the same lesson is to [be] read again, it is confirmed, in their failure to achieve and to maintain the ideals they saw.'
[13] Section 2.4.

Parliament since the late thirteenth century provided the most concrete basis for the development, and emulation elsewhere, of electoral democracy.[14]

In a chapter on pluralism, Patrick Dunleavy and Brendan O'Leary introduced their identification of five 'key features of the intellectual origins of pluralist political science' with an adept survey over a few pages of the key intellectual contributors to liberal democracy.[15] Their overflight of the seventeenth- to nineteenth-century contributors to this intellectual debate began by mentioning John Locke's argument in 1689 'that the state should rest upon consent, and that the governing authorities should never have absolute or monistic power', targeting Thomas Hobbes' contention in 1651 'that vesting absolute power in the government was necessary to avoid an anarchic "war of all against all"'. Montesquieu endeavoured to counter the absolutism of the eighteenth-century monarchies in 1746 by praising the assumed separation of powers in the English constitutional system. In 1787 the American authors of the Federalist Papers attempted to replicate Montesquieu's interpretation of the English system with the understanding that government interference with individuals' natural rights constituted tyranny, which may be countered with the separation of powers and federalism. Madison argued that political representation was not sufficient to counter human egoism and all the 'excesses of direct democracy', but that vertical and horizontal division of sovereignty was required. In praise of American democracy Alexis de Tocqueville in 1835–40 contrasted democratic and aristocratic societies to explain the lingering French tendency to return to authoritarian rule. He described this tendency with reference to the social disruption caused by the disintegration of the traditional feudal hierarchies, replaced only by 'isolated, privatized, and politically apathetic individuals, too disorganized and preoccupied to be free', whereas the Americans had developed a lively civil society.

It is safe to assume that most conceptions of democracy relate to the justification of the authority of those wielding the governmental power of the state. The common response to the question where a government derives its authority from, still is that the people democratically elected (or mandated by other means) their representatives to govern them. After all 'demos' indicates the populace, and 'kratos' authority (or power, which is the less euphemistic expression). But the question must be asked: is this a cogent response given the significant differences between the societies of previous centuries when

---

[14] Section 2.6.
[15] Dunleavy & O'Leary 'Theories of the State' 13–17. The 'key features' listed at 17 are attacks on state monism, the promotion of group and organizational autonomy, vigorous group conflicts, institutional or social checks and balances, and an awareness 'of the dangers of a society where self-interest was the dominant motive and traditional social ties were absent'.

the ideals of democracy were developed and institutionalized, and those of the twenty-first century? Given the elements of coercion implied in the notion of authority, Otfried Höffe's consideration of this matter warrants consideration:

> Some believe that qualified democracy, as a political ideal, puts an end to coercion. This view, which usually remains tacit, may be the reason why the authority to compel is not a topic of dominant legal and democratic theories. Of course, it is true that, in the case of democracy, the origin of the authority to compel changes: it is no longer derived from a (foreign) authority but from those subjected to authority. Moreover, the goal is altered: coercion serves no longer the purposes of those holding it, the rulers, but the citizens themselves. Even a Rousseauvian democracy, which assumes the unity of the rulers and the ruled, maintains penal enforcement, the authority to compel, and requires that the ruled provide for the state. Hence, while the democratic metamorphosis – from an alien authority to one that is self-enforced by those subjected to it – represents a fundamental change, it does not do away with the task of legitimation, nor the authority to compel.[16]

A conceptual problem with governmental authority is that it is very difficult to distribute while at the same time maintaining political consistency and focus. Consequently, political leaders who are entrusted with the authority of the state are endowed with immense personal influence, if not personal *power*: this is demonstrated by the reality that governmental authority, even in the most democratic of orders, is almost always associated with the incumbent of a single office with a title such as 'president', 'premier', 'chancellor', 'governor' or 'prime minister' regardless of how effective such a person's decisions and actions may be subject to institutional controls.[17]

Democracy ideally allows the *demos* to prevent those in power from exceeding the bounds of their *kratos* by political, legal, and moral means. But even the best of the available democratic mechanisms (including the ballot, constitutional litigation, and demonstrations of civil outrage) are notoriously blunt and unwieldy instruments. Put differently, democratic devices alone do not consistently guarantee that elected heads of state or of government will effectively be prevented from conducting themselves in a manner that distinguishes their actions clearly from those of autocrats heading undemocratic governments.[18]

---

[16] Höffe 'Democracy' 22.

[17] The idea that the president of the United States is 'the most powerful person on the planet' and that Angela Merkel is or was during her chancellorship 'the most powerful woman in Europe' is for example often expressed in popular journalistic communication.

[18] It would for instance be an interesting exercise to assess whether the actions of Donald Trump were in 2020 subjected to more effective controls than those of Vladimir Putin.

An age-old foundational question in law is (or should continue to be) what the legal basis is for the authority of the state which empowers its organs to perform legal acts, ranging from making laws, administering them, adjudicating compliance with the law, to enforcing them by punishing or compelling those who fail to comply. This question has been answered in many different ways, the answers invariably being rooted in the responders' *Weltanschauung*.

Deeply rooted in the notions of individualism that emanated from European reasoning following the Reformation, the Peace of Westphalia and the Enlightenment, current Western thinking on the source and legitimacy of governmental authority is still founded upon liberalism. The language of liberal democracy is also reflected in the international constitutional discourse. Thus 'liberal democracy' has achieved the status of a kind of civil religion in Western and westernized countries. Rousseau deemed 'the sanctity of the social contract' to be a core component of the dogma of civil religion,[19] and in 1839, then former US President John Quincy Adams and member of the House of Representatives declaimed: 'Fellow-citizens, the ark of your covenant is the Declaration of Independence. Your Mount Ebal, is the confederacy of separate state sovereignties, and your Mount Gerizim is the Constitution of the United States.'[20]

A core tenet of liberal democracy is the sovereignty of the people. Hardly anyone questions the notion that an entrenched constitution, the supreme law of the land, is the solidified expression of the will of the people, and that a democratically elected government represents the sovereign people. It is therefore widely considered axiomatic that the authority of the state to make laws, administer them and enforce them, is based on the will of the people. Thus, for instance, the editor of a recently published book on jurisprudence opened his introductory chapter with the following remark:

> During the twentieth century, the most influential theories of law have focused almost exclusively on the systems of norms enacted, practised, or recognized by agents and institutions that act on behalf of the modern nation-states (henceforth, 'state law').[21]

This has been the common wisdom for many centuries, but it was solidified in the minds of modern man on the back of the teachings of Western philosophers and the various epic revolutions in America, France, Russia, and China. In these constitutional orders (and their many replicas around the world) 'The

---

[19] Rousseau (Cole's translation) 'Social Contract' Book IV, 8.
[20] Cited by House 'A Tale of Two Kingdoms' 204.
[21] Fabra-Zamora 'Jurisprudence' 1.

People' (be they liberals or communists) are almost similarly recognized as the fount of legal authority.

Ironically, it can hardly be contested that this is an illusion. Neither did 'we the people' write any constitution, nor do the citizens of any country have a significant say in the making of policies, laws or judgments produced by the constitutional institutions of their state. Voters like to believe that their participation in elections (and other forms of public involvement, such as in internal party structures, public demonstrations, publication of opinions) gives meaning and effect to their views, but, when it comes to the actual exercise of authority, the influence of the ordinary members of even majority parties is usually insignificant and that of individuals not in government positions and of minority parties, negligible. Equally, the other bastions of freedom and democracy such as the public media, civil society institutions and academia may be important building blocks in the structures of power, but taken both jointly and separately, their grip on the concrete and routine exercise of governmental authority is weak.

These observations are not intended to be cynical or dismissive of the merits of democracy or motivated by an intention to propose something other or supposedly better than democracy. They are driven by a desire to obtain a deeper understanding of the actual foundations of state authority by not continuing to cling, without further investigation, to the general terminology of democracy as knee-jerk rejoinder to profound questions. It has become urgent, at the very least for the purposes of practicable constitutional comparison, to search for better explanations for the sources of state authority than those that were posited by the fathers of liberal democracy in their endeavours to shift power from monarchists to a collective of 'sovereign' individuals, or those explanations that uphold dictatorships over millions in the name of the 'proletariat'.

It is helpful to examine authority also from the perspective of those who have authority instead of only from the standpoint of the governed. Authority is closely linked, if not synonymous with leadership, and we may begin by registering some distinctions regarding the manner in which leaders obtain authority.[22]

First, a person may obtain authority in a 'natural' manner. The most obvious example would be parents, who are unlikely to strive for parenthood in order to obtain control over their children (this naturally does not preclude overbearing and authoritative parenthood). Without asking for it, however, a parent does have innate authority over a child, which is in most legal orders protected and regulated, even legally demanded, and enforced where the parent is negligent.

---

[22] These remarks are offered on the basis of subjective observation and reason, rather than learned dogma or doctrinal authority.

Parenthood is for the purposes of gaining insight in state authority less relevant, but historically, many sovereigns claimed to have gained their power 'naturally' by means of inheritance.[23]

Secondly, to some, authority comes involuntarily, due to personal attributes of 'natural leadership'. People graced with this characteristic do not always seek to translate their leadership talents into the possession of authority, but many do, and do so for different reasons. At one end of the range of reasons for following up on natural leadership abilities there are noble motives to serve others. At the other end of the scale some (all too many) strive to employ their talents for the mere satisfaction of a base desire for power. In the context of state authority, people-serving leaders would use their abilities unselfishly to promote the interests of society, while self-serving 'natural' leadership would be a tool in the hands of egotistical megalomaniacs to achieve their selfish goals, whatever that might be. Unfortunately, it is common cause that human nature tends to be easily seduced by power. Those who are endowed with the authority of the state notoriously find it hard to resist the seductive opportunities to either use their authority to its fullest – and even to abuse it.

A third category in which people obtain authority is what might be termed 'consequential leadership'. By this I mean situations where a person is focused on performing a function not in order to obtain authority, but with authority inevitably associated with the function. This frequently occurs in the professional world, where engineers, doctors, lawyers, auditors, scholars, and the like find themselves in a position where their knowledge and expertise require them to take the lead, regardless of their desire or otherwise to exercise the consequential authority. In the context of state authority, one might expect to encounter this phenomenon in the ranks of the civil service, and sometimes even at the executive level.

Fourthly, and most importantly for present purposes, there is the category of 'seekers of authority', very often driven by the desire to obtain control or power over others regardless of their personal attributes and leadership abilities (or lack thereof). Sadly, politicians rarely fall outside this category and in many cases democratic systems (unintentionally?) promote the phenomenon of projecting unworthy leaders into positions with access to the power of the state. Few will disagree that twenty-first-century elections in functioning democracies have largely become dominated by spin-doctoring, showmanship, demagoguery, financial capacity, media dominance and persuasive posturing or the backing of influential political organizations – all of which

---

[23] Inherited government authority is not only a historical phenomenon of monarchy, feudalism, and autocracy, but it still persists for instance in modern-day dictatorships such as North Korea.

have consequences including the declining interest of electorates in the democratic process. In states where democracy has not taken root or has become compromised, the authority of leadership inevitably tends to be founded in one form of authoritarianism or another, frequently disguised as democracy. Add thereto the fact that individual governors and government institutions exert their authority over growing numbers of individuals due to the exponential multiplication of the world's population by a factor of around 12 since the 1500s. From the perspective of the voter, the relative effect of the exercise of an individual's democratic rights has been shrinking constantly.

Against this background it is obvious that individual governors and government institutions, however they may have attained their governmental positions, exert their authority over expansively growing numbers of individuals. Seen from below, the relative effect of the exercise of an individual's democratic rights is shrinking steadily. Related to the exponential scale of the increase of the world's demographics, a range of social and consequently legal issues have become current, sometimes even critical. Among these are globalization, intra- and cross-continental migration, the rise of populism, and the extent and ubiquity of electronic and social media. Each of these trends holds challenges for the sustainability of democratic 'business as usual'. These and related questions underscore the relevance of the question whether democracy can (still) explain the nature and source of state authority. Put differently, can the typical political seekers of authority be deemed to wield the immense power of the state legitimately in a globalized, over-populated and digitized world? If not, scholarship has a responsibility to expose the democratic shortfall and to generate more cogent answers.

Among various factors, the emergence of the European Union as a significant force in late twentieth- and early twenty-first-century constitutional thinking and the (in places tenuous) transition of Central and East European states from socialism to constitutional democracy, have inspired much debate on foundational constitutional concepts such as sovereignty, the rule of law and democracy. Thus, for instance, in 2019 András Jakab addressed the 'interconnectedness of the protection of democracy and the rule of law' in his well-documented inaugural address.[24] He listed the following epithets used in scholarly literature published between 2011 and 2019 to describe the retreat and gradual degradation of democracy and the rule of law, not only in Europe, but also in a number of other jurisdictions: an 'illiberal' turn, anti-constitutional populist backsliding, decline of liberal constitutionalism, de-democratization, rule-of-law backsliding, decomposition of constitutional norms, erosion of democracy and constitutionalism, regression of democracy, democratic decay,

---

[24] A translated version appeared as Jakab 'What Can Constitutional Law Do?'

and democratic deconsolidation.[25] He relied on well-respected scholars to point out that, instead of 'traditional military coups', aspiring dictators now 'opt for a more comfortable solution, dismantling the safeguards of democracy and the rule of law gradually, evoking less resistance'.[26] Jakab deems it impossible to pinpoint any single factor as the cause of the erosion of democracy and the rule of law, but lists the following:

- the decline of constant and fervent support for democracy and the rule of law as a key factor in 'the stability of liberal democracies'. Reasons for this include poor economic growth, a rift occurring between the value systems of globalized elites and the rest of the population, and the passing on of the post-war generation that 'valued the benefits of liberal democracy';
- technological and scientific developments such as new technologies for political mobilization and communication technology which have changed political engagement and reading habits;
- the occurrence of terrorist attacks, bringing about responses that contribute to the justification of incursion on fundamental rights and the suspension of some democratic processes.[27]

Jakab significantly finds that 'although constitutional law has an important role to play in the fight against erosion, *on its own*, it is not decisive for the outcome of the process', because constitutional law can only be meaningful in combination with social and political factors. Only partial insight in the health of democracy and the rule of law can be achieved by studying legal rules, taking into account 'the growing chasm between the constitution and constitutional reality'.[28] Ultimately, Jakab finds, prevention of the decline depends on the existence of 'a democratic, rule-of-law-oriented political morality' of a political community.[29]

The large number of published analyses of the tendencies relating to the erosion of democracy and associated constitutional principles (Jakab's list of references covers 40 per cent of the volume of the cited article) indicates consistent (express or implied) concern with the justification of the commanding authority claimed and exercised by governments as the bearers of the authority of the state. The seldomly contested justification rooted in the history of Western political and constitutional thought and constitutional normativ-

---

[25] Jakab 'What Can Constitutional Law Do?' 6.
[26] Jakab 'What Can Constitutional Law Do?' 7. He devotes a further section of his presentation (pages 12–15) to describe the tools of hollowing out democracy by 'very much democratically elected politicians'.
[27] Jakab 'What Can Constitutional Law Do?' 9–12.
[28] Jakab 'What Can Constitutional Law Do?' 15–16.
[29] Jakab 'What Can Constitutional Law Do?' 23.

ity continues to be popular sovereignty, despite the fact that the interaction between the individual will, the will of the sovereign and representation has never been resolved theoretically, also not at the time of the genesis of modern democracy towards the end of the eighteenth and during the nineteenth centuries.[30] And yet –

> The idea of representation proves to be bound to the essence of sovereignty, i.e. to the modern concept of authority in the sense of rational and legitimate authority founded upon everyone's will. Furthermore, it is the hidden kernel of the legitimation of the state's monopoly on power being the foundation of the modern state.[31]

A device other than some process for the determination of the will of many, generically labelled 'democratic', has never been devised, and it seems unlikely that it is possible to do so. According to Ronald Glassman, this is because *homo sapiens* have developed complex political institutions and have developed democracy 'based on our key species characteristic – heightened intelligence and awareness and inter-subjective language skills'.[32]

Numerous explanations for the authority of the few to lead, to dominate over, to prescribe to, and to adjudicate the disputes of and between the many – in short to govern – have been proposed. Taking note of broad categories of these explanations may assist us to contextualize the continued domination of the idea of popular sovereignty, whether it is actually believed in or simply ritualistically echoed in constitutions and in constitutional literature. Three rather broad categories come to mind:

- A *sociological* explanation: humanity cannot function without leadership, and leadership depends on authority.[33]

---

[30] See e.g. the discussion of Hegel's contributions of the time under the heading 'Repräsentation zwischen Einheit und Komplexität' by Duso 'Moderne politische Repräsentation' 113–23.

[31] Free translation by the author of the following passage from Duso 'Moderne politische Repräsentation' 12:
> Der Begriff der Repräsentation erweist sich als wesensmäßig gebunden an denjenigen der Souveränität, d.h. an den modernen Begriff von Herrschaft, im Sinn der rationalen und legitimen Herrschaft, die auf dem Willen Aller beruht, mehr noch: Er ist ihr heimlicher Kern, insofern er jenes Gewaltmonopol zu legitimieren vermag, das grundlegend für die Figur des modernen Staates geworden ist.

[32] Glassman 'Future of Democracy' 5.

[33] Max Weber famously distinguished the legitimation of three types of authority (traditional, charismatic and legal-rational) – see e.g. Harrison 'Weber's Categories of Authority' and Glassman 'Origins' ix–x. The amount of scholarly attention given to Weber's classification dating back to 1922 is indicative of the value of approaching the matter from a perspective different from that of 'the people'.

- A *rationalistic* explanation: Immanuel Kant's categorical imperative which is based on the principle that one should act only in such a way that one can also will that one's maxim should become a universal law.[34]
- An *ontological* explanation: the source of power is inevitably divine.

Each of these categories of justification is prone to difficulties:

- The sociological approach does not clarify the source of authority and does not provide a standard or measure for good leadership.
- The rationalistic explanation suffers from the fact that reason is inevitably subjective. Kant's categorical imperative therefore begs the question: *whose* reason should determine the universal law?
- The ontological reliance on divinity is fraught with the spectacular fragmentation of theological perspectives, broadly divided between on the one hand the deistic view of divine creation followed by the Creator's indifference, and on the other theism, which professes divine creation and the Creator's perpetual involvement in creation.

Theism characterizes the major religions of humanity, including Christianity, Islam, Hinduism, and Judaism. In statistical terms, one might therefore have expected the explanation and justification of state authority to be dominated by theistic justifications of the divine source of all authority. Remarkably, however, twentieth- and twenty-first-century constitutional language is almost devoid of theistic notions, except as adornments in constitutional texts.[35]

Remarkably, the language in terms of which we write and speak about phenomena such as the state, authority, the law, accountability, *and democracy*, is common to leaders in government, whether they are socialist dictators or democratically legitimized republicans. The same language is *de rigueur* among the drafters of contemporary constitutions, be they intended to regulate free and open societies or Marxist-Leninist 'proletarian' states. Legal and political scholarship also speaks this language, while usually ignoring or carefully

---

[34] According to Rosen 'The Philosopher's Handbook' 23, Kant chose to dislodge the 'general will' from its political content and replaced it with the categorical imperative in order to 'liberate ethics from its traditional subordination to the dictates of political prudence'.

[35] In this, the language used in Islamic constitutional documents may perhaps be regarded as an exception. However, one may doubt it if the expressions 'constitutional law' and 'constitutionalism' can legitimately be used in the context of Islamic states in view of the legalistic nature of the religion – no norm being deemed equal or superior to the Sharia. See e.g. the discussion and sources in the extended footnote 99 in Bussani 'Deglobalizing rule of law and democracy' 729.

avoiding confrontation with the fundamental questions regarding the origins or sources of authority.

Answers to the questions concerning the foundations of authority (especially in the form of constitutional powers) are riddled with irony: sociology is more concerned with the effects of the exercise of authority over people than with its origins; rationalists produce convoluted arguments, but consistently fail to produce objective justifications for subjective reasoning; believers in divinity as the source of authority display vastly divergent religious validations of their religions. The crowning irony is that the accepted language in circulation regarding constitutional authority thrives on semiotic plurality.

This is why (at least) constitutional scholars urgently need to reappraise their vocabularies, and explain the meaning of the words and concepts they use by honestly revealing their *Weltanschauung* and openly building their analyses accordingly, including when it comes to the much revered notion of democracy.

7.2 CONTEXTUAL MANIFESTATIONS AND CHALLENGES

Where one encounters the words 'democracy' and 'democratic' in international instruments, constitutions and in scholarly or popular literature, adjectives are not always used to specify the intended meaning. Where adjectives are attached, the reason is usually clear, either as an explicatory enhancement,[36] to distinguish the particular idea from the traditional liberal version,[37] or to convey a specific dogmatic stance.[38]

Let us now first consider the challenges to the notion of democracy as it is currently manifested in the examples of the European Union and on the African continent, and then take a look at more emerging challenges to which democracy is exposed.

7.2.1 Democracy in the European Union

In its birthplace, Europe, democracy today has many faces. Due to the uniqueness of the arrangements upon which the European Union is operating, democracy has distinguishable supra-national and national features. On the

---

[36] Examples are James Fishkin's models of democracy, 'competitive democracy', 'elite deliberation', 'participatory democracy' and 'deliberative democracy' referred to by Blockmans 'Democracy as an Ecosystem' 10.

[37] Such as 'Islamic democracy' and 'socialist democracy' (the latter being promoted by e.g. the Irish Democratic Socialist Party).

[38] Such as 'people's democracy' and 'social democracy'.

one hand, democracy features prominently as a guiding principle in the foundational documents of the EU, while the nature and quality of democracy in the member states vary considerably.

In 1949 the founding members of the Council of Europe confessed in the preamble to the *Statute of the Council of Europe* 'their devotion to the spiritual and moral values which are the common heritage of their peoples and the true source of individual freedom, political liberty and the rule of law, principles which form the basis of all genuine democracy'.

The *European Convention for the Protection of Human Rights and Fundamental Freedoms*, adopted in 1950 in Rome (ECHR), 'reaffirmed' in its preamble the signatories' 'profound belief' that fundamental freedoms 'are best maintained on the one hand by an effective political democracy' and on the other hand by a common understanding of human rights. Reference to what is necessary or appropriate in 'a democratic society' is made throughout the text of the Convention.[39]

In the preamble to the *Treaty on the European Union* (the Maastricht Treaty of 1992 marking a new stage in the process of European integration) the signatories confirmed 'their attachment to the principles of liberty, democracy and respect for human rights and fundamental freedoms and of the rule of law', and expressed their desire 'to enhance further the democratic and efficient functioning of the institutions so as to enable them better to carry out, within a single institutional framework, the tasks entrusted to them'. Title I, Article F 1 of the Treaty provides that 'The Union shall respect the national identities of its Member States, whose systems of government are founded on the principles of democracy'. Regarding the EU's policy on development cooperation Title XVII Article 130u 2 provides that 'Community policy in this area shall contribute to the general objective of developing and consolidating democracy and the rule of law, and to that of respecting human rights and fundamental freedoms'. Title V Article J.1 2 reiterates these objectives regarding the Union's foreign policy.

Clarification of what a democratic system was intended to signify is not to be found in these constituting documents, but some guidance has emerged from European case law, particularly in relation to the right to freedom of expression within the constitutional orders of the member states. Article 10(1) of the ECHR protects the right, and Article 10(2) allows for its limitation insofar as such limitations 'are necessary in a democratic society'. The judgment of the European Court of Human Rights (EctHR) in *Lingens v Austria*

---

[39] Articles 6(1), 8(2), 9(2), 10(2) and 11(2) of the Convention, Articles 2, 3 and 4 of Protocol 4, and the preamble to Protocol 13.

(1986)[40] is on this point the *locus classicus* frequently cited in later case law.[41] Basic conditions for a democratic society in the law of the EU that can be gleaned from the judgment are freedom of expression, which is required for individual self-fulfilment, pluralism, tolerance, broadmindedness, opportunities for the public to discover and form opinions on the ideas and attitudes of political leaders, and freedom of political debate.[42]

Due to the protection of the right to free elections in the First Protocol of the European Convention on Human Rights, the list of characteristics of a democratic society in EU law can be deemed also to include the holding of regular elections conducted by means of a secret ballot allowing 'the people' to freely express their opinion regarding the choice of lawmakers.[43]

Classical elements of liberalism (freedom, individualism, self-fulfilment) are clearly at the root of the EU's formal conception of democracy. However, a vast range of basic understandings, practices, and modes of implementation of these elements exists among the member states, giving cause for growing concern among the Europeans. Richard Young writes about analyses of 'a pan-European democratic crisis' and the suggestion 'that a much messier set of developments defines changes to European democracy':

> In some states, democracy has indeed been in the thralls of existential crisis, and yet in others its current condition is un-dramatic and even modestly improved in some areas. Some EU governments have opened up to new forms of participation, but others have been reluctant to do so. In some there is stifling state control, while in others ungovernable pluralism seems to be the greater peril. In some, party systems have begun to realign, while in others mainstream coalitions have hunkered down

---

[40] EctHR Application no. 9815/82, judgment of 8 July 1986.

[41] For case references following the Lingens-judgment, see e.g. Frowein 'The Transformation of Constitutional Law'.

[42] The core *dicta* are found in paragraphs 41 and 42 of the judgment:
41. ... [T]he Court has to recall that freedom of expression, as secured in paragraph 1 of Article 10 (art. 10-1), constitutes one of the essential foundations of a democratic society and one of the basic conditions for its progress and for each individual's self-fulfilment. Subject to paragraph 2 (art. 10-2), it is applicable not only to 'information' or 'ideas' that are favourably received or regarded as inoffensive or as a matter of indifference, but also to those that offend, shock or disturb. Such are the demands of that pluralism, tolerance and broadmindedness without which there is no 'democratic society'.
42. Freedom of the press furthermore affords the public one of the best means of discovering and forming an opinion of the ideas and attitudes of political leaders. More generally, freedom of political debate is at the very core of the concept of a democratic society which prevails throughout the Convention.

[43] 'The High Contracting Parties undertake to hold free elections at reasonable intervals by secret ballot, under conditions which will ensure the free expression of the opinion of the people in the choice of the legislature.'

in even more self-protective fashion. In some, parliaments have lost power and prestige, while in others they have taken on new functions and begun to reassert themselves over the executive.[44]

Young goes on to point out that in some European countries 'popular antipathy towards core liberal values' drives democratic concerns and identifies three general patterns. First a downward shift of accountability inspiring 'an ethos of bringing democratic control and monitoring down' to the level of the 'apocryphal ordinary citizen'. Secondly a trend towards active democratic engagement in the form of 'the spiralling number of pro-democracy protest, citizen assemblies and civil society initiatives'; and thirdly the realization that the 'democratic decay' will have to be addressed by substantial change at the EU level, with the complication that '[n]ational democracy cannot be protected or enhanced without reform at the EU level; and democratic reform at the EU level will not suffice without reform at the national and sub-national levels'.[45]

From the perspective of the citizens, the EU presents tensions between what Heinz Kleger calls 'normative individualism' and 'normative communitarianism'.[46] The Maastricht Treaty was adopted with the intention to establish 'a citizenship common to nationals' of the member states, and to continue with 'the process of creating an ever closer union among the peoples of Europe, in which decisions are taken as closely as possible to the citizen in accordance with the principle of subsidiarity'.[47] The dilemma that Kleger identified lies in the conception of individual EU citizens being equal participants in EU decision making while the citizens may not feel primarily bound and obliged to the Union, but to the member state whose nationality they possess.[48]

Being a 'supra-national' institution whose organs have since their establishment grown steadily in authority allowing them to enforce measures and decisions on the citizens and societies in the member states without the express concurrence of their governments, unique questions arise related to democracy in the EU. The editors of a collection of essays on this matter stated in their introduction to the volume that the thematic field 'Supranationality and Democracy' has for some time now developed a central area of discourse

---

[44] Young 'Patterns and Particularities in European Democracy' 350.
[45] Young 'Patterns and Particularities in European Democracy' 350–2.
[46] Kleger 'Demokratisches Regieren' 386: 'ein Spannungsverhältnis zwischen normativem Individualismus und normativem Kommunitarismus'.
[47] The preamble to, and Articles A, B, and 8 of the Maastricht Treaty. Article 138a furthermore states that '[p]olitical parties at European level are important as a factor for integration within the Union. They contribute to forming a European awareness and to expressing the political will of the citizens of the Union'.
[48] Kleger 'Demokratisches Regieren' 387.

providing insight in the partly desired and partly disputed political quality of the EU as a form of transnational cooperation unique in the world.[49]

This is a theme that has inspired analysis by some of the most celebrated minds in constitutional law and politics. In Germany, a founding and currently probably the most influential member state, the balance between national and supra-national supremacy or sovereignty has inspired strong (and it must be said, often controversial) judgments delivered by its *Bundesverfassungsgericht*.[50]

In considering the question of democratic legitimation of the EU, Dieter Grimm used the distinction between the constituting *pouvoir constituant* and the constituted *pouvoir constitué*[51] to consider the 'democratic deficit' of the EU. First, he found that in the constituting element the EU could not claim its own legitimacy (the European Parliament is a (weak) factor for legitimation but lacks sufficient representative democratic authority). Secondly, the constituted image of the EU and EU law increasingly bears constitutional qualities, but the more binding norms the EU creates, the more it comes into conflict with national constitutional sovereignty, thereby ironically undermining its legitimacy.[52]

7.2.2 Democracy in Africa

The North Atlantic notions of democracy and colonialism had never been mutually compatible. Although it may be argued that the European colonial masters of Africa up to at least the middle of the twentieth century did in places selectively introduce elements simulating democratic conduct,[53] colonial government was unashamedly guided by the interests of the colonial powers, hardly ever by the interests of the inhabitants of their remote possessions. Only after the withdrawal of the power of the colonizers and the creation of independent states upon the persisting remnants of colonial frameworks during the second half of the twentieth century, did it become feasible for the new African states to introduce simulations of democracy.

---

[49] Abbas, Förster & Richter 'Supranationalität' 1.
[50] Among these are the *Solange* cases (BverfGE 37, 271 and BverfGE 73, 339), *Eurocontrol I* (BverfGE 58, 2), the *Maastricht* case (BVerfGE 89, 155), the *Lisbon* case (BVerfGE 123, 267), and recently the *PSPP* case (BVerfG, Case No. 2 BvR 859/15) (5 May 2020).
[51] Grimm 'Zum Stand der demokratischen Legitimation' 18–26.
[52] Grimm 'Zum Stand der demokratischen Legitimation' 26–35.
[53] E.g. the unfolding of British colonial governance as discussed in section 2.6 of Chapter 2 above regarding the gradual constitutional emancipation of the former colonies and dominions.

No doubt Africa had, at least while most of the continent was dominated by various European colonial powers, virtually no role in the development of the conception of liberal democracy and colonial rule did not provide an example of the merits of democracy to promote their acceptance by African societies.[54] However, general elements of pre-colonial social ordering in Africa (which naturally was by no means uniform across the continent) have been reconstructed by scholars. Decision making by discursive participation and consensus are said to have been typical features of the African social order before it was disrupted by the colonial authorities.

In reconstructions of pre-colonial mores, parallels are drawn with elements of democratic thinking, and possible reasons are identified for contemporary, post-colonial African deviations from Western democracy. The Ghanaian philosopher Kwasi Wiredu describes African consensual democracy and construes a possible relationship with the frequently occurring one-party polities in Africa.[55] Wiredu described the pre-colonial African model for the resolution of issues leading to the attainment of reconciliation as a process that in effect seeks consensus by means of extensive deliberations with a view to overcoming disagreement. The purpose of this model is not to determine 'what is to be done and not what ought to or ought not to be done or what is true or false'. This is a 'non-party system ... in the sense that the system does not involve political parties in the form of entities that compete in order to determine the party that ascends to power, while the losing ones are left out of power'.[56]

African 'consensual democracy' predates the colonial era, but there is evidence that at least traces of it survive as a culturally ingrained attitude.[57]

Nevertheless, African constitutions adopted since the 1960s consistently use the language of Western liberal democracy. Consider for instance section 1(d) of the South African Constitution:

> The Republic of South Africa is one, sovereign, democratic state founded on the following values:
> (d) universal adult suffrage, a national common voters roll, regular elections and a multi-party system of democratic government, to ensure accountability, responsiveness, and openness.[58]

---

[54] See e.g. Venter 'Parliamentary Sovereignty or Presidential Imperialism?' 96–100.
[55] Cf Masaka 'Kwasi Wiredu's Consensual Democracy'.
[56] Masaka 'Kwasi Wiredu's Consensual Democracy' 70.
[57] Mosima 'Inclusive Development' 85.
[58] *Constitution of the Republic of South Africa*, 1996.

Most of these elements are also provided for in current African constitutions[59] and electoral laws, although the effectiveness of their implementation and administration vary. Even where these elements of democracy are consistently applied, a substantial measure of uncertainty exists regarding the actual entrenchment of a liberal democratic ethos in African electorates. Reginald Oduor, a Kenyan philosopher, argues that, in Africa, the status of liberal democracy can be challenged on the grounds of logical inconsistency, impracticability due to the largely communalistic outlook of many Africans, inconsistency between affirmation and action, violation of the right to ethnic identity, and the moral imperative to assert the right to cultural emancipation.[60]

The notion of multi-party democracy, as received in African constitutions from the Western examples, is one of the most important touchstones for determining the viability of the notions of liberal democracy on the continent. It is likely that the ontological disconnect between the constitutionalist foundations of the formal constitutional texts of Africa and the lived socio-cultural realities constitutes a major cause of poorly balanced African political and constitutional practices and formal constitutional identity. This gap has opened democratic politics to political opportunism, as was pointed out by Patrick Tandoh-Offin and Gbensuglo Bukari at the end of their analysis of the frequent political and legal contestations of the outcome of elections in sub-Saharan Africa:

> ... political elites in sub-Saharan Africa have used overt and covert strategies aimed at maintaining or changing the status quo, and this often brings about electoral disputes ... [A]n acceptable electoral outcome is an arbiter of a democratic society and it is imperative that the organisation of elections is given adequate weight in any political system ... [T]he advantage of incumbency and the winner-takes-all concept, ethnicity and sensational media reportage contribute significantly to contentious electoral outcomes. Political leadership in sub-Saharan Africa has failed in its democratic responsibility to aggregate social interests, represent specific constituencies and serve as an intermediary between state and society.[61]

---

[59] Some examples: Preamble to the Constitution of Namibia of 1990, which declaims that the people of Namibia 'have resolved to constitute the Republic of Namibia as a sovereign, secular, democratic and unitary State securing to all our citizens justice, liberty, equality and fraternity', and Article 49 'The election of members [of the National Assembly] shall be on party lists and in accordance with the principles of proportional representation'; Preamble to the Constitution of Kenya of 2010: 'RECOGNISING the aspirations of all Kenyans for a government based on the essential values of human rights, equality, freedom, democracy, social justice and the rule of law' and section 38(2): 'Every citizen has the right to free, fair and regular elections based on universal suffrage and the free expression of the will of the electors ...'.

[60] Oduor 'Liberal Democracy', abstract at 108.

[61] Tandoh-Offin & Bukari 'Towards a Less Contentious Electoral Outcome' 55.

No doubt, accountability, openness and responsivity are the casualties.[62] A telling example of this relates to the constitutional statement of 'basic values and principles governing public administration' listed in section 195 of the South African Constitution of 1996, which include high standards of professional ethics, accountability, good human-resource management and career-development practices, and employment and personnel management practices based on ability, objectivity, and fairness. The South African government has however, over more than two decades, flouted these constitutional values and principles by openly practising a policy mirroring not democratic liberalism, but rather socialist practices described as the 'deployment' across the public service of the 'cadres' of the ruling ANC, with hardly any regard for the principles and values constitutionally prescribed for public administration. The effects of this counter-constitutional practice, described by for instance Elvin Shava and Shingirayi Chamisa, have been devastating. They identify four main issues attending 'cadre deployment', namely patronage or cronyism, skills shortages due to poor training, poor performances in governance and a lack of transparency and accountability.[63]

It stands to reason that, especially from the perspective of the indigent voter, the franchise provides a potential lever of influence over the authorities. Put bluntly, a poor voter's electoral conduct is likely to be determined by the logic of 'if you provide relief for my penury, I will vote for you'. A large proportion of African electorates living in poverty[64] therefore expose democracy on the continent to the scourge of 'vote buying'. In the West the phenomenon of vote buying was however not unknown in the earlier stages of the historical development of electoral systems, for instance in eighteenth-century England. Even in constitutional democracies of the twenty-first century a sophisticated form thereof – although not focused on the poor but on effective 'spin doctoring' – is a well-known and blatant element of electioneering, particularly visible in the presidential elections of the United States.

---

[62] See e.g. Dube 'Enhancing Democratic Accountability'.
[63] Shava & Chamisa 'Cadre Deployment Policy'.
[64] According to the *Institute for Security Studies* https://issafrica.org/iss-today/what-is-the-future-of-poverty-in-africa (accessed 7 May 2020), roughly 40 per cent of people in Africa live with less than US$1.90 a day, people in sub-Saharan Africa are more than twice as likely to live in poverty as those in South Asia, the next poorest region globally, and sub-Saharan Africa accounts for roughly 60 per cent of the global population living in poverty in 2020.

The current occurrence of vote-buying in the African context has received scholarly attention. Chigozie Enwere for example discussed vote-buying in the Nigerian elections of 2019. He concluded:

> Having analysed the syndrome of vote buying in 2019 election and its threat to the principles of free, fair and credible election, vote buying has become a cancer that limits the growth of democratic values and practice in Nigeria, stimulating voter apathy, self-alienation and violence in the electoral process and structure ... Other undercover strategies adopted were the use of clannish, ethnic and religious sentiments to encourage vote buying along tribal and religious lines and interests. This new trend of vote buying poses great threat to [the] existence and practice of modern democracy in Nigeria because vote buying has become an instrumental asse[r]t to determine who wins or loses an election ... we therefore conclude that vote buying is a phenomenon that determines who gets the highest or lowest number of votes, when and how.[65]

Yolanda Sadie, Leila Patel and Kim Baldry empirically investigated the effects of the distribution of food parcels and social grants in South Africa on the behaviour of poor voters. The South African study, which only dealt with three small urban communities, concluded that –

> [M]ore than a quarter of the respondents (with a higher proportion being unemployed rather than employed), would vote for a party that provided food parcels before elections. This suggests that the provision of food parcels to the poor before elections, together with propagating the distribution of social grants as a 'party initiative', can indeed influence the 'floating' vote. It is also likely that, where there is political contestation and competition between political parties in poor communities, vote-buying may to some extent inform electoral strategies.[66]

Despite the apparent liberal democratic idealism reflected in African constitutional texts, even regular multi-party electoral contestation is ostensibly a persistent casualty of endemic African poverty. But it is not only African poverty that should be blamed, nor is it an exclusively African issue. Recording democratic ideals in epic constitutional texts does not ensure the survival of such ideals in societies that do not share the historical experiences or the foundational worldviews of the originating examples. Patrick Glenn, in his general discussion of the nation-state, aptly remarked:

> The internal diversity of states has been obscured for decades by liberal philosophy, by the teaching of the nation-state, and by the concentration of both theorists and

---

[65] Enwere 'Vote Buying Syndrome' 41–2.
[66] Sadie, Patel & Baldry 'Voting Behaviour of Poor People' 136.

historians on a relatively small number of European or anglo-american states that have themselves been heavily committed to a nation-state analysis.[67]

African societies (and others around the globe) cannot simply be assumed to provide an appropriately prepared growth medium for the flourishing of liberal democratic philosophy. Nonetheless, the trappings of liberal constitutionalism actually seem to suit most of the ruling politicians in Africa, because it provides them with mechanisms to consolidate and strengthen their dominance behind the façade of sweet-sounding constitutional documents despite the illusory nature of the theoretical foundations of those founding texts.[68] In the end, it is only civil society, perhaps guided by constitutional scholarship, that may prove able to develop a form of democracy that authentically reflects African worldviews.

7.2.3   Emerging Challenges

It would be possible to survey the manifestation of democracy also in various other parts of the world. For instance, it could be argued that the most spectacular (and oldest) exemplar of electoral democracy involving enormous numbers of voters is that of the United States. Describing the US electoral process, especially presidential elections, as 'spectacular' is justified by factors such as the crucial effects of the vast amounts of money involved,[69] the key role of sensationalist journalistic and social media, systemic acquiescence in spin doctoring methodologies,[70] and the limitation of choices, effectively amounting to a superficial binary alternative between personalities, each nominated by political structures which promote not very precise or predictable policies.[71]

---

[67] Glenn 'Cosmopolitan State' 101.
[68] See e.g. Venter 'Parliamentary Sovereignty or Presidential Imperialism?'.
[69] Howse 'In defense of disruptive democracy' 654:
But the situation in mature liberal democracies today is, arguably, that eligibility for many offices, and certainly the higher offices, is de facto limited to those who either have the ability to attract huge sums of electoral funding (or are privately wealthy) and/or have influence or connections in the established political class, above all the cliques that dominate the leading political parties.
[70] See e.g. Esser, Reinemann & Fan 'Spin Doctors' and Joathan & Lilleker 'Permanent Campaigning' 3:
Research has found it common for governments and representatives to set up communication structures headed by media-relations experts, usually referred to as spin doctors, which attempt to secure positive media coverage, respond to criticism and plan, create and broadcast an official message – processes that have similarities with electoral communication.
[71] See e.g. the following comments by Howse 'In Defense of Disruptive Democracy' 643 made in 2019:

In addition the potential of invasive exploitation of electronic systems relating to elections around the world is accepted as a reality in the twenty-first century.[72] Add to this the advances in technology[73] which allows credible distortion of reality (no longer merely a fictional apocalyptic nightmare, and which obviously holds great potential for the manipulation of credulous public opinion),[74] and one can hardly escape the view that the influence of voters on the manner in which they are governed, is demonstrably waning. These are topics that cannot be pursued here, but the increasing challenges that they present to the integrity of elections should not be ignored when considering the meaning of 'democracy' in constitutional law. For present purposes it is suggested that populism and the nature and diversity of electoral systems are the most prominent factors that have a bearing on the challenges to contemporary democracy.

7.2.3.1 Populism

Many consider the phenomenon 'populism' to represent a unique contemporary challenge to democracy. The recent flood of analyses published by highly regarded constitutional scholars on the subject attests to the high level of concern generated by the phenomenon.[75] When seeking a definition for populism, one is consequently spoilt for choice, but some consensus does exist regarding characteristics frequently associated with the concept.

Paul Blokker also warns that the variety of forms of populism should not be ignored as is often done by 'anti-populists' who tend to equate populism only 'with illiberal, ethno-national, and tendentially authoritarian ideas and practice'. He holds that the overlapping characteristics of populism are

---

> Donald Trump, with the aid of superb campaign manager Kellyanne Conway, exploited the obvious defects of the existing political system in the USA. These defects included the anachronistic Electoral College, voter suppression, and the unresponsiveness of mainstream party politicians to losers from globalization and technological change. Trump was an insider/outsider who mastered the insiders' game and beat them at it. If the Trump Administration is any kind of tyranny it is not a majority tyranny but a minority one; the vast amount of polling that is done in America indicates that there is no majority support for Trump's emblematic policies, such as building a wall with Mexico, fomenting racial confrontation, or overturning established institutions of global governance.

[72] See e.g. Sanger & Perlroth 'Perception Hacks' and Jones 'Defending the 2020 election against hacking'.
[73] See e.g. Barroso 'Technological Revolution, Democratic Recession'.
[74] See e.g. Chesney & Citron 'Deep Fakes'.
[75] See e.g. the papers delivered at symposia on the topic published in 2019 (20) *German Law Journal* (Symposium Title: 'Populism and Constitutionalism') and in 2019 (17(2)) *International Journal of Constitutional Law* 515–660 (Symposium Title: 'Public Law and the New Populism') dealing with the topic in depth.

'a friend-enemy logic in populist political mobilization', 'a critical attitude towards liberal democracy' as being inadequate to promote popular sovereignty, and the emphasis on constituent power. Differentiating between forms of populism, he identifies three 'dimensions': 'inclusionary versus exclusionary forms', 'reformist versus revolutionary forms', and 'national versus transnational manifestations'.[76]

Mark Tushnet distinguishes between a journalistic 'stipulative' approach to populism on the one hand, which refers to a situation where a charismatic leader claims to represent the people in opposition to some kind of an elite, and on the other hand the more academic definitional approach in which criteria like 'a morally pure and unified people' is contrasted with an elite portrayed as corrupt and morally inferior. Populism is seen as a 'mode of political activity' which is given content by 'some version of nationalistic neoliberalism or some version of a similarly nationalistic socialism'.[77]

As Tushnet does, Neil Walker subscribes to Jan-Werner Müller's description of populism as 'a particular moralistic imagination of politics, a way of perceiving the political world that sets a morally pure and unified – but ... ultimately fictional – people against elites who are deemed corrupt or in some other way morally inferior'.[78] Walker rightly laments the reality that scholarship, especially 'the legal academy', is constantly playing a 'game of explanatory "catch-up" with events' when it comes to deal with populism.[79] He then argues that the fashionable preoccupation with populism exposes long-standing tensions and a series of stress factors, or antinomies within modern constitutionalism, and raises 'searching questions to which there are no easy answers'.[80]

Walker's analysis adds justification to the advocacy for reconsidering the meaning of core elements of our constitutional vocabulary in general. This also applies to the manner in which he comments on the linkages between populism and democracy. Citing Paul Blokker, he points out that populists on the one hand express 'a kind of legal resentment against existing structures of constitutional democracy', being 'out of sympathy with deeper features of the modern constitutional inheritance', while simultaneously engaging energetically with the realities of constitutional politics.[81] Walker finds that populism and authoritarian constitutionalism coincide to a large extent, but that there

---

[76] Blokker 'Varieties of Populist Constitutionalism' 342–3.
[77] Tushnet 'Varieties of Populism' 382.
[78] Walker 'Populism and Constitutional Tension' 516 quoting from Müller's book *What is Populism?* (University of Pennsylvania Press, 2016).
[79] Walker 'Populism and Constitutional Tension' 517.
[80] Walker 'Populism and Constitutional Tension' 519.
[81] Walker 'Populism and Constitutional Tension' 519–20.

is a distinction in that, other than in authoritarian constitutionalism, popular sovereignty is a definite component of populist constitutionalism 'because populism assumes that the concrete people are an empirically continuous entity, and so should have their wishes taken account of beyond the constituent moment'.[82] Nevertheless, populism tends, in its one-sided opposition to what they project as an establishment elite and its emphasis on solidarity, towards authoritarianism.

Théo Fournier construes populism as a threat to democracy, the relationship being 'a process of parasitism in which constitutional democracy would be the host and populism would be the parasite'.[83] He describes constitutional democracy, which must balance majority rule and the rule of law, as a 'non-natural ecosystem', therefore being fragile. Populist strategy exploits this fragility by developing a rhetoric tailored to take advantage of the weaknesses inherent in democracy: 'Populist rhetoric refuses any pluralistic vision of the majority. Populist leaders claim to be the spokesperson of the Nation which, because of its unity, can have only one representative'.[84] By manipulating the rule of law and majoritarianism, populists argue that democracy amounts to a tyranny of minorities, and that the (fictional) majority should effect legal and constitutional reforms that would in effect disrupt constitutional democracy.[85]

Subscribing to Alexis de Tocqueville's view of democracy, Robert Howse dampens the unqualified critique of 'disruptive democracy' as populism, because 'in modernity, the People is about the only source of political legitimacy to which one can appeal against the establishment (even if the establishment owes its place in part to democratic institutions)'.[86] He describes some scholarly criticism of populism as 'a sustained defense of elitist liberal democracy', which ignores the merits of other forms of disruptive democratic politics,[87] and denies that there is convincing evidence that making democratic politics less elitist would threaten liberalism.[88] Howse does not seem to subscribe to populism, but he rejects the idea that the 'important agenda of democratic reform' which disrupts liberal democratic politics should be written off as nativist, anti-liberalist, anti-pluralist populism, the real question being 'whether elite liberal democratic politics protect liberty better than stronger, more participatory and representative, i.e. less elitist, forms of democracy,

---

[82] Walker 'Populism and Constitutional Tension' 524–8.
[83] Fournier 'From Rhetoric to Action' 364.
[84] Fournier 'From Rhetoric to Action' 365.
[85] Fournier 'From Rhetoric to Action' 363.
[86] Howse 'In Defense of Disruptive Democracy' 642.
[87] Howse 'In Defense of Disruptive Democracy' 645.
[88] Howse 'In Defense of Disruptive Democracy' 647–50.

and whether elite liberal democratic politics delivers today any of the valid expectations associated with democracy'.[89]

Offensives on the constitutional status quo inspired by various forms of populism in 'mature' democracies, new democracies, and aspirational democracies, but also in undemocratic and illiberal states, have become common. These assaults present much uncertainty about the future of credible democracy (whatever the format). Most certainly populism as a means or process by which comprehensive representation of interests is undermined and replaced by sectional charisma-driven overbearance and suppression of non-aligned interests, should not be described as 'democratic'. The difficulty however lies in the unanswered question of how the progressively apparent shortcomings of systems that identify themselves as 'democratic' might be met. No attempt will be made here to respond to this question, but its mere topicality, accelerated by the wave of populism in many places, must give us additional pause to think (and then say) what we mean in constitutional law when using words such as 'democracy' or 'democratic'.

7.2.3.2 Democratic quality of elections

In the preface to his recently published multi-disciplinary work dealing concretely with representative democracy, Andranik Tangian wrote:

> Today's representative democracy was conceptualized during the American and French Revolutions in the late eighteenth century, when the debates focused primarily on two questions: Who should be represented?, i.e. who is entitled to vote (males or also females, with which civil and property status, etc.) and Who can be a representative? (sons of the constituency or all trusted citizens, taxpayers of a certain level, etc.). The question What should be represented?, i.e. which policies must be pursued on behalf of the electorate, was of secondary importance. Indeed, at that time, the electorate was concerned with very few things like taxation or security, topics like foreign affairs or university regulations were of little interest for most people, and many currently discussed issues, like social security or environmental protection, did not yet exist. Since the population's activities were mainly local and the government operated at a higher level, politicians made decisions with a limited accountability to the electorate.[90]

Tangian deals with the transformation of democratic thinking after the great revolutions, finding that '[i]t turns out that voting, practiced for centuries in simple situations, is not appropriate as a universal tool of democratic decision

---

[89] Howse 'In Defense of Disruptive Democracy' 659–60.
[90] Tangian 'Analytical Theory of Democracy' viii–ix and see also 162–3 concerning the discomfort at the time with popular participation and majority rule.

making'.[91] He, however, seeks to improve democracy by proposing a mixed systemic model combining direct and representative democracy enhanced by policy representation and a 'third vote' mechanism. He points out that different approaches to political philosophy favour different electoral methods by responding differently to the question 'who should be considered, individual electors or the electorate as a single body?' Individual determination favours the election of candidates by name, bringing about a parliament which portrays a miniature of society. Public determination is a method by which candidates are elected on the basis that the policies they promote coincide with the wishes of the electorate.[92] He proposes that the shortcomings of these two methods should be overcome by incorporating in the election process 'a "direct democracy test" – a competitive public examination of the parties, which are evaluated through a special election procedure with embedded referenda'.[93]

These analyses and proposals go to the core of electoral methods and systems and their effects on democracy. In simplified form they can be explained as follows with reference to the general categories of voting methods practised by democracies:

- The representative concept is used in elections where the supposition is that the elected candidate will represent the will of the voters, favouring a system of proportional representation to reflect the nature of society.[94]
- The agency concept of representation assumes representatives to have virtue and competence (similar to lawyers and bankers), mandated by the electorate to act independently, typically employed in a system of constituencies.[95]
- The 'third vote method' is intended to promote policy representation (as distinguished from representatives being (imperfect) intermediaries of the will of the voters and simple majority election often on irrational grounds), facilitated by forms of direct democracy such as plebiscites or referenda on policy issues incorporated in the electoral process.[96]

---

[91] Tangian 'Analytical Theory of Democracy' 177 and the subsequent detailed survey up to page 241, where he concludes that a general understanding of democracy entails elements of government by the people as in Ancient Athens and contemporary Switzerland, a representative system as declared in the recent top-level documents of the EU and the UN, but also 'a demagogic slogan in the struggle for power by opposite parties, as suggested by Weber and Orwell'.
[92] Tangian 'Analytical Theory of Democracy' 504.
[93] Tangian 'Analytical Theory of Democracy' 468.
[94] Tangian 'Analytical Theory of Democracy' 183–4.
[95] Tangian 'Analytical Theory of Democracy' 185–7.
[96] Tangian 'Analytical Theory of Democracy' 354–8.

Tangian's analyses are so comprehensive and persuasive, that no further remarks are required to underscore the fact that, in any constitutional order, there is a direct link between the quality and nature of elections and the quality and nature of the democracy in the particular context. Many related considerations, which will not now be pursued, however remain. Suffice it to simply state that elections that are certified to be 'free and fair' do not in themselves guarantee a credible democratic outcome. The perception of the responsibilities and authority of those who are elected is a determining factor in the consideration of the nature and quality of a democratic order. The condition of the unelected and unrepresented minority remains an intractable democratic conundrum, especially in circumstances where shifts in support for the majority are unlikely. The sheer size of electorates begs the question whether representation is actually achievable in the mega-populations of the twenty-first century. What it comes down to in the end, is the issue of leadership – that indispensable feature of human society. What moves those who seek (also democratic) acquisition of power? To what extent should those who are subject to the decisions and determinations of the leaders be able to inhibit their discretion? How can pathological leadership be avoided?

The problematics surrounding the idea of electoral democracy should not be taken to lead inevitably to the collapse of the concept and its replacement by some other, yet to be discovered mechanism to produce controlled and legitimate governmental authority. What it does lead to is the need, in the constitutional discourse, not to assume that there is a fixed content attached to the expressions 'democratic election' or 'electoral democracy' – possible meanings are legion and one should not leave others with uncertainty about which version reference is being made to when using such expressions.

7.3 THE UTILITY OF 'DEMOCRACY' IN CONSTITUTIONAL LAW

One might bemoan the conceptual fluidity of the democratic notion but cannot escape the fact that constitutional discourse is unable to avoid it. In his analysis of populism, Théo Fournier emphasizes the close linkage between democracy and other key notions of constitutional law:

> Constitutional democracy is a synthesis between the rule of the majority and the rule of law. The rule of the majority proceeds from a procedural vision of democracy. Constitutional democracy elaborates an institutional framework to secure the expression of the majority. This institutional framework consists of free and fair elections to ensure that the expression of the votes actually represents the majority of the citizenry, as well as instruments of representation such as a Parliament used to transform the outcome of the vote into specific policies. The majority in a constitutional democracy can decide the political orientations of the State for the duration of

the mandate ... In a constitutional democracy, the rule of law pillar limits the choices of the majority and protects non-majoritarian individuals from the consequences of not belonging to the majority. The constitution does not only organize majoritarian institutions – its rule of law pillar avoids a coercion of the minority by the majority. The rule of law pillar usually includes a bill of rights and a specific method for constitutional review – a constitutional court being the ideal-type.[97]

However, in this passage various difficulties with our vocabulary are also revealed. There are variations of meaning and substance attributed to 'the rule of law'.[98] The effectiveness, complexity and cost associated with constitutional review as a means of protecting the constitutional rights of minorities are subject to various shades of doubt or qualification in different constitutional orders.[99] Whether (even certified) 'free and fair elections' produce credible representation, even of the majority – which is rarely a consolidated, uniform, united entity – is subject to doubt.[100] In situations where majorities are perpetuated indefinitely due for instance to an inherent inability of minorities to consolidate their opposition (often found in 'new democracies'),[101] it cannot

---

[97] Fournier 'From Rhetoric to Action' 364. Jakab 'What Can Constitutional Law Do?' 7 concisely provided the following widely encountered characterizations of these concepts as point of departure for his discussion of the linkage between democracy and the rule of law, simultaneously referring in a footnote to his own and other publications where 'dilemmas about the definition on the rule of law and democracy' are dealt with:

> In the present paper, democracy means the concurrent presence of the following qualities of any regime: (1) periodically organized fair and free elections, (2) general and equal suffrage, (3) an actually and legally realistic chance of voting the incumbent government out of office, and (4) voters having a real opportunity and the legal means to inform themselves about the performance of the government. Rule of law here means its formal elements in particular, predictability, effectiveness, and clarity as well as substantive elements such as separation of powers and the protection of fundamental rights both in law and in reality. It is evident from the above definitions that the two notions include both factual and legal elements. Of course, this is not the only way to define democracy and the rule of law.

[98] Cf Chapter 8 below.

[99] Cf Chapter 10 below.

[100] In dealing with deliberative democracy, devised to address 'the ignorance and superficiality of the common people', and operating on the basis of representatives voting on alternative propositions, Tangian 'Analytical Theory of Democracy' 218 writes that the role of voting is thereby marginalized:

> Indeed, replacing voting (by secret ballot) with public consensus suppresses the alternative positions of minorities and obscures the true balance of opinions; this runs the risk of turning deliberation into the 'tyranny of majority'. Besides, deliberation is sensitive to rhetorically skilled presenters who can manipulate the audience and, hence, the outcomes.

[101] A typical case in point is South Africa, where the governing formation (the ANC) still markets itself effectively to the demographic majority as a 'revolutionary liberation movement' and has won all regular and well-run 'free and fair' elections since 1994.

be said that election outcomes in for instance constitutional orders established 'as a compromise between the liberationist and liberal narratives'[102] can 'by no means' lead to the oppression of the minority' or that the rule of law protects minorities from the consequences of not belonging to the majority or from coercion of the minority.[103]

A better confirmation that these difficulties are real can hardly be found beyond what John McCormick wrote in 2019:

> A crisis of political accountability plagues contemporary democracy. It has become palpably obvious that elections, even 'free and fair' ones, do not elevate to office individuals who are especially responsive to the political aspirations and expectations of their constituents. Moreover, democratic governments seem decreasingly adept at preventing society's wealthiest members from wielding excessive influence over law- and policy-making.[104] Rather than facilitating popular rule, electoral democracies appear to permit and perhaps even encourage political and economic elites to enrich themselves at the public's expense, and encroach upon the liberty of ordinary citizens. The inability of citizens both to control the behavior of public officials and counteract the power and privilege of the wealthy poses a grave threat to the quality of political representation today; it severely debilitates conditions of liberty and equality within the republics of our age.[105]

And yet, we cannot do without it, as Robert Howse explains:

> Modern (representative) democracy has promised more than a hedge against the purely self-interested rule or exploitative rule of elites, and more than virtual representation – it has also promised government that is meaningfully of, by, and for the People, even if exercised through representative institutions. This is what democrats fought for and sometimes died for in previous centuries in mature liberal democracies, and which is still fought for today in many places. Such government is a logical consequence, arguably, of modernity's rejection of heredity, divine right, aristocratic 'virtue,' tradition, or custom, as valid claims of some to rule over others. We should rule ourselves, not be ruled by our betters. We are citizens, not subjects. No amount of competence or technical knowledge, even if deployed selflessly, can justify overlordship.[106]

One of the problems with the vocabulary of constitutional law is that much of it was not conceived as legal language. 'Democracy' clearly is one of those words. One response against which we need to guard is what Julian Scholtes

---

[102] Croucamp & Malan 'The Theory of Systemic Patronage' 103.
[103] See e.g. Harris 'BEE-ing Chinese'.
[104] South Africa currently provides a typical example of this phenomenon: see e.g. Venter 'State Capture, Corruption, and Constitutionalism'.
[105] McCormick 'The New Ochlophobia?'.
[106] Howse 'In Defense of Disruptive Democracy' 652

calls 'the complacency of legality'.[107] Applied here in simple terms, it is not sufficient to say a particular state is democratic because its constitution says so, or because elections are held. Furthermore, over the time that has elapsed since the conception and constitutionalization of the notion of democracy, it has, with other legal norms, been subjected to unpredictability of how it might be used. What has in fact occurred is 'a massive loss of meaning, due to radical socio-political changes or far-reaching events, and leading to the erosion of our fundamental legal categories and concepts'.[108]

In the end, when one encounters a text or spoken statement produced by a constitutional lawyer in which the word 'democracy' or its derivatives are used, it can mean anything and therefore nothing, except if the author's intention is explained. The addition of adjectives such as 'direct', 'electoral', 'constitutional', 'liberal' (or 'illiberal')[109] can be helpful if the user also explains the intended meaning of the adjective because the combination may also be understood in different ways. When used in constitutional comparison, 'democracy' may first have to be defined meticulously if it is to be useful as *tertium comparationis*.

---

[107] Scholtes 'The Complacency of Legality' 359. On the basis of Joseph de Maistre's question how the people can be sovereign and at the same time not being allowed to exercise their sovereignty, Scholtes responded: 'Normativism does not have an explanation for this. It simply "marginalizes the significance of democratic foundation." Leaning on the complacency of legality, constitutionalism merely assumes that the order is constituted and there is no escaping it.'

[108] Claes, Devroe & Keirsbilck 'The Limits of the Law' 16.

[109] The origin of this notion is ascribed to Zakaria 'The Rise of Illiberal Democracy' 22–3. He described the tendency that he had observed of democracy flourishing while being detached from constitutional liberalism, allowing '[d]emocratically elected regimes, often ones that have been reelected or reaffirmed through referenda' to routinely ignore 'constitutional limits on their power and depriving their citizens of basic rights and freedoms'.

8. Rule of law

According to Nic Barber '[t]he rule of law captures those features of a legal order that are needed for that order to function well'.[1] In an earlier publication Barber argued that 'there are interesting and important differences, as well as marked similarities, between conceptions of the *Rechtsstaat* and conceptions of the rule of law'.[2] Equivalent names for these concepts in other European languages include *état de droit, stato di diritto*, and *el estado de derecho*.

A tendency to either equate or to conceptually merge the notions of the rule of law and the *Rechtsstaat* (literally 'law state' or 'state of law') contributes to the uncertainty of the foundations of the concept. On the one hand, the German term does not translate elegantly into English, and on the other hand its cultural and jurisdictional roots are quite different from those of the rule of law. Although Immanuel Kant never used the word, some attribute the idea of the *Rechtsstaat* to him.[3] It was however Robert von Mohl who coined the term in the first half of the nineteenth century.[4]

The work of the celebrated English constitutional scholar of the late nineteenth century and early twentieth century, Albert Venn Dicey, thrust the idea of the rule of law onto the constitutional stage of the English-speaking world, using the sovereignty of the British parliament as point of departure.[5] Notwithstanding the incompatibility of parliamentary sovereignty with German constitutional law, most Germans use 'rule of law' in English when they actually mean *Rechtsstaat*, or even *Verfassungsstaat*, the latter more accurately translated as 'constitutional state'.

In the context of the European Union, Dimitry Kochenov and Petra Bárd hold that '[t]he essence of the rule of law – which distinguishes it from legality, democracy and other wonderful things – is that the law is constantly in tension with and controlled by other law'.[6] This implies, they go on to say, that *guber-*

---

[1] Barber 'Principles of Constitutionalism' 85.
[2] Barber 'Rechtsstaat and the Rule of Law' 453.
[3] See e.g. Von Hayek 'The Constitution of Liberty' 196–7.
[4] See e.g. Stern 'Staatsrecht' 769, and Scheuner 'Das Wissenschaftliche Lebenswerk von Robert von Mohl'.
[5] Dicey 'Introduction' Chapter IV.
[6] Kochenov & Bárd 'Last Soldier Standing?' 266.

naculum (the law) should always be controlled by *jurisdictio*, law beyond the sovereign's reach.[7]

Martin Krygier, a frequent contributor to the discourse on the rule of law, effectively captured the conceptual problematics we are addressing in this chapter:

> The rule of law is today more talked about in more places by more people than perhaps ever in its history, but that does not mean it is any clearer in meaning or significance, or better understood. Indeed, the term has been put to so many uses in recent years that it is difficult to see how anyone will ever be able plausibly to claim to have cornered the market. Whatever one might propose as the *echt* meaning of the rule of law is precisely that: a proposal. Whether it will and whether it should be accepted, are other matters altogether.[8]

At the level of international law, the United Nations regularly engages in extolling the rule of law, for instance in the preamble of a resolution adopted by the General Assembly on 11 December 2008:[9] '*Reaffirming also* that human rights, the rule of law and democracy are interlinked and mutually reinforcing and that they belong to the universal and indivisible core values and principles of the United Nations.'

If one then wishes to incorporate the rule of law in one's work on constitutional comparison, does the vagueness of the concept render the effort futile? On the other hand, in view of the comprehensive (if not universal) subscription to the idea, can the comparatist afford not to employ it? The question what is to be done with the haziness can however not be ignored.

In an effort to respond to these questions, the first section below will survey recent authoritative engagements intended to attribute meaning and content to the rule of law. In the subsequent section representative examples of endorsements of the rule of law in the constitutional milieu of eight jurisdictions are concisely presented. Against this background a suggestion is made regarding the use of the doctrinal *essentialia* of the rule of law that may be suitable in constitutional comparison.

8.1   ATTRIBUTED MEANINGS

Not surprisingly, scholarship on the rule of law is not limited to, but more concentrated in, the UK and Western Europe, where the notion originated.

---

[7] This distinction is derived from the thirteenth-century writing of Bracton and was brought to modern prominence by McIlwain 'Constitutionalism – Ancient and Modern' (1940) Chapter IV.
[8] Krygier 'Inside the Rule of Law' 77–8.
[9] A/RES/63/128

In 2016 the European Commission for Democracy Through Law (otherwise known as the Venice Commission) of the Council of Europe helpfully published a 'Rule of Law Checklist', identifying 'common features of the Rule of Law, *Rechtsstaat* and *Etat de droit*'.[10] Relying inter alia on the jurisprudence of the European Court of Human Rights, the Commission pointed out that 'the Rule of Law creates a benchmark for the quality of laws protecting human rights',[11] and then goes on to identify five categories of benchmarks and to elaborate on each. The categories are legality, legal certainty, prevention of abuse (misuse) of powers, equality before the law and access to justice.[12]

In their edited volume which investigates the working of the rule of law where state authority can be exercised only to a limited extent, or not at all (a particularly topical theme under the circumstances currently prevailing in a growing number of countries), Linda Hamid and Jan Wouters point out[13] that there is no established definition available for the rule of law, neither in the international, nor the national environments. With reference to the works of Brian Tamanaha,[14] Joseph Raz,[15] and Tom Bingham[16] on the domestic manifestation of the rule of law, and the works of Stéphane Beaulac,[17] Simon Chesterman[18] and Robert McCorquodale[19] on its international application, Hamid and Wouters subscribe to the Venice Commission's identification of the essential elements of the concept. Significantly, they found that, due to the reality that the rule of law is, in its origins and application 'very much State-based', 'a strong RoL at both the national and the international levels

---

[10] Venice Commission 'Rule of Law' 7.
[11] Venice Commission 'Rule of Law' 15.
[12] Venice Commission 'Rule of Law' 17–49.
[13] Hamid & Wouters 'Rule of Law and Areas of Limited Statehood' 10–12.
[14] Tamanaha 'On the Rule of Law', who proposed a distinction between 'formal' or 'thin' aspects of the rule of law and 'substantive' or 'thick' attributes, reminiscent of respectively formal and substantive *Rechtsstaatlichkeit*.
[15] Raz 'The Rule of Law and its Virtue', who presented the rule of law in a positivistic tenor as the rule *by* law, which requires obedience to the law.
[16] Bingham 'The Rule of Law', who associated the rule of law with the protection of human rights.
[17] Beaulac 'The Rule of Law in International Law Today'.
[18] Chesterman 'An International Rule of Law', who argued that the international rule of law should be seen as a political ideal and that 'its applicability to the international level will depend on that ideal being seen as a means rather than an end, as serving a function rather than defining a status'.
[19] McCorquodale 'Defining the International Rule of Law' 279, who wished to show that 'the international rule of law does exist and can be applied internationally, even if it is not yet fully actualized'.

will therefore imply an effective State, in full command of its capacities in both internal and external affairs'.[20]

In an impressive book containing edited contributions to two conferences held in 2017 and 2019 on 'checks and balances in the European legal space', Werner Schroeder addressed the meaning and implications of the rule of law as a value identified in Article 2 of the Treaty of the European Union:

> The Union is founded on the values of respect for human dignity, freedom, democracy, equality, the rule of law and respect for human rights, including the rights of persons belonging to minorities. These values are common to the Member States in a society in which pluralism, non-discrimination, tolerance, justice, solidarity and equality between women and men prevail.[21]

As an amendment to the Amsterdam Treaty, the Lisbon Treaty identified the rule of law as a 'value' instead of (merely?) being a 'principle'. A section of Schroeder's chapter systematically explores the normative character of the rule of law in the EU. He warns against overrating 'terminology issues' in EU law, but finds 'values' in Article 2 to be problematic, 'because it is a meta-legal term'. Values, he argues, being 'beyond the realm of legal norms', must 'guide the individual in decision-making situations to ethically "right" conduct'. Values such as the rule of law, he says, 'are understood as legal norms which do not state specific rights or duties, but which are of a general nature and are in need of being concretised by the legislative, the executive and the judiciary'. Furthermore, as an example of what this means, Schroeder mentions that in the jurisprudence of the Court of Justice of the European Union, the *principle* of legal certainty has been derived from the rule of law (presumably as the guiding *value* (formerly 'principle')). Values in EU law, such as the rule of law, Schroeder construes 'as being ethical, supra-positive norms [having] an orientation and ordering function. They are therefore of an identity-building and legitimacy-creating character'. As a value of EU law, therefore, the rule of law has 'a legal and ethical double-nature. Legal norms concretise values and transform them from the societal system into the legal system'.[22]

Schroeder also construes the rule of law as a value of the EU listed in Article 2 as having a normative character, serving a programmatic function: '... respect by the Member States [for the foundational values] is evoked in Article 2, ... , and for the Union itself this provision serves as characterisation of the classical structural features of the liberal constitutional model', which 'constitutes the

---

[20] Hamid & Wouters 'Rule of Law and Areas of Limited Statehood' 14.
[21] Schroeder 'The Rule of Law As a Value' 108.
[22] Schroeder 'The Rule of Law As a Value' 110–12.

fundament of a membership in the Union'.[23] Where a Member State falls short, there are 'legal consequences as far as [the rule of law] forms the basis of the principle of mutual recognition'.[24]

In his engagement with the basic meaning of the rule of law, Schroeder finds that it has the effect of 'reducing the discretion of public power by subjecting it to means of effective legal and judicial control'. Nevertheless, the broad definition of the concept reveals 'that the rule of law does not constitute a straightforward concept, but rather an aggregate notion for a set of subprinciples which are themselves in need of concretisation depending on the respective context'. The debate on which 'subprinciples' are to be incorporated in the rule of law evokes the distinction between the English legal tendency to emphasize formal legality, whereas the German, Austrian and French read substantive elements of *Rechtsstaatlichkeit* into it.[25] In the end –

> [w]hat remains is the insight that the rule of law constitutes a 'conceptual puzzle' in the Union legal order since there exist different conceptions of its significance and its content beyond its basic meaning that any form of public power must be subordinated to some kind of primary, unchangeable norms. This principle cannot be defined conclusively and it may evolve over time.[26]

For those desiring clarity regarding the meaning of the rule of law the intense engagement with the notion in EU law is encouraging, perhaps eventually also for the purposes of its application in other parts of the world, but the conclusion that, even in Europe, it still 'constitutes a conceptual puzzle', does not provide much gratification. Nevertheless, pledges to and endorsement of the rule of law abound in many constitutional environments around the world.

8.2 CONTEXTUAL VARIATIONS

It is instructive to survey, even briefly, the manner in which the rule of law is understood and utilized in different settings around the world.

Since 2008, the World Justice Project, which describes itself as 'an independent, multidisciplinary organization working to advance the rule of law worldwide', and 'to create knowledge, build awareness, and stimulate action to advance the rule of law worldwide' annually publishes its 'Rule of Law Index

---

[23] Schroeder 'The Rule of Law As a Value' 113.
[24] Schroeder 'The Rule of Law As a Value' 114.
[25] Schroeder 'The Rule of Law As a Value' 117–18.
[26] Schroeder 'The Rule of Law As a Value' 122.

Reports' based on extensive surveys involving 'contributing experts' working in the 128 countries being indexed.[27]

In view of the acknowledgement that 'the rule of law is notoriously difficult to define and measure', the 'conceptual framework' within which the *Index* operates is set out in detail in its introductory pages.[28] First, four 'universal principles' are propounded, namely accountability, just laws, open government and accessible and impartial dispute resolution. These principles are then developed into eight factors, disaggregated into 44 sub-factors to form the framework for the annual survey of the status of the rule of law in each country. The factors that are assessed are constraints on government powers, absence of corruption, open government, fundamental rights, order and security, regulatory enforcement, civil justice, and criminal justice. The *Index* ranks the surveyed jurisdictions (Denmark having been ranked number 1 in 2020 and Venezuela number 128).

The manner in which the rule of law is perceived and employed in the constitutional law of a few selected jurisdictions should provide us with further insights pertinent to our present enquiry.

8.2.1 The United Kingdom[29]

When the Westminster Parliament adopted the Constitutional Reform Act of 2005 which restructured the highest echelons of the British judicial system, it found it necessary to begin in section 1 with the following qualification:

> This Act does not adversely affect –
> (a) the existing constitutional principle of the rule of law, or
> (b) the Lord Chancellor's existing constitutional role in relation to that principle.

The only other reference in the Act to the rule of law is in section 17, which requires the Lord High Chancellor to swear an oath to 'respect the rule of law'. What this provision means was addressed by Chief Justice Lord Bingham in a lecture delivered in 2006. Lord Bingham wrote that, despite the fact that the British courts 'routinely invoked' the rule of law, 'they have not explained what they meant by the expression, and well-respected authors have thrown doubt on its meaning and value'.[30] Against this background he proceeded to provide an exposition of his view on the matter: 'The core of the existing principle is, I suggest, that all persons and authorities within the state, whether

---

[27] World Justice Project 'Rule of Law Index 2020' 202.
[28] World Justice Project 'Rule of Law Index 2020' 9–11.
[29] Ranked no 13 by the World Justice Project 'Rule of Law Index 2020'.
[30] Bingham 'The Rule of Law' 67–8.

public or private, should be bound by and entitled to the benefit of laws publicly and prospectively promulgated and publicly administered in the courts.' To this he added: 'I doubt if anyone would suggest that this statement, even if accurate as one of general principle, could be applied without exception or qualification.'[31]

In the subsequent pages Lord Bingham dealt in some detail with 'breaking down' the principle of the rule of law in various 'sub-rules'. These rules, he suggested, are (key words italicized here) that the law must be *accessible* and so far as possible *intelligible*, *clear* and *predictable*; questions of legal right and liability should ordinarily be resolved by application of the law and *not the exercise of discretion*; the laws of the land should *apply equally* to all, save to the extent that objective differences justify differentiation; the law must afford adequate protection of *fundamental human rights*; means must be provided for *resolving*, without prohibitive cost or inordinate delay, bona fide *civil disputes* which the parties themselves are unable to resolve; ministers and public officers at all levels must *exercise the powers* conferred on them *reasonably*, in *good faith*, for the purpose for which the powers were conferred and *without exceeding the limits* of such powers, thus reflecting the 'well-established and familiar' grounds of judicial review; *adjudicative procedure*s provided by the state should be *fair*, and the existing principle of the rule of law requires compliance by the state with its *obligations in international law*.[32]

To these sub-rules Lord Bingham added that, although this is not generally agreed, 'it seems to me that the rule of law does depend on an unspoken but fundamental bargain between the individual and the state, the governed and the governor, by which both sacrifice a measure of the freedom and power which they would otherwise enjoy'.[33] Lord Bingham's article was soon cited in the Queen's Bench Division,[34] and he himself, presiding over the Lords of Appeal, was called upon to give an opinion on the appeal from the Queen's Bench in the matter.[35]

Besides the disturbing facts of the *Corner House* case (revealing some brutal realities surrounding the global arms trade),[36] both these judgments painfully demonstrate the weaknesses of the rule of law doctrine attributable to its nebulousness. The Queen's Bench for instance, relying on its 'responsibility

---

[31] Bingham 'The Rule of Law' 69.
[32] Bingham 'The Rule of Law' 69–82.
[33] Bingham 'The Rule of Law' 84.
[34] *R (Corner House Research & another) v Director of the Serious Fraud Office* [2008] EWHC 714 (Admin).
[35] *R (Corner House Research & others) v Director of the Serious Fraud Office* [2008] UKHL 60.
[36] Discussed in Venter 'Arms Deals'.

to secure the rule of law', found that the impugned conduct of a senior government official 'failed to recognise that the rule of law required the decision ... to be reached as an exercise of independent judgment, in pursuance of the power conferred by statute'.[37] Lord Bingham however disagreed: 'The issue in these proceedings is not whether [the] decision was right or wrong, nor whether the Divisional Court or the House agrees with it, but whether it was a decision which the Director was lawfully entitled to make. Such an approach involves no affront to the rule of law, to which the principles of judicial review give effect'.[38]

8.2.2   Japan[39]

In 2013 Dimitri Vanoverbeke assessed Japan's campaign since the 1990s to build legal capacity in the East Asian region, thereby becoming an 'exporter' of the rule of law in the region. Being the third-ranking economy of the world, Japan is deemed to be well placed to promote the idea that the rule of law is an essential building block for economic development, but is competing against China with its economy's second world ranking, but pursuing a different approach.[40] By the end of the twentieth century, 'Rule of law became domestically and internationally the corner stone for Japan's foreign policy aiming at forging a "new Japan in the twenty-first century"' as 'an alternative to the efforts by the US/IMF and to the Chinese pragmatic approach, in efforts to build an environment favorable for economic growth in a global economy'.[41] Thus, the rule of law is promoted as a means for the achievement of economic prosperity.

In 1990 Noriho Urabe opened his comparative discussion of the rule of law by stating that 'it seems that in Japan the term "Rule of Law" (ho no shihai) is used less often than the word *Rechtsstaat* (hochi-koku or hochi kokka), or "state based on law" or "ruled by law"', and went on to explain:

> The *hochi kokka* means something like a state that preserves the public peace or protects people from crime. This is far different from the Anglo-American concept of the Rule of Law. Therefore, when Japanese legal scholars discuss the Rule of Law, the first problem to be discussed is the difference between the Rule of Law and the *Rechtsstaat*, both of which have been imported into Japanese law despite their disparate origins in Anglo-American and German law.[42]

---

[37] Paras 170 and 171 of the judgment (note 34 above).
[38] Para 41 of the judgment (note 35 above).
[39] Ranked no 15 by the World Justice Project 'Rule of Law Index 2020'.
[40] Vanoverbeke 'Exporting the rule of law' 368–69.
[41] Vanoverbeke 'Exporting the rule of law' 370–1.
[42] Urabe 'Rule of Law and Due Process' 61.

Vanoverbeke found that in Japan, the rule of law differs in practice from other jurisdictions in that it is very difficult for individuals to sue state authorities successfully, and, although the rule of law 'is discussed as a protection against abuses by state authority ... very exceptionally the concept of the rule of law is used in connection with human rights and democracy despite persisting issues with e.g. the death penalty, human trafficking and minorities'. Nevertheless, he concluded that '[t]he rule of law is indeed an ambivalent concept in Japan but maybe this is an advantage for Japan as an exporter of the rule of law'.[43]

8.2.3   United States of America[44]

Citing the iconic 1803 judgment in *Marbury v Madison*, Robin Charlow closely associated the American notion of the rule of law with the primacy and supremacy of the Constitution: 'Our Constitution also serves as a universal rule of law. We all agree that the Constitution governs everyone and that no one, not even our highest and mightiest officials, is exempt from its dictates', but then recognizes the difficulty that, 'in a fashion quite perplexing to Continentals, our constitutional rule of law is incredibly indeterminate. The sparse and often enigmatic words in the text of our Constitution permit many and diverse interpretations'.[45]

The American doctrine on rule of law seems to amount to an affirmation of the binding nature of the law, the highest source of which is the Constitution. The following description on the 'US Courts' website seems to confirm this:

> Rule of law is a principle under which all persons, institutions, and entities are accountable to laws that are:
> - Publicly promulgated
> - Equally enforced
> - Independently adjudicated
> - And consistent with international human rights principles.[46]

---

[43] Vanoverbeke 'Exporting the rule of law' 380–1.
[44] Ranked no 21 by the World Justice Project 'Rule of Law Index 2020'.
[45] Charlow 'America's Constitutional Rule of Law' 90. See also Charlow 'American Constitutional Analysis'.
[46] US Courts www.uscourts.gov/educational-resources/educational-activities/overview-rule-law (accessed 12 March 2021).

The American Supreme Court frequently associates the rule of law with *stare decisis*. A recent example:

> In the words of THE CHIEF JUSTICE, *stare decisis*' 'greatest purpose is to serve a constitutional ideal – the rule of law.' *Citizens United v. Federal Election Comm'n*, 558 U. S. 310, 378 (2010) (concurring opinion).
> This Court has repeatedly explained that *stare decisis* 'promotes the evenhanded, predictable, and consistent development of legal principles, fosters reliance on judicial decisions, and contributes to the actual and perceived integrity of the judicial process'.[47]

In the United States the rule of law therefore serves the purpose of ensuring that the binding content of the laws is accessible to all, including those empowered to exercise authority under the laws. Put differently, the American rule of law's primary functions appear to be legal certainty and accountability.

8.2.4 South Africa[48]

Because the rule of law has been enshrined as a foundational value in the relatively young constitutional order of South Africa,[49] the notion has drawn a comparatively extensive amount of judicial attention.

A 1997 dictum of the Constitutional Court established a direct link between the concepts 'rule of law' and 'constitutional state',[50] which has since then

---

[47] Kavanaugh, J concurring in part in *Ramos v Louisiana* 590 U.S. ___ (2020) 2.
[48] Ranked no 45 by the World Justice Project 'Rule of Law Index 2020'.
[49] Section 1 of the *Constitution of the Republic of South Africa*, 1996, which is strongly entrenched against amendment by section 74(1), provides (italics added):
  The Republic of South Africa is one, sovereign, democratic state *founded on the following values*:
  (a) Human dignity, the achievement of equality and the advancement of human rights and freedoms.
  (b) Non-racialism and non-sexism.
  (c) Supremacy of the constitution and *the rule of law*.
  (d) Universal adult suffrage, a national common voters roll, regular elections and a multi-party system of democratic government, to ensure accountability, responsiveness and openness.
[50] *Prinsloo v Van der Linde* 1997 (3) SA 1012 para 25 (italics added):
  In regard to mere differentiation *the constitutional state* is expected to act in a rational manner. It should not regulate in an arbitrary manner or manifest 'naked preferences' that serve no legitimate governmental purpose, for that would be inconsistent with the *rule of law and the fundamental premises of the constitutional state*. The purpose of this aspect of equality is, therefore, to ensure that the state is bound to function in a rational manner. This has been said to promote the need for governmental action to relate to a defensible vision of the public good, as well as to enhance the coherence and integrity of legislation.

frequently been cited and relied upon by the Court.[51] By 2012 an analysis of the Constitutional Court's jurisprudence could confirm that the notion of South Africa as a constitutional state had been developed in the process of interpretatively marrying *Rechtsstaatlichkeit* and the rule of law:

> (T)he South African constitutional state may be defined as a state in which: (a) the constitution prevails over all law and all actions of the state; (b) fundamental rights are acknowledged and protected through the independent authority of the judiciary to enforce the bill of rights and the constitution; (c) separation of powers is maintained; (d) all government action is required to be legally justified; (e) the state has a duty to protect fundamental rights; (f) legal certainty is promoted; (g) democracy and the rule of law are maintained; (h) a specific set of legal principles apply; and (i) an objective, normative system of values guides the executive, legislature, and the judiciary.[52]

The South African rule of law therefore incorporates both the formal ('thin') and substantive ('thick') elements of the rule of law. The link between *stare decisis* and the rule of law is also emphasized from time to time, but only as one of its concrete characteristics.[53]

8.2.5　China[54]

In 2006 Wenxian Zhang of the Jilin University in Changchun, China wrote about 'constructing a socialist rule of law' against the background of the exigencies of globalization, finding that globalization of the economy, public affairs, human rights, environment, and law were 'pushing forward the transformation of China's rule of law'.[55] He identified three relevant phases of legal reform, beginning with the constitutional revision in the late 1970s, leading to the new constitution of 1982, representing the replacement of 'the wrong class struggle centered path' with 'an economic construction centered strategy' and enabling legislative reforms 'signalling the twilight of the spring for the rule of law'.[56]

The second reform in the 1990s took the form of adapting the constitution and the legal system to support a socialist market economy, conceived as a shift from a 'state-run economy' to a 'state-owned economy' allowing for private

---

[51] See e.g. *Mahlangu v Minister of Labour* 2021 (2) SA 54 (CC) paras 71 and 154.
[52] Venter 'South Africa: a Diceyan Rechtsstaat?' 736.
[53] See e.g. *Sonke Gender Justice NPC v President of the Republic of South Africa* 2021 (3) BCLR 269 (CC) para 47.
[54] Ranked no 88 by the World Justice Project 'Rule of Law Index 2020'.
[55] Zhang 'China's Rule of Law' 472.
[56] Zhang 'China's Rule of Law' 480–1.

involvement in economic operations, the protection of human rights and the inviolability of 'private lawful properties'.[57] No doubt these reforms created an environment in which China could build its still burgeoning economy.

The third reform Zhang identified as getting underway was inspired by globalization and involves legal adaptation to conform to the requirements of China's membership of the World Trade Organization and 'its increasing integration into the structure of global governance'. This third phase is manifested in the 'reformation of political and legal systems', the restructuring of the legal system to account for the country's international obligations and internal legal adjustments, and the transformation of the legal culture ('legal spirits') to 'be associated with market economy, democratic politics, spiritual civilization and eco-civilization and rational spirits and values that correspond to the pattern and trend of globalization'.[58]

Writing in 2019 in a journal sponsored by the China Society for Human Rights Studies, Zhang further reported:

> China has met the basic needs of over a billion people, has basically made it possible for people to live decent lives, and will soon bring the building of a moderately prosperous society to a successful completion. The needs that have to be met to enable people to live better lives are increasingly broad. Not only have people's material and cultural needs grown; their demands for democracy, rule of law, fairness and justice, security, and a better environment are increasing. The new and incremental needs for a better life of the people are human rights needs. To respond to the people's demands for democracy, the rule of law, fairness, justice, security, dignity, the environment and development is to respond to the people's high-standard demands for human rights.[59]

From the internal perspective of a scholar with express sympathies for the powers that be in China, these comments are enlightening. They exude an ambition for progress towards a universally accepted doctrine on the rule of law, albeit from a subjective, if not unique, socialist point of view.

Less sympathetic, but also hopeful, is the perspective from Hong Kong of Clara Wong, writing about the introduction of 'e-Justice' composed of 'e-Litigation, e-Discovery, e-Filing, e-Evidence, e-Service, e-Hearing and e-Judgment' as part of China's ongoing reform process. She concluded that the e-Justice reform is intended to strengthen the 'rein' of the Chinese Communist Party and improve its legitimacy, but nevertheless, 'it is hoped that the reform

---

[57] Zhang 'China's Rule of Law' 482.
[58] Zhang 'China's Rule of Law' 482–5.
[59] Zhang 'Human Rights Jurisprudence' 270.

would provide greater incentives for China to undertake more substantive reforms, and eventually steer China towards a "thicker" form of rule of law'.[60]

That the Chinese Communist party-state is in the process of developing its own version of the rule of law in order to enhance its international and internal acceptance is interesting: could this be the beginnings of a new, 'socialist' version of an indeterminate global notion of governmental legitimacy?

8.2.6 Russia[61]

Various translations into English (italics added) of the first sentence of Article 1 of the Constitution of the Russian Federation of 1993 are available: Russia is 'a democratic federal *law-bound State* with a republican form of government';[62] 'a democratic federative *law-governed state* with a republican form of government';[63] 'a democratic, federal, *rule-of-law state*'.[64] Gordon Smith stated in 2008 that 'The meaning of "rule-of-law state" (*pravovoe gosudarstvo*) also remains ill-defined and less than fully realized in practice',[65] and offered the following conclusion at the end of the book:

> The Constitution itself was the product of a violent confrontation between President El'tsin and remnants of resistance in the Russian parliament in 1993. From this perspective and in light of the track records of other democratizing states, the development of constitutionalism and rule of law in Russia has been remarkable. Yet, not surprisingly, it also remains a work in progress.[66]

Some six years later, Gadis Abdullaevich Gadzhiev, judge of the Constitutional Court of the Russian Federation, confirmed the conceptual, linguistic and translation difficulties surrounding the notion of the rule of law in Russia, noting that rule of law is usually considered in Russian constitutional doctrine to be an element of the broader concept of the 'legal state' (*Rechtsstaat*) both encapsulated in *verhovenstvo prava* (primacy of the law).[67] Gadzhiev pointed

---

[60] Wong 'E-Justice Reform in China'.
[61] Ranked no 94 by the World Justice Project 'Rule of Law Index 2020'.
[62] See www.constitution.ru/en/10003000-02.htm (accessed 15 March 2021).
[63] HeinOnline 'World Constitutions Illustrated – Constitution of the Russian Federation, 1993 – As Amended to 2020 – Constitutional Court [consulted 2020] – English' (15 March 2021). The German translation (Constitutional Court [consulted 2021]) uses the phrase 'demokratischer föderativer Rechtsstaat', and the French translation (Constitutional Court [consulted 2021]) the translation is 'un État démocratique, fédéral, un État de droit'.
[64] Smith & Sharlet 'Russia and its Constitution' xxiii.
[65] Smith & Sharlet 'Russia and its Constitution' xxiv.
[66] Smith & Sharlet 'Russia and its Constitution' 192–3.
[67] Gadzhiev 'The Russian Judicial Doctrine of the Rule of Law' 209–12.

out that '[t]he rule of law is also radically different from the system of views represented by such legal notion as *verhovenstvo zakona* (the supremacy of statute law)',[68] that various methodological problems still need to be solved to establish a Russian model of the rule of law, including 'ontological problems' such as the nature of human rights, justice and the law.[69] Perhaps idealistically, in Gadzhiev's opinion '[t]he nucleus of the rule of law idea in Russia is the belief that the independence of the court as a constitutional principle is one of the primary pillars of constitutionalism'.[70]

Whether current Russian politics is or will become conducive to the further development of judicial independence, a consistent rule of law concept, and supportive constitutional doctrine, remains an open question.[71]

8.3 ESSENTIALS OF AN OVERBURDENED CONCEPT

No doubt, when one refers to the 'rule of law' the intention is to convey a complex of legal conceptions, mostly – but not exclusively – related to constitutional law. Every user of the expression may have a different rendering of this multifaceted notion in mind. For the purposes of constitutional comparison it is not tenable (as it may have been some time ago) to limit the meaning of the concept to its Diceyan roots, nor to consider it to be a full substitute for either or both *Rechtsstaatlichkeit* and *Verfassungsstaatlichkeit*, although much of the substance attributed in some representations to the rule of law seems to have been sourced from the extensive German theorization on the ideal formal ('thin') and substantive or material ('thick') characteristics of the constitutional state.

From the brief survey above it may also be deduced that the rule of law should not be seen as a universal remedy for anything or everything that can go wrong in society. Thomas von Danwitz, judge at the Court of Justice of the European Union, aptly captured this perspective in 2014:

> [E]ven in democratic societies in which the rule of law is traditionally respected in principle, it is not self-evident that the rule of law will in fact be observed when legislation has to meet new challenges. In that respect it should be stressed that the democratic nature and all public transparency of the political process are not sufficient to ensure the rule of law. For the protection of minorities and, in particular,

---

[68] Gadzhiev 'The Russian Judicial Doctrine of the Rule of Law' 219.
[69] Gadzhiev 'The Russian Judicial Doctrine of the Rule of Law' 220–1.
[70] Gadzhiev 'The Russian Judicial Doctrine of the Rule of Law' 221.
[71] See e.g. Popova 'Putin-Style Rule of Law'.

of individuals, a reasonably intense judicial review both of individual decisions and legislative acts appears indispensable to effectively ensure the rule of law.[72]

It seems to be impossible in contemporary constitutional discourse to avoid reference to the rule of law. It is clearly unacceptable to allow comparatists to impose their own jurisdictional or other subjective connotations of the concept on the rest of the constitutional community. Due to the diversity of possible meanings that can be attributed to the idea, it is equally unacceptable for anyone to assume that some unexplained preferred version should be accepted by others without clear delineation.

Despite the flood of characterizations of the rule of law, which, if compiled, produces an impressively long list, it may be possible to extract the most essential elements to serve as a common basis for the purposes of mutually understandable communication in constitutional comparison. Viewed from a perspective of outcome, rather than prerequisites, and merging formal and material notions, it is suggested that the expression 'rule of law' universally evokes at least two attributes of a constitutional order being associated with the expression: *legal certainty* and *non-arbitrariness*.

Legal certainty requires access of everyone who is subject to or affected by a legal norm. This means that the norm concerned in terms of which the state is empowered to exercise authority must reasonably be knowable and stable.

Non-arbitrariness is the legal corrective on unchecked discretionary conduct. This means that the rule of law can only be said to be operational in a constitutional order to the extent that objective legal criteria have to be complied with for the discretionary exercise of state authority for it to be binding. This is usually manifested as a legal limitation on the exercise of executive and administrative power.

In short: the rule of law is absent from a constitutional order where the state and its organs exercise power in unpredictable ways which cannot be restrained effectively by legal means. Conceptions of constitutionalism, which is the topic of the next chapter, depend in many cases on some notion of the rule of law.

---

[72] Von Danwitz 'The Rule of Law in the Recent Jurisprudence of the ECJ' 1346.

9. Constitutionalism

According to Maurizio Fioravanti constitutionalism is all about the limitation of public powers, and it developed along with the modern state itself.[1]

Anyone interested in constitutional comparison cannot escape dealing with constitutionalism.[2] In a similar vein as with several other concepts with which this book is concerned, constitutionalism is often identified, or annexed ideologically, by attaching adjectives to it, such as 'liberal' (and 'illiberal'),[3] 'political', 'legal',[4] 'authoritarian',[5] 'popular',[6] 'revolutionary',[7] and more.[8] A recent addition to this list is 'transformative constitutionalism', which originated in the 1990s in the milieu of the then new South African constitution,[9] and has since been received and adapted for the purposes of constitutional comparison (at least) in Latin America.[10]

There is a significant theoretical overlap between constitutionalism and various other concepts discussed in this book,[11] which suggests that it often serves the purpose of a terminological scaffold supporting (especially liberal)

---

[1] Fioravanti 'Constitutionalism' 263.

[2] Aspiring to make a contribution to the field of constitutional comparison, I have made various published attempts at coming to grips with this concept. See e.g. Venter 'The Many Faces of Constitutionalism' and Venter 'Constitutionalism and Religion' Chapter 3.

[3] See e.g. Drinóczi & Bień-Kacała 'Illiberal Constitutionalism'.

[4] See e.g. Latham-Gambi 'Political Constitutionalism and Legal Constitutionalism'.

[5] See e.g. García & Frankenberg 'Authoritarian Constitutionalism'.

[6] See e.g. Gargarella 'Popular Constitutionalism'.

[7] See e.g. Albert 'Revolutionary Constitutionalism'.

[8] See e.g. Tushnet 'Varieties of Constitutionalism' and Frankenberg 'Between Magic and Deceit' 94–107.

[9] See e.g. Venter 'The Limits of Transformation'.

[10] See e.g. Vilhena, Baxi & Viljoen 'Transformative Constitutionalism'; Riegner 'Transformativer Konstitutionalismus'; Von Bogdandy 'Überstaatlicher Transformativer Konstitutionalismus'; and Samararatne 'From South Africa to Sri Lanka'.

[11] For instance, in a contribution to a law journal based in Ethiopia, Bazezew 'Constitutionalism' 359, Maru Bazezew presented the following as basic elements of constitutionalism: popular sovereignty, separation of powers (checks and balances), responsible and accountable government, rule of law, an independent judiciary, respect for individual rights, respect for self-determination, civilian control of the military and police governed by law, and judicial control.

constitutional discussion. Constitutional comparison therefore has no choice but to scramble around on this scaffold in an effort to produce comprehensible results holding value for an understanding of the field of constitutional law and its further development.

In the first section below the vast range of meanings attributed to 'constitutionalism' is probed, revealing its terminological inexactitude. The second section highlights a few examples of regional and jurisdictional applications of the concept. Given the fluidity of the term, the chapter ends with some thoughts on how it might be employed in constitutional comparison, taking note of the attendant caveats.

9.1 ATTRIBUTED MEANINGS

In her textbook aimed 'to handily introduce the science of constitutions and western constitutional law to university under-graduate and graduate students',[12] Andrea Buratti attributes connotations of the historical and conceptual essentials of North Atlantic constitutional law to constitutionalism in the following definition:

> The notion of 'constitutionalism' identifies a political doctrine that first appeared in England during the seventeenth century, and quickly spread throughout North America and Western Europe, becoming the leading political doctrine of the three revolutions of the Modern Age.
> Since its origins, constitutionalism has striven to achieve the goal of **limiting political power** through the acquisition of three legal tools: (i) the adoption of a **written constitution**, prescriptive toward the institutions of the state and suitable to act as paramount law upon its acts; (ii) the **separation of powers of the state**; (iii) the legal protection of a wide range of **individual rights**. Constitutionalism is, therefore, the legal outcome of philosophical doctrines of the Modern Age – jusnaturalism, contractarianism, and their political synthesis, liberalism – with which it shares not only theoretical premises, but also political goals.[13]

A distinct difficulty with the concept is that, beyond the obvious suggestion that it involves some notion of a *constitution*, it does not, on the face of it, reveal specific qualities. The adjective 'constitutional' is linked to '-ism', implying doctrine, theory, system, practice, or characteristics. This generality (vagueness if you will) allows for almost unbounded possibilities of signification of the term. Günter Frankenberg for instance finds an explanation for a linkage by authoritarian regimes with constitutionalism in the attractiveness

---

[12] Buratti 'Western Constitutionalism' v.
[13] Buratti 'Western Constitutionalism' 2.

of using 'constitutions as popular signs of decorum that offer another imaginative alternative to the one inhabited in the everyday'.[14]

In most cases where constitutionalism is invoked, it suggests the existence of a doctrine involving constitutional elements or characteristics, and, except when mustered to highlight or critique shortcomings indicated by an adjective such as 'authoritarian', it is usually meant to indicate a good or desirable state of affairs. Nevertheless, discussions of constitutionalism frequently begin with an acknowledgment of the indeterminacy of the notion, followed by filling it with some characteristics:

> Thus constitutionalism is a rather diffuse concept that seeks to ensure that certain values predominate in the conduct of government by organs of the state, and to overcome obstacles to that end with which Locke and Montesquieu were familiar. The values include legality (constitutionality) and the rule of law, but no less fundamental are democratic accountability, fundamental rights (especially liberty), and avoidance of arbitrary power; and among the favoured methods of modern constitutionalists to give effect to these values is use of the judicial system.[15]

The 'fillings' of constitutionalism vary, but there is considerable consensus that liberal democracy rooted in West European constitutional, philosophical and political history up to at least the middle of the twentieth century serves as general point of departure. Günter Frankenberg brilliantly (and critically) summarizes the 'orthodoxy of constitutionalism' in a few pages,[16] the core being 'the assumption that (modern) constitutionalism brings forth an institutional ensemble forging a free political order sustained by a coherent scaffolding of legality/constitutionality – constitutional democracy'.[17]

Elsewhere[18] I comparatively surveyed the application of the notion in various constitutional orders in an attempt to extract typical elements of constitutionalism. A tabulated presentation of the findings was prefaced with the remark that the elements needed to be understood to have 'fuzzy boundaries and variable descriptions because different proponents of constitutionalism see

---

[14] Frankenberg 'Authoritarian Constitutionalism' 36.
[15] Ziegler, Baranger & Bradley 'Constitutionalism and the Role of Parliaments' 6–7.
[16] Frankenberg 'Authoritarian Constitutionalism' 7–10. In the text supported by note 58 at 12–13 Frankenberg mentions the diverse forms that constitutionalism has taken since the nineteenth century: 'They display a wide range of – liberal, illiberal, and aliberal – scaffolds buttressing the constitutional construction of political authority. They testify to constitutionalism's astounding flexibility as a normative framework for democracy, its plasticity as an ideological cover narrative of political authority, and its scaffolding of legality for state action (performance).'
[17] Frankenberg 'Authoritarian Constitutionalism' 8.
[18] Venter 'Constitutionalism and Religion' 46–83.

things differently', but that, for the purpose, it seemed useful to focus on the rule of law/*Rechtsstaat*/constitutional state as a core doctrinal element. From that exercise it emerged that one might distinguish between doctrinal components, substantive (normative) qualities, and structural (formal) elements of constitutionalism. Rule of law (and its siblings), democracy and popular sovereignty belong in the doctrinal category, substantive qualities include non-arbitrary government, legal certainty and the separation of powers, and the structural elements include independence of the judiciary, the maintenance of public order, protection of fundamental rights, legitimate democratic elections, and representative and accountable government. This should not be understood to be an exhaustive list of the qualities of constitutionalism, because various further aspirational characteristics and elements may be added as they are found in the literature and assorted constitutional arrangements. Nevertheless, the listed elements frequently crop up in discussions involving liberal constitutionalism.

The American constitutional historian CH McIlwain undertook a remarkable pre-war study of the development of 'the Anglo-Saxon brand' of constitutionalism (which he defined as having one essential quality, namely 'a legal limitation on government').[19] His focus was primarily on English constitutional law. In a series of lectures in 1938 and 1939 McIlwain emphasized the need to counter arbitrariness by balancing political power by legal means:

> The people have now replaced the king in these political matters of government; but even in a popular state, such as we trust ours is, the problem of law *versus* will remains the most important of all practical problems. We must leave open the possibility of an appeal from the people drunk to the people sober, if individual and minority rights are to be protected in the periods of excitement and hysteria from which we unfortunately are not immune. The long and fascinating story of the balancing of *jurisdictio* and *gubernaculum*, of which I could give only the barest outline here, should be, if we could study it with an open mind, of some help in adjusting and maintaining today the delicate balance of will and law, the central practical problem of politics now as it has been in all past ages. The two fundamental correlative elements of constitutionalism for which all lovers of liberty must yet fight are the legal limits to arbitrary power and a complete political responsibility of government to the governed.[20]

Constitutionalism as a catch-all concept reflecting liberal democracy has also been employed as a means to problematize some of the characteristics of liberal democracy, for instance Martin Loughlin and Neil Walker's statement

---

[19] McIlwain 'Constitutionalism – Ancient and Modern' (1940, 1947) 21: 'it is a legal limitation on government; it is the antithesis of arbitrary rule; its opposite is despotic government, the government of will instead of law'.

[20] McIlwain 'Constitutionalism – Ancient and Modern' (1940, 1947) 137.

that 'Modern constitutionalism is underpinned by two fundamental though antagonistic imperatives: that governmental power ultimately is generated from the "consent of the people" and that, to be sustained and effective, such power must be divided, constrained, and exercised through distinctive institutional forms'.[21] In his discussion of the paradox of constitutionalism discernible in the proliferation of populism, Julian Scholtes found that the 'emergence of populism as a political force does not create any new tensions, it merely highlights the tension that is inherent in constitutional democracy in the first place'.[22]

The idea of a constitution often (perhaps usually) provides an anchor for the idea of constitutionalism, despite the absence of universal consensus on the meaning and content of 'the constitution'.[23] Riccardo Prandini's observations on the nature of constitutions are useful as a conceptual framework (although we should here avoid becoming immersed in the intricacies of political sociology). Prandini believes that constitutions perform four main functions, namely establishing 'a legitimacy principle for political power', regulating 'the conditions for the real exercise of powers', instituting 'the boundaries between the political system and the other subsystems (e.g. civil society)', and determining 'the ultimate goals of the polity'. He finds that the 'modern territorial-state configuration' has spread around the world in the twentieth century, causing constitutionalism to have become 'the most influential frame of reference for a legitimate regulatory framework of any national political community'.[24] Prandini opened his chapter with the following interesting comment:

> We are living through a new constitutional era, and we are overwhelmed by strange constitutional–constituent experiences. It is not a time of exceptional politics, as exists during the founding episodes of modern constitutions. It does not represent a demise of constitutionalism, since there is no such unique real thing to be demised. And it does not represent a transmutation because nothing is really mutating: there is only an emerging new form. We are facing a living and latent process of morphogenesis which reframes the very idea of constitution in a way which is more adequate to world society.[25]

---

[21] Loughlin & Walker 'Paradox of Constitutionalism' 1.
[22] Scholtes 'The Complacency of Legality' 360.
[23] Witness e.g. Nic Barber's remark in Barber 'Constitutional State' 75:
The content of the constitutions of states is remarkably unclear. We should anticipate that particular constitutional rules will be disputed and debated – such rules are, after all, often vague or incomplete – but even the scope of the constitution appears ambiguous. It is far from obvious what rules should be counted as part of the state's constitution, and what rules, in contrast, act on the state indirectly, mediated through other institutions and groups.
[24] Prandini 'Morphogenesis' 312.
[25] Prandini 'Morphogenesis' 309.

It may be that in the decade since the publication of these observations 'exceptional politics' have become more prevalent, breeding increased vagueness surrounding constitutionalism. This may also be the reason for the ever-expanding range of 'constitutionalisms' cropping up in the literature, a sample of which follows by way of illustration of the phenomenon.

9.1.1 Post-liberal Constitutionalism

Jorge M Farinacci-Fernos argues that many of the younger constitutions in Latin America and Africa have a *teleological* (substantive, programmatic, purposive) nature, usually associated with the rise of socio-economic rights since World War II, providing not merely a constitutional framework, but 'premised on substantive purpose', including 'a specific view on what, why and how society should be'.[26] These characteristics he believes are compatible with constitutionalism properly understood:

> Constitutionalism is made up of core elements which are shared by all constitutionalist systems, on top of which additional, though not constitutive, elements can be incorporated, as long as they are compatible with the core. In that sense, two things become clear: (1) there is such a thing as constitutionalism, which includes an inherent constitutive core; and (2) there are multiple articulations of constitutionalism, which include additional elements that, although compatible with the inherent core, can actually contradict each other. In the end, we can see that liberal-democratic constitutionalism is merely one of many equally legitimate and effective constitutionalist systems.[27]

9.1.2 Popular Constitutionalism

According to Bertrall Ross, writing from an exclusively US American perspective, 'popular constitutionalism remains a theory in search of a workable method', although its theory is clear, namely that 'the people should have the final say in determining the meaning of the Constitution'. This stands in contrast to the preference of judicial supremacy in the sense of the Supreme Court being awarded 'supreme authority over constitutional meaning'[28] and it is required due to 'the view that the Constitution's meaning is not fully determined by its text'.[29] In order to argue for 'administrative constitutionalism' Ross further unpacks various versions of popular constitutionalism, namely direct input from the populace in the process of the determination of the

---

[26] Farinacci-Fernos 'Post-Liberal Constitutionalism' 32–3.
[27] Farinacci-Fernos 'Post-Liberal Constitutionalism' 3.
[28] Ross 'Administrative Constitutionalism' 1785.
[29] Ross 'Administrative Constitutionalism' 1792.

meaning of the Constitution, mediated popular constitutionalism in the form of the legislature (Congress) and the executive (the President), construing constitutional meaning in response to social pressure and widely held societal values:

> A popular constitutionalism for the modern era requires a recognition of both the role of agencies as constitutional actors, as loci for popular input in constitutional meaning determinations, and as catalysts for popular debate about the Constitution. In fact, in a context in which social movement activity is infrequent, Congress is dysfunctional, and the President for the most part stays out of constitutional disputes, administrative agencies are arguably the lead popular constitutional actors that compete with the constitutional supremacy of the courts.[30]

Donald Hutt, a Chilean champion of popular constitutionalism, holds that 'popular constitutionalism must secure and foster republican liberty and deliberation among citizens, against a background of egalitarian conditions demanded by a principle of political equality I call Equality of Access and Deliberation'.[31] Republicanism entails freedom from dependence on the will of others, and deliberative democracy requires collective decisions to be taken inclusively by means of deliberation among all who may potentially be affected thereby.[32] He describes the commonwealth parliamentary model of Canada, New Zealand and the United Kingdom, in which the effect of proposed legislation on rights is reviewed by 'elective branches of government' prior to adoption, and a decoupling of judicial review from judicial supremacy as 'an intermediate model of constitutionalism'.[33]

It seems fair to deduce that proponents of popular constitutionalism are essentially engaged in efforts to concretize and improve democratic decision making in the complex political societies of this era. A certain distrust in varying degrees (frequently well-founded) of elected representatives, executive government, administrative structures, and the judiciary – in short the bearers of authority in modern states – seems to inspire the aspirations of popular constitutionalists.

9.1.3 Transformative Constitutionalism

A politically inspired conception of 'transformation' of society, conceived as a means to achieve ideological goals not supported by the constitutional text, emerged around the 1980s in the mobilizing language of South Africa's African National Congress (ANC), which has since 1994 been the governing

---

[30] Ross 'Administrative Constitutionalism' 1821.
[31] Hutt 'Deliberative, Republican, and Egalitarian Institutional Alternatives' 187.
[32] Hutt 'Deliberative, Republican, and Egalitarian Institutional Alternatives' 188.
[33] Hutt 'Deliberative, Republican, and Egalitarian Institutional Alternatives' 197.

party. Socialism is undeniably the underpinning dogma of this language. Although the concept does not appear in the text of the Constitution, it has been introduced progressively into legislation and the political vernacular, leading since 2004 to incorporation in the language of the Constitutional Court.[34]

The coining of the concept must be credited to Karl Klare, a long-standing exponent of Critical Legal Theory,[35] which explains its attractiveness, at least partly, for those who prefer to interpret the law in terms of politics. Regardless of its origins and ideological baggage, the linking of 'transformative' to constitutionalism provides much scope for its application in various contexts. Dealing with the constitutional law of Brazil, India and South Africa, Upendra Baxi for instance wrote:

> The transformative imagery in each one of the three BISA [Brazil/India/South Africa] constitutionalisms decisively turns back on any nostalgic reinvention of past. Each seeks to affirm the disinvention of the collective past. The Indian constitution-makers decisively repudiated calls to creatively adapt the heritage of syncretic Hinduism; instead and with intense normative rigour they wrestled with some ancient wrongs such as the practices of untouchability, of the Hindu patriarchy, and of agrestic serfdom. Even as the spirit of Ubuntu presides over the making of the South African constitution, this does not revive any pre-colonial visions of 'African' governance, rights, and justice. The Brazil constitutionalism now valiantly seeks, normatively at least, to restore indigenous people's rights as human rights.[36]

Probably after taking note of the notion originating in the South Africa jurisprudence and literature, the Constitutional Court of Colombia introduced the notion of transformative constitutionalism in judgments concerning the rights of indigenous peoples and Afro-descendants,[37] from where the concept migrated to the Inter-American Court of Human Rights and the construction of the development of a *ius constitutionale commune en América Latina*.[38] These developments hold the promise of considerable expansion and further develop-

---

[34] See Venter 'The Limits of Transformation' and *Bato Star Fishing v Minister of Environmental Affairs* 2004 (4) SA 490 (CC).

[35] Klare 'Legal Culture and Transformative Constitutionalism'.

[36] Baxi 'Preliminary Notes on Transformative Constitutionalism' 28. In their concluding chapter Vilhena, Baxi & Viljoen 'Transformative Constitutionalism' identified at 618 'the main features of transformative constitutionalism as a political and moral foundation of the BISA societies' along 'three axes', namely 'the material/symbolic aspects of transformative constitutionalism; the political space created by constitutions and occupied by civil society; and finally constitutional openness to international human rights law'.

[37] A key judgment is the Court's Decision T-129 of 2011: also see Herrera 'Judicial Dialogue and Transformative Constitutionalism'.

[38] See e.g. Von Bogdandy 'Überstaatlicher Transformativer Konstitutionalismus' and Riegner 'Transformativer Konstitutionalismus'.

ment, possibly affecting constitutional scholarship around the world – a space to be watched closely by constitutional comparatists.[39]

9.1.4 Autocratic (Authoritarian) Constitutionalism

According to Kim Lane Scheppele legalistic autocrats 'justify their actions through elections and then use legal methods to remove the liberal content from constitutionalism'. This occurs where '[d]emocracy and constitutionalism may come into conflict', and '[t] he end result ... is simple majoritarianism, which can lead quickly to illiberalism'.[40]

An edited volume appeared in 2019 bearing the title 'Authoritarian Constitutionalism' with chapter contributions by authors from a wide range of jurisdictions where authoritarian constitutionalism was diagnosed. Günter Frankenberg's introductory chapter bears the subtitle 'coming to terms with modernity's nightmares'. He opens his analysis by mentioning the 'dark shadows' over the human rights and liberal democracy of the twentieth and early twenty-first centuries: 'No ultimate triumph of liberalism, then, and certainly no end of history – rather, further struggle between the "gentle" authority of democracy and the brutish, patriarchal forces of authoritarianism.'[41] In contradistinction to liberal democracy's justifications for legitimate authority, 'the tropes of consent, democracy, trust, the social contract, and (real) discourse', Frankenberg shows that 'authoritarian ideologies "explain away" coercion, violence, and inequality by invoking necessity, self-preservation, security, and whatever else community may require'.[42]

9.1.5 Global Constitutionalism

Due to the endemic lack of means to enforce obligations under international law, international legal scholarship and jurisprudence tend to seek to remedy the shortfall with efforts to 'constitutionalize' international law. Enter the notion of 'global constitutionalism', rooted in normative universalism.

In 2012 a new journal was launched with the title *Global Constitutionalism*. In the editorial of the inaugural edition, the journal's *raison d'être* was explained with reference to a judgment of the European Court of Justice (the *Kadi* case of 2008), which, according to the editors, 'demonstrates how the interaction between different political and legal orders impacts on the fun-

---

[39] See e.g. Samararatne 'From South Africa to Sri Lanka'.
[40] Scheppele 'Constitutional Coups and Judicial Review' 556–7.
[41] Frankenberg 'Authoritarian Constitutionalism' 1.
[42] Frankenberg 'Authoritarian Constitutionalism' 2.

damental rights of individuals in ways that deserve much more attention. It is; therefore, a good example of how constitutional questions and claims are emerging beyond the state and how they require the input of different disciplines at the intersection of law and politics'.[43]

In 2017 two of the editors of *Global Constitutionalism* published an edited volume professing 'a recognition that the international order cannot be understood without an understanding of constitutional theory'.[44] Judging from recent literature, challenges to the viability of the notion seem to be on the increase: citing among others Ran Hirschl's 2018 article,[45] Elvira Mendez-Pinedo found evidence, especially in Iceland, 'that global constitutionalism is not the only game in town'.[46]

In 2018 Martin Belov edited a book 'meant to present in a multi-discursive and critical manner the current clash between national and post-national, national and supranational, Westphalian and post-Westphalian constitutionalism'. The author of the first chapter, Jean-Bernard Auby concluded:

> The idea of global constitutionalism as a means of disciplining normative pluralism in legal globalisation is not only a good idea: it is a necessity. In the globalised world, national constitutions become, as it were, partial constitutions. They control only part of the legal relations in which the legal order concerned is inscribed. This is compounded by the fact that global constitutional or quasi-constitutional instruments are essential for the international promotion of certain fundamental principles: it is clear that a certain amount of submission to these principles is a necessary counterweight to globalisation.[47]

The proponents of global constitutionalism appear to strive to resolve political and international legal conflicts by extending the ideals of liberal constitutionalism to the realm of global inter-state relations, working on the assumptions of normative universalism.

---

[43] Wiener, Lang, Tully, Maduro & Kumm 'Global Constitutionalism' 1. Four years later, alarmed by negative developments during 2014, the editorial Dunoff, Wiener, Kumm, Lang & Tully 'Hard Times' 1 raised the question whether 'at least certain elements of global constitutionalism have provisionally peaked or even entered a period of decline'.

[44] Lang & Wiener 'Handbook on Global Constitutionalism' (from the text of the blurb).

[45] Hirschl 'Opting Out of "Global Constitutionalism"'.

[46] Mendez-Pinedo 'Constitutional/Judicial Resistance to European Law in Iceland' 397.

[47] Auby 'Global Constitutionalism and Normative Hierarchies' 44.

9.2 CONTEXTUAL VARIATIONS

In addition to the range of generic manifestations of constitutionalism discussed in section 9.1 above, one can find a variety of further attributions of the notion, contextualized jurisdictionally or regionally. A brief glance over some of these is sufficient to illuminate the phenomenon.

9.2.1 East Asia

The range of constitutional arrangements currently prevalent in the East Asian region is wide, but there is a long-standing ontological history linking the region's denizens: Confucianism. With a focus of the Republic of (South) Korea, Chaihark Hahm wrote in 2002:

> In place of Confucian values like filial piety or ritual propriety, Koreans nowadays prefer to speak in terms of individual rights and describe their country as a 'liberal democracy' ... Similarly, the average Korean probably knows more about what Kant or Marx said than what Confucius or Mencius taught, while Christianity and Buddhism are by far the more visible religions of modern Korea.
> Yet ... the persistence of the Confucian tradition is often noted as an important factor in describing or explaining contemporary Korean society. Confucianism apparently has an invisible grip on the people's everyday life and behavior. Even with no formal voice to defend it, Confucianism seems to inform the way people interact with one another, and the way they make sense of the world around them. Indeed, it may be that because Confucianism exists in a less visible and more diffuse state, it is exerting an unconscious and therefore more powerful influence on their lives.[48]

Bui Ngoc Son cites various scholars who 'have demonstrated the Confucian influences in various dimensions of the contemporary societies in mainland China, Hong Kong, Japan, Singapore, South Korea, Taiwan and Vietnam'. He goes on to reject the idea that Confucianism is in conflict with Western constitutionalism, as well as an approach which seeks to find compatibilities in Confucianism with Western constitutionalism on the assumption that the latter should be seen as the universal standard. He proposes a mixed approach in which elements of Confucian tradition are combined with elements of Western constitutionalism 'to produce a distinctive model of East Asian constitutionalism'.[49]

Following a discussion of classical, imperial, and modern Confucian constitutionalism, Son proposes 'a normative theory of mixed constitutionalism', which 'has implications for the development of both established constitution-

---

[48] Hahm 'Law, Culture, and the Politics of Confucianism' 269–70.
[49] Son 'Confucian Constitutionalism in East Asia' 10–18.

alist polities (Japan, South Korea, and Taiwan) and transforming constitutional systems (China and Vietnam) in East Asia'.[50]

9.2.2 South Africa

The introduction of the essentials of Western constitutionalism in South Africa in 1994 under circumstances that lacked a political and social history supporting expectations for such a turn of events[51] has created space for localized scholarly and judicial applications of the concept. Thus far, in the judgments of the Constitutional Court 'constitutionalism' has mostly been used as a conceptual reference to constitutional values and characteristics,[52] and linked on occasion to 'transformative' ideals.[53] In addition to the introduction of the notion of transformative constitutionalism referred to above in section 9.1.3, constitutional scholars such as Heinz Klug have associated South African constitutionalism with decolonization[54] and argued that it represents a means to counter 'state capture'.[55]

9.2.3 Various

Many more parochial, thematic (for instance religious or doctrinal) understandings and applications of constitutionalism can be found in most existing constitutional orders. Mere mention of a few examples will have to suffice here.

Despite the historic adaptability of the uncodified *British* constitution, Sionaidh Douglas-Scott argues that recent developments, especially around the Brexit process, have caused constitutionalism to be under attack through '[t]he dilution or eradication of human rights, the attacks on judicial review, as

---

[50] Son 'Confucian Constitutionalism in East Asia' 208.
[51] See e.g. Venter 'Liberal Democracy: the Unintended Consequence'.
[52] E.g. *Economic Freedom Fighters v Speaker, National Assembly* 2016 (3) SA 580, para 1, rather histrionically: '... public-office bearers ignore their constitutional obligations at their peril. This is so because constitutionalism, accountability and the rule of law constitute the sharp and mighty sword that stands ready to chop the ugly head of impunity off its stiffened neck', and reference to the office of the Public Protector, established by the Constitution as '... an important cog in our constitutionalism as it and the others were created to "strengthen constitutional democracy"' in *Public Protector v Commissioner for the South African Revenue Service* [2020] ZACC 28, para 44.
[53] See e.g. *Beadica 231 CC v Trustees for the time being of the Oregon Trust* 2020 (5) SA 247 (CC) and *King N.O. v De Jager* [2021] ZACC 4.
[54] Klug 'Decolonisation, Compensation and Constitutionalism'.
[55] Klug 'Transformative Constitutions and the Role of Integrity Institutions'.

well as a growing reliance on executive sovereignty claiming legitimacy from a popular mandate, all lead[ing] to a diminishing of the rule of law'.[56]

Navraj Singh Ghaleigh describes *Japanese* constitutionalism as neither legal nor political, but 'bureaucratic'.[57]

Baogang He finds that '[m]any socialist constitutionalist arguments contain a core of liberal elements – like democracy and fundamental civil and political rights – on the one hand, while rejecting other liberal elements (like the constitutional elevation of the individual over civil society), on the other. In other words, *China* is warming up to the idea of constitutional hybridity'.[58]

Muhammad Siddiq Armia finds various degrees of adherence to Islamic constitutionalism in countries such as Saudi Arabia, Brunei and *Indonesia*, concluding about the latter that 'even though this country does not explicitly declare of adhering to Islamic constitutionalism, but in practice, it adopts the principles that exist in Islamic constitutionalism and applies them in a number of legal rules'.[59]

Louis Kotzé and Paola Villavicencio Calzadilla considered the potential of environmental constitutionalism expressed in the constitutional protection of rights of nature in the *Ecuadorian* Constitution of 2008.[60]

9.3 ACCOUNTING FOR FLUIDITY

'Constitutionalism' can hardly be understood to be more than a conceptual banner under which a wide range of dogmatic battles may be fought, depending on the adjective placed before it, or the definition ascribed thereto. No doubt liberal constitutionalism is the genealogical model for the spectrum of evolutionary mutations, each having been conceived as an expression of varying circumstantial ideological and political desires. With a pinch of irony one might even be forgiven for thinking that constitutionalism can be made to mean almost anything one wishes it to mean. Nevertheless, the wide expanse of constitutional law literature where it is used, albeit variously, suggests that constitutionalism is embedded in the vocabulary of constitutional lawyers, not to be pushed aside despite its extreme fluidity.

Seen positively, constitutionalism's pluriformity and terminological popularity allows for it to be a useful tool in constitutional comparison, not in itself as a stable referential anchor, but as a notion that may be defined almost

---

[56] Douglas-Scott 'Illiberal Constitutionalism' 36.
[57] Ghaleigh 'Neither Legal Nor Political?'.
[58] He 'Socialist Constitutionalism in Contemporary China' 194.
[59] Armia 'Implementing Islamic Constitutionalism' 447.
[60] Kotzé & Villavicencio Calzadilla 'Somewhere between Rhetoric and Reality'. See also Sajeva 'Do We Need Earth Jurisprudence?'.

arbitrarily to serve as a tailor-made *tertium comparationis*. Michael Riegner quite convincingly opened his analysis of 'transformative constitutionalism' with the statement that constitutional comparison is not what it used to be, because it has become geographically globalized, methodologically diversified, and pluralized regarding participants, which means that European and North American liberal constitutionalism has become but one among a number of types of constitutional statehood.[61]

Having noted the immense width of employment possibilities for 'constitutionalism' it stands to reason that no comparatist can be suffered to use the notion without explanation: failing to explain the jurisdictional, epistemological, or disciplinary (constitutional, international legal, supra-national, historical, environmental, etc.) context in which the comparatist wishes to be understood, will leave the audience in the dark, at sea, wallowing in an ocean of possible meanings. Given the sensitivities attending the globalization of constitutional law, employing the classic liberal democratic configuration of constitutionalism as comparative standard is likely to be perceived as patronising liberal arrogance, especially if it goes undefined.

On the other hand, those proposing novel applications of the notion used to promote specific agendas (for instance universalist, counter-anthroposcenic or authoritarian programmes) may find that their efforts may be met with scepticism and suspicions of opportunism.

In short, they who speak or write 'constitutionalism' would be well advised to explain themselves before proceeding to engineer conceptual or comparative constructs using this useful but slippery notion as foundation.

---

[61] Riegner 'Transformativer Konstitutionalismus' 265–6:
Verfassungsvergleichung ist nicht mehr das, was sie einmal war. Sie hat sich geografisch globalisiert, methodisch diversifiziert und personell pluralisiert. Rechtsordnungen in Asien, Afrika und Lateinamerika erweitern den europäisch-nordamerikanischen Horizont der Disziplin ... Vor diesem Hintergrund erscheint der liberale Konstitutionalismus, wie er in Europa und Nordamerika überwiegend verstanden wird, als einer von mehreren Typen von Verfassungsstaatlichkeit – ein wichtiger, ja dominanter, aber gleichwohl nur regionaler Typus.

10. Judicial review

Legal adjudication of disputes is an immanent feature of the law, and has since time immemorial been such. Since the existence of law is closely associated with the state,[1] it is unthinkable not to conceive judicial authority as being a specific facet of the authority of the state. Put differently, courts of law can hardly be imagined outside the scope of the exercise of authority by the state.

No wonder, then, that judicial power features prominently in the doctrine of the separation of powers as one of the three pillars of the structure of the law and the constitution. When properly constituted and well-functioning courts adjudicate decisively and authoritatively over most civil and criminal matters, one can hardly expect any doubts to be raised over the justification of their authority to do so – the judgment of a court is the accepted outcome of the well-regulated legal process, designed to deliver justice, and balance rights in a fair, objective and structured manner. It is the law in action, at its best.

However, seen from our present focus on constitutional law, it is in principle a conceptual curiosity that the judiciary is an integral organ of the state exercising state authority, while also bearing the responsibility and power to pronounce conclusively on the lawfulness of the actions of the state itself, performed by its other organs. What is the source of this considerable power of the courts, and why should judges be entrusted with such conclusive authority beyond private and criminal law?

The source of the proposition that constitutional review jurisdiction is problematic is the assumption that 'the people' are the depository of state sovereignty and their democratically elected representatives are entrusted with the authority to make laws and to administer them. Judges can seldom claim that they are representative of the electorate. How can it then be that the judiciary is given the authority to determine whether legislative and administrative actions are lawful, even to the point of effectively declaring them null and void? Problems can be solved, dilemmas not. From the perspective of the doctrine of popular sovereignty, this is a dilemma.

The insoluble difficulties emanating from explanations of state authority based on popular sovereignty complicate the explanation of judicial authority,

---

[1] For the moment leaving behind consideration of the possibility of defining law as not exclusively being dependent on the authority of the state.

but also affect the justification of constitutional amendment. Richard Albert made this clear in the following passage:

> Stated most simply, constituent power theory proposes a rigid division of labor between the people and their representatives in government: only the people may found an altogether new constitution while their representatives in government are authorized to act in their name to do no more than change a constitution in harmony with the constitution's own terms. Yet constituent power theory refers to the people as an amorphous whole, with neither quantification nor qualification of who the people are, how they exercise their power, and when we know their actions are valid. Where the constitution does not entrench two tracks of rules of change, the rule of mutuality gives shape to constituent power theory by establishing a rebuttable presumption that the people exercise their constituent power when they speak in the same way they did when they wrote the constitution to begin with.[2]

Populism thrives on this dilemma. In his analysis of populist thinking, Théo Fournier shows how the fragility of democracy due to its inherent paradoxes lends itself to rhetorical and political exploitation, also regarding the role of the judiciary:

> The balance between majority rule and rule of law makes constitutional democracy a nonnatural ecosystem. How natural is it to claim to be a democratic regime while, at the same time, constraining the choice of the majority? How does one justify the final and binding authority of a constitutional court – a non-elected body – against the willingness of the Parliament – the national representation? Arguing that the constitution legitimizes this unnatural balance is even more unnatural. How does one justify that rules written decades ago – by a generation often no longer alive – can constrain a contemporary majority? If the principle of a constitution is accepted, why then restrain its amendments to a supra-majority?[3]

---

[2] Albert 'Constitutional Amendment and Dismemberment' 6.

[3] Fournier 'From Rhetoric to Action' 365. One may assume that by 'natural' Fournier meant 'logical' or 'reasonable'. In the same volume the negative attitude of populists towards judicial review was also pointed out by Julian Scholtes, Scholtes 'The Complacency of Legality' 353:
> Not only are populist platforms often at odds with constitutionally entrenched rights, but populists also reject the constraints on political power that emanate from these rights. In short, populism rejects constitutionalism. Populism 'deems that nothing supersedes the general will of the people[.]' The power of courts is thus a significant thorn in the side of many populists. Populists brand courts as enemies of the people and lash out against unelected judges who 'overstep ... their authority'.

On the one hand the rule of law[4] and constitutionalism[5] usually require, as a self-evident attribute, that a court or courts will have review jurisdiction rooted in their authoritative interpretation of constitutional and other legal texts. On the other hand, various influential voices can be heard protesting, or warning from divergent dogmatic stances against judicial dominance. In addition to the emerging populist push-back mentioned by Fournier, expressions such as the 'countermajoritarian difficulty', 'juristocracy', 'the judicialisation of politics', and 'the new constitutionalism' are in circulation.

Given these ambiguities, the first section below is devoted to a survey of attitudes and theories relating to judicial review in order to contextualize them in the second section as they are practised in a few jurisdictions representative of the major models. In the third section remarks relating to the essential nature and justification of the authority of the judiciary are offered.

10.1 CONSTITUTIONAL REVIEW: ORIGINS AND CONTESTATION

10.1.1 Origins

Understandably, the following *dictum* of the English chief justice Sir Edward Coke in the famous case of Dr Bonham (1610) has served as an historical justification for judicial review of legislation: 'the common law will control Acts of Parliament, and sometimes adjudge them to be utterly void; for when an Act of Parliament is against common right and reason, or repugnant, or impossible to be performed, the common law will control it and adjudge such Act to be void'.[6] However, the striking down of parliamentary legislation could in essence not be aligned with the cornerstone of English constitutional law, the sovereignty of Parliament, thereby creating a conundrum for the justification

---

[4] The Venice Commission considers review of the exercise of legislative and executive powers by an independent and impartial judiciary for constitutionality and legality to be an integral component of the rule of law: Venice Commission 'Rule of Law' 16.

[5] In 2016 Mark Tushnet remarked in Tushnet 'Varieties of constitutionalism' 2:
Over the past several decades we have learned how to subdivide liberal constitutionalism. There is political constitutionalism, identified by Richard Bellamy and others, theorizing parliamentary supremacy as a form of limited government. Alternatively, there is judicial constitutionalism (sometimes misleadingly referred to as 'legal' constitutionalism), in which courts enforce limitations on government power. And within judicial constitutionalism we find strong-form review and judicial supremacy, and weak-form or dialogic review.

[6] *Thomas Bonham v College of Physicians* 8 *Co. Rep.* at 118a, 77 *Eng. Rep.*, 652.

of Coke's judgment. A possible solution was offered by Richard Helmholz, remarking that both Blackstone and Coke –

> ... accepted the existence of natural law, and the traditions of natural law embraced both positions ... Invocation of the law of nature was no idiosyncrasy on their part. A commonplace of the legal culture of their times held that certain general principles of justice were part of human nature, formed within us by God. These principles were common to all men, they were constant and immutable, and they provided the necessary foundation of all human law. Although the limited character of our understanding prevented men from knowing them fully, the basic tenets were accessible in part through human reason and observation. Many were stated in venerable legal maxims. Moreover, they were capable of application in legal practice. They could decide the outcome of litigation. Indeed under certain circumstances they were capable of rendering a statute inoperative – 'void' if we follow Coke's terminology. Bonham's Case was in fact a relatively simple example of the application of the law of nature to its facts.[7]

Parliamentary sovereignty was however not a factor with which the US Supreme Court had to contend in its 1803 judgment in *Marbury v Madison*.[8] As Chief Justice Marshall pointed out in the final paragraphs of the judgment, the oath of office of judges imposed primary allegiance to the Constitution as the supreme law of the land, and to other laws of the United States 'only which shall be made in pursuance of the Constitution'. The Chief Justice closed the matter with the following dictum, which may be said to resonate to this day in many a constitutional order around the world:

> Thus, the particular phraseology of the Constitution of the United States confirms and strengthens the principle, supposed to be essential to all written Constitutions, that a law repugnant to the Constitution is void, and that courts, as well as other departments, are bound by that instrument.

It is safe to assume that contemporary teachings on judicial review as phenomenon are based on the judgment in *Marbury v Madison*, being the *locus classicus* from which the idea of judicial 'testing' of state conduct against the demands of the constitutional text sprouted. Over time, the propagation of the idea of judicial review proceeded piecemeal and in diverse forms and modes of application, producing interesting variations and configurations, some of which warrant mention for the purposes of outlining a topical contemporary understanding of the notion. Stated simply, judicial review is not a monosemic concept, although some broad categories can be recognized.

---

[7] Helmholz 'Bonham's Case' 331.
[8] 5 U.S. (1 Cranch) 137 (1803).

Two American papers published in the early 1970s provided helpful basic data in this regard. First, Mauro Cappelletti explained the distinction between centralized and decentralized systems of judicial review, namely bestowing on all judicial organs the jurisdiction to adjudicate on the constitutionality of legislation (and presumably also non-legislative state conduct) in decentralized systems, and in centralized systems on only one particular judicial institution.[9] Keith Rosenn surveyed judicial review in the Latin American states. Despite having 'civil law' legal orders, various interesting variations of constitutional review were developed in the region already during the nineteenth century, inspired by their northern neighbour. Rosenn discussed instances of centralized (Mexico), decentralized (Argentina, Brazil, El Salvador, Venezuela, and partly Colombia) and mixed-mode (Bolivia, Chile, Costa Rica, Haiti, Honduras, Panama, Paraguay, and Uruguay) approaches to judicial review. Various procedural mechanisms for bringing constitutional matters before the courts were developed in South American states, including *habeas corpus* (*recurso de amparo de la libertad*), *mandado de segurança* (writ of security), *amparo* (support or protection), 'popular action' (*acción popular*), and 'representation'.[10]

During the twentieth century, specialized constitutional courts entrusted with review jurisdiction were established in many countries, pioneered in 1920 by the republican constitution of Austria, followed by Ireland in 1922, Japan in 1947, and Germany in 1949. In the second half of the century the German model was followed widely in Central and Eastern Europe during the wave of constitution-writing after the fall of the USSR. Its own version of constitutional judicial review was introduced in Canada with the adoption of the *Canadian Constitution Act* of 1982, and in the still ongoing procession of constitution-writing in many places, almost every current constitution provides for some form of judicial review jurisdiction, be it in a decentralized, centralized, or mixed-model form, and with more or less efficacy.[11]

If the history and legacy of *Marbury v Madison* may be described as a success story, the extent of misgivings and reservations about judicial review, undoubtedly stimulated by contrary ontological and epistemic premises, cannot (yet?) be said to threaten its survival, but the qualms certainly expose the need to delve deeper into the nature, justification, and limitations of judicial authority, if not constitutional authority itself.

---

[9] Cappelletti 'Judicial Review in Comparative Perspective' 1033–9.
[10] Rosenn 'Judicial Review in Latin America'.
[11] See further Müller-Freienfels 'Zur Rangstufung rechtlicher Normen' 8; Koopmans 'Courts and Political Institutions' 35–44; Weber 'Typen der Verfassungsgerichtsbarkeit' 37–41; and Arnold & Martínez-Estay 'Rule of Law, Human Rights and Judicial Control of Power'.

10.1.2 Contestation

A simplified characterization of the 'countermajoritarian difficulty' (or 'dilemma'), can be expressed as a question: how is it that unelected and unaccoutable judges are allowed to frustrate or destroy legislation adopted by a democratically elected legislature? Academic literature on the subject is vast and dispersed over a wide spectrum of attitudes. One of the most articulate American opponents to judicial review of legislation is Jeremy Waldron, whose publications on the matter bring together the essential arguments, and who also takes into consideration (extra-American) comparative material.

In a chapter devoted to the matter in a book published in 2016, Waldron distinguishes various forms of judicial review.[12] First, 'strong' versus 'weak' judicial review, the first being the target of his attack, namely a situation where courts may refuse to apply a statute or to modify its effect, or even to render it completely void. Weak judicial review takes the form of a judicial finding of incompatibility with protected rights, thereby facilitating legislative rectification. Even weaker judicial review may take the form of judicial attempts at interpreting legislation violating rights to avoid such violation, without any legal effect on the legislature.

Canada represents an 'intermediate case', where the courts may decline to apply legislation they find to be in conflict with constitutional rights, but the legislatures are empowered constitutionally to adopt such laws 'notwithstanding' their incompatibility. Further distinctions occur between judicial review based only on the protection of rights and protection also of other constitutional arrangements (for instance federal relationships, elections, and legislative procedure), *ex post* review (after the promulgation of the statute) and abstract *ex ante* review by a special tribunal as part of the legislative process, and review jurisdiction shared by a number of courts, or limited to a specialized constitutional court.[13]

Despite his criticism of the phenomenon, circumstances may, according to Waldron, justify judicial review:

> Maybe there are circumstances – peculiar pathologies, dysfunctional legislative institutions, corrupt political cultures, legacies of racism, and other forms of endemic prejudice – in which these costs of obfuscation and disenfranchisement are worth bearing for the time being. But defenders of judicial review ought to start making their claims for the practice frankly on that basis – and make it with a degree of humility and shame in regard to the circumstances that elicit it – rather

---

[12] Waldron 'The Core of the Case against Judicial Review' 195–245.
[13] Waldron 'The Core of the Case against Judicial Review' 199–202.

than preaching it abroad as the epitome of respect for rights and as a normal and normatively desirable element of modern constitutional democracy.[14]

These are however not the circumstances that Waldron has in mind in his opposition to review jurisdiction over legislation. He opposes it under circumstances where the existence in a society of four conditions are assumed: democratic institutions 'in reasonably good working order; judicial institutions, again in reasonably good order to adjudicate on disputes and to uphold the rule of law; majority commitment to individual and minority rights; and 'persisting, substantial, and good-faith disagreements' about what the protected rights actually amount to.[15] Waldron bases his opposition to judicial review on two grounds: it distracts the attention from the 'real issues at stake when citizens disagree about rights' by involving 'side issues about precedent, texts, and interpretation', and, secondly, it is 'politically illegitimate', because –

> ... by privileging majority voting among a small number of unelected and unaccountable judges, it disenfranchises ordinary citizens and brushes aside cherished principles of representation and political equality in the final resolution of issues about rights.[16]

A glance at the rest of the literature on the matter reveals that Waldron's views are far from a generally accepted stance (which does in any event not exist). My survey elsewhere[17] gave an indication of how different people deal with the topic.

Bert van Roermund for instance highlighted three other arguments against constitutional adjudication: the separation of powers requires the legislature itself, not the courts, to ensure that its laws are adopted lawfully in accordance with the constitution; the courts should be spared from involvement in political controversy such as the validity of laws adopted by a democratic majority; and courts' jurisdiction to overturn the actions of other organs of the state undermine legal certainty until the validity thereof has been tested judicially.[18]

From a review of three comprehensive papers by Barrie Friedman on the American history of the countermajoritarian difficulty, I have distilled

---

[14] Waldron 'The Core of the Case against Judicial Review' 244–5.
[15] Waldron 'The Core of the Case against Judicial Review' 202–12.
[16] Waldron 'The Core of the Case against Judicial Review' 199.
[17] Venter 'Global Features' 83–113.
[18] Van Roermund 'Constitutional Review' 5–6.

elsewhere[19] the following characteristics of the phenomenon, which occur in a range of jurisdictional circumstances:

- For the countermajoritarian difficulty to arise, the decision of a court must indeed run against the will of the majority of those affected by the decision.
- The following four factors form a framework within which the countermajoritarian difficulty and its American history may be described: the measure of judicial interference with popular will; the current public sentiment regarding the degree to which government should be 'popular', i.e. reflect the 'will of the people'; attitudes regarding the meaning of the Constitution, i.e. whether it is relatively fixed or open; and the degree of acceptance that judicial decisions are supreme.
- Since the late twentieth century the tendency has been to justify judicial review as a means to satisfy the need to protect minority rights.
- Methods that may be employed (and which had been propagated from time to time in the United States) to solve the countermajoritarian difficulty include 'court-packing', jurisdiction-stripping, holding referenda, judicial recall, legislative override and the election of judges.
- 'Understanding the relationship between judicial review and politics is essential to determining the appropriate bounds of political pressure placed upon ... the ... judiciary.'[20] In this regard an important conclusion made by Friedman is: 'It is ironic that when the real world stakes are high, legal rules may be most important; yet, there is at those times the greatest pressure on those rules to give way to political expediency.'[21]

What Friedman has called 'the central obsession of modern [American] constitutional scholarship'[22] has also been engaging scholars in other constitutional orders to varying degrees of intensity.[23] Different labels are attached to concerns over the exercise of judicial review authority, such as 'juristocracy', 'the judicialisation of politics' and 'the new constitutionalism'.

Despite the ongoing debate in the US over its advisability, a number of twentieth-century constitutions make explicit provision for ultimate judicial

---

[19] Venter 'Global Features' 86–7.
[20] Friedman 'Reconstruction's Political Court' footnote 7.
[21] Friedman 'Reconstruction's Political Court' 65.
[22] Friedman 'The History of the Countermajoritarian Difficulty, Part One' 344–5.
[23] See e.g. Shakhray & Popova 'Countermajoritarian Institutions in the Russian Constitution' and Dent & Kroeze 'Minority Rights in the South-African Context'.

control over constitutionality, for instance in Japan,[24] Colombia,[25] Angola,[26] Romania[27] and Morocco.[28]

Somewhat unexpectedly, the term 'juristocracy' appears to have been coined in England as long ago as 1923 in connection with the functions of a Bar Association: 'It is not suggested that democracy should be replaced by juristocracy – if one may coin such a barbarous hybrid ...'[29] By 1988 Abram Chayes could cite three publications to which he referred as 'a good deal of soul-searching about our "juristocracy", often reaching sharply negative conclusions'.[30] A seminal book by Ran Hirschl may be said to have canonized the term in the current constitutional vocabulary.[31]

Looking at it from a New Zealand perspective, John Smillie described the adoption in 1990 of the *New Zealand Bill of Rights Act* as a shift from *parliamentary* democracy to *constitutional* democracy, remarking, with evident distaste, that New Zealand seemed 'to be moving towards an American-style "juristocracy" in which the judges of the highest court have the final say on controversial issues of morality and social policy', a synonym being 'legal constitutionalism'.[32]

Citing examples from constitutional orders as widely separated as Japan, Honduras, India and Canada, Richard Albert characterized the 'problem of juristocracy' thus:

> One of the most important trends in constitutionalism since the last great war is what Ran Hirschl has described as 'juristocracy' – the rise of courts to the highest seat of power. Political actors have chosen, for strategic reasons of hegemonic self-preservation, to confer the power of judicial review on courts. Over time, juristocracy has brought increasingly more matters into the purview of judicial authority, leading to what Hirschl has called the judicialization of 'mega-politics,' described as 'core political controversies that define the boundaries of the collective or cut through the heart of entire nations.' These controversies include matters commonly thought to raise distinctly political questions: macroeconomic planning, national security, electoral procedures, secession and independence, the formation of collective identity, and the kinds of nation-building processes that have historically remained beyond the realm of judicial control. The problem of juristocracy

---

[24] Section 81 of the Japanese Constitution of 1947.
[25] Chapter 4 of the Constitution of Colombia of 1991.
[26] Article 180 of the Constitution of Angola of 2010.
[27] Title V of the Constitution of Romania of 1991.
[28] Title Viii of the Constitution of Morocco of 2011.
[29] Anonymous editorial 'Solicitors' Journal & Weekly Reporter'. (Reading this remark a century after it was written, the epithet 'barbarous hybrid' one feels justified to experience a measure of amusement.)
[30] Chayes 'How Does the Constitution Establish Justice?' 1039.
[31] Hirschl 'Towards Juristocracy'.
[32] Smillie 'Who Wants Juristocracy' 183.

is therefore a problem of democratic participation; courts commonly suffer from a democratic deficit relative to other political branches insofar as courts are out of the reach of electoral politics and the accountability they entail.[33]

It seems therefore that 'juristocracy' and the countermajoritarian difficulty are aspects of the same phenomenon, the first at most being a specie of the genus countermajoritarianism.

One view of constitution-writing, constitutions and constitutional law is that they represent crystallized politics.[34] If this is correct, one might ask whether it should be strange that constitutional review has a political dimension taking the form of the 'judicialisation of politics'. Ary Nogueira opened his recent survey of research on this topic as follows:

> In recent decades, the world has experienced a new phenomenon without precedent, the expansion of judicial and legal discourse in all social relations. Courts are now called upon to resolve controversies that were previously seen as purely political. Every day, people resort to the judiciary to have their most basic needs met; the judicial form interferes throughout the public administration, so much so that the expression 'administrative process' has become a common occurrence.[35]

Following the literature, Nogueira found that the main criticism of the judicialization of politics and judicial activism is founded upon concerns regarding legitimacy, judicial capacity, and independence.[36] That the theme is not isolated to certain regions or constitution types is clear from the spectrum of jurisdictions from which the matter is being aired.[37]

No doubt, the growing involvement of constitutional adjudication in political and other social issues raises the topicality of the countermajoritarian difficulty. Some refer to this as the 'new constitutionalism', Tamas Gyorfi's

---

[33] Albert 'Constitutional Amendment and Dismemberment' 66–7.

[34] Widner & Contiades 'Constitution-writing Processes' 60 e.g. provide the following description:
> ... constitution-drafting procedures may shape political behavior in ways that have little to do with the actual substantive terms accepted. The models they set may influence whether citizens channel conflict into non-violent forums, enter sustained dialogue, and adopt constitutional principles as part of the vocabulary of popular politics. Some constitutions remain pieces of paper that command little attention from political elites or ordinary citizens, while others have become focal points for political debate and the source of norms that shape everyday behavior.

[35] Nogueira 'State of the Art Research in the Judicialization of Politics' 670.

[36] Nogueira 'State of the Art Research in the Judicialization of Politics' 684–5.

[37] See e.g. Balme 'The Judicialisation of Politics and the Politicisation of the Judiciary in China'; Yusuf 'Robes on Tight Ropes' (Nigeria); and Malila 'The Zambian Judiciary on Trial'.

argument against it being one of the most comprehensive (and abstract).[38] Gyorfi's focus is on established, well-functioning democracies, and he promotes 'political liberalism' to confine the scope of political decision making as a justification for a 'weak', rather than a 'strong' form of judicial review. '[I]n mature democracies the case for a strong constitutional court is not compelling and, as a general rule, the power to specify the meaning of abstract human rights provisions should be conferred on the legislature.'[39] To address the problems of the 'new constitutionalism', Gyorfi pleads for 'institutional conservatism', 'institutional experimentalism, innovation and radicalism'.[40]

10.2 CONTEXTUAL VARIATIONS

For present purposes enough has been said above about judicial review in the United States where it originated in its contemporary form, and continues to stand out as the primary example of decentralized, strong constitutional review jurisdiction.[41] The US Constitution also still stands out as the original example of constitutional dualism (entrenched constitutional supremacy; constituent versus constituted power; popular sovereignty)[42] as distinct from the monism of the British constitution also reflected in some common law jurisdictions such as New Zealand, where parliamentary sovereignty survives, although not wholly unchallenged.[43] Examples from selected constitutional orders demonstrate the effect of these distinctions.

10.2.1 United Kingdom

The run-up to, and consequences of, Brexit have been imbued with considerations of parliamentary sovereignty. This has convincingly been ascribed to 'institutional incompatibilities between the EU's over-constitutionalization and the UK's parliamentary sovereignty'.[44]

---

[38] Gyorfi 'New Constitutionalism' 151, canvassing for scepticism over the proliferation of American dualism, finding that 'in mature democracies there is no compelling reason to introduce the strong form of judicial review'. See also my review of the book in 2017 (20) *PER/PELJ* https://journals.assaf.org.za/index.php/per/article/view/2426/2693 (accessed 20 April 2021).
[39] Gyorfi 'New Constitutionalism' 168.
[40] Gyorfi 'New Constitutionalism' 258.
[41] For the distinction between 'decentralized' and 'centralized', see notes 9–11 and the associated text above, and for 'strong' and 'weak', see Waldron 'The Core of the Case against Judicial Review' and Gyorfi 'New Constitutionalism'.
[42] See e.g. Gyorfi 'New Constitutionalism' 4–5.
[43] See e.g. Smillie 'Who Wants Juristocracy'.
[44] Schmidt 'No Match Made in Heaven' 781.

The Supreme Court of the United Kingdom was seized twice with executive conduct concerning Brexit and parliamentary sovereignty. In both cases the exercise of the royal prerogative by the executive was involved. Based on the view that the conduct of international relations is a matter of prerogative, the government was of the opinion in 2017 that giving notice to the EU of the UK's intention to leave the Union did not require the involvement of Parliament. The Court however found that 'ministers cannot give Notice without prior sanction from the UK Parliament'[45] because changes in domestic law would be the effect of leaving the EU.

In 2019 the Prime Minister prorogued Parliament for an unduly long period, denying members at a crucial stage the opportunity to debate the terms of the Brexit withdrawal. The unanimous bench determined that the attempted prorogation was unlawful and void, and stated that two fundamental constitutional principles were relevant in this case:

> The first is the principle of Parliamentary sovereignty: that laws enacted by the Crown in Parliament are the supreme form of law in our legal system, with which everyone, including the Government, must comply. However, the effect which the courts have given to Parliamentary sovereignty is not confined to recognising the status of the legislation enacted by the Crown in Parliament as our highest form of law. Time and again, in a series of cases since the seventeenth century, the courts have protected Parliamentary sovereignty from threats posed to it by the use of prerogative powers, and in doing so have demonstrated that prerogative powers are limited by the principle of Parliamentary sovereignty.[46]

Notably, the UK Supreme Court's claim of jurisdiction to sanction unconstitutional conduct does not, due to the sanctity of parliamentary sovereignty, extend to 'testing' the validity of legislation duly adopted by Parliament. The essential element distinguishing British constitutional law from that of constitutional orders with 'strong' judicial review is the settled principle of the sovereignty not of 'the people', but of Parliament. Brexiteers and some scholars argued that parliamentary sovereignty was impinged upon by the United Kingdom's membership of the EU.[47]

---

[45] *R (Miller) v Secretary of State for Exiting the European Union* [2017] UKSC 5, para 115.

[46] *R (Miller) v The Prime Minister; R (Cherry) v Advocate General for Scotland* [2019] UKSC 41, para 41.

[47] McConalogue 'The British Constitution Resettled?' for instance stated at 442: 'Where the UK Parliament has become less sovereign due to the incremental removal of parliamentary power over policy and law under EU membership, it additionally provided an executive-legislature accountability gap in the UK constitutional system.'

To the contrary, Stuart White has recently argued that 'unstable points in the traditional [British] constitution' post-Brexit may cause the balance of constitutional primacy to swing away from Parliament in favour of the executive:

> We have seen how Brexit – the 2016 referendum, followed by the UK's exit from the EU – puts additional pressure on pre-existing instabilities in the UK's traditional constitution. One possible outcome is evolution within the legal framework of the traditional constitution towards a populist democracy, in which the UK executive is strengthened in relation to the judiciary, to parliament and to the devolved governments, and in which the referendum possibly has a more central political role than in the past. In this scenario, the UK's trajectory following Brexit can be seen as a variant of a wider 'post-liberal' or 'populist' shift in contemporary democratic political systems.[48]

Although the constitutional trajectory of Britain after Brexit can of course not be predicted with certainty, it is noteworthy that, as far back as 2014, the President of the Supreme Court of the United Kingdom at the time expressed some wistful thoughts on the possibility of a written constitution and a constitutional court:

> We have a proud and successful history with a pragmatic, rather than principled, approach to law and legal systems, and we have managed pretty well without a constitution. But times change, and the fact that we managed well without a constitution in a very different world from that which we now inhabit may be a point of limited force when applied to the present. So long as things remained much the same, the argument based on the status quo was hard to resist. However, if, and it is a big 'if' which is ultimately a political decision, our system of government is going to be significantly reconsidered and restructured, there is obviously a more powerful case for a written constitution. Writing a constitution may help focus minds on the details of the restructuring, and, once the restructuring has occurred, a new formal constitution should provide the new order with a clarity and certainty which may otherwise be lacking.[49]

10.2.2 Germany

The German Federal Constitutional Court (*Bundesverfassungsgericht*), established in 1951, may currently be considered to be the prime example of the centralized European model of constitutional review. Its historical roots are

---

[48] Stuart White, 'Brexit and the Future of the UK constitution' 2021 *International Political Science Review* 1–15 https://journals.sagepub.com/doi/10.1177/0192512121995133 (accessed 21 April 2021) 11.

[49] Speech by Lord Neuberger at the Legal Wales Conference 2014 on 10 October 2014, para 33 www.supremecourt.uk/docs/speech-141010.pdf (accessed 22 April 2021), and see also para 31.

said to go back to the nineteenth century. Between the two World Wars courts with review jurisdiction existed in Austria, Czechoslovakia, Liechtenstein, and Spain. Hans Kelsen is credited for conceiving the model and inspiring its implementation in Austria in 1920.[50] Many new constitutions that have been adopted since the middle of the twentieth century follow the German model.

In terms of Article 20(2) of the German Federal Constitution (the *Grundgesetz*) of 1949, all the authority of the state vests in the people (*das Volk*). This is understood to include the judicial authority, as shown in the opening formula used by the German courts in their judgments: *Im Namen des Volkes* (in the name of the nation). Article 93(1) of the *Grundgesetz* provides a comprehensive exposition of the jurisdiction of the *Bundesverfassungsgericht* and it is further specified in the applicable legislation, the *Bundesverfassungsgerichtsgesetz* of 1951. In terms of §1(1) of this statute, the Court is autonomous and independent (*selbständig* and *unabhängig*) of all other constitutional organs. §31 renders the decisions of the Court binding on all organs of state and awards the status of legislation (*Gesetzeskraft*) to decisions on specified topics relating to constitutionality. The field of jurisdiction of the Court ranges from disputes between organs of state (*Organstreit*), disputes over federal issues, 'abstract' norm control,[51] 'concrete' norm control,[52] and individual constitutional complaints (*Verfassungsbeschwerde*).

The title of Ulrich Haltern's thesis suggests that the *Bundesverfassungsgericht* follows a constitutional theory balanced between populism and progressivism. He sees the German political process as a non-hierarchical, competitive process of continuous negotiation in which many groups, distinguished in terms of various criteria such as ethnicity, religion, social status, etc., participate.[53] According to him, the Court distinguishes between state and society, the latter being composed of groups engaged in a competition for power while the state is required to ensure that the playing field is equal for all, which implies that the weaker components of society must be protected and provided with means to compete freely.[54] Haltern also found that John Stuart Mill's teachings on liberalism underpin the Court's approach in its application of Article 2 of

---

[50] See e.g. Schlaich 'Das Bundesverfassungsgericht' 1–4, 7–8 and 55–6; Comella 'The European Model of Constitutional Review' 461–3; and Moreso 'Kelsen on Justifying Judicial Review'.

[51] Article 93(2) of the *Grundgesetz*, concerning the determination of the compatibility of legislation with the *Grundgesetz* without it being raised in specific litigation.

[52] In terms of Article 100(1) of the *Grundgesetz*, where a court considers that a statute on whose validity the Court's decision depends is unconstitutional, the proceedings have to be stayed in order to have its constitutionality determined.

[53] Haltern 'Verfassungsgerichtsbarkeit, Demokratie und Misstrauen' 120.

[54] Haltern 'Verfassungsgerichtsbarkeit, Demokratie und Misstrauen' 142–5.

the *Grundgesetz*, which guarantees everyone's rights to self-fulfilment, life, physical integrity, and personal freedom,[55] but considered this combined pluralistic and liberalistic approach to be contradictory, causing the courts to be drawn into having to adjudicate over a growing range of social controversies.[56]

Amidst the unrivalled sophistication of German constitutional law and doctrine, the mundane question regarding its popular legitimacy in relation to the rest of the constitutional system has also received much attention, especially from political scientists. An example is Uwe Kranenpohl's 2009 article under the (translated) title 'The Social Legitimacy of Constitutional Review or: Why Germans Love their *Bundesverfassungsgericht*',[57] who reported various reasons for the Court's popularity. Among these are: the traditional saturation of German society with the idea of the *Rechtsstaat*, of which the Court is deemed to be a paragon; the Court's apolitical image, elevated above the political parties, free from pressures from politicians and above their contests and quarrels, focused on harmonized conflict resolution in accordance with the law; and the Court's charisma born from factors such as its unique presentation and closed consultation procedures and a 'secretive aura'. In 2001 the serving President of the Court, Jutta Limbach famously raised the question in a speech celebrating the first 50 years of the Court's existence whether the popularity of the *Bundesverfassungsgericht* might be ascribed to a political distrust of democracy.[58]

The standing and jurisprudence of the *Bundesverfassungsgericht* as the apex court of probably the most influential member state of the European Union relative to the Court of Justice of the European Union and the European Court of Human Rights is a topical theme in current literature,[59] but for present purposes this does not need to be pursued further.

10.2.3 France

As Marie-Claire Ponthoreau and Fabrice Hourquebiec pointed out 50 years after the establishment of the *Conseil Constitutionnel*, constitutional review

---

[55] Haltern 'Verfassungsgerichtsbarkeit, Demokratie und Misstrauen' 157–8. See in particular the Court's judgment in its Brokdorf judgment in 1985 *BverfGE* 69, 315 (346) concerning the process of the formation of political opinion.
[56] Haltern 'Verfassungsgerichtsbarkeit, Demokratie und Misstrauen' 161–8.
[57] Kranenpohl 'Die gesellschaftlichen Legitimationsgrundlagen der Verfassungsrechtsprechung'.
[58] Cited in Venter 'Global Features' 96.
[59] E.g. (among very many) Paris 'Constitutional Courts and the European Court of Human Rights', and Wendel 'Das Bundesverfassungsgericht als Garant der Unionsgrundrechte'.

is a relatively new phenomenon in France, and in a category of its own: 'Although very remote from French legal tradition, the CC is solidly rooted in the French political system.'[60]

The *Conseil Constitutionnel* was established in 1958 in terms of Title VII of the French Constitution of 4 October 1958, with jurisdiction over the conduct of elections of the President of the Republic (Article 58) and of the members of the National Assembly and Senators (Article 59), the conduct of referenda (Article 60). Article 61 allows the *Conseil Constitutionnel* to rule on the conformity with the Constitution of various forms of legislation *prior* to its promulgation (review *ex ante*), and since 2010 Article 61-1 and a subsequently adopted 'Institutional Act', *ex post* review jurisdiction was added. The requirement for *ex post* review is that, 'during proceedings in progress before a court of law, it is claimed that a legislative provision infringes the rights and freedoms guaranteed by the Constitution'. The matter may then be referred to the *Conseil Constitutionnel* by the *Conseil d'Etat* or by the *Cour de Cassation*.

Constitutional review in France is therefore centralized, and recently became 'strong', since Article 62 of the Constitution provides that 'A provision declared unconstitutional on the basis of article 61 shall be neither promulgated nor implemented', and that 'A provision declared unconstitutional on the basis of article 61-1 shall be repealed as of the publication of the said decision of the Constitutional Council or as of a subsequent date determined by said decision'.

A slightly surprising feature of French constitutional adjudication, pointed out by Ponthoreau and Hourquebiec, is that France lacks a consolidated charter of constitutionally protected rights: it is only in the preamble to the Constitution that the French people proclaimed 'their attachment to the Rights of Man and the principles of national sovereignty as defined by the Declaration of 1789', listing only the original 'first generation' rights.[61] A *Charter of the Environment and Standards of Environmental Protection* of 2004 was incorporated in the Constitution in 2005, and in a 2008 judgment the *Conseil Constitutionnel* recognized the constitutional status of the rights set out therein.[62] Due to the lack of a consolidated catalogue of fundamental rights, the *Conseil Constitutionnel* might have followed an approach of applying the Constitution only literally, but has chosen to follow a constructive interpretation, nevertheless leaving room for some uncertainty about what the extent of the superior constitutional norms (the *bloc de constitutionnalité*) is.[63]

---

[60] Ponthoreau & Hourquebiec 'The French Conseil Constitutionnel' 269.
[61] Ponthoreau & Hourquebiec 'The French Conseil Constitutionnel' 270.
[62] Decision no. 2008-564 DC of 19 June 2008, para 18.
[63] Ponthoreau & Hourquebiec 'The French Conseil Constitutionnel' 277–8.

10.2.4 South Africa

Having had British colonial constitutional foundations for almost two centuries (complete with the primacy of parliamentary sovereignty) before adopting a comprehensive supreme constitution in 1994, the South African judiciary has had to undergo a complete renewal. First, a new tribunal, the Constitutional Court, was set up with final jurisdiction over constitutional matters. Secondly, constitutional jurisdiction was awarded to most of the existing superior courts, subject however to the final determination by the Constitutional Court.[64]

Thus decentralized and strong constitutional review was introduced to South Africa, in effect fundamentally transforming the legal system as a whole from a mixed Roman-Dutch, common law and indigenous legal order to one dominated by a constitution as the supreme law of the land, conceived according to the late twentieth-century model of constitutionalism as interpreted authoritatively by the judiciary. In time the judicial system has been systematically adapted and refined in a process of converting a judiciary lacking constitutional review jurisdiction into one that bears the final responsibility for interpreting and overseeing conformity with the Constitution.

Initially, the previous apex court retained its position as final adjudicator in all non-constitutional matters, but in 2013 a constitutional amendment rendered the Constitutional Court 'the highest court of the Republic'.[65] Section 2 of the current (1996) Constitution provides that law or conduct inconsistent with the Constitution is invalid, and section 172(1) explicitly requires courts to declare any law or conduct that is inconsistent with the Constitution to be invalid to the extent of its inconsistency. Orders of a High Court declaring national or provincial legislation or conduct of the President to be constitutionally invalid requires confirmation by the Constitutional Court.[66] At the request of the President, or of one-third of the members of the National Assembly, the Constitutional Court may determine the constitutional validity of legislation *ex ante*,[67] but *ex post* judgments on constitutionality[68] occurs more frequently.

Over the first 25 years of the life of the Constitutional Court, it has performed a key role in the development of a South African notion of constitutionalism. The legitimacy of its judgments has been buttressed by mechanisms such as *en banc* adjudication, comprehensive (sometimes exhaustive) justificatory argumentation and commitment to the defence of the integrity of the Constitution,

---

[64] Chapter 7 of the *Constitution of the Republic of South Africa*, 1993.
[65] Section 167(3)(a) of the Constitution as amended by the *Constitution Seventeenth Amendment Act*, 2012.
[66] Sections 169(1) and 172 of the 1996 Constitution.
[67] Sections 79 and 80 of the 1996 Constitution.
[68] Sections 167–9 of the 1996 Constitution.

but is constantly being challenged under circumstances in Waldron's words quoted above at note 14 of a set of 'peculiar pathologies, dysfunctional legislative institutions, corrupt political cultures, legacies of racism, and other forms of endemic prejudice'.[69]

Relatively frequent adverse decisions of unconstitutionality against parliamentary legislation and executive action have been taken by the courts, especially the Constitutional Court. Adverse political reaction is inevitable, and a range of devices used by governments to respond to judgments unfavourable to them may be identified. Isabeau Steytler recently discussed ten such 'tactics for striking back and clamping down' under circumstances of a shift from parliamentary sovereignty to constitutional supremacy, with specific reference to South Africa.[70] She found a pattern of steady escalation in the employment of such tactics in South Africa since 1994, peaking during the Zuma presidency from 2009 to 2018 during which open political attacks on the judiciary, manipulation of the appointment process of judges, flouting the law during court procedures to disable the effects of the negative outcome, and openly employing delaying mechanisms to postpone final adjudication indefinitely, proliferated.[71]

10.2.5 Dysfunctional Constitutional Review

At the end of his comprehensive survey of the growth of judicial review as an almost self-evident feature of contemporary constitutionalism, Stephen Calabresi concluded:

> I think that what is truly distinctive about the post-1945 experience of constitutionalism is ... the written constitutionalization of judicial review of federal legislation, executive actions under written bills of rights, and of a Madisonian system of checks and balances ... What is distinctive about the post-1945 constitutions is that they have actually worked because they have been accompanied by 'the rise of

---

[69] Also see Venter 'Independence and Accountability of the South African Judiciary'.

[70] Steytler '"Striking Back" and "Clamping Down" in South Africa'. At 365–6 she identified the following ten tactics: delaying tactics using the judicial process; repeating decisions after following the correct procedure censured by the court; adopting legislation retrospectively validating faulty government conduct; simply disobeying court orders; legislatively diverting jurisdiction away from the ordinary courts; limiting *locus standi* to for instance only those personally affected by government conduct; abuse of legal costs by raising them or denying legal aid; legislation adopted to relieve the government from liability before the courts to comply with international obligations; the appointment of executive-minded judges; and undermining the independence of the judiciary.

[71] Steytler '"Striking Back" and "Clamping Down" in South Africa' 374–82.

global systems of checks and balances' and by 'the rise of global judicial review' ... Between 1945 and 2021, the common law world rejected the Westminster Model in favor of the U.S. Model of judicial review, and the civil law world rejected France's historical disapproval of judicial review in favor of the German Model of judicial review, which is now triumphant in all civil law nations, including France.[72]

Seen thus, one might say that judicial review jurisdiction has become the constitutional vogue: without it, a country's constitutional order might be denigrated as being out of sync with the 'democratic' world. This may be a reason for the emergence of apparent, but dysfunctional regimes of judicial review, of which some Central and Eastern European examples increasingly crop up.[73] Kim Lane Scheppele described this form of retrogression in terms of a 'constitutional coup', including court packing and jurisdiction stripping:

> A *constitutional* coup is constitutional because there is no break in legality, never a moment when a government does something formally illegal to attain its desired goals. It is nonetheless a *coup* because the end result turns the prior constitutional order on its head without a legitimating process to confirm the changes. Through a series of perfectly legal moves the constitutionally devious leaders of a state can achieve a substantively anti-constitutional result, including, in the extreme case, transforming a state in plain sight from a constitutional democracy to an autocracy, all the while appearing to honor the constitution.[74]

The apparent retreat of effective constitutional review in states where principled adherence to constitutional values is being replaced by nominal 'constitutionalism' speaks at least as loudly about the underlying political problematics as do the various theoretical claims of countermajoritarianism in its different forms: opposition to review jurisdiction on constitutional grounds over legislative and executive conduct is founded on assumptions about the legitimacy of state authority (such as liberalism, populism and positivism), which should be accounted for when assessing the desirability of judicial review.

10.3 THE ESSENCE OF JUDICIAL AUTHORITY

When considering judicial review authority, the focus is understandably on constitutional review in the sense of courts' jurisdiction to determine the constitutional lawfulness of especially legislative, but also executive and other actions taken in the process of exercising the authority of the state.

---

[72] Calabresi 'The Global Rise of Judicial Review' 443–4.
[73] See the references to 'illiberal constitutionalism' in Chapter 9 above, and the sources cited there, and also Bugarič 'Central Europe's Descent into Autocracy'.
[74] Scheppele 'Constitutional Coups and Judicial Review' 51–2.

However, to gain a clear perspective on its essence, one needs to consider that constitutional jurisdiction often also extends to the adjudication of individual disputes without direct involvement of the state, and also that constitutional review is only one form of adjudicatory authority (other forms being administrative, criminal and civil law adjudication). The various forms of judicial authority are clearly distinguishable from one another, but they have a common foundation: it is in itself an exercise of state authority, entailing the resolution of disputes in terms of the law in all its manifestations, its underlying values and principles, and for the purposes of maintaining social order in the pursuance of justice. The essential reasons for a court having constitutional review jurisdiction can hardly be detached from the reasons for having jurisdiction at all.

But a question – very hard to answer – must be asked: why *do* courts have the authority to adjudicate at all? Providing an answer may be even more difficult than explaining the power of the government and the legislature. Those who profess the sovereignty of the people have succeeded for centuries in building elaborate theories based on the notion that rulers and legislators exercise whatever powers they have on behalf of the 'sovereign people', but where do the judges fit in this scheme of things? In fact, at the centre of the countermajoritarian argument that judicial control over the constitutionality of legislation lacks legitimacy, lies the assertion that judges do not represent the 'people'.

With no fear of contradiction, one can state that adjudication has been a feature of human social life as far back in history as can be reached. Does this ancient phenomenon across cultures perhaps not mean that judicial authority is an existential characteristic of social order?

In the sense of the competence of a court to adjudicate on the validity of conduct measured against the interpretation of binding legal norms, judicial (review) authority is an essential feature of a functional legal order. Assessment of the fairness and legitimacy of judicial authority in concrete instances requires consideration of more than its origins and theoretical justification. Equally (if not more) crucial, are considerations of the legitimacy of judicial appointments, and the independence and professional ethics of the judges and legal practitioners. This, again, is a topic that cannot here be pursued further in detail, other than referring to the insightful analysis by Michal Bobek and David Kosař of the difficulties attending global attempts (with specific reference to post-Soviet reforms in Central and Eastern Europe) to ensure judicial independence in the process of reforming judiciaries. They cite global and European efforts to develop standards (mostly formulated by judges) for the administration of a judiciary,[75] and find them lacking because their application has not succeeded in ensuring two of the most important desired outcomes: 'open, transparent and competitive access to the judicial profession' and 'the focus on the quintessential nature of judging: Independent and impartial decision-making in an individual case, delivered in a speedy way, and of a reasonable quality. For that, individual guarantees on a micro-level together with strong individual judges are essential.'[76]

The issues surrounding judicial review and its justification evoke some of the most profound considerations in the field of constitutional law, because, I would suggest, constitutional adjudication very often transcends mere legal norms, deals with and purports to resolve moral issues, ontological premises, and notions of justice. Jeremy Waldron called these 'watershed issues', being 'major choices that any modern society must face' which are to be settled legislatively in legal orders with weak-form or no judicial review, and judicially where strong-form review prevails.[77]

For judicial review, and for that matter all judicial authority to be recognized as legitimate and justifiable, trust in the objectivity, skills, fairness, and wisdom of judges is a prerequisite – regardless of the judicial model – strong, weak, centralized, decentralized or in any combination thereof. In her consideration of 'adjudication as applied moral theory' Iris van Domselaar considers a liberal perspective on reciprocity,[78] proffering in its place what she calls a 'neo-aristotelian' approach, which 'does not rely on moral theory for the justification of judicial decisions, but rather on these decisions being made by a virtuous judge'.[79]

The involvement of *reciprocity* in the consideration of the ideals for and justification of judicial authority holds much promise, despite some variation

---

[75] These include the United Nations' *Basic Principles on the Independence of the Judiciary* of 1985 and the 2002 *Bangalore Principles of Judicial Conduct*, the Council of Europe's 1994 *Recommendation No. R (94) 12 to Member States on the Independence, Efficiency and Role of Judges*, and *Opinion no. 10(2007) of the Consultative Council of European Judges (CCJE) to the attention of the Committee of Ministers of the Council of Europe on the Council for the Judiciary at the service of society*: Bobek & Kosař 'Global Solutions, Local Damages' 1258–63.

[76] Bobek & Kosař 'Global Solutions, Local Damages' 1292.

[77] Waldron 'Judicial Review of Legislation' 438.

[78] Van Domselaar 'A Neo-Aristotelian Notion of Reciprocity'. At 223 she cites John Rawls' summary of 'liberal reciprocity': 'our exercise of political power is proper only when we sincerely believe that the reasons for our political action may reasonably be accepted by other citizens as a justification of those actions' (which seems to me to resonate with Kant's 'categorical imperative').

[79] Van Domselaar 'A Neo-Aristotelian Notion of Reciprocity' 245.

in emphasis regarding its meaning, because, as I have argued elsewhere,[80] the truly universal principle of reciprocity and judicial endeavour to achieve objectivity founded upon this principle, offer solutions to some of the most intractable difficulties inherent in contemporary constitutionalism.

---

[80] Venter 'Constitutionalism and Religion' 79–83 and 230–40.

11. Constitutional comparison and terminology

It is possible to argue that almost all knowledge, be it obtained inductively by naïve or conscious empirical observation, or deductively by means of logical reasoning and systematic ordering, is gained by means of comparison. Such an argument would assume that perceptions of reality are relative and contextual, requiring comparison in order to validate observation.[1] Regardless of the salience of such an argument, there can be little doubt that both unplanned (involuntary inductive) and intentional (deductive, scientific) comparison very often assist us in gaining what we perceive to be 'knowledge'. How, for instance, would a lawyer be able to distinguish between judicial review and appeal, between domestic and international regulation, between criminal and civil procedure, between personal and political fundamental rights, without comparison?

Epistemological analysis aside, legal, and especially constitutional, comparison[2] has achieved the status of an essential tool for the acquisition of knowledge of constitutional law in our globalized world.[3] As is the case with

---

[1] E.g. the rise or fall of ocean temperature by single degrees as opposed to temperature variations of hundreds of degrees on the International Space Station indicate relative and contextual meanings of 'warm' and 'cold'. Thus, it may be argued that valid knowledge of the effects of temperature variation depends on comparison.

[2] I prefer, despite its wide currency, not to use the term 'comparative constitutional law' because it suggests the existence of a body of legal norms, while it, even as a growing field of scholarly endeavour and education, is devoid of legal normative or prescriptive characteristics. This is acknowledged by Reimann 'Neighbouring Disciplines' 14:
> comparative law is a *method* of studying law and a stock of *academic knowledge*, while the other 'international' disciplines consist (at least largely) of positive legal rules. In other words, there is no comparative *law* (only the comparative study and knowledge of it), but there *is* foreign, private and public international, and transnational *law*.

[3] Clicking on the 'search' function of the websites of major legal publishing houses or academic libraries with the term 'comparative constitutional law' produces thousands of results listing recently published books explicitly or indirectly dealing with the field. This means more than the mere popularization of the field: it demonstrates the liberation of constitutional studies from parochial navel-gazing, driven by, inter alia, globalization.

all lawyers, the constitutional comparatist is entirely dependent on the words, the language, definitions, the *lexis* of constitutional law. In a recent publication on comparative constitutional theory (focused on liberal constitutional theory), the editors were primarily concerned –

> ... with the clarification of concepts important to the activity of comparative theorizing (which if done well will translate into a more applied vernacular). Thus many of the ideas and analytical constructs that have become ubiquitous in the field of comparative constitutional law remain largely under-theorized, frequently applied to all manner of things that are dissimilar in significant respects.[4]

Here lies the core problem with which this book is concerned: comparatists from different constitutional jurisdictions, subscribing to varying ontological persuasions, rooted in unlike educational traditions and working in constitutional orders with dissimilar historical backgrounds and traditions of governance, adjudication, and practice, are all constrained to express themselves comparatively using the same words. Elemental 'constitutional' words such as those discussed in the preceding chapters more than often bear different contextual meanings, potentially curtailing the potential of clear and effective comparative communication.

This chapter explores the implications for comparative constitutional scholarship and state practice of the ongoing variance, mutation, and diversity of meaning of the words and concepts in our strange, and often inconsistent constitutional vocabulary identified in the preceding chapters.

In the first section the nature of constitutional comparison is revisited. What is it that constitutional comparatists do, why do they do it, should it really be acknowledged as a discipline within the legal encyclopaedia, and why has it become such a widespread activity? The second section is concerned with comparative methodology and the complications for the comparative method produced by the unstable language of constitutional law. In the third section conclusions are drawn concerning the implications for constitutional comparison of the fluidity of constitutional language, keeping in mind that comprehensive methodological consistency in the field of constitutional comparison will remain, at best, a fragile ideal.

11.1 THE NATURE OF CONSTITUTIONAL COMPARISON

'Constitutional law' being what it is, namely the complex of binding legal norms in terms of which *a particular state* and its organs are established, and

---

[4] Jacobsohn & Schor 'Comparative Constitutional Theory' 5.

the operation, functions, relationships among the organs, and between them and the citizens of the state concerned are regulated, can easily be mistaken for an isolated, inward-looking discipline dealing only with national history and parochial idiosyncrasies. The inclination to commit such an error can be compounded by the fact that the constitutional law of every state is indeed unique. This is due to the inevitability of the distinctive historical, social, political, economic, and cultural considerations that give rise to the founding of a state, but significantly also because of the operation of the always present foundational notion of *sovereignty*. The sovereignty of a state conceptually precludes the external imposition of constitutional norms upon the state as a legal entity, its organs, nationals, and citizens.[5]

Comparing the constitutional law of various states, on the other hand, is not at all unusual or rare. Constitutional comparison is an almost instinctive and hardly avoidable choice when constitutions are designed, exactly because of the unfeasibility of isolating the impact of the historical, social, political, economic, and cultural considerations relevant in one place from those prevailing in the rest of the world.[6] No doubt these factors have an impact on the interpretation of the constitutional law of a particular state. The interpretation and implementation of a constitution is obviously the remit of judges and practising lawyers (who are notoriously not all competent comparatists), but it is constitutional scholarship that has developed constitutional comparison into an intellectual industry, inundated with ontological, epistemological, doctrinal, dogmatic, cultural, and ideological considerations. The field (which it seems to have become) therefore presents a fractured appearance, which justifies avoidance of the concept 'comparative constitutional law', suggestive of consolidated normativity in favour of the *activity* 'constitutional comparison'.[7]

Scholarly comparison in science is a universal phenomenon, likely in most cases to encounter common challenges relating to difference and similarity. Imaginary comparative research projects in the agricultural, economic, biological, historical (and other) sciences might for instance pursue the following themes: meat production by the Sámi in Finland, by Argentinian Gauchos and by Australian ranchers; the impact on human health of beverages produced by

---

[5] Many an instance can however be cited where foreign, and even international prescripts concerning constitutional norms of embryonic or reconfigured states had had to be complied with, but at the moment of the achievement of sovereignty, the constitutional law of the sovereign state becomes indigenous, in principle (if not always in practice) beyond the pale of the rest of the world.

[6] Goderis & Versteeg 'Transnational Constitutionalism' 125 e.g. argues that, through coercion, competition, learning and acculturation as mechanisms, 'modern-day constitutions have become transnational constitutions'.

[7] Cf the remark in note 2 above.

Colombia (coffee), South Africa (Rooibos) and Sri Lanka (tea), and marketing strategies employed by the producers of Irish whiskey, Caribbean rum and Japanese saké. In such projects, researchers will encounter the need to justify their comparisons, will have to seek a balance in their interpretation of similarity and difference, and will have to account for their own predilections brought about by, among other things, their cultural and educational backgrounds. For constitutional comparatists it is not different.

11.2 METHODOLOGY AND CONSTITUTIONAL LANGUAGE

What a proper comparative method is, is an issue of intense debate (sometimes with extreme acerbity).[8] It is a debate that cannot be expected ever to subside or to be 'won' by any school of thought, exactly because comparative methodology is profoundly dependent upon ontological and epistemological premises. It may however be possible to glean valuable elements from various methodologies to promote a measure of comprehensive cogency. To this end, and to demonstrate the impact of the sponginess of the terminology of constitutional law on the practice of constitutional comparison, taking a bird's eye view of the methods in circulation which are propounded for constitutional comparison may be helpful.

The picture of intellectualized methodological approaches to comparison in law, including constitutional law, can be equated with a seascape speckled with remote islands. One of these islands is inhabited by an energetic, if motley population of 'Crits', some also working in constitutional law.[9] Another is populated by (mostly American) teachers of 'comparative constitutional law',[10] and the island of European constitutional scholarship concentrates on issues related to the balancing of domestic constitutional and supra-national (EU)

---

[8] Among the most odious examples of unethical scholarly vitriol is Pierre Legrand's accusation hurled at renowned comparatists, with whose methods he differed, of being 'tenaciously delusional' and 'stubbornly disingenuous': Legrand & Munday (eds) 'Comparative Legal Studies' 247–8. Perhaps there is some truth in 'Sayre's law', which has been expressed eloquently in the Wall Street Journal's quotation on 20 December 1973 of Wallace Stanley Sayre: 'Academic politics is the most vicious and bitter form of politics, because the stakes are so low.'

[9] Exemplified by Günter Frankenberg's brilliant publications, such as Frankenberg 'Between Magic and Deceit' and Frankenberg 'Critique'.

[10] Prominent in this category are professors such as Vicky Jackson and Mark Tushnet (who have published or edited various books jointly and separately under the title 'comparative constitutional law' since 1999, the latest being four volumes by Jackson & Versteeg 'Comparative Constitutional Law').

law.[11] There is also the island of legal pluralism,[12] and others visible on the horizon, but more difficult to distinguish through the mists of theorization.[13] Although their foci may sometimes coincide, comparative methodology is not necessarily the binding force among those toiling on any of these 'islands': *none of them can however escape the bonds of the ecumenical vocabulary of constitutional law.*

Little more than listing the most prominent methodological variations in constitutional comparison can be achieved here.[14] The methodologies are seldom particularly 'constitutional', among other reasons because, by the time comparative constitutional scholarship became prominent,[15] methods for comparison in law, especially in private law, had already been established, allowing for much borrowing from especially the continental private law comparatists.[16] In time, constitutional comparison developed to a point where Jaako Husa could state that –

> ... comparative constitutional law has freed itself from the paradigmatic grip of a private law-oriented comparative study of law. This has brought new approaches and an openness towards various methods not familiar from doctrinal comparisons. In short, the suffocating epistemic embrace of private law-focused legal doctrine has all but died out.[17]

Most settled and widely advocated (and also most denigrated) is functionalism and variations on the theme (functionalism not being a uniform idea).[18] The

---

[11] See e.g. Miller & Zumbansen 'Comparative Law as Transnational Law' and Von Bogdandy et al. 'Defending Checks and Balances in EU Member States'.

[12] See e.g. Tamanaha, Sage & Woolcock 'Legal Pluralism and Development' and Tusseau 'Debating Legal Pluralism and Constitutionalism'.

[13] For instance, without knowledge of the relevant languages, it is difficult to identify or categorize the comparative work done beyond the hegemonic domain of North Atlantic scholarship, although measuring Islamic, socialist, and other legal orders against Western constitutional notions is often encountered: cf e.g. Matronardi 'Recht und Kultur'. See also the identification of elements of uniqueness emerging elsewhere, discussed in Dann, Riegner & Bönnemann 'The Global South and Comparative Constitutional Law'.

[14] I have surveyed the field before, e.g. Venter 'Global Features' 37–51, and will therefore only cite a few additional publications on the subject for reference purposes.

[15] See e.g. Hirschl 'The Continued Renaissance of Comparative Constitutional Law'.

[16] See e.g. Bignami 'Formal Versus Functional Method in Comparative Constitutional Law'.

[17] Husa 'Comparative Methodology and Constitutional Change' 25.

[18] See e.g. Whytock 'Legal Origins, Functionalism, and the Future of Comparative Law', the sources cited in Venter 'Global Features' 38–41, and Zumbansen 'Review' of Frankenberg's 'Comparative Law's Coming of Age?' 1074–7.

appeal of functionalism lies in its apparent neutral neatness and assumptions of universalism: the messiness of the history, cultural context and social effects of a legal norm is often deemed to be of secondary importance as soon as the similarity of the function of the norm is construed as comparator (to borrow a term from the field of electronics).[19]

Another widely advocated group of comparative methods relies on the observation that constitutional ideas are mobile. Labels attached to this approach are 'transplantation',[20] 'migration',[21] and 'borrowing'.[22] An advantage of this approach is that it provides a locus from where the comparative exercise may depart, namely the constitutional order serving as the perceived origin of the concepts being compared.

Distaste for liberalism, legalism, 'mainstream orthodoxy', rejection of the emphasis on similarity, and preoccupation with 'the Other',[23] have inspired 'critical' scholars to develop unique and complex alternative comparative matrices.[24]

Woven into various points in the fabric of comparative methodologies is a further plethora of concepts employed in the practice of constitutional comparison. Among them there are universalism versus contextualism,[25] dialogical interpretationism,[26] and an emphasis on constitutional change as a distinct field, which 'is methodologically open and flexible because it encompasses all sorts of comparisons ranging from the study of formal amendment procedures to analysing more subtle mechanisms of change'.[27]

Despite (or perhaps because of) the immense volume of literature on comparative methodology, not many judges and students of constitutional law concern themselves overly much with the raging debates over their own methods of comparison – and simply go ahead to compare, merrily incorporating 'comparative' in the titles of their publications or judicial remarks,

---

[19] Cf e.g. Peters & Schwenke 'Comparative Law beyond Post-Modernism' 808–10.
[20] See e.g. Donovan 'Human Rights: From Legal Transplants to Fair Translation', and (critical of transplantation) Carvalho 'Law, Language, and Knowledge'.
[21] See e.g. Brang 'Carl Schmitt and the Evolution of Chinese Constitutional Theory'.
[22] See e.g. Tsai 'Considerations of History and Purpose in Constitutional Borrowing'.
[23] See e.g. Peters & Schwenke 'Comparative Law beyond Post-Modernism' 802, 811–12.
[24] An interesting example is the comparative 'grid' proposed by Günter Frankenberg in Frankenberg 'Critique' 84, and the demonstration of its application at 118.
[25] Murkens 'Preservative or Transformative?'.
[26] See e.g. Dhooghe, Franken & Opgenhaffen 'Judicial Activism at the European Court of Justice'.
[27] Husa 'Comparative Methodology and Constitutional Change' 41.

leaving it to readers who may want to bother to work out if the resultant comparative work was inspired by one or the other methodological doctrine or approach. One might sometimes even wonder whether a particular methodologically undefined comparison was made inductively, based on superficial, cherry-picking observation, or done based on (carefully concealed) rigorous deductive reasoning. But no comparatist can escape the methodological undercurrents, as Ralf Michaels neatly sketched the scene in 2002 by showing that it is very broadly tied to the perennial epistemological poles, natural law and positivism.[28] *And yet, constitutional comparatists have only one universal constitutional vocabulary, regardless of their leanings towards natural law or positivism, or of their disregard for theoretical justification.*

The turbulent vista over the sea of constitutional comparison, showing capital ships firing broadsides in battles over methodological propriety while floating on a stagnant surface of methodological apathy, leaves the constitutional comparatist with difficult choices, compounded by the terminological vagaries considered in the previous chapters. So, why not leave it to those endlessly quibbling metaphysically minded theorists?

The answer is simple: neutrality is impossible and compromises between incompatible views inconceivable.[29] The interwoven histories, terminology and interlinked theoretical foundations of constitutional orders will be invisible only to the uninitiated or ignored by the obtuse, because the answer to the question how it should be done depends on the questioner's personal worldview. True liberals (still apparently in the majority among authors on constitutional comparison) base their comparisons on the assumption of popular sovereignty and the primacy of individual autonomy. Those with

---

[28] Michaels 'Im Westen nichts Neues?' 100:
... Vergleichung im strikten Sinne [setzt] einerseits Verschiedenheit, andererseits Gleichartigkeit (das tertium comparationis) der Untersuchungsgegenstände voraus [...]. Im klassischen Spannungsverhältnis zwischen potenziell universalem Vernunft- oder Naturrecht einerseits, nationalem positivem Recht andererseits, fiel damit die Rechtsvergleichung zwischen beide Stühle. Natur- und Vernunftrechtler waren – jedenfalls, soweit sie ihr Fach spekulativ betrieben – an der Vergleichung verschiedener Rechtsordnungen ebensowenig interessiert wie die Pandektisten, weil es für beide nur eine echte Rechtsgrundlage gab: Vernunft, Natur, christliche Ethik einerseits, römisches Recht andererseits. Fehlte es hier also an der Verschiedenheit unterschiedlicher Forschungsgegenstände, so bezweifelten Positivisten andererseits die Vergleichbarkeit verschiedener Rechtsordnungen – für sie war jeder ausländische Rechtssatz irrelevant, weil er für sie nicht bindend sein konnte (und weil sie mit der Auslegung der neuen Gesetzbücher genug zu tun hatten).

[29] To mention but one example: Frankenberg's assault on 'mainstream orthodoxy' as 'legoscentric, positivist and Anglo-Eurocentric' (Frankenberg 'Critique' 14) effectively demonstrates the incompatibility of contesting comparative methodologies.

a post-modern inclination deal with constitutional law comparatively as an essentially political, economic or social discipline expressed in words having interminable normative fluidity. Functional comparison may serve positivists well, and true socialists should not have much use for constitutional comparison at all, except perhaps to obtain an understanding of how the rest of the world thinks about limitations on the authority of the state.

The upshot is that the constitutional comparatist cannot be neutral. That, I would argue, speaks for sound scholarship, because neutrality, properly understood, signifies detachment, disinterest, non-engagement, uncaring blandness and disregard for one's personal convictions – an attitude incompatible with honest scientific investigation.[30] What is however required as an essential element of unbiased investigation, promising results persuasive to, or at least legitimate in the eyes also of those with different foundational perspectives, is *objectivity*.

To achieve objective analysis requires concentrated hard work and a conscious effort. Where the pursuit of neutrality would demand the ability to be completely detached from the desired outcome of an investigation (which really is humanly impossible), objectivity calls for the express acknowledgement of one's inability so to be mindlessly detached, and recognition of the responsibility to be fair-minded in the pursuit of an unprejudiced result. Whereas the notion of neutrality supposes the ability to disengage feeling and preference, objectivity actively requires an effort to be even-handed, despite one's inescapably extant predilections. Ironically, objectivity depends on the acknowledgment of preconception, whereas a claim of neutrality may amount to an attempt to conceal prejudice.

When it comes to (constitutional) comparison, it is objectivity that may allow one to avoid the cloister of a single comparative method.[31] An objective

---

[30] In an excellent dissection of the notion of neutrality, Watson 'Rethinking neutrality' shows that its meaning is all but clear-cut, finding (at 27) that –

> ... many theorists writing about neutrality as a political ideal are operating without the benefit of a coherent and plausible conception of what it is to act neutrally, and that in the interests of conceptual clarity it would be preferable if they spoke not of 'neutrality', but rather of 'public justifiability', or 'equal accommodation', or 'equal impact' (depending on the particular emphasis of particular scholars).

Watson *ibid* proposes instead 'volitional neutrality', 'according to which acting neutrally requires that an actor refrains from conduct engaged in for the purpose of helping or hindering a particular party in a given contest, as well as conduct that the actor believes is likely to cause such an effect'.

[31] It is not always clear if multi-method comparative approaches are moved by motives of objectivity, but it is not uncommon, e.g. Whytock 'Legal Origins, Functionalism, and the Future of Comparative Law' 1879: 'After all, different approaches are appropriate for different endeavors'; Örücü 'The Enigma of Comparative

measurement of the tenability of the results of another's comparative exercise, also considering the underlying epistemology of the method, is possible, among other reasons because it allows for comparing the outcomes of further projects achieved with methods based on dissimilar foundational views. Such an objective appraisal then provides one with a sound foundation for the assessment of various outcomes, explicitly based on one's own predilections. Objectivity thus facilitates judgement based on the revelation of one's ever-present premises, whereas neutrality presumes the (impossible) ability to 'switch off' preconception, while actually engaging it.

11.3 COMPARING WITH ESSENTIAL MEANING

There may be various purposes for undertaking a project of constitutional comparison, including a taxonomic classification of constitutional orders, gaining an improved understanding of a – especially the comparatist's own – constitutional order, finding or promoting universal constitutional principles or phenomena, deepening understanding of the historical or theoretical development of constitutional concepts, processes and systems, enriching insights for the purposes of constitution-writing, and more.[32] But, regardless of methodological preference, the instability of the language of constitutional law represents the soft underbelly of constitutional comparison, however approached.

To demonstrate, consider the following statement:

> *The comparative quality of the constitutional order of the state of any nation whose citizens participate in the democratic establishment of their sovereign government under the rule of law may, for the purposes of judicial review, be measured in terms of compliance with the tenets of constitutionalism.*

To many a constitutional lawyer this assertion may appear to be self-evidently correct. However, eight key concepts are employed here which were found in

---

Law' 64 concluded on the question whether different comparative approaches are incompatible, that there is ample scope in a particular case to use any one of the following: 'universalism, functionalism, culture, legal history, unity of common law, convergence and the *ius commune novum*, difference and identity, competition of legal rules and transposition.'

[32] In a small textbook on research methodology in law intended for a readership of students and early-career researchers (Venter *Legal Research* 50–62), I pointed out that a project in legal comparison should not be mere mechanical compilation, the selection of materials to be compared should be relevant and comparable, the comparison should be approached systematically, be done for a legitimate purpose (as opposed to mere academic adornment), should be clear on what the materials are being compared against, and that the reasons for dealing with the topic comparatively should be justified.

the chapters above to bear multiple or indeterminate meanings. If these findings are correct, the legitimacy and cogency of every project of constitutional comparison can be expected to depend on a coherent explication (or at the very least a clear and perceptible implication) of what the comparatist means with the core constitutional expressions employed in the project. No doubt there would be those who would deem this proposition to be overly cumbersome, but it would be difficult to deny its logic, given the findings reported in the previous chapters.

> As an ubiquitous construct of human society, the *state* is both the subject and object of constitutional law, and therefore the study of its juridical qualities should be the ultimate goal of the craft of constitutional comparison. However, being the stuff of profound and interminable theorization among constitutional lawyers, there is no consensus regarding its substance or the legal requirements for its establishment, existence, and functioning.[33]
>
> In the popular political vernacular, nationhood often anachronistically serves as an expression of statehood, but '*nation*' bears a multitude of alternative meanings, and constitutional theory has contributed very little to revoke the anachronistic suggestion of synchronicity between 'state' and 'nation'.[34]
>
> *Sovereignty* as justification for holding power is widely (if varyingly) attributed to the sovereignty of 'the people'. In constitutional law the notion presents itself as a relic from the history of the evolution of modern statehood. It has lost its original substance, causing popular sovereignty, based on fictional assumptions and constructions, to notionally contradict state and governmental sovereignty.[35]
>
> *Citizenship* (often confusingly equated with nationality) can be regarded both from the perspective of the individual citizen (whose legal status is determined thereby), and of the state (whose existence is closely linked to a citizenry). This reciprocal link is confirmed by the reality that the authority of the state can only be exercised by human hands acting as organs of the state, but globalization, supranationalism, large-scale migration and various non-legal disciplines' attraction to the concept tend to dilate the boundaries of its meaning in law.[36]
>
> The transfer of the authority of 'the people' to (at least some of) the governing institutions of a state by means of a *democratic* process

---

[33] Chapter 5 above.
[34] Chapter 3 above.
[35] Chapter 4 above.
[36] Chapter 6 above.

is routinely deemed to legitimize the exercise of constituted powers. This is a claim made in constitutional orders spread across the whole spectrum, causing 'democracy' to mean almost anything, and therefore potentially nothing. The addition of adjectives such as 'direct', 'electoral', 'constitutional', 'liberal' (or 'illiberal'), 'people's', etc. can be helpful if the user simultaneously explains the intended meaning of the adjective, because the combination may also be understood in different ways.[37]

Reference to the *rule of law* implicates a complex of legal conceptions, but almost every user of the expression may have a different notion in mind of the compound of conceptions populating the idea. The existence of partially comparable doctrines in Continental legal orders (especially *Rechtsstaatlichkeit* and *Verfassungsstaatlichkeit*) adds to the range of possible elements, both of a formal and substantive nature.[38]

The width of meaning attributable to *constitutionalism* is compounded by the fact that it is usually intended to incorporate a range of conceptions in the common constitutional vocabulary with indefinite or variable meaning. Mention of constitutionalism in comparative context may therefore lack persuasive meaning where the comparatist fails to explain the jurisdictional, epistemological, or disciplinary (constitutional, international legal, supra-national, historical, environmental, etc.) context in which it is used.[39]

The controversies surrounding *judicial review* jurisdiction founded upon constitutional sanction are many. Justifying it evokes some of the most profound considerations in the field of constitutional law, also because constitutional adjudication very often transcends questions of lawfulness and legitimacy, and purports to resolve not only the finer points of constitutional interpretation, but also moral issues, ontological points of departure, and notions of justice.[40]

Where does this leave the constitutional comparatist? A blunt answer might be a moralistic exclamation: 'watch your language!' – but this is not about moralization. It concerns the heart of what has developed from dispersed academic cottage enterprises of constitutional comparison to an immense global scholarly and judicial industry in which practically anyone working in constitutional law must be involved in order to validate their status as constitutional lawyers.

As constitutional comparison grows in importance, there is an inexorably increasing need for coherent comparative language, because its absence may

---

[37] Chapter 7 above.
[38] Chapter 8 above.
[39] Chapter 9 above.
[40] Chapter 10 above.

cause the whole effort to come to naught, losing any claim to consistency, brought about by fragmented attribution (or lack thereof) of intended meaning and inevitable factional preferences.[41] Overcoming the disjointed nature of the language of constitutional comparison is simply unachievable.

Linguistic coherence however does not require uniformity, but it demands contextualization: cogent comparison of statehood, sovereignty, democracy, constitutionalism, and judicial authority among others is obviously precluded if the comparatist uses their meaning in one constitutional order or set of orders to analyze or evaluate others which are rooted in dissimilar conceptual soil.

Equally important are the implications for comparison of the constitutional law of compatible or interlinked constitutional orders without making the comparatist's conceptual premises clear. For instance, assessing the role of the rule of law in British constitutional law by using an American understanding of the notion can hardly be convincing, but it may serve a useful purpose if attributes common to the expression in both contexts (for instance the pursuit of legal certainty and the promotion of non-arbitrariness) are extracted and applied in order to produce comparative insights.[42]

For comparatists taking the problems caused by the liquidity of core constitutional terms into serious consideration (as opposed to arrogantly proceeding on the assumption that subjective personal, jurisdictional or regional terminological, epistemic and ontological preferences should self-evidently dominate the world of comparison), the options for the improvement of comparative constitutional communication are limited, although I would submit that pursuing such improvement warrants persistent consideration.

Two clear options present themselves, both inevitably involving additional encumbrances on the work of the constitutional comparatist: first explicitly stating the preferred definitions of the constitutional concepts to be used in a comparative project, and secondly, working towards a solidification – rather than further diversification – of our common constitutional vocabulary. The merits of the second option are recommended to all constitutional comparatists as an ideal and perpetual quest.

---

[41] Although constitutional comparison resides in the ambit of the humanities and social sciences, the point might also be demonstrated from an (admittedly not directly transferable) example from the science of physics: imagine the confusion among physicists if each awarded their own meaning to concepts such as energy and mass in their efforts to explain the laws of thermodynamics.

[42] See Chapter 8 above.

Epilogue

PURPOSE

The purpose of writing this book was to accentuate the implications of a known phenomenon which is too seldom acknowledged: the capriciousness of the language essential to comparative work in constitutional law. The idea was not to attempt to resolve the problem, but to shine a spotlight on it.

This was motivated by what I consider to be a need to draw the attention of practitioners of constitutional comparison to two features of our work. The first is the proposition that comparatists should strive towards objectivity in the use of constitutional language and also in their choice of comparative method in order to produce persuasive results. Many constitutional comparatists (like most lawyers and scientists in all fields) tend to present their views with confidence as 'truth', without however providing an ontological and epistemological context within which to assess the value of their insights. Secondly, the writing of the book was motivated by the desire to emphasize the need for comparatists to acknowledge that there is no way around the given that one's worldview determines the outcomes of one's scholarly (also comparative) work. The two propositions (objectivity and the inescapability of worldview) may at first sight appear to be contradictory, but, if one accepts that objectivity (distinguished from neutrality) actually depends on the acknowledgement of predilection,[1] it becomes clear that the propositions are mutually reinforcing.

Here a legitimate question would be whether the author is accusing others of what he is guilty himself. Not so, I would argue. First consider again briefly the nature of objectivity, worldview and the mysticism of constitutional theory before weighing a few remarks on my personal conviction pertinent to the study of constitutional law.

OBJECTIVITY

I would suggest that the test for the objectivity with which the analyses were done in the foregoing chapters is whether obvious ontological and epistemo-

---

[1] Cf the reasoning presented in section 11.2 of Chapter 11 above.

logical predilection characterizes the presentation of the various theoretical approaches that were discussed. Although I will admit below to compelling personal convictions inspiring strong likes and dislikes, the intention was to highlight, as objectively as possible, the linguistic problem which bedevils cogent constitutional comparison, by identifying the terminological trends current in the world of constitutional law. Arguing for my terminological preferences was not a central goal, and insofar as inklings of my prejudices might be discernible, the purpose was not to bury them as though it would be possible to achieve 'neutrality'. The intention was to inspect the sources and manner of application of the concepts that were considered as fairly (objectively) as possible in order to expose the plurality of understandings of common concepts. Assessing whether these concepts are compatible with my subjective convictions, and presenting my understanding of the truth, would require a different kind of project, launched under a banner providing a recognizable ontological point of departure.

The purpose of an objective analysis must not be to conceal unspoken premises, but, on the one hand to accumulate valid data, and then, when the occasion arises, to assess the assembled information from an explicitly principled perspective indicative of an intention of open subjectivity. Where one's worldview deviates (as mine does) from the major ontological trends, it would be quixotic to present it to the world in the expectation that adherents of prevailing schools of thought would be persuaded to deviate from their own various courses. At best, expounding one's subjective views would strengthen the convictions of those who share yours, and hopefully be interesting to those who do not. The present undertaking is however not an attempt either to show those with whom I disagree how wrong their premises are or how indisputable mine presumably are, but to emphasize how damaging to legitimate constitutional comparison the terminological murkiness with which constitutional lawyers have to work, actually is.

WORLDVIEW

This was therefore not the occasion to launch into an evaluation of the material that was dealt with, based on a personal worldview (such evaluation may nevertheless warrant future efforts). It may however serve a purpose to present a preliminary outline of my take on a few important issues in constitutional law that I have touched upon in the body of this book.

Seen from the perspective of the terminologically dominant trend in constitutional law, a reading of what is presented above might reveal my capital crime: a distrust of Liberalism. Even if this offence against the norm might be evident, my alternative preferences may be slightly obscure, except perhaps negatively, in that I also do not subscribe to illiberal constitutionalism or populism. I find some of the work produced by the 'Crits' fascinating because of its intellectual depth, but at the same time profoundly objectionable due to its (sometimes even choleric, gloomy or anarchic) inconclusiveness. Constitutional socialism is distasteful to me because of its inherently unprincipled centralization of the power of government, only ostensibly in the name of 'the people' and religion-dominated systems of governance (for instance Islam and other forms of theocratic attempts at masking absolutism) are incapable of offering objective fairness to unbelievers.

Life is unfathomably complex. Science and scholarship represent our efforts to come to grips with the complexities of human life in a cosmos so vast and immeasurable, that we can achieve little more than going on to investigate, hypothesize, theorize – only to reach preliminary, potentially reversible conclusions. To depend on the 'certainties' of our scientifically manufactured knowledge, however meticulously constructed, is to rely on uncertainty. Where the 'exact' sciences study, hypothesize, theorize and sometimes produce spectacular practical achievements – mostly based on often inexplicable phenomena found in nature assumed to be immutable – the humanities and social sciences deal with fluid data gleaned from observation of inconstant objects: human society, human thought, human conflict, human weakness.

Among these sciences is the study of juridical law. The notion of law itself is open to a range of understandings. An understanding of law as enforceable rules regulating human society, produces the need to systematize that bloated body of norms into manageable components. Common to the whole complex of legal normativity is a profound question: why are legal norms enforceable by some people (or institutions of society) over others? This is a question that should engage all students of the law, but the discipline of constitutional law, by its nature, forces its proponents to take a position, at least by implication and even sub-consciously, on the matter. Constitutional law is in the end all about power – its study concerns answering the question from where the power of and in the state originates, how it is regulated, how it is exercised, how it can be limited.

But 'power' is an ugly word because it suggests scarcely qualified dominance of those subject to it by those who have it. More discerning is the euphemism for power: authority. 'Authority' more diplomatically suggests an ability to maintain order, but not necessarily with overwhelming might. Nevertheless, it is impossible to imagine human society functioning in a void without authority – it is an indispensable thread in the fabric of human society, enabling order and government, resulting in normativity: *law*. Every one of us encounters authority in many forms throughout life, and our responses thereto vary.

No wonder then that one's understanding or explanation of the source of authority marks the point of ontological and epistemic parting of many ways: without compromise, one's perception of the foundations upon which authority stands is determined by one's most profound understanding of the world.[2] Simply put, it is a matter of incontestable belief. Incontestable because it is at its foundation not a matter of external, rational persuasion or debate, but of nuclear conviction. In those substantively subscribing to a religion, it is grounded in faith.

CONSTITUTIONAL LAW DEMYSTIFIED

A human society without some hierarchical structure of authority can only exist briefly before it disintegrates. Social order depends on authority. Deciding effectively on behalf of a society about alternative courses to be taken, and producing normation for the functioning of the society, are actions which would not be possible if not accompanied by the obligation of those subject to the norms to comply with the norms.[3] Unfortunately, however, a tendency among those in authority to abuse their privileged positions seems to be an inborn human trait which can only be resisted by the engagement of moral conviction, and where such does not suffice, by means of legal fiat or insurrection.

Preventing or curbing the undue exploitation of attained authority requires the means to limit, and if necessary to withdraw or terminate, the ability to exercise it. Where such termination occurs, an immediate need for reallocation of the revoked authority arises. Recognition of these inherent characteristics of human society and the desire for stability and progress has, since time immemorial, demanded the devising of mechanisms to maintain social order while the complexity of society constantly increases. In history various social artefacts developed in order to regulate authority, quite frequently (especially in less developed societies) monocratic rule, but eventually the idea of the state, which is established and stabilized by law – constitutional law.

Demystifying constitutional sovereignty by recognizing that it is external to the state would relieve the constitutional lawyer from choosing between or creating and adjusting power fictions based on intra-statal social elements such as fear for crude human vulgarity, hopes for collective wisdom, rational individualism (alternatively communal comity), ideological social constructs, and such like. The ambit and remit of demystified constitutional law (especially viewed comparatively) encompasses the study of the fascinating spectrum of solutions to the problem of balancing governing power within the state – itself

---

[2] Consider the religious attitudes of the founders of modern constitutional thinking discussed in section 2.9 of Chapter 2 above.
[3] Is this not also an indispensable insight for the construction of social compact theories, foundational to popular sovereignty?

probably the most ubiquitous virtual artefact of human society created by means of constitutional norms.

Demystified constitutional law is, on the other hand, far from a collection of desiccated, abstract, merely posited rules. In the substrates of almost every facet of constitutional law one can discover their historical and ontological origins, which makes constitutional interpretation, be it judicial or scholarly, a captivating enterprise inevitably requiring engaging the precepts of the interpreter's worldview. This is where scholarly objectivity is called for – to study and appraise the material for what it is, taking note of where it came from, knowing that your own basic premises will constrain you to approve or to disapprove, to support or oppose that which your analyses reveal according to your convictions.

The effort to make your observations objectively, consciously avoiding premature judgemental shortcuts, enables one to assess in a manner consistent with one's foundational understanding of the world. Such objective study is fundamentally different from pretentions of neutrality, which can only achieve the obfuscation of prejudice, because neutrality is unachievable, a figment of the imagination, demanding one to be untrue to one's inescapable personal convictions.

My understanding of the essence of authority, and therefore of constitutional law, is determined by my Christian belief. Now, such a bland statement can no doubt evoke various responses, covering a range of possibilities such as instant termination of academic communication, prejudicial incredulity, sympathetic tolerance, religious opposition, empathetic commiseration, suspicions of naïveté and dogmatism, and more. But hold on! What follows is not an attempt to persuade, to convert or even to defend a position considered by many to be indefensible as a scientific perspective. It is no more than a concise (admittedly unapologetic) demonstration of the influence of worldview on some of the core elements of constitutional law.

'Christian belief' can mean many things to many people, even among the millions who self-identify as Christians. Much of the divergence can be attributed to ecclesiastical dogmatism, fabricated mysticism, misrepresentation, syncretism, embarrassing episodes in church history, and ignorance. A major difficulty is that the practice of religious faith in any manifestation involves commuting between rationality and unquestioning acceptance, the latter shared only by fellow believers. This is most certainly not to subscribe to the notion that faith is purely emotional and devoid of reason: understanding one's belief is eminently rational, even if much of it is not inspired by scientific logic. It must however be emphasized that this does not apply to the Christian faith alone – it is a characteristic of all ontological and epistemic creeds, including those that shun religion.[4]

Let us now briefly consider a few implications of this worldview for attributing meaning to constitutional language.

SOVEREIGNTY AND AUTHORITY

Among the distinguishing features of the Christian belief relevant to my understanding of constitutional law is the conviction that there is only one, sovereign God who created everything known and unknown to humanity and who continues to determine the flow of history, that personal deliverance into eternal life is only possible, and also guaranteed, through belief in the death and resurrection of Christ, and that the Bible contains a reliable, authoritative explication of divine revelations relevant to belief, sufficient for true faith. None of these elements of faith provide the means to persuade others rationally of their truth, but my and other Christians' belief in them is real, and they are indispensably foundational to the Christian worldview. Importantly, those who say that they agree with those tenets of the Christian faith and still seek to explain constitutional (or any other) authority with reference to natural law, popular sovereignty, political, economic, or historical chance, should urgently investigate the solidity of their basic beliefs, or must reconsider their views on constitutional matters.

Since constitutional law is concerned at its core with the source and justification of the authority of the state, a foundational Christian insight is captured in the following remarkable passage in Romans 13:1–7:[5]

> 1 Let everyone be subject to the governing authorities, for there is no authority except that which God has established. The authorities that exist have been established by God. 2 Consequently, whoever rebels against the authority is rebelling against what God has instituted, and those who do so will bring judgment on themselves. 3 For rulers hold no terror for those who do right, but for those who do wrong. Do you want to be free from fear of the one in authority? Then do what is right and you will be commended. 4 For the one in authority is God's servant for your good. But if you do wrong, be afraid, for rulers do not bear the sword for no reason. They are God's servants, agents of wrath to bring punishment on the wrongdoer. 5 Therefore, it is necessary to submit to the authorities, not only because of possible punishment but also as a matter of conscience. 6 This is also why you pay taxes, for the authorities are God's servants, who give their full time to governing. 7 Give to everyone what

---

[4] Is it for instance reasonable for a rationalist to consider human logic to be a reliable source of knowledge without investing blind trust in the unprovable reliability of the mind?

[5] The translation is taken from the New International Version (UK). This is naturally by far not the only Scriptural proclamation of the sovereignty of God.

you owe them: if you owe taxes, pay taxes; if revenue, then revenue; if respect, then respect; if honour, then honour.

Historically this text has of course been abused by rulers and governors to justify claims to divine and absolute power,[6] but the real and obvious crux of the passage is to be found in its proclamation of the *exclusive* seat and source of sovereignty: God. Attributing sovereignty to the state, for instance on the assumption that sovereignty belongs to and emanates from 'the people', is therefore inconsistent with a foundational biblical datum: it contradicts cosmic divine sovereignty at least as much as despotism does.

This does not relieve any constitutional lawyer from the requirement to engage with the core issue of the justification of state authority. On the contrary, it removes doctrinal myopia by deploying a supra-statal lens: sovereignty properly understood is not an artefact of the state, the law, government, the people, electorate, parliament, or constitution, but divine sovereignty is the source of at best the *autonomy* of those people and institutions endowed by law to exercise authority on behalf of the state. No institution of human society or individual human is competent to be 'sovereign' in the sense of having ultimate, indivisible and unquestionable power or authority, not accountable to any other authority: bearing such competency is as far beyond human capability as it is to create life or matter from nothing, or to predict the future.

A fair question flowing from this perspective on sovereignty is what its implications are for the study of constitutional law, and specifically for an understanding of current constitutional concepts. A generalized response is, perhaps surprisingly, that it has a demystifying effect, the reason being that the clarification of the core question of constitutional law (the ultimate source of the state's authority) removes the need to rely on speculative mythology devised as rationalized, unknown, and therefore imagined contractarian history.

THE STATE AND THE LAW

The state, being a human construct, is composed of and managed by people. These people constituting the state are known as citizens, identified as such in legal terms, and linked to a delimited part of the planet's surface. The citizenry, their common claim to be associated with their demarcated land, governed under discernible legal authority, together distinguish one particular state from

---

[6] See e.g. Aguilera-Barchet 'History' 54–5, text and footnotes under the heading 'From Imperator to Dominus', and the influential writings of Jean Bodin referred to above in section 2.4 of Chapter 2.

all others. The laws of the state can only be conceived, formulated, prescribed and applied through human agency. The nature, content and effect of those laws can (and should) be determined objectively, but deciding whether they are appropriate, is another matter. Assessing law involves questions not only of effectiveness, fitness and practicability, but also considerations of fairness, justice and justification. These considerations are concerned with morality, and morality is deeply rooted in conviction – worldview.

Moral considerations are inexorably present in the making, study, qualitative assessment and application of the law. No wonder then, that there is an age-old tendency to search for ideal, extra-statal legal standards against which the quality of posited legal norms can be measured. The most common expression of this idea is to be found in the notion of natural law, but all natural law theories are incurably flawed because of the difficulty of 'finding' the norms of natural law by means of fallible human reason. They are not to be found in some codex, neither of divine, nor of temporal origin. 'Natural law' can only be fabricated through cerebral effort, producing no more than predisposed results as varied as the worldviews of the fabricators. The law under which a society functions, also its constitutional law, must therefore be evaluated morally for what it is, as it is concretely manifested.

This leaves the lawyer searching for standards for the assessment and justification of legal norms with little more than personal convictions regarding the frail conceptions of justice, fairness, integrity, legitimacy, reasonableness, and so on. The point is not that the search for proper standards is futile – the point is that honesty requires acknowledgement of the subjective nature of one's views regarding which criteria are appropriate for the validation of legal norms. Those views depend wholly on the observer's worldview. Naturally views on such matters tend to congeal into clumps of common conviction, from which schools of thought and even dogmatic doctrines are developed.

Currently in constitutional law the most influential doctrine is typified by the expression 'liberal constitutionalism'. Despite its generality, the core of this doctrine has, especially due to the social, economic, and political successes that it has facilitated, much to recommend itself. However, typical of a dominant dogma, proponents of liberal constitutionalism tend to underestimate the shortcomings attributable to its internal contradictions, insoluble dilemmas and paradoxes.[7] It is clear that various pillars of liberal constitutionalism are under attack in the twenty-first century, placing them in danger of crumbling.[8]

CHALLENGE

If this book has succeeded in exposing some of the difficulties inherent in assuming the universal validity of one kind of meaning assigned to core concepts of constitutional law, especially for constitutional comparison, it has also identified a clear challenge: to devise alternative conceptual approaches based on other worldviews – including the Christian faith.

---

[7] Having devoted a complete book to thoroughly analyze (in a typically post-modern fashion) the works of major Western philosophers, Johan van der Walt, *The Concept of Liberal Democratic Law* (Routledge, 2020) 247 presented the following definition:
> Liberal democratic law consists of an anomic, unnatural, inorganic, nominalist and non-spiritual system of non-actualisable but adequately socialist legislative rules that govern, reflect and sustain the divided life of societies that manage to sustain sufficiently forceful poetic fictions to compensate for the grey lack of heroism that they will have to endure during the time that remains.

[8] The more obvious evidence of this involves democracy (Chapter 7 above) and constitutionalism (Chapter 9 above), but it is to be found also in the inconsistency of meaning of core constitutional concepts considered in the other chapters.

Bibliography

Abbas, N, Förster, A & Richter, E (eds) *Supranationalität und Demokratie, Staat – Souveränität – Nation* (Springer, 2015)
Ackerman, B 'The Emergency Constitution' 2020 (1) *Journal of Constitutional Law* 9–64
Ackerman, B *We the People – Foundations* (Harvard University Press, 1991)
Adams, GB 'The Descendants of the Curia Regis' 1907 (13.1) *The American Historical Review* 11–15
Adepoju, AT & Basiru, AS 'The State and Crisis of Citizenship in Contemporary Africa: Revisiting the Globalization Thesis' 2019 (6.2–3) *African Journal of Democracy and Governance* 202–26
Aguilera-Barchet, B *A History of Western Public Law – Between Nation and State* (Springer, 2015, translated from the original Spanish edition of 2011)
Al-Ali, Z & Thiruvengadam, AK 'The Competing Effect of National Uniqueness and Comparative Influences on Constitutional Practice' in Tushnet, M, Fleiner, T & Saunders, C (eds) *Routledge Handbook of Constitutional Law* (Routledge, 2013) 427–42
Albert, R 'Constitutional Amendment and Dismemberment' 2018 (43.1) *Yale Journal of International Law* 1–84
Albert, R (ed) *Revolutionary Constitutionalism – Law, Legitimacy, Power* (Hart Publishing, 2020)
Allenby, BR 'Information Technology and the Fall of the American Republic' 2019 (59.4) *Jurimetrics* 409–38
Anonymous Editorial Listing of 'Current Topics' in 1922–1923 (67) *Solicitors' Journal & Weekly Reporter* 254 (published in London, England)
Arake, OJ 'The Actualization of Independent State of Palestine: Palestine Liberation Organization's Contribution and the Emergence of HAMAS' 2018 (7.1–2) *International Journal of Advanced Legal Studies and Governance* 47–62
Arato, A *The Adventures of Constituent Power* (Cambridge University Press, 2017)
Arjomand, SA *Constitutionalism and Political Reconstruction* (Brill, 2007)
Armia, MS 'Implementing Islamic Constitutionalism: How Islamic Is Indonesia Constitution?' 2018 (15.2) *Al-'Adalah* 437–50
Arnold, T & Martínez-Estay, JI (eds) *Rule of Law, Human Rights and Judicial Control of Power – Some Reflections from National and International Law* (Springer, 2017).
Auby, J-B 'Global Constitutionalism and Normative Hierarchies' in Belov, M (ed) *Global Constitutionalism and Its Challenges to Westphalian Constitutional Law* (Hart Publishing, 2018) 38–48
Badura, P *Staatsrecht – Systematische Erläuterung des Grundgesetzes* 7. Auflage (CH Beck, 2018)
Balke, F *Figuren der Souveränität* (Wilhelm Fink Verlag, 2009)
Balkin, JM 'Promise of Legal Semiotics' 1991 (69) *Texas Law Review* 1831–52
Balme, S 'The Judicialisation of Politics and the Politicisation of the Judiciary in China (1978–2005)' 2005 (5) *Global Jurist* [i]–41

Baofu, P *The Rise of Authoritarian Liberal Democracy – A Preface to a New Theory of Comparative Political Systems* (Cambridge Scholars Publishing, 2007)
Barber, NW *The Constitutional State* (Oxford University Press, 2010)
Barber, NW *The Principles of Constitutionalism* (Oxford University Press, 2018)
Barber, NW 'The Rechtsstaat and the Rule of Law' 2003 (53) *University of Toronto Law Journal* 443–54
Barroso, LR 'Technological Revolution, Democratic Recession, and Climate Change: The Limits of Law in a Changing World' 2020 (18.2) *International Journal of Constitutional Law* 334–69
Bates, CA 'Law and the Rule of Law and Its Place Relative to Politeia in Aristotle's Politics' in Huppes-Cluysenaer, L & Coelho, NMMS (eds) *Aristotle and The Philosophy of Law: Theory, Practice and Justice* (Springer, 2013) 59–75
Bauböck, R (ed) *Migration and Citizenship – Legal Status, Rights and Political Participation* (Amsterdam University Press, 2006)
Bauböck, R, Ersbøll, E, Groenendijk, K & Waldrauch, H (eds) *Acquisition and Loss of Nationality, 1 & 2: Country Analyses – Policies and Trends in 15 European Countries* (Amsterdam University Press, 2006) Volume 1
Baume, S 'Hans Kelsen and the Case for Democracy' *E-INTERNATIONAL RELATIONS* 18 December 2020 www.e-ir.info/2013/05/08/hans-kelsen-and-the-case-for-democracy/ (accessed 17 June 2021)
Baxi, U 'Preliminary Notes on Transformative Constitutionalism' in Vilhena, O, Baxi, U & Viljoen, F (eds) *Transformative Constitutionalism: Comparing the Apex Courts of Brazil, India and South Africa* (Pretoria University Law Press, 2013) 19–47
Bazezew, M 'Constitutionalism' 2009 (3.2) *Mizan Law Review* 358–69
Beaulac, S 'The Rule of Law in International Law Today' in Palombella, G & Walker, N (eds) *Relocating the Rule of Law* (Hart Publishing, 2009) 197–224
Beaumont, KM 'Jurisprudence' 1939 (9) *Revue Aeronautique Internationale* 24–46
Beckenbach, N & Klotter, C *Gleichheit und Souveränität – Von den Verheißungen der Gleichheit, der Teufelslist der Diktatur und dem schwachen Trost der Nivellierung* (Springer, 2014)
Belov, M (ed) *Global Constitutionalism and Its Challenges to Westphalian Constitutional Law* (Hart Publishing, 2018)
Benhabib, S *Transformations of Citizenship – Dilemmas of the Nation-state in the Era of Globalization* (Koninklijke van Gorcum, 2001)
Beyer, M *Making Abbé Sieyès and Jürgen Habermas Meet: Constitution-Making in the Supranational Setting* (European Institute of Public Administration, 2005)
Bierbach, JB *Frontiers of Equality in the Development of EU and US Citizenship* (Springer, 2017)
Bignami, F 'Formal Versus Functional Method in Comparative Constitutional Law' 2016 (53.2) *Osgoode Hall Law Journal* 442–71
Billig, M *Banal Nationalism* (Sage Publications, 1995)
Bingham, Lord 'The Rule of Law' 2007 (66.1) *Cambridge Law Journal* 67–85
Blackstone, W *Commentaries on the Laws of England* (published in 1774)
Blockmans, S 'Democracy as an Ecosystem' in Blockmans, S & Russack, S (eds) *Deliberative Democracy in the EU – Countering Populism with Participation and Debate* (Rowman & Littlefield, 2020) 1–19
Blokker, P 'Varieties of Populist Constitutionalism: The Transnational Dimension' 2019 (20) *German Law Journal* 332–50
Bobek, M & Kosař, D 'Global Solutions, Local Damages: A Critical Study in Judicial Councils in Central and Eastern Europe' 2014 (15.7) *German Law Journal* 1257–92

Boogaard, G 'Wer ist das Volk?' 2017 (178.4) *Rechtsgeleerd Magazijn THEMIS* 144–47

Bosniak, L 'Making Sense of Citizenship' in 'Denaturalizing Citizenship: A Symposium on Linda Bosniak's *The Citizen and the Alien* and Ayelet Shachar's *The Birthright Lottery*' 2011 (9) *Issues in Legal Scholarship* 1–17

Bosniak, L *The Citizen and the Alien* (Princeton University Press, 2006)

Bowen, HV, Mancke, E & Reid, J (eds) *Britain's Oceanic Empire: Atlantic and Indian Ocean Worlds, c. 1550–1850* (Cambridge University Press, 2012)

Brang, L 'Carl Schmitt and the Evolution of Chinese Constitutional Theory: Conceptual Transfer and the Unexpected Paths of Legal Globalisation' 2020 (9.1) *Global Constitutionalism* 117–54

Brewer, DJ *Ancient Egypt: Foundations of a Civilization* (Routledge, 2014)

Broekman, JM & Backer, LC *Lawyers Making Meaning* (Springer, 2013)

Brown, G (ed) *The Universal Declaration of Human Rights in the 21st Century: A Living Document in a Changing World – A Report by the Global Citizenship Commission* (Open Book Publishers, 2016)

Bugarič, B 'Central Europe's Descent into Autocracy: A Constitutional Analysis of Authoritarian Populism' 2019 (17.2) *International Journal of Constitutional Law* 597–616

Buratti, A *Western Constitutionalism – History, Institutions, Comparative Law* 2nd ed (Springer, 2019)

Burch, M 'The United Kingdom' in Blondel, J & Müller-Rommel, F (eds) *Cabinets in Western Europe* 2nd ed (Macmillan, 1997)

Bussani, M 'Deglobalizing Rule of law and Democracy: Hunting Down Rhetoric Through Comparative Law' 2019 (67.4) *American Journal of Comparative Law* 701–44

Butler, EC 'Diversity Jurisdiction and Juridical Persons: Determining the Citizenship of Foreign-Country Business Entities' 2018 (97.1) *Texas Law Review* 193–224

Calabresi, SG 'The Global Rise of Judicial Review since 1945' 2020 (69.3) *Catholic University Law Review* 401–44

Calvin, J *The Institutes of the Christian Religion* translation by Henry Beveridge 1845 (Christian Classics Ethereal Library, Grand Rapids) https://ccel.org/ccel/c/calvin/institutes/cache/institutes.pdf (accessed 11 June 2021)

Cappelletti, M 'Judicial Review in Comparative Perspective' 1970 (58.5) *California Law Review* 1017–53

Carey, HM & Gascoigne, J (eds) *Church and State in Old and New Worlds* (BRILL, 2010)

Carvalho, EM de *Semiotics of International Law* translated by LC Fonseca (Springer, 2011)

Carvalho, J 'Law, Language, and Knowledge: Legal Transplants from a Cultural Perspective' 2019 (20) *German Law Journal* 21–45

Charlow, R 'American Constitutional Analysis and a Substantive Understanding of the Rule of Law' in Silkenat, JR, Hickey, JE & Barenboim, PD *The Legal Doctrines of the Rule of Law and the Legal State (Rechtsstaat)* (Springer, 2014) 251–66

Charlow, R 'America's Constitutional Rule of Law: Structure and Symbol' in Sellers, M & Tomaszewski, T (eds) *The Rule of Law in Comparative Perspective* (Springer, 2010) 89–99

Chayes, A 'How Does the Constitution Establish Justice' 1988 (101) *Harvard Law Review* 1026–42

Chernilo, D *The Natural Law Foundations of Modern Social Theory* (Cambridge University Press, 2013)
Chesney, B & Citron, D 'Deep Fakes: A Looming Challenge for Privacy, Democracy, and National Security' 2019 (107.6) *California Law Review* 1753–820
Chesterman, S 'An International Rule of Law' 2008 (56.2) *American Journal of Comparative Law* 331–62
Chinkin, C & Baetens, F *Sovereignty, Statehood and State Responsibility* (Cambridge University Press, 2015)
Cladis, MC *Public Vision, Private Lives: Rousseau, Religion, and 21st-Century Democracy* (Oxford University Press, 2003)
Claes, E, Devroe, W & Keirsbilck, B 'The Limits of the Law' in Claes, E, Devroe, W & Keirsbilck, B (eds), *Facing the Limits of the Law* (Springer, 2009) 1–24
Collings, J 'What Should Comparative Constitutional History Compare' 2017 (2) *University of Illinois Law Review* 475–96
Comella, VF 'The European Model of Constitutional Review of Legislation: Toward Decentralization?' 2004 (2.3) *International Journal of Constitutional Law* 461–91
Coomaraswamy, R 'The Contemporary Challenges to International Human Rights' in Sheeran, S & Rodley, N (eds) *Routledge Handbook of International Human Rights Law* (Routledge, 2013) 127–39
Cooper, R *The Post-modern State and the World Order* (Demos, 1996)
Cornelissen, S, Cheru, F & Shaw, TM (eds) *Africa and International Relations in the 21st Century* (Palgrave Macmillan, 2012)
Croucamp, PA & Malan, L 'The Theory of Systemic Patronage and State Capture. The Liberal Democratic Project and its Regime Contenders' 2018 (10.4) *African Journal of Public Affairs* 86–105
Crowe, J & Lee, C (eds) *Research Handbook on Natural Law Theory* (Edward Elgar Publishing, 2019)
Dalla-Pozza, D & Williams, G 'The Constitutional Validity of Declaration of Incompatibility in Austalian Charters of Rights' 2007 (12.1) *Deakin Law Review* 1–39
Dann, P, Riegner, M & Bönnemann, M (eds) *The Global South and Comparative Constitutional Law* (Oxford University Press, 2020)
Dauchy, S, Matyn, G, Musson, A, Pihlajamäki, H & Wijffels, A (eds) *The Formation and Transmission of Western Legal Culture – 150 Books that Made the Law in the Age of Printing* (Springer, 2016)
De Groot, G-R & Luk, Ngo Chun 'Twenty Years of CJEU Jurisprudence on Citizenship' 2014 (15.5) *German Law Journal* 821–34
Dent, K & Kroeze, IJ 'Minority Rights in the South-African Context: An Exploration of the Counter-Majoritarian Dilemma' 2015 (26) *Stellenbosch Law Review* 518–31
Dhooghe, V, Franken, R & Opgenhaffen, T 'Judicial Activism at the European Court of Justice: A Natural Feature in a Dialogical Context' 2015 (20.2) *Tilburg Law Review* 122–41
Di Fabio, U *Die Staatsrechtslehre und der Staat* (Ferdinand Schöningh, Paderborn 2003)
Di Lizia, F 'More than Just a Humble Abode: The Implications of Constitutional Citizenship Rights for Passport Law' 2019 (44) *University of Western Australia Law Review* 116–56
DiCenso, J *Kant, Religion, and Politics* (Cambridge University Press, 2011)
Dicey, AV *Introduction to the Study of the Law of the Constitution*, 3rd ed (MacMillan & Co, 1889)

Dicey, AV *Introduction to the Study of the Constitution* first published in 1885 (8th ed 1915)

Dixon, R 'Introduction – Public Law and Populism' 2019 (20) *German Law Journal* 125–8

Donovan, JM 'Human Rights: From Legal Transplants to Fair Translation' 2017 (34.3) *Wisconsin International Law Journal* 475–534

Dörr, O & Schmalenbach, K (eds) *Vienna Convention on the Law of Treaties – A Commentary* (Springer, 2012)

Douglas-Scott, S 'Brexit, the Referendum and the UK Parliament: Some Questions about Sovereignty' 2016 (June 28) *UK Constitutional Law Blog* 22 December 2020 https://ukconstitutionallaw.org/2016/06/28/sionaidh-douglas-scott-brexit-the-referendum-and-the-uk-parliament-some-questions-about-sovereignty/ (accessed 17 June 2021)

Douglas-Scott, S 'The United Kingdom: Lurching Toward Illiberal Constitutionalism in 3 Episodes' paper given at Cardozo/Columbia Colloquium on Illiberal Constitutionalism and the Future of Constitutional Democracy (2020) https://ssrn.com/abstract=3554855 (accessed 8 April 2021)

Dowdle, MW & Wilkinson, MA 'On the Limits of Constitutional Liberalism: In Search of Constitutional Reflexivity' in Dowdle, MW & Wilkinson, MA (eds) *Constitutionalism Beyond Liberalism* (Cambridge University Press, 2017)

Drinóczi, T & Bień-Kacała, A 'Illiberal Constitutionalism: The Case of Hungary and Poland' 2019 (20) *German Law Journal* 1140–66

Dube, F *Enhancing Democratic Accountability through Constitutionalism in South Africa* (LLD Thesis North-West University, Potchefstroom) 2019

Dugard, J *International Law – A South African Perspective* 4th ed (Juta, 2011)

Dunleavy, P & O'Leary, B *Theories of the State – The Politics of Liberal Democracy* (Macmillan Education, 1987)

Dunoff, JL, Wiener, A, Kumm, M, Lang, AF & Tully, J 'Hard Times: Progress Narratives, Historical Contingency and the Fate of Global Constitutionalism' 2015 (4.1) *Global Constitutionalism* 1–17

Duso, G *Die moderne politische Repräsentation: Entstehung und Krise des Begriffs* translated from the Italian by Peter Paschke (Duncker & Humblot, 2005)

Dworkin, R *Sovereign Virtue – The Theory and Practice of Equality* (Harvard University Press, 2000)

Enwere, C 'Vote Buying Syndrome in 2019 Election: A Threat to Modern Democracy in Nigeria' 2019 (3.2) *Journal of Nation-building & Policy Studies* 25–43

Esser, F, Reinemann, C & Fan, D 'Spin Doctors in the United States, Great Britain and Germany' 2001 (6.1) *The International Journal of Press/Politics* 16–45

Fabra-Zamora, JL (ed) *Jurisprudence in a Globalized World* (Edward Elgar Publishing, 2020)

Farinacci-Fernos, JM 'Post-Liberal Constitutionalism' 2018 (54.1) *Tulsa Law Review* 1–48

Ferrari, GF (ed) *Introduction to Italian Public Law* (Giuffrè Editore, 2008)

Financial Times London 28 June 2019 www.ft.com/content/670039ec-98f3-11e9-9573-ee5cbb98ed36 (accessed 8 July 2019)

Finnis, NJ 'Natural Law Theory – Its Past and Its Present' in Marmor, A *The Routledge Companion to Philosophy of Law* (Routledge New York, 2012) 16–30

Fioravanti, M 'Constitutionalism' in Canale, D, Grossi, P & Hofmann, H (eds) *A History of the Philosophy of Law in the Civil Law World, 1600–1900* (Springer, 2009) 263–300

Fleiner, T & Basta Fleiner, LR *Constitutional Democracy in a Multicultural and Globalised World* translated from German by Katy Le Roy (Springer, 2009)

Förster, S *Philanthropic Foundations and Social Welfare: A Comparative Study of Germany, Sweden and the United Kingdom (England)* (Springer, 2020)

Fournier, T 'From Rhetoric to Action: A Constitutional Analysis of Populism' 2019 (20) *German Law Journal* 362–81

Frankenberg, G 'Authoritarian Constitutionalism: Coming to Terms with Modernity's Nightmares' in García, HA & Frankenberg, G (eds) *Authoritarian Constitutionalism* (Edward Elgar Publishing, 2019) 1–36

Frankenberg, G *Comparative Constitutional Studies – Between Magic and Deceit* (Edward Elgar Publishing, 2018)

Frankenberg, G *Comparative Law as Critique* (Edward Elgar Publishing, 2016)

Frankenberg, G *Political Technology and the Erosion of the Rule of Law* (Edward Elgar Publishing, 2014)

Frankenberg, G 'Review of Mehring, R *Carl Schmitt – Aufstieg und Fall* (CH Beck, 2009)' in 2011 (50.1) *Der Staat* 156–60

Friedberg, JJ 'Brexit, the Misrepresentation of Democracy, and the Rock of Gibraltar' 2020 (5.1) *University of Bologna Law Review* 209–25

Friedman, B 'Reconstruction's Political Court' 2002 (91.1) *The Georgetown Law Journal* 1–66

Friedman, B 'The History of the Countermajoritarian Difficulty, Part One: the Road to Judicial Supremacy' 1998 (73.2) *New York University Law Review* 333–433

Friedman, B 'The History of the Countermajoritarian Difficulty, Three: The Lesson of Lochner' 2001 (76.5) *New York University Law Review* 1383–455

Frowein, JA 'The Transformation of Constitutional Law through the European Convention on Human Rights' 2015 (35) *Human Rights Law Journal* 1–8

Gadzhiev, GA 'The Russian Judicial Doctrine of the Rule of Law: Twenty Years After' in Silkenat, JR, Hickey, JE & Barenboim, PD *The Legal Doctrines of the Rule of Law and the Legal State (Rechtsstaat)* (Springer, 2014) 209–28

Gagnon, A-G & Tremblay, A (eds) *Federalism and National Diversity in the 21st Century* (Palgrave Macmillan, 2020)

Galloro, C 'Das heutige Völkerrecht: ius gentium oder ius inter gentes?' 2018 (9) *Journal on European History of Law* 80–98

Gao, Quanxi, Zhang, Wei & Tian, Feilong *The Road to the Rule of Law in Modern China* (Springer, 2015)

García, HA & Frankenberg, G (eds) *Authoritarian Constitutionalism* (Edward Elgar Publishing, 2019)

Gargarella, R 'Popular Constitutionalism' in Sellers, M & Kirste, S (eds) *Encyclopedia of the Philosophy of Law and Social Philosophy* (Springer, 2020) https://doi.org/10.1007/978-94-007-6730-0_112-2

Geddis, A 'Parliamentary Government in New Zealand: Lines of Continuity and Moments of Change' 2016 (14.1) *International Journal of Consitutional Law* 99–118

Gehring, P 'Force and "Mystical Foundation" of Law: How Jacques Derrida Addresses Legal Discourse' 2005 (6.1) *German Law Journal* 151–69

Gerhard, J & Lengfeld, H *Wir, ein europäisches Volk? – Sozialintegration Europas und die Idee der Gleichheit aller europäischen Bürger* (Springer 2013)

Gerson, LP's Review of Mor Segev, *Aristotle on Religion* in 2018.06.01 *Notre Dame Philosophical Reviews* published electronically at https://ndpr.nd.edu/

Ghaleigh, NS 'Neither Legal Nor Political? Bureaucratic Constitutionalism in Japanese Law' 2015 (26.2) *King's Law Journal* 193–212

Gible, DM *The Territorial Peace Borders, State Development, and International Conflict* (Cambridge University Press, 2012)

Giri, AK 'Social Theory and Asian Dialogues: Cultivating Planetary Conversations' in Giri, AK (ed) *Social Theory and Asian Dialogues – Cultivating Planetary Conversations* (Palgrave Macmillan, 2018)

Giuliani, A 'What is Comparative Legal History? Legal Historiography and the Revolt against Formalism, 1930–60' in Moréteau, O, Masferrer, A & Modéer, KÅ (eds) *Comparative Legal History* (Edward Elgar Publishing, 2019)

Glassman, RM *The Future of Democracy* (Springer, 2019)

Glassman, RM *The Origins of Democracy in Tribes, City-States and Nation-States* (Springer, 2017) (Four Volumes)

Glenn, HP *The Cosmopolitan State* (Oxford University Press, 2013)

Glenn, P 'Legal Cultures and Legal Traditions' in Van Hoecke, M (ed) *Epistemology and Methodology of Comparative Law* (Hart Publishing, 2004) 7–20

Glover, TR *Democracy in the Ancient World* (Cambridge University Press, 1927)

Goderis, B & Versteeg, M 'Transnational Constitutionalism – A Conceptual Framework' in Galligan, DJ & Verteeg, M (eds) *Social and Political Foundations of Constitutions* (Cambridge University Press, 2013) 103–33

Goldini, M 'Rousseau's Radical Constitutionalism and Its Legacy' in Dowdle, MW & Wilkinson, MA (eds) *Constitutionalism Beyond Liberalism* (Cambridge University Press, 2017) 227–53

Greene, A 'Emergency Powers in a Time of Pandemic' (Bristol University Press, 2020)

Greenfeld, L *Mind, Modernity, Madness: The Impact of Culture on Human Experience* (Harvard University Press, 2013)

Greenfeld, L *Nationalism – Five Roads to Modernity* (Harvard University Press, 1992)

Greenfeld, L *The Spirit of Capitalism: Nationalism and Economic Growth* (Harvard University Press, 2001)

Greenfeld, L & Wu, Zeying (eds) *Research Handbook on Nationalism* (Edward Elgar Publishing, 2020)

Grimm, D 'A Long Time Coming' 2020 (21) *German Law Journal* 944–9

Grimm, D 'Zum Stand der demokratischen Legitimation der Europäischen Union nach Lissabon' in Abbas, N, Förster, A & Richter, E (eds) *Supranationalität und Demokratie, Staat – Souveränität – Nation* (Springer, 2015) 17–36

Grossi, P *Das Recht in der europäischen Geschichte* translated from Italian by Gerhard Kuck (CH Beck, 2010)

Grotenhuis, R *Nation-Building as Necessary Effort in Fragile States* (Amsterdam University Press, 2016)

Gunn, TJ 'The Complexity of Religion and the Definition of "Religion" in International Law' 2003 (16) *Harvard Human Rights Journal* 189–215

Gyorfi, T *Against the New Constitutionalism* (Edward Elgar Publishing, 2016)

Habermas, J 'Human Rights and Popular Sovereignty: The Liberal and Republican Versions' 1994 (7.1) *Ratio Juris* 1–13

Hahm, C 'Law, Culture, and the Politics of Confucianism' 2002 (16.2) *Columbia Journal of Asian Law* 253–302

Haldén, P *Stability without Statehood Lessons from Europe's History before the Sovereign State* (Palgrave Macmillan, 2011)

Haley, JO *Law's Political Foundations – Rivers, Rifles, Rice, and Religion* (Edward Elgar Publishing, 2016)

Hallam, H *The Constitutional History of England* 5th ed Vol I (Murray, London, 1846)
Hallaq, WB '"Muslim Rage" and Islamic Law' 2003 (54.6) *Hastings Law Journal* 1705–19
Haltern, UR *Verfassungsgerichtsbarkeit, Demokratie und Misstrauen: das Bundesverfassungsgericht in einer Verfassungstheorie zwischen Populismus und Progressivismus* (Duncker & Humblot, 1998)
Hameiri, S *Regulating Statehood State Building and the Transformation of the Global Order* (Palgrave Macmillan, 2010)
Hamid, L & Wouters, J (eds) *Rule of Law and Areas of Limited Statehood – Domestic and International Dimensions* (Edward Elgar Publishing, 2021)
Harris, KL 'BEE-ing Chinese in South Africa: A Legal Historic Perspective' 2017 (23.2) *Fundamina* 1–20
Harrison, PM 'Weber's Categories of Authority and Voluntary Associations' 1960 (25.2) *American Sociological Review* 232–7
Hartmann, J, Meyer, B & Oldopp, B *Geschichte der politischen Ideen* (Westdeutscher Verlag, 2002)
Hasebe Y & Pinelli, C 'Constitutions' in Tushnet, M, Fleiner, T & Saunders, C (eds) *Routledge Handbook of Constitutional Law* (Routledge, 2013) 9–19
Hatschek, J *Englische Verfassungsgeschichte bis zum Regierungsantritt der Königin Viktoria* 2nd ed (Scientia Verlag, 1978)
He, Baogang 'Socialist Constitutionalism in Contemporary China' in Dowdle, M & Wilkinson, M (eds), *Constitutionalism Beyond Liberalism* (Cambridge University Press, 2017) 176–94
Hegel, GWF *Elements of the Philosophy of Right* translated by HB Nisbet, edited by Allen W Wood (Cambridge University Press, 1991)
Heidemann, DH & Stoppenbrink, K (eds) *Join, or Die – Philosophical Foundations of Federalism* (De Gruyter, 2016)
Helmholz, RH 'Bonham's Case, Judicial Review, and the Law of Nature' 2009 (1.1) *Journal of Legal Analysis* 325–54
Herrera, JC 'Judicial Dialogue and Transformative Constitutionalism in Latin America: The Case of Indigenous Peoples and Afro-descendants' 2019 (43) *Revista Derecho del Estado* 191–233
Hesse, K *Grundzüge des Verfassungsrechts der Bundesrepublik Deutschland* 19th revised ed (CF Müller, 1993)
Hidalgo, O (ed) *Der lange Schatten des Contrat social – Demokratie und Volkssouveränität bei Jean-Jacques Rousseau* (Springer, 2013)
Hiebert, JL 'The Human Rights Act: Ambiguity about Parliamentary Sovereign' 2013 (14.12) *German Law Journal* 2254–74
Hilker, J *Grundrechte im deutschen Frühkonstitutionalismus* (Dunckler & Humblot, 2005)
Himsworth, CMG 'In a State No Longer: The End of Constitutionalism?' 1996 *Public Law* 639–60
Hirschi, C *The Origins of Nationalism – An Alternative History from Ancient Rome to Early Modern Germany* (Cambridge University Press, 2012)
Hirschl, R 'Opting Out of "Global Constitutionalism"' 2018 (12.1) *Law & Ethics of Human Rights* 1–36
Hirschl, R 'The Continued Renaissance of Comparative Constitutional Law' 2010 (45.10) *Tulsa Law Review* 771–80
Hirschl, R *Towards Juristocracy: The Origins and Consequences of the New Constitutionalism* (Harvard University Press, 2004)

Hochstrasser, TJ *Natural Law Theories in the Early Enlightenment* (Cambridge University Press, 2004)
Hoexter, C & Olivier, M *The Judiciary in South Africa* (Juta, 2014)
Höffe, O *Democracy in an Age of Globalisation* (Springer, 2007)
Holmberg, S 'Dynamic Representation from Above' in Rosema, M, Denters, B & Aarts, K (eds) *How Democracy Works: Political Representation and Policy Congruence in Modern Societies* (Amsterdam University Press, 2011) 54–76
House, HW 'A Tale of Two Kingdoms: Can There Be Peaceful Coexistence of Religion within the Secular State?' 1998–1999 (13) *Brigham Young University Journal of Public Law* 203–92
Howse, R 'Epilogue: In Defense of Disruptive Democracy – A Critique of Anti-populism' 2019 (17.2) *International Journal of Constitutional Law* 641–60
Htun, Su Yin 'Legal Aspects of the Right to Nationality Pursuant to Myanmar Citizenship Law' 2019 (3.2) *Journal of Southeast Asian Human Rights* 277–99
Huber, J *Guicciardinis Kritik an Machiavelli* (Deutscher Universitats-Verlag, 2004)
Hughes, PL & Fries, RF (eds) *Crown and Parliament in Tudor Stuart England* (Putnam 1959)
Huppes-Cluysenaer, L & Coelho, NMMS (eds) *Aristotle and The Philosophy of Law: Theory, Practice and Justice* (Springer, 2013)
Husa, J 'Comparative Methodology and Constitutional Change' in Contiades, X & Fotiadou, A (eds) *Routledge Handbook of Comparative Constitutional Change* (Routledge, 2021) 25–44
Hutt, DB 'Deliberative, Republican, and Egalitarian Institutional Alternatives for Popular Constitutionalism' 2021 (48) *Revista Derecho del Estado* 183–214
Ipsen, J *Staatsrecht I (Staatsorganisationsrecht)* 8. Aufl. (Luchterhand, 1996)
Jackson, VC & Versteeg, M (eds) *Comparative Constitutional Law* (Routledge, 2021)
Jacobsohn, G & Schor, M (eds) *Comparative Constitutional Theory* (Edward Elgar Publishing, 2018)
Jakab, A 'What Can Constitutional Law Do against the Erosion of Democracy and the Rule of Law? On the Interconnectedness of the Protection of Democracy and the Rule of Law' 2020 (6) *Constitutional Studies* 5–34
Jany, J *Legal Traditions in Asia – History, Concepts and Laws* (Springer, 2020)
Jellinek, W: Georg Jellinek, *Allgemeine Staatslehre* (Springer-Verlag 1921)
Joathan, Í & Lilleker, DG 'Permanent Campaigning: A Meta-Analysis and Framework for Measurement' *Journal of Political Marketing* DOI: 10.1080/15377857.2020.1832015 published online 23 October 2020
Johri, S *Lectures on Constitutional Law* (Central Law Publications, 2016)
Jones, CJ *Constitutional Idolatry and Democracy – Challenging the Infatuation with Writtenness* (Edward Elgar Publishing, 2020)
Jones, DW 'Defending the 2020 election against hacking: 5 questions answered', 14 September 2020 *The Conversation* https://theconversation.com/defending-the-2020-election-against-hacking-5-questions-answered-146055 (accessed 13 November 2020)
Kant, I *Immanuel Kant – Groundwork of the Metaphysics of Morals*, translated by Mary Gregor (Cambridge University Press, 1997) translation of Kant's text as published online by Jeffrey W Bulger found at https://learn.canvas.net › courses › files › download (accessed 9 June 2021)
Kelly, D 'Revisiting the Rights of Man: Georg Jellinek on Rights and the State' 2004 (22.3) *Law and History Review* 493–529

Kelsen, H 'Sovereignty' in Paulson, SL & Paulson, BL (eds) *Normativity and Norms – Critical Perspectives on Kelsenian Themes* (Clarenden Press, 1998) 525–36

Kim, Kyung Mi *The Korean Developmental State* (Palgrave Macmillan, 2020)

Klare, KE 'Legal Culture and Transformative Constitutionalism' 1998 (14) *South African Journal on Human Rights* 146–88

Kleger, H *Demokratisches Regieren – Bürgersouveränität, Repräsentation und Legitimation* (Nomos, 2018)

Klingemann, H-D & Fuchs, D *Citizens and the State: A Changing Relationship?* (Oxford University Press, 1998)

Klug, H 'Decolonisation, Compensation and Constitutionalism: Land, Wealth and the Sustainability of Constitutionalism in Post-Apartheid South Africa' 2018 (34.3) *South African Journal on Human Rights* 469–91

Klug, H 'Transformative Constitutions and the Role of Integrity Institutions in Tempering Power: The Case of Resistance to State Capture in Post-Apartheid South Africa' 2019 (67.3) *Buffalo Law Review* 701–42

Knight, WSM *The History of the Great European War* Volume I (Caxton Publishing Company, September 1914)

Knudson, J 'The Influence of the German Concepts of Volksgeist and Zeitgeist on the Thought and Jurisprudence of Oliver Wendell Holmes' 2002 (11) *Journal of Transnational Law & Policy* 407–20

Kochenov, D & Bárd, P 'The Last Soldier Standing? Courts Versus Politicians and the Rule of Law Crisis in the New Member States of the EU' in Ballin, EH, Van der Schyff, G & Stremler, M (eds) *European Yearbook of Constitutional Law 2019* (Asser Press, 2020)

Koontz, TJ 'Religion and Political Cohesion: John Locke and Jean Jacques Rousseau' 1981 (23) *Journal of Church & State* 95–115.

Koopmans, T *Courts and Political Institutions* (Cambridge University Press, 2003)

Körtvélyesi, Z 'Nation, Nationality, and National Identity: Uses, Misuses, and the Hungarian Case of External Ethnic Citizenship' 2020 (33.3) *International Journal for the Semiotics of Law* 771–98

Kotzé, LJ & Villavicencio Calzadilla, P 'Somewhere between Rhetoric and Reality: Environmental Constitutionalism and the Rights of Nature in Ecuador' 2017 (6.3) *Transnational Environmental Law* 401–33

Koulish, R 'Sovereign Bias, Crimmigration, and Risk' in Guia, MJ, Koulish, R & Mitsilegas, V (eds) *Immigration Detention, Risk and Human Rights* (Springer, 2016) 1–16

Kranenpohl, U 'Die gesellschaftlichen Legitimationsgrundlagen der Verfassungsrechtsprechung oder: Darum lieben die Deutschen Karlsruhe' 2009 (56.4) *Zeitschrift für Politik* 436–53

Krygier, M 'Inside the Rule of Law' 2014 (III,1) *Rivista di filosofia del diritto* 77–98

Krzan, B 'Poland and International Courts: A Centennial Perspective' 2020 (9.1) *Polish Review of International and European Law* 99–124

Kyriazis, D 'The PSPP judgment of the German Constitutional Court: An Abrupt Pause to an Intricate Judicial Tango' 6 May 2020 *European Law Blog* https://europeanlawblog.eu/2020/05/06/the-pspp-judgment-of-the-german-constitutional-court-an-abrupt-pause-to-an-intricate-judicial-tango/ (accessed 26 December 2020)

Lang, AF & Wiener, A (eds) *Handbook on Global Constitutionalism* (Edward Elgar Publishing, 2017)

Latham-Gambi, A 'Political Constitutionalism and Legal Constitutionalism – an Imaginary Opposition?' 2020 (40.4) *Oxford Journal of Legal Studies* 737–63

Law, DS 'Constitutional Archetypes' 2016 (95) *Texas Law Review* 153–243
Law, J (ed) *A Dictionary of Law* 8th edn (Oxford University Press, 2015)
Legrand, P & Munday, R (eds) *Comparative Legal Studies: Traditions and Transitions* (Cambridge University Press, 2003)
Lepsius, O 'Georg Jellinek's Theory of the Two Sides of the State ("Zwei-Seiten-Lehre des Staates")' in Ladavac, NB, Bezemek, C & Schauer, F (eds) *The Normative Force of the Factual – Legal Philosophy Between Is and Ought* (Springer, 2019) 5–28
Lessnoff, M *Social Contract* (Macmillan 1986)
Llanque, M 'Der Begriff des Volkes bei Rousseau zwischen Mitgliedschaft und Zugehörigkeit' in Hidalgo, O (ed) *Der lange Schatten des Contrat social – Demokratie und Volkssouveränität bei Jean-Jacques Rousseau* (Springer, 2013) 31–52
Lombardo, M *Critique of Sovereignty – Book I: Contemporary Theories of Sovereignty* (Punctum Books, 2015)
Loughlin, M & Walker, N (eds) *The Paradox of Constitutionalism – Constituent Power and Constitutional Form* (Oxford University Press, 2007)
Loup, RM *Geschiedenis van het Engelsch Kiesrecht* (Brill, 1879)
Luard, E *A History of the United Nations* Volume 1 (Macmillan, 1982)
Lyon, B *A Constitutional and Legal History of Medieval England* 2nd ed (New York, 1980)
Mackintosh, JP *The British Cabinet* 3rd ed (Stevens & Sons, 1977)
Mäder, W *Vom Wesen der Souveränität* (Duncker & Humblot, 2007)
Malila, M 'The Zambian Judiciary on Trial: Politicisation of the Judiciary or Judicialisation of Politics' 2011 (42) *Zambia Law Journal* 63–152
Maloy, JS 'The Aristotelianism of Locke's Politics' 2009 (70.2) *Journal of the History of Ideas* 235–57
Mancini, M 'The Non-Abdication Rule in Canadian Constitutional Law' 2020 (83.1) *Saskatchewan Law Review* 45–84
Mandelbaum, MM *The Nation/State Fantasy – A Psychoanalytical Genealogy of Nationalism* (Palgrave Macmillan, 2020)
Martin, R 'Two Cities in Augustine's Political Philosophy' 1972 (33.2) *Journal of the History of Ideas* 195–216
Masaka, D 'Kwasi Wiredu's Consensual Democracy and One-party Polities in Africa' 2019 (38.1) *South African Journal of Philosophy* 68–78
Matronardi, P 'Recht und Kultur: Kulturelle Bedingtheit und universaler Anspruch des juristischen Denkens' 2001 (61.1) *Zeitschrift für ausländisches öffentliches Recht und Völkerrecht* 61–83
Maus, I 'Liberties and Popular Sovereignty: On Jurgen Habermas's Reconstruction of the System of Rights' 1995 (17.4–5) *Cardozo Law Review* 825–82 (a translated version of 'Freiheitsrechte und volkssouveranitat: Zu Jurgen Habermas' rekonstruktion des systems der rechte' which appeared in 1995 (26.4) *Rechtsteorie* 507–62)
May, NM, Ides, A & Grossi, S *Constitutional Law – National Power and Federalism* 8th edn (Wolters Kluwer, 2019)
McConalogue, J 'The British Constitution Resettled? Parliamentary Sovereignty after the EU Referendum' 2019 (21.2) *The British Journal of Politics and International Relations* 439–58
McConnell, MW 'Why is Religious Liberty the "First Freedom"?' 2000 (21) *Cardozo Law Review* 1243–66
McCormick, J 'The New Ochlophobia? Populism, Majority Rule, and Prospects for Democratic Republicanism' in Elazar, Y & Rousselière, G (eds) *Republicanism*

and the Future of Democracy (Cambridge University Press, 2019) Chapter 7 (pre-publication citation drawn from Howse, R 'Epilogue: In Defense of Disruptive Democracy – A Critique of Anti-Populism' 2019 (17.2) *International Journal of Constitutional Law* 641–60, at 645–60)

McCorquodale, R 'Defining the International Rule of Law: Defying Gravity?' 2016 (65.2) *International and Comparative Law Quarterly* 277–304

McIlwain, CH *Constitutionalism – Ancient and Modern* (Cornell University Press, 1940)

Mendez-Pinedo, ME 'Constitutional/Judicial Resistance to European Law in Iceland. Sovereignty and Constitutional Identity vs. Access to Justice under the EEA Agreement' 2020 (10.3) *Juridical Tribune* 390–418

Menski, W *Comparative Law in a Global Context – The Legal Systems of Asia and Africa* 2nd ed (Cambridge University Press, 2006)

Michaels, R 'Im Westen nichts Neues?' 2002 (66) *Rabels Zeitschrift* 97–115

Miller, RA & Zumbansen, P (eds) *Comparative Law as Transnational Law* (Oxford University Press, 2012)

Mitra, SK 'Introduction: Citizenship as Cultural Flow – Shifting Paradigms, Hybridization, or *Plus ça Change*?' in Mitra, SK (ed) *Citizenship as Cultural Flow, Transcultural Research* (Springer, 2013) 1–20

Moltchanova, A *National Self-Determination and Justice in Multinational States* (Springer, 2009)

Montesquieu, Charles de Secondat, Baron de *The Spirit of the Laws 1748* translated by Thomas Nugent 1752 (Batoche Books, Kitchener 2001)

Moreso, JJ 'Kelsen on Justifying Judicial Review' in Cleves GR (ed) *Ecos de Kelsen: Vidas, obras y controversias* (Universidad Externado de Colombia, 2012) 354–78 (English translation at https://papers.ssrn.com/sol3/papers.cfm?abstract_id= 2595560 (accessed 22 April 2021)

Moréteau, O 'The Words of Comparative Law' 2019 (6) *Journal of International and Comparative Law* 183–208

Mosima, PM 'Inclusive Development: Some Perspectives from African Communitarian Philosophy' 2019 (8.1) *Filosofia Theoretica: Journal of African Philosophy, Culture and Religions* 69–94

Müller-Freienfels, W 'Zur Rangstufung rechtlicher Normen' in Institute of Comparative Law (ed) *Law in East and West/Recht in Ost und West* (Waseda University Press, 1988) 3–39

Murkens, JEK 'Preservative or Transformative? Theorizing the UK Constitution Using Comparative Method' 2020 (68.2) *The American Journal of Comparative Law* 412–40

Mylonas, H 'Nation-Building' in Oxford Bibliographies DOI: 10.1093/OBO/9780199743292-0217 www.oxfordbibliographies.com/view/document/obo-9780199743292/obo-9780199743292-0217.xml#obo-9780199743292-0217-div2-0001 (accessed 14 October 2020)

Neuberger 'Legal Wales Conference 2014 on 10 October 2014' www.supremecourt.uk/docs/speech-141010.pdf (accessed 22 April 2021)

Neuvonen, PJ 'A Revised Democratic Critique of EU (Citizenship) Law: From Relative Homogeneity to Political Judgment' 2020 (21) *German Law Journal* 867–3

Ngigi, S & Busolo, DN 'Devolution in Kenya: The Good, the Bad and the Ugly' 2019 (9.6) *Public Policy and Administration Research* 9–21

Nogueira, AJA 'State of the Art Research in the Judicialization of Politics' 2020 (11.3) *Beijing Law Review* 670–89

Oake, RB 'Montesquieu's Religious Ideas' 1953 (14.4) *Journal of the History of Ideas* 548–60

Oduor, RMJ 'Liberal Democracy: An African Critique' 2019 (38.1) *South African Journal of Philosophy* 108–22

O'Kelly, C 'Nationalism and the State' in Bellamy, R & Mason, A (eds) *Political Concepts* (Manchester University Press, 2003) 52–64

Orgad, L *The Cultural Defense of Nations – A Liberal Theory of Majority Rights* (Oxford University Press, 2015) [page references to Adobe Digital Editions numbering]

Örücü, E *The Enigma of Comparative Law – Variations on a Theme for the Twenty-first Century* (Springer, 2004)

Paris, D 'Constitutional Courts and the European Court of Human Rights: A Comparative Perspective' 2017 (77) *Zeitschrift für ausländisches öffentliches Recht und Völkerrecht* 623–49

Parker, G, Brundsen, JG & Fleming, S 'Brexit Trade talks Buffeted by EU Covid Relief State Aid Row' 17 December 2020 *Financial Times* www.ft.com/content/2f508f4d-22e2-4deb-8d42-77a7c31fc53c (accessed 20 January 2021)

Paulson, SL 'The Very Idea of Legal Positivism' (English Text) 2011 (102) *Revista Brasileira Estudos Politicos* 139–66

Peters, A & Schwenke, H 'Comparative Law beyond Post-Modernism' 2000 (49.4) *International and Comparative Law Quarterly* 800–34

Pfetsch, FR 'European Citizenship: A Concept of Interrelatedness and Conditionality' in Mitra, SK (ed) *Citizenship as Cultural Flow, Transcultural Research* (Springer, 2013) 87–106

Pies, I 'Introduction: Corporate Citizenship and New Governance – The Political Role of Corporations' in Pies, I & Koslowski, P (eds) *Corporate Citizenship and New Governance – The Political Role of Corporations* (Springer, 2011) 1–6

Plato *The Seventh Letter* http://classics.mit.edu/Plato/seventh_letter.html (accessed 10 June 2021)

Ponthoreau, M-C & Hourquebiec, F 'The French Conseil Constitutionnel: An Evolving Form of Constitutional Justice' 2008 (3.2) *Journal of Comparative Law* 269–84

Popova, M 'Putin-Style "Rule of Law" & the Prospects for Change' 2017 (146.2) *Dædalus, the Journal of the American Academy of Arts & Sciences* 64–75

Popović, D *Comparative Government* (Edward Elgar Publishing, 2019)

Prandini, R 'The Morphogenesis of Constitutionalism' in Dobner, P & Loughlin, M (eds) *The Twilight of Constitutionalism* (Oxford University Press, 2010) 309–326

Pyke, J *Constitutional Law* (Palgrave Macmillan, 2013)

Quadrio, PA 'Religious Particularism, Anti-somatism and Elitism in "Mystical Anarchism"' in Welchman A (ed) *Politics of Religion/Religions of Politics* (Springer, 2015) 29–49

Rahmatian, A 'Friedrich Carl von Savigny's Beruf and Volksgeistlehre' 2007 (28) *Journal of Legal History* 1–30

Rawls, J 'Justice as Fairness' 1958 (67.2) *The Philosophical Review* 164–94

Raz, J 'The Rule of Law and its Virtue' in Raz, J *The Authority of Law: Essays on Law and Morality* (Clarendon Press, 1979) 208–28

Reidy, DA & Riker, WJ (eds) *Coercion and the State* (Springer, 2008)

Reimann, M 'Comparative Law and Neighbouring Disciplines' in Bussani, M & Mattei, U (eds) *The Cambridge Companion to Comparative Law* (Cambridge University Press, 2012) 13–34

Riegner, M 'Transformativer Konstitutionalismus und offene Staatlichkeit im regionalen Verfassungsvergleich mit Lateinamerika' in Baer, S, Lepsius, O, Schönberger, C, Waldhoff, C & Walter, C (eds) *Jahrbuch des Öffentliches Rechts der Gegenwart* Band 67 (Neue Folge) (Mohr Siebeck, 2019) 265–99

Rosen, S (ed) *The Philosopher's Handbook* (Random House, 2000)

Rosenn, KS 'Judicial Review in Latin America' 1974 (35) *Ohio State Law Journal* 785–819

Ross II, BL 'Administrative Constitutionalism as Popular Constitutionalism' 2019 (167.7) *University of Pennsylvania Law Review* 1783–1821

Rousseau, J-J *The Social Contract or Principles of Political Rights* (1762, translated by Cole, GDH) https://constitution.org/2-Authors/jjr/socon.txt (accessed 21 October 2020)

Rousseau, J-J *The Social Contract* (1762, translated by Bennett, J, 2017) www.earlymoderntexts.com/assets/pdfs/rousseau1762book1.pdf (accessed 8 June 2021)

Runhua, Z *The Constitutional and Legal Development of the Chinese Presidency* (Lexington Books, Lanham, 2015)

Ryan, FW *Constitutional Law* 3rd ed (Round Hall, 2018)

Sadie, Y, Patel, L & Baldry, K 'A Comparative Case Study of the Voting Behaviour of Poor People in Three Selected South African Communities' 2016 (15.6) *Journal of African Elections* 113–38

Sajeva, G 'Do We Need Earth Jurisprudence? Looking for Change in New Old Friends' 2020 (20.2) *Diritto & Questioni Pubbliche* 13–28

Samararatne, D 'From South Africa to Sri Lanka: Prospects of Travel for "Transformative Constitutionalism"' 2020 (15) *Asian Journal of Comparative Law* 45–68

Sánchez, SI 'Nationality: The Missing Link between Citizenship of the European Union and European Migration Policy' in Guild, E, Rotaeche, CJG & Kostakopoulou, D (eds) *The Reconceptualization of European Union Citizenship* (Brill Nijhoff, 2014) 65–87

Sanger, DE & Perlroth, N '"Perception Hacks" and Other Potential Threats to the Election' 28 October 2020 *The New York Times* www.nytimes.com/2020/10/28/us/politics/2020-election-hacking.html (accessed 9 November 2020)

Scheppele, KL 'Constitutional Coups and Judicial Review: How Transnational Institutions can Strengthen Peak Courts at Times of Crisis (With Special Reference to Hungary)' 2014 (23.1) *Transnational Law and Contemporary Problems* 51–118

Scheuner, U 'Der Rechtsstaat und die Soziale Verantwortung des Staates. Das Wissenschaftliche Lebenswerk von Robert von Mohl' 1979 (18.1) *Der Staat* 1–30

Schlaich, K *Das Bundesverfassungsgericht – Stellung, Verfahren, Entscheidungen 3. Auflage* (CH Beck, 1994)

Schmidt, SK 'No Match Made in Heaven. Parliamentary Sovereignty, EU over-Constitutionalization and Brexit' *Journal of European Public Policy* 2020 (27.5) 779–94

Schmitt, C *Political Theology Four Chapters on the Concept of Sovereignty* (translated by George Schwab) (University of Chicago Press, 2005) (original title published in 1922: *Politische Theologie: Vier Kapitel zur Lehre von der Souveranitat*)

Schmitt, C *Politische Theologie: Vier Kapitel zur Lehre von der Souveräntät* (Berlin, 1922, 9th ed by Duncker & Humblot, Berlin, 2009)

Scholtes, J 'The Complacency of Legality: Constitutionalist Vulnerabilities to Populist Constituent Power' 2019 (20) *German Law Journal* 351–61

Schonfeld, WR 'The Classical Marxist Conception of Liberal Democracy' 1971 (33.3) *The Review of Politics* 360–76

Schroeder, W 'The Rule of Law As a Value in the Sense of Article 2 TEU: What Does It Mean and Imply?' in Von Bogdandy, A et al. (eds) *Defending Checks and Balances in EU Member States – Taking Stock of Europe's Actions* (Springer, 2021) 105–26

Schwab, G 'Introduction' in Carl Schmitt's *Political Theology – Four Chapters on the Concept of Sovereignty* (University of Chicago Press, 2005)

Segev, M *Aristotle on Religion* (Cambridge University Press, 2017)

Setzer, H *Wahlsystem und Parteienentwicklung in England* (Suhrkamp, 1973)

Sevastik, P (ed) *Aspects of Sovereignty – Sino-Swedish Reflections* (Martinus Nijhoff, 2013)

Shakhray, S & Popova, S 'Countermajoritarian Institutions in the Russian Constitution of 1993 as an Instrument Ensuring Constitutional and Political Stability' 2018 (5) *BRICS Law Journal* 78–92

Shava, E & Chamisa, SF 'Cadre Deployment Policy and its Effects on Performance Management in South African Local Government: A Critical Review' 2018 (37.1) *Politeia* 1–18.

Sherman, GE 'Jus Gentium and International Law' 1918 (12.1) *The American Journal of International Law* 56–63

Shklar, JN 'Jean-Jacques Rousseau and Equality' 1978 (107.3) *Daedalus* 13–25

Simpson, DP *Cassell's New Latin-English English-Latin Dictionary* (Cassell, 1959)

Skey, M & Antonsich, M (eds) *Everyday Nationhood – Theorising Culture, Identity and Belonging after Banal Nationalism* (Palgrave Macmillan, 2017)

Smillie, J 'Who Wants Juristocracy' 2006 (11.2) *Otago Law Review* 183–96

Smith, GB & Sharlet, R (eds) *Russia and its Constitution: Promise and Political Reality* (Martinus Nijhoff Publishers, 2008)

Smith, RM 'Beyond Sovereignty and Uniformity: the Challenges for Equal Citizenship in the Twenty-first Century' (Book Review) 2009 (122) *Harvard Law Review* 907–36

Son, Bui Ngoc *Confucian Constitutionalism in East Asia* (Routledge, 2016)

Spadafora, A 'George Jellinek on Values and Objectivity in the Legal and Political Sciences' 2017 (14.3) *Modern Intellectual History* 747–76

Spawforth, A *Greece and the Augustan Cultural Revolution* (Cambridge University Press, 2012)

Spector, C 'Was Montesquieu Liberal? *The Spirit of the Laws* in the History of Liberalism' in Geenens, R & Rosenblatt, H (eds) *French Liberalism from Montesquieu to the Present Day* (Cambridge University Press, 2012) 57–72

Starck, C *vMangoldt/Klein/Starck Das Bonner Grundgesetz* Band 1 (Verlag Franz Vahlen, 1999)

Stern, K *Das Staatsrecht der Bundesrepublik Deutschland* Band I, 2. Aufl. (Beck, 1984)

Stewart, I 'The Critical Legal Science of Hans Kelsen' 1990 (17.3) *Journal of Law and Society* 273–308

Steytler, I '"Striking Back" and "Clamping Down" in South Africa: Responding to Adverse Judicial Decisions Under Systems of Parliamentary Sovereignty and Constitutional Supremacy' 2020 (12) *Hague Journal on the Rule of Law* 363–86

Strauss, L *Natural Right and History* (University of Chicago Press, 1953)

Strumia, F *Supranational Citizenship and the Challenge of Diversity – Immigrants, Citizens and Member States in the EU* (Nijhoff, 2013)

Stubbs, W *The Constitutional History of England in its Origin and Development* 2nd ed Vol III (Clarendon Press, 1878)

Tamanaha, BZ *On the Rule of Law* (Cambridge University Press, 2004)

Tamanaha, BZ, Sage, C & Woolcock, M (eds) *Legal Pluralism and Development – Scholars and Practitioners in Dialogue* (Cambridge University Press, 2012)

Tandoh-Offin, P & Bukari, GA 'Towards a Less Contentious Electoral Outcome in Sub-Saharan Africa' 2019 (2.2) *Africa Journal of Public Sector Development and Governance* 29–59

Tangian, A *Analytical Theory of Democracy – History, Mathematics and Applications* (Springer, 2020)

The Guardian London 28 June 2019 www.theguardian.com/world/2019/jun/28/western-leaders-defend-liberal-order-putin-obsolete-claim-donald-tusk (accessed 8 July 2019)

Tiedemann, P *Religionsfreiheit – Menschenrecht oder Toleranzgebot?* (Springer, 2012)

Trnavci, G 'The Meaning and Scope of the Law of Nations in the Context of the Alien Tort Claims Act and International Law' 2005 (26.2) *University of Pennsylvania Journal of International Economic Law* 193–266

Tsai, RL 'Considerations of History and Purpose in Constitutional Borrowing' 2019 (28.2) *William & Mary Bill of Rights Journal* 517–40

Tushnet, M 'Varieties of Constitutionalism' 2016 (14.1) *International Journal of Constitutional Law* 1–5

Tushnet, M 'Varieties of Populism' 2019 (20) *German Law Journal* 382–9

Tusseau, G (ed) *Debating Legal Pluralism and Consitutionalism – New Trajectories for Legal Theory in the Global Age* (Springer, 2020)

Tzanakopoulou, M *Reclaiming Constitutionalism – Democracy, Power and the State* (Hart Publishing, 2018)

Ullmann, U *A Short History of the Papacy in the Middle Ages* 2nd ed (Routledge, 2003)

Urabe, N 'Rule of Law and Due Process: A Comparative View of the United States and Japan' 1990 (53.1) *Law and Contemporary Problems* 61–72

Van der Vyver, JD 'The Right to Self-determination of Cultural, Religious and Linguistic Communities in South Africa' 2011 (14.4) *PER (Potchefstroom Electronic Law Journal)* 1–28

Van der Walt, J *The Horizontal Effect Revolution and the Question of Sovereignty* (De Gruyter, 2014)

Van Domselaar, I 'A Neo-Aristotelian Notion of Reciprocity: About Civic Friendship and (the Troublesome Character of) Right Judicial Decisions' in Huppes-Cluysenaer, L & Coelho, NMMS (eds) *Aristotle and The Philosophy of Law: Theory, Practice and Justice* (Springer, 2013) 223–47

Van Gelder, HAE *The Two Reformations in the 16th Century* (Martinus Nijhoff, 1964)

Van Roermund, B (ed) *Constitutional Review – Verfassungsgerichtsbarkeit – Constitutionele Toetsing* (Kluwer, 1993)

Vanoverbeke, D 'Exporting the Rule of Law in East Asia: Japan's Experiences from the 1990s to Present' 2013 (46.2) *Revue Belge de Droit International Belgian Review of International Law* 364–81

Venice Commission *Rule of Law Checklist* (European Commission for Democracy Through Law, Council of Europe, 2016)

Venter, F 'Arms Deals, Bribery and Political Interference: How (Im)potent the (Rule of) Law?' 2008 (125.4) *South African Law Journal* 633–42

Venter, F *Constitutional Comparison* (Juta/Kluwer, 2000)

Venter, F *Constitutionalism and Religion* (Edward Elgar Publishing, 2015)

Venter, F *Global Features of Constitutional Law* (Wolf Legal Publishers, 2010)

Venter, F 'Independence and Accountability of the South African Judiciary' in Hirsch Ballin, E, Van der Schyff, G & Stremler, M (eds) *European Yearbook of*

Constitutional Law 2019 – Judicial Power: Safeguards and Limits in a Democratic Society (Asser Press, 2020) 171–96

Venter, F *Legal Research – Purpose, Planning and Publication* (Juta, 2018)

Venter, F 'Liberal Democracy: the Unintended Consequence. South African Constitution-writing Propelled by the Winds of Globalisation' 2010 (26) *South African Journal on Human Rights* 45–65

Venter, F 'Parliamentary Sovereignty or Presidential Imperialism? – The Difficulties of Identifying the Source of Constitutional Power from the Interaction Between Legislatures and Executives in Anglophone Africa' in Fombad, CM (ed) *Separation of Powers in African Constitutionalism* (Oxford University Press, 2016) 95–115.

Venter, F 'Rethinking the Language of Constitutional Comparison' 2017 (33.1) *South African Journal on Human Rights* 72–96

Venter, F 'Review of Gyorfi "New Constitutionalism"' 2017 (20) *PER/PELJ* https://journals.assaf.org.za/index.php/per/article/view/2426/2693 (accessed 20 April 2021)

Venter, F 'South Africa: a Diceyan Rechtsstaat?' 2012 (57.4) *McGill Law Journal* 721–47

Venter, F 'State Capture, Corruption, and Constitutionalism in South Africa' in Fombad, CM & Steytler, N (eds) *Corruption and Constitutionalism in Africa – Revisiting Control Measures and Strategies* (Oxford University Press, 2020) 69–89

Venter, F 'The Limits of Transformation in South Africa's Constitutional Democracy' 2018 (34.2) *South African Journal on Human Rights* 143–66

Venter, F 'The Many Faces of Constitutionalism – Contemporary Challenges' in Fleiner, T (ed) *Five Decades of Constitutionalism: Reality and Perspectives (1945–1995)* (Helbing & Lichtenhahn, 1999) 21–45

Venter, F 'The Separation of Powers in New Constitutions' in Baraggia, A, Fasone, C & Vanoni, LP (eds) *New Challenges to the Separation of Powers* (Edward Elgar Publishing, 2020) 105–22

Verovšek, P 'Brexit and the Misunderstanding of Sovereignty' *Social Europe* 26 December 2020 www.socialeurope.eu/brexit-and-the-misunderstanding-of-sovereignty (accessed 9 December 2020)

Vilhena, O, Baxi, U & Viljoen, F (eds) *Transformative Constitutionalism: Comparing the Apex Courts of Brazil, India and South Africa* (Pretoria University Law Press, 2013)

Voigt, R *Der moderne Staat – Zur Genese des heutigen Staatsverständnisses* (Springer, 2015)

Von Bernstorff, J 'Georg Jellinek and the Origins of Liberal Constitutionalism in International Law' 2012 (4.3) *Goettingen Journal of International Law* 659–75

Von Bogdandy, A 'The Current Situation of European Jurisprudence in the Light of Carl Schmitt's Homonymous Text' *MPIL Research Paper Series* No. 2020–08 https://papers.ssrn.com/sol3/papers.cfm?abstract_id=3561655 (accessed 15 December 2020)

Von Bogdandy, A 'Überstaatlicher Transformativer Konstitutionalismus – Bemerkenswertes vom Interamerikanischen System für Menschenrechte' 2019 (58) *Der Staat* 41–56

Von Bogdandy, A, Bogdanowicz, P, Canor, I, Grabenwarter, C, Taborowski, M & Schmidt, M (eds) *Defending Checks and Balances in EU Member States – Taking Stock of Europe's Actions* (Springer, 2021)

Von Bogdandy, A, Wolfrum, R, Von Bernstorff, J, Dann, P & Goldmann, M (eds) *The Exercise of Public Authority by International Institutions – Advancing International Institutional Law* (Springer, 2010)

Von Danwitz, T 'The Rule of Law in the Recent Jurisprudence of the ECJ' 2014 (37) *Fordham International Law Journal* 1311–46
Von Hayek, FA *The Constitution of Liberty* (Routledge, 1960)
Walbank, FW 'Nationality as a Factor in Roman History' 1972 (76) *Harvard Studies in Classical Philology* 145–68
Waldrauch, H 'Methodology for Comparing Acquisition and Loss of Nationality' in Bauböck, R, Ersbøll, E, Groenendijk, K & Waldrauch, H (eds) *Acquisition and Loss of Nationality, 1 & 2: Country Analyses – Policies and Trends in 15 European Countries* (Amsterdam University Press, 2006) Volume 1, 105–19
Waldron, J 'Judical Review of Legislation' in Marmor, A (ed) *Routledge Companion to Philosophy of Law* (Routledge, 2012) 434–48
Waldron, J 'Kant's Legal Positivism' 1996 (109) *Harvard Law Review* 1535–66
Waldron, J 'The Core of the Case against Judicial Review' in Waldron, J *Political Political Theory* (Harvard University Press, 2016) 195–245
Walker, N 'Populism and Constitutional Tension' 2019 (17.2) *International Journal of Constitutional Law* 515–35
Walker, N 'The Sovereignty Surplus' 2020 (18.2) *International Journal of Constitutional Law* 370–428
Ward, L *John Locke and Modern Life* (Cambridge University Press, 2010)
Watson, M 'Rethinking Neutrality: A Conceptual Analysis' 2021 (46.1) *Journal of Legal Philosophy* 1–28
Weber, A 'Typen der Verfassungsgerichtsbarkeit und Rezeptionsprobleme' in Starck, C (ed) *Fortschritte der Verfassungsgerichtsbarkeit in der Welt Teil I* (Baden-Baden, 2004)
Weber-Fas, R *Staatsdenker der Moderne* (Mohr Siebeck, 2003)
Weiler, JHH 'A Nation of Nations?' 2019 (17.4) *International Journal of Constitutional Law* 1301–6
Wendel, M 'Das Bundesverfassungsgericht als Garant der Unionsgrundrechte' 2020 (75.4) *JuristenZeitung* 157–68
Wesemann, A *Citizenship in the European Union – Constitutionalism, Rights and Norms* (Edward Elgar Publishing, 2020)
White, S 'Brexit and the Future of the UK Constitution' 2021 *International Political Science Review* 1–15 https://journals.sagepub.com/doi/10.1177/0192512121995133 (accessed 21 April 2021)
Whytock, CA 'Legal Origins, Functionalism, and the Future of Comparative Law' 2009 (6) *Brigham Young University Law Review* 1879–906
Widner, J & Contiades, X 'Constitution-writing Processes' in Tushnet, M, Fleiner, T & Saunders, C (eds) *Routledge Handbook of Constitutional Law* (Routledge, 2013) 57–69
Wielgus, S 'The Genesis and History of *Ius Gentium* in the Ancient World and the Middle Ages' 1999 (47.2) *Roczniki Filozoficzne/Annales de Philosophie / Annals of Philosophy* 335–51
Wiener, A, Lang, AF, Tully, J, Maduro, MP & Kumm, M 'Global Constitutionalism: Human Rights, Democracy and the Rule of Law' 2012 (1.1) *Global Constitutionalism* 1–15
Wilkinson, MA 'The Reconstitution of Post-war Europe: Liberal Excesses, Democratic Deficiencies' in Dowdle, MW & Wilkinson, MA (eds) *Constitutionalism Beyond Liberalism* (Cambridge University Press, 2017) 38–78
Wilms, H *Staatsrecht I – Staatsorganisationsrecht unter Berücksichtigung der Föderalismusreform* (Kohlhammer, 2007)

Wilson, EE 'Kant's Moral Philosophy' in Garrett, A (ed) *The Routledge Companion to Eighteenth Century Philosophy* (Routledge, 2014) 442–64

Wimmer, H *Die Modernisierung politischer Systeme* (Böhlau Verlag, 2000)

Witte, J *God's Joust, God's Justice – Law and Religion in the Western Tradition* (Wm B. Eerdemans Publishing, 2006)

Wong, C 'E-Justice Reform in China: A Committed Move towards the Rule of Law, or Old Wine in New Bottles?' 2020 (14) *Hong Kong Journal of Legal Studies* 81–112

World Justice Project *Rule of Law Index 2020* https://worldjusticeproject.org/our-work/research-and-data/wjp-rule-law-index-2020 (accessed 9 March 2021)

Worster, WT 'Territorial Status Triggering Functional Approach to Statehood' 2020 (8.1) *Penn State Journal of Law and International Affairs* 118–80

Wright, G *Religion, Politics and Thomas Hobbes* (Springer, 2006)

Young, BW *Religion and Enlightenment in Eighteenth-Century England: Theological Debate from Locke to Burke* (Clarendon Press, 1998)

Young, R 'Patterns and Particularities in European Democracy' in Blockmans, S & Russack, S (eds) *Deliberative Democracy in the EU – Countering Populism with Participation and Debate* (Rowman & Littlefield, 2020) 349–55

Yusuf, HO 'Robes on Tight Ropes: The Judicialisation of Politics in Nigeria' 2008 (8) *Global Jurist* [i]–31

Zakaria, F 'The Rise of Illiberal Democracy' November/December 1997 (76.6) *Foreign Affairs* 22–43

Zhang, W 'China's Rule of Law in the Globalization Era' 2006 (1.4) *Frontiers of Law in China* 471–85

Zhang, W 'Human Rights Jurisprudence in the New Era' 2019 (18.3) *Journal of Human Rights* 265–83

Ziegler, KS, Baranger, D & Bradley, AW (eds) *Constitutionalism and the Role of Parliaments* (Hart Publishing, 2007)

Zumbansen, P 'Review' of Frankenberg, G 'Comparative Law's Coming of Age? Twenty Years after Critical Comparisons' 2005 (6.7) *German Law Journal* 1073–84

Index

Abbas, Förster & Richter 95, 155
absolutism 7, 21, 23–4, 26, 37, 47, 62, 65, 83, 142, 235, 239
abuse 18, 24, 69, 86, 146, 172, 216, 236
abuse of power 24
academia 2, 9, 13, 70, 86–7, 125, 145, 160, 162, 193, 206, 221–3, 225, 229, 231, 237
accountability 86, 150, 154, 156, 158, 164, 168, 175, 179, 187, 196, 208, 210
Ackerman 79, 87
Adams 31
Adams, John Quincy 144
Adepoju & Basiru 94
aequitas 19, 20
Afghanistan 55, 135
Africa 2, 16, 36, 39, 69, 92, 94–5, 114, 117, 119, 139, 151, 155–60, 179–80, 185, 190, 192–3, 215–6
agency 78, 165, 240
Agenda for Sustainable Development 139
agnosticism 44, 84
Aguilera-Barchet 16–7, 37, 40, 58, 60–3, 80, 82–3, 104, 111, 129–30, 134, 239
Al-Ali & Thiruvengadam 71
Albert 170, 185, 200, 207–8
Alfons III 19
Alfons X 19
Allenby 140
Allgemeines Landrecht 64
Allgemeine Staatslehre 105–7
American Revolution 17, 29, 38, 62, 131, 164
Amsterdam Treaty 173
Anderson 70

Anglicans 31–2
Angola 207
anthropocentrism 18, 20, 50
anthropology 50, 55, 57
Aquinas 48, 60
Arake 91
Arato 29
arbitrariness 18–9, 22, 25, 179, 184, 187–8, 232
Argentina 132, 203
Argentine 223
aristocracy 142, 168
Aristotle 16, 45–6
Arjomand 75
Armia 197
Arnold & Martínez-Estay 203
Articles of Confederation 132
artificial intelligence 53
Asia 2, 8, 39, 58, 69, 81, 117, 158, 177, 195–6
aspirational 46, 87, 115, 139, 157, 164, 168, 188, 191
atheism 44, 49, 84
Athens 16, 17, 59, 141, 165
Atlantic Charter 66
Auby 194
Auguste 19
Augustinus 46
Augustus 46
Ausnahmezustand 54, 79
Australia 4, 35–6, 86–7, 112, 223
Austria 22, 37–9, 63–4, 152, 174, 203, 212
Austro-Hungarian Empire 40, 76
authoritarian constitutionalism 162, 193
authoritarianism 9, 51, 53, 70, 141–2, 147, 161–3, 185–7, 193, 198

authority/power 1–3, 6, 11–14, 17–25, 27, 29–35, 38, 41–2, 45–7, 50, 53, 55, 57, 61–3, 66, 72–3, 75, 78, 80–85, 88–9, 92–3, 95–9, 101–4, 109–10, 112–13, 117–19, 122, 136, 138–51, 154–5, 166, 172, 175–6, 178–80, 184–5, 187, 189–91, 193, 199–201, 203, 206, 210, 212, 217–18, 228, 230–1, 2359
autocracy 33, 35, 53, 76, 139, 146, 217
autonomous will 27
autonomy 17, 26–8, 36, 52, 112, 117, 127, 129, 142, 212, 227, 239

Babylonia 104
Bacon 37
Badura 4, 38
Balke 24
Balkin 56
Balme 208
Bangladesh 135
Baofu 10
Barber 5, 10, 121, 136–7, 170, 189
Barroso 161
Bates 16
Bauböck 129
Bauböck, Ersbøll, Groenendijk & Waldrauch 128
Baudrillard 9
Baume 80
Baxi 6, 192
Bazezew 185
Beaulac 172
Beaumont 66
Beckenbach & Klotter 103
Belgium 65, 128
belief 5, 11, 21, 25, 27, 42, 44, 48, 51, 81, 120, 152, 183, 236–8
belonging 21, 74, 75, 125, 126, 128, 135, 137, 168
Belov 194
Benhabib 124
Bentham 60
Beyer 84
Bierbach 132
big bang 44
Bignami 225
Billig 55
Bill of Rights 32, 64, 114–16, 216

Bingham 172, 175–7
Bismarck 39
Blackstone 34, 202
Blockmans 151
Blokker 161–2
Bobek & Kosař 219
Bodin 23, 49, 62, 83, 239
Bolivia 203
Boogaard 92
Bosniak 124, 134
Botswana 139
Bowen, Mancke & Reid 33
Brang 226
Brazil 192, 203
Brewer 58
Brexit 86, 90, 98, 110, 196, 209, 210–211
Britain 18, 30, 33, 35, 37, 40, 41, 42, 66, 71, 211
British colonial constitutional law 33–6, 88, 215
British colonialism 33
British Commonwealth 36
British constitution 36, 86, 196, 209
British constitutional law 188, 210, 232
British Empire 30, 33–4, 36
Broekman & Backer 56
Brown Report 42
Brunei 197
Buddhism 195
Buddhist 135
Bugarič 76, 217
Bundesverfassungsgericht 95–6, 155, 211–13
Buratti 186
Burch 33
Bürgerliches Gesetzbuch 64
Bussani 150
Butler 123
Byzantium 17

C2G2 124
cabinet 30–32
Caesar 46
Calabresi 216–17
Calvin 32, 34, 47
Calvinism 31
Canada 33–6, 80, 86–8, 112, 119, 139, 191, 203–4, 207
Canadian Constitution Act 87, 203

Index

canon law 18–20, 60
Cape Colony 35
Cape of Good Hope 34
Cappelletti 203
Caracalla 130
Carey & Gascoigne 119
Carvalho 56, 226
categorical imperative 150, 219
catholic 46
Central Europe 75
Ceylon 35
Charlemagne 46
Charles II 32
Charles X 38
Charlow 178
Charter of the United Nations 67, 90
Chartres 18
Chayes 207
Chernilo 22
Chesney & Citron 161
Chesterman 172
Chile 203
China 16, 42–4, 53, 58, 104, 139, 144, 168, 177, 180–182, 195–7, 208, 226
Chinkin & Baetens 103
Christian 37, 46–8, 50–51, 135, 237–8, 241
Christianity 51, 150, 195
Churchill 66
Cicero 17, 46, 59
cidade 131
citizen 2, 48, 50–51, 54, 59, 65, 74, 94, 97, 99, 102–3, 111, 114–15, 117, 122, 124–38, 143, 145, 154, 157, 164, 168–9, 191, 205, 208, 219, 223, 229, 239
citizenry 76, 94, 127–8, 137–8, 166, 230, 239
citizenship 2–3, 28, 65, 68, 72, 76, 94–5, 101, 123, 123–138, 154
citta 131
city of God 47
city states 16, 57–8, 103, 108
ciutat 131
civilized state (*état civil*) 25
civil law 20, 25, 203, 217–18
civil liberties 73
civil religion 144

civil society 74, 124, 142, 145, 154, 160, 189, 192, 197
civis 129–31
civitas 59, 61, 82, 103, 129, 130–131
Cladis 50–51
Claes, Devroe & Keirsbilck 169
clientelism 76
Code Civil 64
coercion 20, 27, 78, 103, 143, 167–8, 193, 223
Coke 201–2
Collings 15
Colombia 192, 203, 207, 224
colonialism 20, 29, 30, 33–7, 39–40, 42, 71, 86, 88–9, 92, 94, 102, 105, 155–6, 192
Comella 212
comita curiata 59
comitia tributa 59
comity 18, 236
common law 19, 109, 217, 229
communalism 81, 157
communism 40, 43, 76, 81, 181–2
communitarianism 95, 154
Community Law 95–6
comparative constitutional history 15
comparative constitutional law 3, 221–5
comparative law 15, 221
comparative method 222, 224, 228, 233
Confucianism 195
Congress of Vienna 63
Conseil Constitutionnel 213–4
Conseil d'Etat 214
consensual democracy 156
Constantine I 46
constituent power 88, 162, 200
constitution 4–5, 29–30, 38, 43, 54–5, 58, 64, 71–2, 75, 79–80, 86–8, 92, 98, 104, 113–15, 118, 136, 139–40, 145, 148, 167, 169, 179–80, 182, 185–6, 189, 192, 199–200, 203, 205, 210–211, 215, 217, 223, 239
constitutional comparison 3, 6, 9–10, 13, 15, 57, 99, 100–102, 104, 122, 125, 135, 138, 141, 145, 169, 171, 183–6, 197, 221–7, 229–34, 241
Constitutional Convention 29
constitutional coup 217
Constitutional Court of South Africa 215

constitutionalism 3, 5–6, 13, 28–9, 31, 33, 39, 48, 54, 62, 81, 94, 109, 112, 115, 131, 140, 147, 150, 162–3, 169, 182, 183–98, 200–201, 206–8, 215–17, 220, 229, 231–2, 234, 240–241
constitutionality 187, 201, 203, 207, 212, 214–15, 218
constitutionalization 92, 169, 209, 216
constitutional law 1–2, 4, 10–11, 13, 15–16, 28, 30, 44–6, 56–8, 68, 71, 73, 77–9, 82, 84, 86–7, 89–92, 95, 98, 102, 105–8, 112, 114, 120–122, 129, 131, 134–35, 137–8, 141, 148, 150, 155, 161, 164, 166, 168, 170, 175, 183, 186, 192, 198–9, 201, 208, 219, 221–4, 226–7, 229–41
constitutional review 167, 199, 203, 208–9, 211–13, 215–18
constitutional state 102, 109–10, 179, 183, 188
constitutional supremacy 87, 94, 99, 144, 202, 215
constitutional values 158, 196, 217
constitution-making 29–30
Constitution of the Republic of South Africa 55, 63, 73–4, 87, 93, 114–17, 119, 156, 158, 179, 192, 215
constitution-writing 43, 77, 203, 208, 229
contextualization 4, 232
contextualism 226
Convention Relating to the Status of Refugees 136
convictions 44, 49, 52, 81, 94, 228, 233–4, 236–8, 240
Coomaraswamy 89
Cooper 101
Cornelissen, Cheru & Shaw 102
cosmopolitan 6, 37, 102, 108–9
cosmos 21, 48, 235, 239
Costa Rica 203
Council of Europe 152, 172, 219
countermajoritarian difficulty 201, 204–6, 208
countermajoritarian dilemma 204

country 10, 17, 34, 36–7, 40, 51, 61, 66, 71–2, 76, 93, 98, 108, 117, 123, 125, 127–8, 130, 133–4, 136, 141, 144–5, 175, 197
Court of Justice of the European Union 96, 129, 173, 183, 193, 213
Covenant of the League of Nations 66
Critical Legal Theory 5, 9, 81, 105, 124, 192, 224, 226, 235
Critique of Pure Reason 52
Critique of the Power of Judgment 52
Cromwell 32
cronyism 158
Croucamp & Malan 168
Crowe & Lee 48
Crown 30–36, 61–2, 75–6, 80, 82, 85, 123, 132, 210
Crown Colony 35
culture 10–11, 13, 15, 18–19, 39, 46, 52, 55–8, 63, 65–6, 68, 70, 74, 76, 81, 90, 93–4, 102, 126, 128, 131, 137, 140, 157, 170, 181, 218, 223–4, 226
curia 31, 58
curia regis 31
custom 22, 168
customary law 19–20
Czechoslovakia 212
Czech Republic 133

Dalla-Pozza & Williams 87
Dann, Riegner & Bönnemann 225
Dauchy 22
decentralization 93
Déclaration des droits de l'homme et du citoyen 63
Declaration of Independence 34, 55
decolonization 196
deconcentration 93
deconstruction 9
deductive reasoning 227
De Groot & Luk 129
deism 49, 51, 119, 150
De Jure Belli Ac Pacis 60
De L'Esprit des loix 51
democracy 88, 92, 139–169, 171, 213

democratic 25, 38, 40, 69, 71, 73, 75, 86, 90, 93, 95, 97, 101–2, 113–14, 116, 124, 139, 140–143, 146–9, 151–61, 163–4, 166, 168–9, 179, 181–3, 187–8, 190–191, 200, 205, 208, 211, 217, 229–30
demography 1, 18, 42, 53, 59, 125, 147, 167
demos 142–3
demystification 236–7, 239
Denmark 63, 175
Dent & Kroeze 206
Derrida 9
Descartes 37
Deutsche Bund 63–4
devolution 94
Dhooghe, Franken & Opgenhaffen 226
dialogical interpretation 226
DiCenso 52
Dicey 85, 87, 170, 180, 183
dictatorship 29, 139, 145, 148, 150
dictatorship of the people 29
Di Fabio 106
dignity 6, 27–8, 62, 72, 116, 173, 179, 181
Di Lizia 123
diplomacy 68, 71
divine 20, 23–4, 31–2, 92, 98, 104, 150, 168, 238–40
divine law 109
divinity 150, 151
Dixon 141
doctrine 10, 21, 48, 62, 72–3, 77, 85–6, 106, 114, 122, 145, 171, 176, 178, 181–3, 186–8, 196, 199, 213, 223, 225, 227, 239–40
dogma 11, 16, 44, 114, 120, 144–5, 192, 240
dogmatism 6, 8, 11, 97, 122, 128, 151, 197, 201, 223, 237, 240
domestic 15, 36, 50, 55, 128, 172, 210, 221, 224
dominions 36, 86, 155
Donovan 226
Dörr & Schmalenbach 68
Douglas-Scott 86, 196, 197
Dowdle 3, 10, 11
Drinóczi & Bień-Kacała 185
dualism 87–8, 209
Dube 158

Dugard 123
Dumbarton Oaks 41
Dunleavy & O'Leary 102, 142
Dunoff, Wiener, Kumm, Lang & Tully 194
Durham Report 35
Duso 149
Dutch legal order 35, 92
Dworkin 79

Eastern and Central Europe 8, 147
Eastern Europe 203, 217, 218
economics 1, 8, 12, 15, 19–20, 23, 26, 29, 35–6, 39–42, 53–4, 57–8, 67, 69–71, 81, 89, 92, 94, 105, 111, 124, 137, 148, 177, 180–181, 223, 228, 238, 240
Ecuadorian 197
education 19, 54, 57, 72, 106, 116–17
Edward I 32
egalitarianism 69
Egypt 16, 58, 104
elections 32, 35, 76, 88, 97, 99, 140, 142, 145–6, 153, 156–61, 164–69, 179, 188, 193, 204, 207, 208, 214, 231
elite 148, 157, 162, 168, 208
elitism 70, 94, 140, 151, 162–4
El Salvador 203
Emile 51
emperor 20, 39, 46, 47, 82, 83, 98
empiricism 37
Engels 81
England 1, 23, 25, 30–6, 38, 50, 61–2, 69, 85–6, 97, 113, 141–2, 158, 186, 201, 207
English Common Law 35, 85, 201, 209, 215
English constitutional history 30–1, 33
English Revolution 62
Enlightenment 16, 18, 21–3, 50, 62, 144
environmental constitutionalism 197, 231
Enwere 159
epistemology 6–10, 42, 52–3, 84, 107–8, 198, 203, 223–5, 227, 229, 231–5, 238
equality 22, 25–6, 51, 60, 62, 70, 72, 75, 84, 90, 113, 116, 139, 141, 157, 168, 172–3, 179, 191, 205

Eridu 57
Esser, Reinemann & Fan 160
ethics 49, 52, 84, 150, 158, 173, 218
ethnic 55, 61, 63, 65–6, 68, 70, 72, 76, 90, 92, 93, 126–8, 131, 157, 159, 212
ethnology 55
ethnos 55
ethos 43, 154, 157
EU law 96–7, 127, 138, 153, 155, 173–4, 225
Eurocentric 2, 39, 227
Europe 2, 8, 15, 18– 21, 29, 38–9, 46, 60–64, 66, 69, 74, 76, 82, 95, 102, 104, 128–9, 131, 143, 147, 151–2, 154, 174, 219
European Commission 110
European Council 8, 97–8
European Court of Human Rights 86, 91, 152, 172, 213
European Parliament 97
European Union 86, 95–8, 110–111, 127–9, 133, 138, 140, 147, 151–5, 165, 170, 173–4, 209–11, 213
evolutionism 44
extremism 53, 55, 69

Fabra-Zamora 144
fairness 60, 139, 158, 181, 218–9, 235, 240
faith 44, 50, 67, 176, 205, 236–8, 241
family 17, 57–9, 73–5, 78, 108, 114, 130, 136, 145
fantasy 105
Far East 57, 66
Farinacci-Fernos 190
fascism 40
federalism 87, 93, 109, 112–13, 142, 182
Ferrari 4, 103
feudalism 18–20, 30, 43, 61, 82, 142, 146
fiction 3, 24, 28, 80, 83–4, 99, 107, 138, 161–3, 230
Finland 223
Finnis 16
Fioravanti 185
First British Empire 33
Fleiner & Basta Fleiner 57, 84
Forrest 134

Förster 111, 155
Foucault 9, 105
four freedoms 41–2
Fournier 163, 166–7, 200–201
France 19–20, 23, 25, 34, 38–40, 43, 61, 63–5, 69, 71, 74, 82, 134, 144, 213–14, 217
franchise 33, 158
Frankenberg 3, 6, 9, 54, 64, 79, 81, 83, 185–7, 193, 224–7
Frankfurt Constitution 38
freedom 20, 22, 24, 26–7, 32, 42, 66, 70, 90, 101, 106, 116, 124, 136, 139, 145, 152–3, 157, 173, 176, 191, 213
French Constitution 214
French legal order 21, 29, 31, 35, 39, 61, 63, 174, 214
French Revolution 29, 37, 38, 62, 130–131, 164
Friedberg 90
Friedman 205–6
Friedrich Wilhelm IV 38
Frowein 153
functionalism 225, 229
fundamental rights 96, 175, 180, 214, 221

Gadzhiev 182–3
Gagnon & Tremblay 112
Galileo 37
Galloro 60
Gao, Zhang & Tian 43
García & Frankenberg 185
Gargarella 185
gatekeeping 54
Geddis 87
Gehring 9
Gellner 70, 105
General Assembly 41, 67, 91, 139, 171
genos 58
gens 58–61, 129
geography 1, 17–18, 36, 67, 74, 92, 102, 119–20, 122, 124, 187, 189
Gerhard & Lengfeld 129
German constitutional law 213
German Historical School 64
German nation 38, 72
German Reich 72, 103

Germany 4, 23, 38–41, 43, 64, 72, 96, 97, 112–13, 131, 155, 203, 211
Gerson 45
Geschichtliche Rechtswissenschaft 64
Ghaleigh 197
Ghana 55, 93
Gible 103
Giri 2
Girsu 57
Giuliani 64
Glassman 16, 149
Glenn 6, 10, 31, 37, 39, 46, 102, 108–9, 159–60
global 2, 3, 7–8, 10, 19, 28, 36–7, 40, 42, 55, 89, 93, 124, 129, 158, 161, 176–7, 181–2, 193–4, 217–18, 231
globalization 39, 53, 70, 102, 123–4, 134, 147–8, 161, 180–181, 194, 198, 221, 230
global north 123
global south 8, 123
Glover 141
God 23–4, 32, 39, 47–50, 55, 62, 73, 80, 84, 118–20, 202, 238–9
Goderis & Versteeg 223
Goldini 26
Goldoni 26
good life 24
government 13, 25, 29, 30–33, 38–9, 49, 51, 54, 66, 70, 72–4, 76, 87, 91, 93–4, 103, 110–111, 113, 115, 117–19, 139–50, 152, 156–8, 160, 164–5, 167, 168, 175, 177, 179, 185, 187–8, 191, 200–201, 206–11, 216–18, 229, 235, 239
Great Depression 40
Greece 13, 38, 58, 65, 140
Greene 54
Greenfield 55, 61–2, 69–70
Greenfield & Wu 70
Grimm 95–7, 155
Grossi 18–23, 30, 47, 48
Grotenhuis 75
Grotius 22, 30, 48, 60
Grundgesetz 38, 72, 95–7, 113–18, 128, 212–13
Grundnorm 80
Grundrechte 38, 64
gubernaculum 171, 188

Gunn 44
Gyorfi 3, 87, 208–9

habeas corpus 203
Habermas 73, 79, 84
Hahm 195
Haiti 203
Haldén 102
Haley 2
Hallam 31
Hallaq 81
Haltern 212–13
Hameiri 102
Hamid & Wouters 172–3
Harris 74, 168
Harrison 149
Hartmann, Meyer & Oldopp 16
Hatschek 31
He 148, 169, 197
Hegel 64, 99, 149
Heidemann & Stoppenbrink 112
Hellas 16–17, 32, 59, 141
Helmholz 202
Henry VIII 31
Herrera 192
Hesse 106
Hidalgo 84
Hiebert 86
Hilker 38
Himsworth 101
Hindu 135, 192
Hinduism 150, 192
Hirschi 55
Hirschl 6, 194, 207, 225
historiography 15
history 3–4, 10, 12, 15–17, 21, 30, 39, 43, 55, 58, 64, 69, 73, 80, 83–84, 103–4, 110, 122, 125, 134, 137, 146, 158–9, 186, 198, 201, 222–3, 227, 229, 231, 237–8
Hobbes 16, 23–4, 28, 49, 79, 142
Hochstrasser 22
Hoexter & Olivier 87
Höffe 140, 143
Holmberg 140
Holy Roman Empire 46
homo homini lupus 24
homo sapiens 149
Honduras 203, 207
Hong Kong 181, 195

hostis 129–30
Hotmann 21
House 144
House of Commons 32, 49, 80
Howse 160, 163–4, 168
Htun 126
Huber 48, 89
Hughes & Fries 31–2
humanism 20–21, 62
human nature 24, 27, 84, 202
human reason 23, 44, 48, 202, 240
human rights 8, 41–2, 44, 52, 72, 87, 89–90, 96, 124, 129, 152, 157, 171–3, 176, 178–9, 180–181, 183, 192–3, 196, 209
Human Rights Act 86
Human Rights and Popular Sovereignty 79
Human Rights Committee 129
Hungary 72, 75
Huppes-Cluysenaer & Coelho 16
Husa 225–6
Hutt 191

Iceland 132, 194
idealism 11, 17, 92, 94, 159
ideology 8, 185, 187, 191–2, 197, 223, 236
illiberal 26, 53, 76, 141, 147, 161, 164, 185, 187, 217, 231, 234
illusion 11, 44, 145
Il Risorgimento 39
imperium 103
Imperium Christianum 46
independence 31–3, 38, 40, 42, 65, 89, 90–91, 111, 183, 188, 207–8, 216, 218
indeterminacy 28, 135, 187
India 4, 33, 35, 42, 53, 135, 192, 207
indigenous 35, 93, 94, 114, 192, 215, 223
individual 13, 18, 20, 22, 24–8, 30, 32, 39, 45, 47, 51, 62–3, 70–71, 80, 82, 95, 101, 123, 125, 128, 131, 135, 138, 147, 149, 152–4, 165, 173, 176, 184–6, 188, 195, 197, 205, 212, 218–19, 227, 230, 239
individualism 20, 94, 144–5, 153–4, 236
Indo-European 58
Indonesia 105, 197

industrial revolution 53
injustice 53, 115
Inter-American Court of Human Rights 192
International Bill of Human Rights 42
International Covenant on Economic, Social and Cultural Rights 116
international law 1, 4, 12–13, 37, 42, 44, 53, 55–6, 59–60, 66–7, 72–3, 77, 87, 89–90, 98, 104, 110–112, 117, 120, 123–6, 128–9, 138–9, 151, 171–2, 176, 178, 181, 192–4, 198, 216, 221, 231
law of nations 25, 59
international relations 36, 60, 67, 79, 89, 91, 111, 117, 124, 125, 210
Ipsen 114
Ireland 4, 33, 55, 113, 115–19, 134, 151, 203, 224
irrationality 3, 44
Islam 81, 105, 113, 117, 120, 140, 150–151, 197, 225, 235
Italy 4, 23, 38–40, 47, 82, 103, 131
ius civile 59–60
ius commune 19, 20, 229
ius gentium 59–60
ius inter gentes 60
ius sanguinis 126

Jackson & Versteeg 224
Jacobsohn & Schor 222
Jain 135
Jakab 147–8, 167
Jany 57–8
Japan 41–2, 55, 66, 177–8, 195–6, 203, 207
Japanese 41, 43, 58, 177, 197, 207, 224
Jellinek 72, 105–8
Jesus 51
Joathan & Lilleker 160
Johri 4
Jones 72, 161
journalism 110, 143, 160, 162
Judaism 150
judicial activism 208
judicial authority 3, 28, 30, 54, 199, 203, 207, 212, 218–9, 232
judicial independence 183, 218
judicialisation of politics 206, 208

judicial review 87, 88, 95, 109, 176–7, 184, 191, 196, 200–207, 209–10, 216–17, 219, 221, 229, 231
jurisdictio 171, 188
juristic person 123
juristocracy 201, 206–8
justice 2, 13, 19, 22, 28, 45, 84, 93, 95, 101, 113, 157, 172–3, 175, 181, 183, 192, 199, 201–2, 218–19, 231, 240
Justinian 19, 60, 115

Kaiserreich 63
Kant 23, 26–8, 42, 52, 73, 107, 150, 170, 195, 219
Kavanaugh 179
Kelly 63, 105
Kelsen 80–81, 89, 212
Kenya 93–4, 139, 157
Kim 111
king 19, 20, 26, 30–32, 34, 37–9, 47, 61–2, 82, 91, 98, 196
Klare 192
Kleger 99, 154
Klingemann & Fuchs 129
Klug 196
Knight 65–6
Knudson 64
Kochenov & Bárd 170
Koontz 50
Koopmans 203
Korea 81, 139, 146, 195–6
Körtvélyesi 56, 75–6, 90, 102, 135
Kosovo 55, 91
Kötz 15
Kotzé & Villavicencio Calzadilla 197
Koulish 123
Kranenpohl 213
kratos 142, 143
Krygier 171
Krzan 91
Kulturnation 65
Kyriazis 96–7

labour 57
Lacan 105
Lagash 57
Lang & Wiener 194
Latham-Gambi 185

Latin America 117, 185, 190, 203
leadership 18, 21, 57–8, 145–6, 149–50, 157, 166
League of Nations 40, 66, 89, 111
legal certainty 172–3, 179–80, 184, 188, 205, 232
legalism 23, 81, 226
legality 86, 169, 170, 172, 174, 187, 189, 200–201, 217
legal pluralism 78, 122, 225
legal scholarship 19, 21, 56, 69, 193
legislative authority 88
legislative sovereignty 88
legitimacy 61–2, 80, 83–4, 90, 92, 97, 144, 155, 163, 173, 181–2, 189, 197, 208, 213, 215, 217–18, 230–231, 240
Legrand & Munday 224
Leibnitz 37
Lepsius 105, 107
Lessnoff 84
Leviathan 23, 24, 49, 79, 81
liberal constitutionalism 3, 9, 10, 30, 40–41, 52–4, 79, 81, 93, 94, 147, 160, 173, 188, 194, 197–8, 201, 222, 240
liberal democracy 6, 8, 11, 28, 40, 42–3, 52, 70, 76, 80–82, 92–5, 142, 144–5, 148, 156–7, 159–60, 162–4, 168, 187–8, 193, 195, 198
liberal individualism 66
liberalism 3, 6, 8–11, 24–6, 40, 42–3, 47, 50, 52–3, 61–2, 69, 79, 81, 94–5, 144–5, 153, 158–9, 163, 169, 186, 193, 212, 217, 226–7
liberty 25–6, 28, 38–9, 47, 62, 66, 70, 82, 95, 152, 157, 163, 168, 187–8, 191
Licinius 46
Liechtenstein 125, 212
Limbach 213
lingua 1, 59, 61, 129
Lisbon Treaty 127, 173
Livy 59
Llanque 51
local 30–32, 34–5, 39, 55, 73, 113–15, 123, 135, 164
Locke 16, 22–5, 28, 30, 48, 50, 63, 83, 142, 187
Lombardo 103

Loughlin & Walker 140, 189
Louis IX 19, 82
Louis Philippe 64
Louis VI 82
Louis VII 82
Louis XVIII 38
Loup 32
loyalty 46, 68, 76, 115, 134
Luard 40–41
Luther 47
Luxemburg 63, 96, 132
Lyon 31, 32
Lyotard 9

Maastricht Treaty 91, 96, 152, 154
Machiavelli 16, 23, 48, 62, 82, 131
Mackintosh 33
Mäder 24
Madison 142, 178, 202, 216
Magna Carta Libertatum 30
Magnum Concilium 31
majestas 83
majoritarianism 163, 167, 193
Malila 208
Maloy 16
Mancini 88
Mandelbaum 58, 105
marriage 114, 133, 136
Marshall 202
Martin 47
Marx 26, 81, 195
Marxism 81, 150
Masaka 156
mathematics 21, 44
Matronardi 225
Maus 73
May, Ides & Grossi 4
McConalogue 210
McConnell 50–51, 131
McCormick 168
McCorquodale 172
McIlwain 171, 188
mediaeval 18–20, 32, 47, 60
Meineke 65
Mendez-Pinedo 194
Menski 2
Merkel 143
Mesopotamia 16, 57, 104
methodology 6, 183, 222, 224–5, 227, 229

Mexico 161, 203
Michaels 227
Middle Ages 17–18, 20, 46, 61, 103, 109
migration 74, 123–4, 129, 147, 230
military 34, 39, 53, 70–71, 91, 134, 148, 185
Mill 212
Miller & Zumbansen 225
minority 24, 75, 145, 161, 163, 166–8, 173, 178, 183, 188, 205, 206
Mitra 123
Model Parliament 32
modernity 20, 24, 43, 163, 168, 193
Moltchanova 103
monarch 19, 22–3, 32, 37, 61–2, 82
monarchy 37, 62–3, 140, 142, 145
monism 87–8, 142, 209
monotheism 49
Montesquieu 16–17, 23, 25, 51–2, 142, 187
Montevideo Convention 72, 111–12
morality 13, 22, 24, 27, 41–2, 48, 50–51, 53, 120, 131, 143, 148, 152, 157, 162, 192, 207, 219, 231, 236, 240
Moreso 212
Moréteau 12
Morgan 58
Morocco 140, 207
morphogenesis 5, 189
Mosima 95, 156
Müller 162
Müller-Freienfels 203
Murkens 226
Muslim 81, 117, 135
Myanmar 126–27, 128
Mylonas 74
mysticism 47, 233, 237
mythology 53, 239

Namibia 93, 133, 157
Napoleon 17, 29, 37, 63
natio 59, 61, 129
nation 37–8, 55–6, 58, 60, 63–4, 68–77, 90, 92, 102, 105, 111, 123, 126, 132, 135, 137, 139, 163
national assembly 38
national emergency 54
national identity 76, 90
nationalism 38–9, 55–6, 59, 61–3, 68–71, 128

nationalistic 55, 70, 162
nationality 13, 18, 62, 67–8, 70, 75–6, 95, 101, 123–38, 154, 223, 230
national minorities 76
nation-building 74–5, 207
nationhood 39, 55–6, 58, 61–2, 64–5, 68–9, 71, 75, 94, 128, 230
nation-state 23, 37, 39, 52, 61, 65, 71, 90, 102, 105, 124, 131, 159
naturalization 76, 133, 134
natural law 21–4, 38, 47–8, 62, 84, 109, 202, 227, 238, 240
natural sciences 21
natural state (état naturel)) 25
nature 18, 20–22, 24, 27–8, 197, 235
Nederlanderschap 128
Netherlands 38, 63, 64, 89, 92, 128
Neuberger 211
neutrality 8, 12, 59, 82, 102, 226–9, 233–4, 237
Neuvonen 129
Newton 37
New Zealand 35–6, 86–7, 191, 207, 209
Ngigi & Busolo 94
Nigeria 93, 112, 159, 208
Nogueira 208
Norman Conquest 30
North Atlantic 3, 8, 10, 15, 39–40, 42–3, 58, 81, 83, 94, 155, 186, 225
Nottebohm 125

Oake 51, 52
objectivity 22, 48, 101, 107, 158, 199, 219–20, 228, 233–4, 237, 240
Oduor 81, 157
O'Kelly 62, 63
oligarchy 9
Ontario 35
ontology 7, 44, 81, 84, 98, 150, 157, 183, 195, 203, 219, 222–4, 231–5, 237–8
Orgad 75
organs of state 74, 81, 89, 118–19, 184, 187, 203, 205, 212, 222, 230
Örücü 228
Ottoman Empire 40

Pakistan 105, 113–14, 116–18, 120, 134–5, 139–40
Palestine 91
Panama 203
paradox 140, 189, 200, 241
Paraguay 203
Paris 38, 213
Parker, Brundsen & Fleming 110
Parliament 31–6, 39, 82, 85–7, 93, 116, 123, 142, 154–5, 166, 175, 200–201, 210–211
parliamentary sovereignty 31, 71, 85–8, 170, 209–10, 216
Parsi 135
party-state 182
patriarchy 57, 192–3
patriotism 55
patronage 158
Paulskirchenverfassung 64
Paulson 108
Peace of Versailles 36, 40
Peace of Westphalia 37, 144
people 19, 23–4, 26, 35, 42–3, 47–8, 53, 55, 57–8, 60–61, 63, 65–6, 68, 72–3, 75, 81–4, 87–8, 93, 97, 99, 107, 139, 151, 158, 162–3, 167–8, 171, 181, 188, 195, 200, 208, 214, 218, 235, 239
peoples 27, 60, 62, 66–7, 90, 113, 117, 129, 152, 154, 192
people's capitalism 53
peregrinus 129–30
Persia 58, 104
Peters & Schwenke 226
Pfetsch 127
philosophy 1, 4, 9–11, 16–17, 19–21, 23, 26–9, 36, 39, 44–5, 47–9, 54, 80, 103, 144, 159–60, 165, 186–87
phratria 58
Pies 124
Plato 16, 45–6
plebiscite 86, 88, 165
Poland 38, 91
polis 16, 45, 59
political community 10, 99, 135, 148, 189
political liberalism 209
political party 33, 139, 156, 159–60, 213
political science 5, 73, 105, 124, 141–2, 213
Political Theology 79–80

politics 1, 2, 5, 8, 9–10, 12–13, 15–19, 22–4, 29–30, 32–3, 35, 39, 40–43, 45–8, 50–53, 55, 57–9, 62, 64–6, 68–71, 76, 78–80, 83–6, 90–92, 94, 97, 99, 101, 103, 110, 120, 123–4, 129, 133, 140, 143, 146–8, 150, 152–7, 159–66, 168–9, 181, 183, 185–94, 196–7, 200–201, 204–9, 211–14, 216–17, 219, 223–4, 228, 230, 238, 240
Pomponius 59
Ponthoreau & Hourquebiec 214
pontifex maximus 46
pope 20, 47, 82, 98
Pope Leo III 46
Popova 183
Popović 65, 103, 131
popular constitutionalism 190–191
popular sovereignty 25, 52, 61, 63, 69, 73, 76, 83–4, 86, 88, 90, 92, 94–5, 97–9, 149, 162–3, 185, 188, 199, 209, 218, 227, 230, 236, 238
popular will 139, 206
populism 26, 53, 76–7, 81, 98, 128, 141, 147, 161–4, 166, 189, 200–201, 211–12, 217, 235
populus 60–61, 82, 129, 130
Portugal 19, 22, 38, 131
positivism 28, 78, 108, 122, 217, 227
post-modernism 6, 9, 80–81, 101, 105, 227, 241
pouvoir constituant 29, 72, 155, 209
pouvoir constitué 29, 155, 209
poverty 158–159
Prandini 5–6, 10, 189
predilections 224, 228–9
prejudice 204, 216, 228, 237
premises 7, 11, 13, 44, 81, 98, 127, 179, 186, 203, 219, 224, 229, 232, 234, 237
presidential imperialism 88
princeps legibus solutus est 115
principle 19, 28, 33–5, 49, 60, 62–3, 66–7, 69, 71, 78, 83, 85–90, 93, 97, 113, 115, 117–20, 126, 139, 148, 150, 152, 154, 157–9, 173–80, 183, 189, 191, 194, 197, 199, 200, 202, 205, 208, 210, 214, 220, 223, 229
private law 2, 17, 64, 225

proletariat 145, 150
property 20, 22, 24, 47–8, 106, 115–16, 134, 164
Protestantism 21, 46, 49–50
Prussia 22, 37–9, 63–4
psychology 1, 11, 50, 57
public interest 26, 82, 116
public law 2, 12, 17, 27, 60, 64, 123, 134, 141
public weal 82
public welfare 139
Puritans 31–2
Putin 8, 143, 183
Pyke 4

Qing dynasty 43
Quadrio 50
quasi-democracy 53
Quebec 35
Qu'est-ce que le tiers-état? 79

Rahmatian 64
rationalism 27–8, 37, 49, 52, 149–51, 179, 181, 236–8
rationality 92
Rawls 84, 219
Raz 172
Rechtsstaat 13, 110, 170, 172, 174, 177, 180, 182–3, 188, 213, 231
Rechtswissenschaft 63, 106
reciprocity 219
referendum 63, 86, 88, 92, 165, 169, 206, 211, 214
Reformation 20, 31, 46, 144
regional 18, 30, 55, 87, 104, 186, 232
regnum 103
Reichsverfassung 64
Reidy & Riker 103
Reimann 15, 221
religion 16, 20, 32, 44–52, 54–5, 57–9, 62, 71, 74–5, 81, 84, 93, 105, 115–16, 119–20, 123, 131, 137, 150–151, 159, 195–6, 212, 235–8
Religion within the Boundaries of Mere Reason 52
Renaissance 17–18, 21, 31, 62, 103
representation 32, 63–4, 66, 73, 98, 142, 160, 165, 167, 191, 199–200, 203
representative government 35

republic 30, 51, 113, 129, 130, 182, 191, 203
responsible self-government 35
res publica 103, 129
Rex est imperator in regno suo 82
Riegner 185, 192, 198
rights 2, 22, 24–7, 30–32, 38, 42, 52, 65, 67, 73, 83, 86, 89–90, 96, 109, 112–17, 128, 130–132, 134–9, 142, 147–8, 152, 167, 169, 173, 181, 185–8, 192, 194–5, 197, 199–200, 204–6, 213–14
Rohingya 127
Roman Church 18, 20, 46, 60, 82, 108
Roman-Dutch law 215
Roman Empire 17–18, 46, 59, 103, 130
Romania 75, 207
Roman law 2, 19, 21, 82, 129, 130, 136
Roman Republic 103
romanticism 51, 61, 63–4, 68, 83
Rome 17, 46, 58–9, 130–131, 152
Rooseveldt, Eleanor 41
Rooseveldt, Franklin 41, 66
Rosen 150
Rosenn 203
Ross 190, 191
Rousseau 22–3, 25–6, 50–51, 63, 83, 131, 141, 144
royal prerogative 86, 210
rule of law 28, 44, 52, 90, 113, 119, 139, 147–8, 150, 152, 157, 163, 166–7, 170–85, 187–8, 196–7, 200–201, 205, 229, 231–2
Runhua 43–4
Russia 8, 37–8, 41, 43, 53, 55, 69, 112–16, 118–20, 144, 182–83, 206
Ryan 4

Sacrum Imperium Romanum 20
Sadie, Patel & Baldry 159
Sage & Woolcock 225
Saint Denis, de 82
Sajeva 197
Samararatne 185, 193
Sánchez 127
Sanger & Perlroth 161
Sargon I 104
Saudi Arabia 197
Savigny 63–4, 83

Saxoferrato, de 82
Sayre's law 224
Scheppele 193, 217
Scheuner 170
Schlaich 212
Schmidt 209
Schmitt 79, 80, 83, 226
Scholtes 168–69, 189, 200
Schonfeld 81
Schroeder 173–74
Schwab 79
science 9, 12, 19, 21–2, 37, 54, 56–7, 63, 81, 99, 106, 148, 186, 221, 223, 232, 235, 237
scientific 105, 228
Scotland 61–2, 210
Scripture 20, 238
Second British Empire 34
secular 20, 24, 37, 46, 50, 75, 120, 157
secularism 44, 51, 52, 84
Segev 45
self-determination 67, 89–91, 97, 113, 185
self-interest 27–8, 142
semiotics 56, 151
separation of church and state 49
separation of powers 24–5, 28, 88, 142, 167, 180, 185–6, 188, 199, 205
Serbia 75
Setzer 33
Sevastik 103
Shakhray & Popova 206
Shava & Chamisa 158
Sherman 59–60
Shklar 26
Shotoku Taishi 58
Shuruppak 57
Sieyès 29, 79, 84
Sikh 135
Simpson 130
Singapore 195
Sippar 57
Skey & Antonsich 69
Slovakia 75
Smillie 207, 209
Smith 134–5, 182
Smith & Sharlet 182
social contract 22, 24, 26–8, 38, 47, 77, 83–4, 99, 144, 193, 236, 239

socialism 10, 40, 53, 81, 139, 147, 150–151, 158, 162, 180–182, 197, 225, 235, 241
social justice 140, 157
social order 18, 23, 52, 68, 98, 156, 218, 236
social welfare state 111
society 1, 5, 16–20, 28, 46–8, 51, 54, 57–8, 61, 69, 78, 81, 83, 95, 97, 101, 106, 110, 116, 139, 142, 146, 152–3, 157, 165–6, 168, 173, 181, 183, 189–91, 195, 205, 212–13, 219, 230, 235–7, 239–40
socio-economic rights 190
sociology 1, 55, 69, 80, 105, 149, 150–151, 189
Son 195–6
South Africa 36, 72–4, 86, 93, 114, 119, 139, 156, 167–8, 179–80, 191–2, 196, 215–16, 224
South America 16
soverain 98
sovereign 78–99
sovereignty 3–4, 20, 23–4, 26, 28–9, 33, 62–4, 68–9, 70, 72–3, 75–6, 78–93, 95–9, 101, 103, 111, 119, 124, 127, 140, 142, 144, 147, 149, 155, 169–70, 197, 199, 201–2, 209–10, 214–15, 223, 230, 232, 236, 238–9
sovereignty of Parliament 80, 201
Sovereign Virtue 79
soziale Staatslehre 106
Sozialstaat 110
Spadafora 105
Spain 19, 38, 65, 212
Spanish legal order 35, 38, 61, 131
Sparta 16–17
Spawforth 46
Spector 25
spin-doctoring 146, 158, 160
sport 70
Sri Lanka 185, 193, 224
Staat 23, 103–4, 106–7, 110
Staatsangehörigkeit 72, 128
Staatsnation 65
Staatsrecht 4, 38, 105–6, 170
Staatsrechtslehre 106
staatsreg 105
Staatsvolk 72, 73

Staatswissenschaft 106
Starck 114
stare decisis 179, 180
state 1–2, 4, 6, 9–10, 12–13, 16–18, 20–30, 36, 38–43, 45–52, 54–5, 58–9, 61–3, 65, 68, 71–4, 76–93, 97–99, 101–123, 126–30, 133–9, 142–5, 147–50, 153, 156–7, 160, 169–70, 172–3, 175–80, 184–9, 194–5, 199, 202–3, 212–13, 217–18, 222–3, 228–30, 235–6, 238–9
statehood 3, 13, 16, 65, 68, 72, 75, 91, 95, 98, 101–3, 109–12, 122, 133, 198, 230, 232
statelessness 126–7
state of disaster 54
state of nature 22, 24, 28
status 26, 36, 62, 69, 71–2, 74, 76, 90–91, 107, 114, 119, 123, 126, 128, 130, 134–8, 157, 210, 230
Statute of Westminster 36
Stern 170
Stewart 80–1
Steytler 216
Strauss 21
Strumia 129
Stubbs 31
Sumeria 104
superanus 98
supra-national 95, 97–8, 101, 125, 129, 135, 151, 154–5, 194, 198, 224, 231
Supreme Court of the United Kingdom 210–211
Switzerland 38, 112, 165

Taiwan 91, 195–6
Tamanaha 172, 225
Tandoh-Offin & Bukari 157
Tangian 164–7
technology 39, 53, 140, 147–8, 161
terminology 1–3, 8–9, 43, 54–5, 68, 77, 91, 104, 112, 123, 125, 128, 185–6, 197, 227, 232–4
territorial integrity 40, 119
tertium comparationis 169, 198, 227
theism 150
theology 19–20, 48–50, 80–81, 83, 150

Index

the people 13, 23–4, 26, 38, 47, 55, 57, 59, 61, 63–5, 68, 72, 75, 82–3, 87–8, 92–4, 97, 99, 101, 118, 123, 132, 135, 139, 140, 142, 144–5, 149, 153, 157, 162, 165, 169, 181, 188–9, 190, 195, 199–200, 206, 210, 212, 230, 235, 239
the Sovereign 51, 131
Third British Empire 35
third estate 29
Third World 8
Tiedemann 44
Tocqueville 142, 163
totalitarianism 26, 40
tradition 6, 8–9, 22, 43, 48, 83, 108–9, 123, 140, 168, 195, 214
transformation 92, 164, 180–181, 185, 191–2, 196, 198
transformative constitutionalism 185, 192, 196, 198
transnational 124, 155, 162, 221, 223
transplantation 226
Treaty of Trianon 76
tribuno 59
Trnavci 60
Trump 143, 161
truth 22, 44, 47, 52, 84, 99, 107, 224, 233–4, 238
Tsai 226
Tsar 37
Tushnet 81, 162, 185, 201, 224
Tusk 8
Tusseau 225
two cities 46
two kingdoms 47
two powers 47
two swords 47
Tzanakopoulou 131

Ubaldis, de 82
Uganda 93
Ukraine 75
Ullmann 82
Ulpianus 115
Umma 57
UN Commission on Human Rights 41
United Kingdom 33, 66, 71–2, 86–7, 98, 171, 175, 191, 209, 210–211, 238

United Nations 40–42, 66–7, 89–91, 136, 139, 165, 171, 219
United States of America 4, 40–41, 43, 59, 71, 88–9, 128, 132, 139–40, 143–4, 158, 160–161, 177–8, 190, 206
  citizen 131–32
  Congress 29, 63, 88, 191
  Constitution 25, 30, 88, 132, 144, 209
  Continental Congress 29
  Declaration of Independence 29, 33, 144
  federalism 112
  Federalist Papers 142
  monism 88
  republic 37
  Supreme Court 80, 87, 132, 179, 190, 202
Universal Declaration of Human Rights 41, 66, 127
universalism 22–3, 193–4, 226, 229
universality 1–3, 7, 9, 19, 21, 25, 37, 42, 46, 50, 52, 59–60, 67, 84–5, 99, 108, 141, 150, 156–7, 164, 171, 175, 178, 183, 189, 195, 220, 223, 227, 229, 241
Ur 57
Urabe 177
urbanization 19, 42, 59, 74
urbs 59, 131
Uruguay 203
Uruk 57
USSR 42–3, 53, 203

vagueness 4, 13, 61, 68, 125, 171, 186, 190
value 2, 5, 21, 40, 71, 85, 107, 124, 148–9, 173, 179, 186, 233
values and principles 158, 171, 218
Van der Vyver 90
Van der Walt 80, 241
Van Domselaar 219
Van Gelder 20, 49, 131
Vanoverbeke 177–8
Van Roermund 205
Vattel, de 68
Venezuela 175, 203
Venice Commission 172, 201

Venter 3, 7, 9, 29, 33, 41, 45, 47, 84, 87–8, 101–2, 109, 134, 138, 156, 160, 168, 176, 180, 185, 187, 192, 196, 205–6, 213, 216, 220, 225, 229
Verfassung des Deutschen Reiches 38
Verfassungsrecht 106
Verfassungsstaat 110, 170, 183, 198, 231
Verovšek 98
Victoria 35
Victor Immanuel II 39
Vietnam 133, 195–6
Vilhena, Baxi & Viljoen 185, 192
Voigt 23, 103, 110
Volk 63–4, 72–3, 92, 128–9, 212
Volksgeist 64
volonté générale 26
Voltaire 63, 83
Von Bernstorff 105, 111
Von Bogdandy 79, 111, 185, 192, 225
Von Danwitz 183
Von Hayek 170
Von Mohl 170
vote-buying 159

Walbank 59, 65, 129
Waldrauch 133, 134
Waldron 28, 204–5, 209, 216, 219
Wales 61, 211
Walker 10, 85, 162, 163
wall of separation 50
Ward 24, 28
Watson 228
Weber 24, 26, 149, 165, 203
Weber-Fas 24, 26
Weiler 76
Weimar Constitution 38, 115
Weimar Republic 39–40
Wendel 213
Wesemann 129
Western 2–3, 8–9, 16–18, 20, 22–3, 27, 37, 39, 41–4, 46, 48, 53, 60, 81, 95, 144, 148, 156–7, 171, 186, 195–6, 225, 241

Western Europe 8, 18, 20, 37, 171, 186
Western Sahara 91
West-Indies 33
Westminster 35, 37, 88, 175, 217
We, the people 73–4, 93
White 49, 211
Whytock 225, 228
Widner & Contiades 208
Wielgus 60
Wiener, Lang, Tully, Maduro & Kumm 194
Wilkinson 3, 10–11, 40
William I 30
will of the people 93, 144
Wilms 64, 72
Wilson 27
Wimmer 102
Wiredu 156
Witte 44
Wong 181, 182
World Justice Project 174–5, 177–8, 179–80, 182
worldview 9, 44, 52, 78, 84, 144, 151, 159, 160, 227, 233–4, 237–8, 240–241
World War I 6, 36, 39–40, 59, 75, 79
World War II 40, 53, 66, 72, 79, 92, 190
Worster 90–91
Wright 49
WTO 56

Young 50, 153, 154
Yusuf 208

Zakaria 169
Zambia 93
Zeitgeist 64
Zhang 43, 180–181
Ziegler, Baranger & Bradley 187
Zimbabwe 55, 139
Zouche 60
Zumbansen 225